Southern Illinois University Press

CARBONDALE AND EDWARDSVILLE

FEFFER & SIMONS, INC.

LONDON AND AMSTERDAM

PAUL WEISS

BEYOND ALL APPEARANCES

Library of Congress Cataloging in Publication Data

Weiss, Paul, 1901–
  Beyond all appearances.

  1. Man.   2. Reality.   3. Phenomenology.   4. Ideals (Philosophy)
5. Knowledge, Theory of. I. Title.
B945.W396B48   191   74–5484
ISBN 0–8093–0617–4

The quotation from "Description Without Place" from The Collected
Poems of Wallace Stevens, *copyright 1923, 1931, 1935, 1936, 1937,
1942, 1943, 1944, 1945, 1946, 1947, 1948, 1949, 1950, 1951, 1952,
1954 by Wallace Stevens, is reprinted by permission
of Alfred A. Knopf, Inc.*

BOOKS BY PAUL WEISS

Beyond All Appearances (1974)

Cinematics (forthcoming)

The God We Seek (1964)

History: Written and Lived (1962)

The Making of Men (1967)

Man's Freedom (1950)

Modes of Being (1958)

Nature and Man (1947)

Nine Basic Arts (1961)

Our Public Life (1959)

Philosophy in Process, Vol. 1: 1955–1960 (1966)

Philosophy in Process, Vol. 2: 1960–1964 (1966)

Philosophy in Process, Vol. 3: 1964 (1968)

Philosophy in Process, Vol. 4: 1964–1965 (1969)

Philosophy in Process, Vol. 5: 1965–1968 (1971)

Philosophy in Process, Vol. 6: 1968–1971 (forthcoming)

Reality (1938)

Religion and Art (1963)

Right and Wrong: A Philosophical Dialogue Between Father and Son,
with Jonathan Weiss (1967)

Sport: A Philosophic Inquiry (1969)

The World of Art (1961)

PRINCIPAL CONTRIBUTIONS BY PAUL WEISS

American Philosophers at Work, edited by Sidney Hook (1956)

American Philosophy Today and Tomorrow,
edited by H. M. Kallen and Sidney Hook (1935)

The Concept of Order, edited by Paul Kuntz (1968)

Contemporary American Philosophy, edited by John E. Smith (1970)

Design and Aesthetics of Wood, edited by Eric A. Anderson
and George F. Earl (1972)

Dimensions of Mind: A Symposium, edited by Sidney Hook (1960)

Evolution in Perspective, edited by G. Schuster and G. Thorson (1971)

The Future of Metaphysics, edited by Robert Wood (1970)
Human Values and Economic Policy: Proceedings,
edited by Sidney Hook (1967)
Law and Philosophy, edited by Sidney Hook (1964)
Moments of Personal Discovery, edited by R. M. MacIver (1952)
Moral Principles in Action, edited by R. Anshen (1952)
Philosophical Interrogations, edited by S. and B. Rome (1964)
Philosophy and History, edited by Sidney Hook (1963)
Science, Philosophy, and Religion: Proceedings (1941–)

EDITED WORKS BY PAUL WEISS

Collected Papers of Charles Sanders Peirce (six volumes),
editor, with Charles Hartshorne (1931–35)

FOR KING LUI WU

A great architect and a great friend

CONTENTS

PREFACE

Some fifteen years ago in *Modes of Being* I tried to make evident what the ultimate realities were, by themselves and in relation to one another. Since they are neither prominent nor unmistakable, I have thought it desirable to show how we can move to them from where we now are. One of the primary objectives of the present enterprise is to do this. The effort allows one to take the earlier portion of this work as the first part of a two volume study, of which *Modes of Being* is the second—provided that *Modes of Being* be corrected in accord with suggestions and criticisms made in *Philosophy in Process*. The present work, though, was conceived and written independently of the other, and contains new explorations and developments, particularly regarding the nature of man, what finally ought to be, and the problems which beset reflective thought.

P. W.

Washington, D. C.
May 1973

INTRODUCTION

The first part of this work begins with appearances, which are actualities and finalities factually together. It then attempts to show how those appearances make possible a move into their sources and, particularly, into the actualities to which the appearances are normally ascribed.

The second part contains an account of the opportunities which appearances and actualities provide for a movement into the finalities. The main emphasis is on the tracing of contexts back to their sources. Once this is done, it is possible to see the law-abiding cosmos as a product of the way in which actualities and finalities are involved with one another.

The third part brings these results to bear on the understanding of man. They are relevant to him because he, in contradistinction from all other actualities, instantiates all the finalities in the very act of maintaining himself in opposition to them. He alone, as a consequence, is an individual with rights, provides a test of truth, has a persistent identity, and makes himself immortal in ways not possible to any other reality. A fresh answer is then made available to the question inherited from Descartes hundreds of years ago, as to just how men differ from animals and, particularly, machines, what man's task is, and the nature of the Ideal he is to realize.

The work, as a whole, offers one illustration of the way in which a final Ideal is realized. This Ideal, in the guise of the ultimate objective for knowledge, is filled out with a systematic account of what is real. We end and must end where we began—with less than all there is. But this less is at last seen to be not only less than what ought to be, but to stand outside the most complete possible fulfillment. The most complete possible fulfillment will always defy and be defied by that which fulfills it.

[2]

Appearances are products, the outcome of the juncture of controlled contexts and the exhibitions of actualities. They are not dependent for their presence on men or any other perceivers. But, both as individuals and as social beings, men add to those objective appearances. They modify them, overlaying them with interpretations, distortions, and additions. What is daily confronted are such modified appearances, altered still further by perspective, media, idiosyncracies, and special conditions.

Appearances have textures. A movement through those textures is a movement toward the realities which contribute constituents to the appearances. When we begin at an appearance and trace a constituent back to its source, along the route provided by the texture, we engage in a symbolization of the source. By symbolizing, we penetrate into the reality from the position of its textured appearance. All of us have some acquaintance with individual actualities and with the different finalities, because we all make symbolic use of appearances. Conventional signs, externally referring terms, and detached hypotheses are special cases, delimited and degenerate versions of a fundamental symbolization.

Knowledge of appearances is preceded by an act of attention. This imposes a boundary on a limited area, holding it off from the rest of the world of appearances. The boundary is not respected by the sources of the appearances; the appearances are pulled away from those boundaries by the realities which make the appearances possible.

Because of the boundaries, some of the appearances are able to have a role in our economy. They are unities reflected on, remembered, articulated, judged, and acted through. All the while, the realities, through the agency of the contributions they make to the appearances, keep those appearances related to one another across those boundaries. A knowledge of the appearances as they exist apart from us requires the assumption of attitudes which are in consonance with the way in which appearances are in fact related outside the boundaries that we introduce.

[3]

The exhibitions of actualities are contextualized. They are subject to common controls and are caught up in relations that no actualities can account for or abrogate. The resultant appearances exhibit sets of features, each testifying to the presence of a distinctive finality.

Appearances contrast, conflict with, and supplement one another to constitute an aesthetic vibrating whole. No matter what their sources, the appearances are also all on a footing, one no more and no less a genuine appearance than any other. Reasoning, plans, and predictions are possible because the appearances, in addition, are subject to laws. They are also contemporaries in time, related across space, and are relevant to one another because they are outcroppings of what is involved in causal chains. And they are united in a single totality.

Each type of contextualized feature provides evidence of a distinct finality. To move from the feature to the finality, one must engage in a distinctive act of symbolization. This begins with the texture, and penetrates, under the influence of the finality, into the finality.

A movement to a finality can also begin at an actuality. This occurs when one seeks the appropriate object of awe, reverence, or some other form of the emotion of wonder. The activity begins at any one of an endless number of possible positions in an actuality, and stops at any one of an endless number of possible positions in the finality. It is always possible to have begun somewhat deeper inside an actuality, and always possible to have ended somewhat further within a finality. Only the actuality itself can be at its own center;

only the finality itself enjoys its own inwardness. We know that there is always more beyond the points at which we begin and end, because we are aware of the absenting resistance of the realities with which we deal.

Actualities and finalities are not merely together as a matter of fact so as to constitute appearances; they are also involved with one another. They affect one another and do what they can to internalize the qualifications to which they are subject. The scene of their interplay is the cosmos, where the actualities and the finalities together constitute a single whole, at once unitary and diversified. Here the actualities are governed in common ways, and the finalities meet a plurality of challenges.

[4]

Actualities come to be and pass away, but while they are, they are real, not reducible to other realities. Each maintains itself against other actualities; each exhibits itself and thereby provides constituents of appearances; each is a unique individual, maintaining itself against a primal Substance, in the very act of instancing this in the shape of a distinctive substance.

Each actuality is unique, but it is only the uniqueness of man that is enriched by all the finalities. Attempts to understand him as some kind of complicated animal or machine are plausible only when abstraction is made of what he is from within, and therefore from the way he deals with the different finalities and what these make possible.

Man has the ability to maintain himself against all finalities. Only he is internally a substance, with a being, a nature, an existence, and a unity enriching this, thereby making possible a distinguishable self, reason, mind, sensibility, and person. Only, he, consequently, has an enriched individuality, with rights, a basis for determining truth, an identity, and an immortality, not possible to other actualities.

All other actualities, like man, are subject to all the finalities. But these others remain simply subject to one or more of the finalities; they never manage to maintain themselves in opposition to them. Like man, they are substances which have internalized qualifications due to Substance. Their inability, though, to internalize the qualifications to which all the finalities other than Substance subject them, leaves those substances comparatively empty.

Men alone are able to stand away from all finalities and all actualities. As a consequence, they are able to know that the universe is made up of actualities and finalities, and to see that these realities are not only together factually in the guise of appearances, and are involved with one another in a cosmos, but that they are also necessarily together in an ideal, homogeneous, minimal way. This last is a constant, in terms of which the value of what is now the case can be measured.

[5]

The irreducible multiplicity of realities that make up the totality of what there is precludes the assumption of just one outlook on everything. To envisage anything, one must adopt the position of an actuality or of some finality. But impurities, abstractions, paradoxes, difficulties, and sometimes contradictions, which the assumed position entails, provide indications of the need and right to assume other positions.

One can know realities as subjected to some privileged one. The limitations of the partial views are overcome by the assumption of privileged positions by what had been previously taken to be subordinate. When each of the finalities is in turn treated as privileged, when each is recognized to have an absolute moment in terms of which the rest are to be envisaged, justice can be done to all.

To deal with each finality as occupying a privileged position is still to leave over two issues. The frame in which the privileged position is adopted must, if it impose special conditions, be itself supplemented by the use of other frames. And there must be a way to envisage all the results at the same time; otherwise one will encompass all there is, but only sequentially, and never have all the frames and all the privileged positions with their different emphases together within a single outlook.

The Ideal, which serves as man's goal and the measure of his achievements and excellence, offers a position in terms of which all realities can be understood. By itself it is only a possibility, a constant indeterminate, which is now more or less adequately filled out by the realities together. Whatever there is realizes and instantiates the Ideal at the same time that the Ideal stands away from it in the form of a union not yet fully embodied.

The Ideal is an ought to be that is itself less than what ought to be, at once intelligible, an objective, a demand, and a reality. It defines perfection to be a union in which all the realities, while maintaining their integrity, are harmoniously united. It is best portrayed in a neutral, universal, speculative, abstract, categorial counterpart of the myths which nations employ to express dramatically what they have gradually and only partially grasped of the objective toward which all should strive and which all should realize.

A myth is a likely but luring story for a segment of mankind. Philosophy is myth sobered and universalized, allowing one to see how, despite their irreducible differences, realities are always together, and could be together in better ways than they now are.

[6]

The major theses are:

1. There are no primitive, unmistakable data.
2. All beginnings are arrived at.
3. Knowledge adds to the known.
4. The known is continuous with knowledge, and with objects as they exist apart from knowledge.
5. Appearances are products, constituted of factors contributed by actualities and finalities.
6. Some appearances occur apart from men.
7. Appearances have textures which are continuous with actualities and finalities.

8. Symbolic knowledge is a primary mode of knowing realities; it begins with an appearance and terminates in the source of one of its factors.

9. Things manifest themselves; they are substances which are subject to, but do not instance any other finality but Substance.

10. Animals both manifest and display themselves in relation to one another; some of them are responsive. All instance other finalities besides Substance, but none is able to instance Being.

11. Men alone instance all the finalities; they alone exhibit themselves in expressions, as well as in manifestations, displays, and responses.

12. Knowledge is articulate; it divides what is bounded, and reunites it to constitute a claim.

13. Realities are not controlled by the boundaries knowledge imposes.

14. Appearances are pulled on by realities via the factors those realities contribute to the appearances.

15. Appearances are related to one another apart from the boundaries knowledge introduces.

16. Men know a world of appearances, because their attitudes allow them to anticipate what lies outside the borders of the boundaries they impose.

17. Appearances are interrelated in a single aesthetic whole.

18. Appearances are coordinated, equal in status.

19. Appearances are subject to laws.

20. Appearances are extended; they are related in space, and in time, and are relevant to one another.

21. Appearances are units in a single governing unity.

22. Contexts are factors in the constitution of appearances.

23. A symbolic use of a context begins a penetration into a finality.

24. Finalities qualify actualities.

25. Actualities maintain themselves against the finalities whose qualifications they internalize.

26. A transcendent dialectic begins at the qualifications that finalities impose on actualities.

27. Any beginning of a transcendence could have been preceded by

others; any ending of a transcendence could be followed by others.

28. The cosmos is the product of the interplay of actualities with finalities.

29. Men are actualities who are able to maintain themselves in opposition to all other actualities and all the finalities.

30. Men internalize qualifications stemming from all the finalities.

31. Men have natural rights.

32. Men provide bases for primary truths.

33. Men are self-identical through change.

34. Men are immortalized while they live.

35. Men have a power to organize ideas, acts, and occurrences in ways beyond the capacity of other actualities.

36. The final Ideal is a union of all realities. Its terms are homogeneous with their relation, and are internal to one another.

37. The final Ideal has a reality distinct from the realities as they now are severally and together.

38. The worth of anything is measured by what is done and not done to realize the Ideal.

39. Men are obligated to realize the final Ideal.

40. Incapable of fully realizing the final Ideal, men are inescapably defective and criticizable.

PART 1

DEPTH VECTORS

1

THE BEGINNING

Controlling Summary: Inquiry must begin here, where one now is. But this here could be in the familiar, commonsense, daily world; in the common world which is a transsocial version of this; in the underlying public world known to science; in the natural world of manifested actualities; or in the cosmos constituted of interacting actualities and finalities.

We are now in the commonsense world. We can move to the others by following the lead of evidences now available.

To read a philosophic work is to know what it says, and perhaps to learn from it. Some of its claims might subtend all others. It is conceivable, too, that an able reader might disentangle what was sound in it from what was not. But no reader, even one scrupulously careful, shrewd, and critical, could know, simply by reading, what the claims of the work presupposed, what they really meant, or what they involved. Such knowledge is a product of reflection. It involves evaluation, analysis, and criticism. Not to engage in these is to fail to grasp the philosophic import of a philosophy. It is to become acquainted with a writer, but not with a thinker or with the world he was trying to portray. He who does not engage in them independently of the author will fail to be a philosopher in his own right. He will become acquainted with a man or his world, perhaps,

3

but will not be prepared to meet the author on common ground. The philosophy might be known but would never be possessed.

No one should just read a philosophic work. To benefit from it, one must be prepared to consider fundamental issues, some of which the author may himself have neglected to face. To allow what a philosopher says to pass unchallenged is to attend to him in a non-philosophic spirit. The challenge, hopefully, will be presented in the work and may be successfully met there, but this one can know only if one challenges it oneself as well.

But should one not read a philosophic work to learn, if not the answers, at least the questions which underlie all others? To demand of a reader that he ask these questions, is this not to make him already one who has no need to attend to the book at all? The conclusion would be unavoidable, were it not that the questions which the reader should ask and even independently formulate, are stated and insistently provoked by the philosophic work itself. One learns to judge a philosophic work, even adversely, by learning from it. It prompts one to stand away while remaining most attentive to it; at its best, it teaches one how to move beyond it.

Whatever a philosophic work says ought to be sympathetically restated, and critically examined. Its presuppositions should be exposed. It has little value if it does not make possible a better understanding of what is, and what is known. This does not preclude—indeed, it invites—a joint intellectual adventuring on the part of both writer and reader. One thing is certain: for neither will there be neat answers to self-sufficient, well-formulated questions.

A philosopher tries to grapple with what every man should sooner or later find basic and perplexing. He wants to clarify central issues and to get close to the final answers. But it is not for him to decide whether he has done so or not.

A philosophy is too powerful to be let in without resistance. It could affect the reader's outlook on the world and on himself; it could lead to a too ready adoption or rejection of long sanctioned views, and a too ready dismissal of disciplines and positions which the philosophy is not flexible or broad enough to accommodate.

Scepticism and criticism should slow the pace of every phil-

osophic study. But a philosophy is also fragile. It makes little head-
way against insensitivity, and finds itself perpetually intruded upon
by familiar but not realiable ideas, categories, distinctions, and beliefs. One of its main functions is to arouse thought, to awaken and
redirect. It asks others to think through, to assess, and at the same
time to be flexible and steady. Author and reader must, despite the
printed page, despite difference in age and experience, training and
knowledge, philosophize together.

[2]

Where shall we begin? It is tempting to say, "With the familiar, daily, commonsense world," for it is the function of philosophy
to clarify what we know and where we are, and not to substitute for
this what is only an imagined universe, or even one more real, noble,
or elegant, if such there be. Yet common sense is too confused, too
capricious, too disorganized, too overrun with superstition, convention, the arbitrary, the dogmatic, the vague, and the unclear to
allow anyone to use it for more than a starting point—something
less than a true beginning foreshadowing the end that is to be
attained. One is prompted, therefore, to turn instead to mathematics,
logic, and scientifically established truths; these seem to offer sound
bases from which to make a confident intellectual beginning. It
seems wise to accept only what these sustain or justify. There is
necessity in them; they are clear and insistent; they allow one to
know much that otherwise would remain obscure or would have
been entirely unknown. But we do not and we cannot begin with
them. No one of these powerful sources of reliable knowledge
grounds itself; each presupposes other realities which we must first
know in order to be able to get to them, with warrant and dis-
patch. Each is had only if one has moved to them from some other
position. The nature of that position and the move from it need
to be justified and accounted for.

Better than a beginning with some formal discipline is one
which attends to root questions and perplexities. Such disturbances
exhibit us in disequilibrium. They are true beginnings, for of them-

selves they prompt, lead, and perhaps even take us elsewhere. But they—or wonder, as Aristotle designated the state of being in a primary disequilibrium—are either externally provoked or are integral to what occasions them. But if externally provoked, they will not tell us where to move; if integral, we will, on confronting what occasions those questions and perplexities, be inescapably forced away from there. The position at which we then arrive will be one from which we will be forced to move again for a similar reason, or it will be where the movement comes to an end. No inquiry will ever reach a satisfactory answer, or it will be brought abruptly to a final close.

Unsatisfied inquiry is inevitable if particulars raise transcendent or cosmic questions and we have only particulars with which to answer them. But an inquiry can be satisfied without making an end to all questioning. This occurs when the answers, though satisfactory, are themselves questions directed at that which originally was directed at them. To end a line of questioning it is not necessary to end all questions. The questions that particulars raise about ultimates are answered by those ultimates, but these in turn raise questions about the particulars.

Genuine root questions are provoked by what answers them. They are inseparable from the realities that make good their deficiencies. Each expresses the fact that it is distinguished from but connected with what completes it.

Descartes has only an externally determined doubt. If he made no attempt to raise questions, all would remain calm for him forever. His problems are self-made, deliberately introduced into the contents he faced. The pragmatists, by contrast, have a doubt that is thrown up by the confronted subject matter. They hope they can reach a point where they do not need to inquire further—as though thinking were disagreeable and intellectual quiescence a desirable goal. They would have no questions if they were not rudely disturbed. The Hegelian, instead, finds a disequilibrium wherever he rests. No attained position is stable for him, not even the position of the Absolute, for this is achieved only by mind, and not in its full concreteness, in nature and in history. But his road is already laid out; there is no genuine inquiry in his world, but only rediscovery. His universe is closed; it only seems to be open, and then only so far as men are ignorant and finite. His questions are all answers to one grand question: how he stands in relation to what is ultimately real.

All fail to see that, ontologically, every question is an answer, and every answer a question. The transient points to the eternal, and the eternal to the transient. Disequilibrium is not just a disagreeable state to overcome, nor is it confined only to men. Each question, grounded in what is, is so far satisfactory; each terminates in what else is needed, but which in turn has need of that which needs it.

Inquiry, and particularly a systematic one, is inevitable, but only after we, our subject matter, or both together, have matured. It is not doubt but an openness, not the inchoate but the mellowed that most clearly leads us elsewhere. It is not the defect of deficiency but the defect of being fully what it is that makes for disequilibrium. When the pear is ripe it is about to fall from the tree.

The question "where should we begin" evidently has two answers. We should begin with what sets us off for elsewhere. And we must begin here. To combine the two answers is to begin here with what is already thrusting us beyond itself.

[3]

There is no other place, there can be no other place to start than where we are. And that is here. Here is where we now are, and here is where we will continue to be for a while. But that "here," where is it? The obvious answer is, "In this room, holding a book, on the couch, near the desk." But to be obvious is not necessarily to be free from ambiguity. The room and these objects, are these the familiar items of everyday? Or are they the room and objects when freed from all social conditioning? Both are "here."

The *daily*, familiar, commonsense world, in which we move about with little thought, is well grooved by habit, convention, and common language. Its distinctive "here" is where effective action occurs. A transsocial version of this, a *common* world, is where strangers meet. It escapes from some of the limitations imposed by different societies, their practices and discourses; its "here" is at the core of the "heres" of different familiar worlds. There is also a *public* world in which little of the daily world is found. Arrived at through the help of scientific techniques, it is often expressed in formulae beyond the capacity of any but specialists to master. Its "here" is where scientists set the zeros for their spaces and times. Different from this, but sometimes coinciding, is a *natural* world constituted of individual actualities manifesting themselves to some degree, but largely hidden except to those who know how to probe beneath surfaces. "Here" in that world is wherever an actuality is active. And, then, there is the *cosmos* in which the actualities interplay with one another and with whatever finalities there may be. In that cosmos, "here" is where each affected actuality is. There are other "heres" as well. The worlds of history, religion, art, all have distinctive "heres."

Were there no "here" in the daily world, there would be no originating of a practical act. If there were no "here" in the common world, we and members of other societies would not have a common referent near us. Were there no "here" in the public world, there would be no place or date for anything, once we had freed ourselves and what we confront from all social and personal notes. Without a "here" in the natural world, there could be no actualities close by. Did the cosmos not contain a "here," nothing in that cosmos would be locatable in relation to us.

Usually, if we acknowledge that we are "here" in one world we will have to take at least a moment or so to move to the "here" in another. We will then be "here" in the one at one moment, and "here" in the other at a subsequent moment, and this despite the fact that the "heres" are not entirely sunderable from one another.

For most men "here" relates only to a position near them in their daily, familiar world. That world is lived in and lived with. Overrun with quick supposition and expectation, it shows the effects of fear and hope. It has rough edges and has neither a steady quality nor a fixed population. "Here" in that domain is close to where its designator's body is, the normal starting point of action.

An infant is born into the daily world. It comes into a family which is already burdened with multiple accretions and habituated in many practices. But the infant knows nothing of this. The infant, not yet fitted into its parents' world, is at once natural and cosmic; it arrives at a place in the daily world only after a period of learning and training. Taught and disciplined, the infant only gradually becomes a functioning part of it. And once it is in the daily world, it is usually content to stay there. Occasionally, though, it will make momentary moves into the others.

No normal man is denied some glimpse into the depths of other actualities; none is altogether unaware of finalities. The unreflecting responsiveness and the simple innocence that is characteristic of almost every infant is still present in the calculated answers and the settled knowledge of the mature. All of us remain open to the presence of realities which play little or no role in our practices and observations. Indeed, our lives could not continue long, if we remained entirely in the daily world. For an effective laying hold of objects, for anticipating the effects of actions, for a knowledge open to all men, it is necessary to be aware of common, natural, and cosmic objects as well.

[4]

The daily, familiar world has a nature and course of its own. All must learn to adjust to its tendencies. Each individual inevitably modifies it. The shards of his individual experiences and needs are quite near its surface. Since it is partly an individualized product, no precise, detailed account of the daily world can avoid all reference to personalized variations in it. But it is only partly personalized. Partly, it is also constituted by men existing together with one another. Together they make it, and it makes them.

Practical needs prompt men to attend mainly to the items in their daily world. There they distinguish and classify in accord with established habits of thought and need. Language, routines, rituals, superstitions, beliefs, knowledge, and action play a role in making that world take shape. Value-laden, it reflects the import of dominant folktales and myths. These, reverberating with distant triumphs and terrors, express in vivid terms the differences men discern between bravery and cowardice, honesty and hypocrisy, good and ill will, and the dangers which virtue, vice, innocence, and success entrain. The result is a world envisaged from the position of a particular society.

Accepted practices reveal what is in fact believed to be true. To adopt those practices at established times is to be reasonable in a society. To be a member of it is to use classifications acceptable to others; it is to judge and speak, usually unreflectingly, but in accord with well-established rules. Making occasional stabs at explanation and clarification, men in a society draw somewhat similar conclusions from what they all assume.

This is where men spend their days; it is here that they find what is important for their welfare. Living in the light of traditions, they signalize important and recurrent events by established ceremonies, stories, and activities. After a while, almost everyone acquires a good stock of reliable, impersonal knowledge, gathered in idleness, backed by observation, and controlled by rough experiments. Little of this is clear; much of it is mixed with what is unreliable. Some of it is overpersonalized, qualified by shared opinion and indurated belief, not always sound. But some of it is objective enough to allow men to know what holds, not only in their own but in any society, and even for any man. Seamen and farmers, hunters and swimmers know some transsocial truths.

Clear distinctions are difficult to make. Lacking discipline, one is able to stand steadily apart only for a while. Yet stand apart one must, if matters are to be carefully and dispassionately examined. The ordinary man is unable to do this well or for long. Consequently, he is unable to formulate muscular theories that can be checked by others, or that can be altered to conform to what the evidence reveals. Though his expectations are frequently justified, his analyses are poor and his generalizations too quick. Hard questions, rare cases, complex issues baffle him. When he cannot ignore them, he deals with them in inadequate terms. Well-certified data,

mathematics and logic, persistent universal laws do not interest him much. Nor is he altogether at home with what is minute, cosmic, private, or forever. The formal, the theoretical, the transcendental, the speculative attract him, if made dramatic; they do not, if allowed to stand out in their stark beauty. Attending and recording carelessly, he reasons without regard for the conditions that govern validity. He does not know that what seems to be diverse—a horse and a bat—might be closely related, or that what seems to be very similar—a porpoise and a shark—are quite different. Since well-grounded predictions are beyond his capacity or concern, he must guess, play hunches, follow habituated patterns. Distinctions sanctioned by practice or usage control him unduly; too readily he takes linguistic divisions and combinations to provide him with good portrayals of realities. Impatient with subtlety, detailed argument, or with what takes considerable time to make its nature clear, the ordinary man is good on what in his society is of vital importance or of immediate practical value, but is not a safe guide as to just what in fact is, apart from all human need, custom, or predilection. Nevertheless, he knows some things which do not depend on his society for their truth or value. He adds correctly and he rightly fears, both by making distinctions which are appropriate also to the course of other societies, and by escaping societal bonds altogether.

[5]

Societies differ. They face different environments, and solve their problems in different ways. At the same time they exhibit a common punctuation. All have a place for similar crucial occurrences defining a common world, a world for all men. Birth, maturation, death, male and female, young and old, leader and follower, earth, water, and sky, the sacred and profane are acknowledged in all societies, though not distinguished in the same ways. They provide common divisions which enable men to escape some of the limitations of their familiar and social worlds.

Crucial occurrences make it possible to isolate what is at root identical in all societies. This, which is common, is not the truly public or natural. To get to these we would have to return to the familiar world, and, instead of looking for punctuating occurrences which are duplicated in other societies, free it from all societal accretions.

It is enough for daily living to make a crude and ragged collection of what is socially assumed to be matter of fact. Were such collections everywhere alike, they would characterize a common world where all men belong. Men would then form a single body whose separation into different societies would be of relatively minor moment. But we find no such common collections—only the crucial common divisions and events.

To find what is real, to arrive at a world not affected by personal, societal, or even transsocietal divisions, it is necessary not only to cut behind all idiosyncratic interpretations, but also behind both distinctive and common societal acceptances. One way of doing this is to follow the lead of the exact sciences, and to occupy oneself with what is public. Another is to symbolize or speculate so as to arrive at actualities in a natural world, or at the cosmic interplay of these with finalities.

Cosmic realities are grasped at the edge of the familiar. What we daily know are appearances rooted in them. The appearances allow us to penetrate to these others. But the demands of society and the enticements of the senses quickly narrow our range and stop short our penetrations, with the consequence that actualities and finalities become just faint backgrounds for the familiar world.

The public world is the familiar purged of convention and arbitrary supposition. It is that at which science hopes to arrive. For most men it is almost completely hidden by conventions and practical alignments; for the others it is skewed by factors it takes a later generation, with its own distinctive, unknown bias, to discover. But it is now well enough known to enable one to assess and correct many of the beliefs and outlooks long held by men, both inside and outside a particular society.

The familiar world is sufficiently final and real for most practical purposes, but the public world is final and real apart from those purposes. In compensation, there is a richness and a satisfaction obtainable from the familiar that is not possible in the public. Though it is not as steady or as open to mathematical and logical thought as the other, the familiar is enlivened by daily expectations and evaluations. In turn, the public world finds no place for the robust, gross, familiar objects which provide the evidence for the particles that the public world is, with good reason, thought to contain.

[6]

The ordinary man is often wiser than some of his philosophic defenders; he stubbornly insists that he makes contact with realities existing outside the familiar, common, or public world. Not only is he not altogether unaware of the existence of actualities, but he has some knowledge of their differences. Though he tends to exaggerate the power or intelligence of what is not human, he rightly takes men and animals to differ in kind and not only in degree, sometimes because of what he discerns behind their appearances. To be sure, he classifies the living roughly into the harmless, the useful, the useless, and the dangerous, the landlocked, the flying, and those that live in the water, even after he has learned that there are good reasons for making other classifications. But whatever the classifications, he rightly sees himself and other living beings to be realities, contrasting in nature and activity, in value and in promise from inanimate beings, themselves also divided into the useful, the useless, the harmful, and the harmless, and then cross-classified as hard or soft, big or small, and the like. More important, both the inanimate and the animate are sometimes correctly dealt with by him as part of a natural world for which personal, societal, and scientific categories are not entirely appropriate.

Rarely does the ordinary man remain long on the surface of things, or simply relate items to others that are alongside, in the past, or in the future. Again and again he looks beyond what is before him, sometimes turning toward individual—and occasionally toward other final—realities outside the confines of the daily, common, or public world. Confidently, and often justifiably, he takes smiles, snarls, hesitant movements, shifts of the eyes, laughter, and tears to provide evidences of the character and sometimes even of the intent of men and other living beings.

He is deceived occasionally. Since everyone is an ordinary man, immersed in the affairs of the daily world a good deal of the time, no one, no matter how knowledgeable or sophisticated, detached or controlled, can be rightly said to have an infallible grasp of what is the case. All can be fooled. There are rogues, actors, hypocrites, men who know how to dissemble. It is not too difficult to assume a role which misleads quite a number for a while. The ordinary man, in fact, becomes so confident at times that it is legitimate and illuminating to move from what is manifest to what grounds this, that he readily accepts the conclusions of graphologists, phrenologists, and others who claim to have refined the art of finding out what is from what appears. It would be precipitate to translate the need to be cautious here into a denial that men can and do penetrate beyond appearances. There is warrant for moving from appearances to their sources, from surface to depth. Biography would be just fiction, description, or groundless assertion if it did not lead us to know what beings are from what they show themselves to be.

The specifics of the attempt to penetrate the surface of the familiar will occupy us later. For the time being, it is sufficient to point up the fact that we have here the promise of a method of discovery which could lead far from what might be learned by its crude use. An occasional genius has seen this. Freud is an example. He made evident how aberrational expressions and acts can be taken to be revelatory of unsuspected motives and drives. The conclusions he reached, though abhorrent to and initially rejected by ordinary men, were the outcomes of their own rough methods, refined and persistently pursued.

Inquiry must take its start *in* the familiar world, because that is where one initially is. That familiar world is the product of the interplay of men with other actualities, under the limitations which tradition and need impose. The actualities not only affect one another; they bear the marks of what occurred, and are conditioned by what can occur. Men's attitudes and activities add another layer to the encrusted result, to yield a world where they daily live and act.

The familiar, commonsense world baffles us again and again. We try to find better paths within it than those we now have, so that we can live in it with greater confidence and success. Practical enterprises strengthen, mend, and lengthen the fragile, fragmented, brief lines which seem to connect the items that we want and need. Theoretical science steps back from that world in the attempt to find more fundamental realities and connections which will provide a more stable and intelligible account of what occurs.

Inquiry need not remain in the familiar world. It can move into the realities beyond it. This is possible because those realities not only make the appearances of the familiar world possible, but enable the appearances to function as symbols of them. Because realities maintain a hold on the appearances with which the inquiry begins, inquiry can reach them.

The familiar is most available and first known. We can occupy ourselves with its details as long as we like. Sometimes we speak as though we keep inside it all the time, but, despite our persistent concern for what occurs there, we find it opening up again and again to leave us facing dark depths. We are then already on the road away from the familiar toward something quite different.

The familiar is porous. It seems solid only if we stolidly ignore what is outside it and with which we are already in contact. But it is understood only after we have come to know what is beyond it. What is known is part of what is still to be known, and what is still to be known is already discernible. We know the familiar before we know what is beyond it, but we understand the familiar only because we have come to know what is beyond it. If we are to know what is now before us, we must know what is now only discernible.

We start with the familiar in any case. We must also begin with it in order to understand what has reality apart from all of us. This requires that the familiar be clarified by what is now only faintly grasped beyond it.

Knowledge begins where we now are; but we are also already elsewhere. We can make a directed move toward that elsewhere because the beginning, and every step thereafter, is guided by it. Were they not so guided, it would be possible to end anywhere— perhaps even in some more obscure part of the familiar world. There is a principle governing directed action and the pursuit of knowledge: To make a good beginning it is necessary to attend to the controlling end. This has a correlate in a principle governing reflection: To understand a beginning it is necessary to begin with an achieved end.

The familiar world is too much the creature of deniable conditions to allow one to speak of it as though it were a tightly bounded domain, without openings into other realms. There is enough insight into what lies beyond it to prompt anyone to refuse to attend solely to the routinized, or to remain entirely on the familiar surface of the encountered. Since the ordinary man has neither the ability nor the interest to know how much distortion in fact occurs, or how to get rid of it, he is not in a position to determine to what degree his daily world exhibits conventions and unsupported supposition. But any attempt to bypass his world will be defeated the first time an attempt is made to quiet hunger. And any attempt to rectify his world will inevitably make use of agencies, at least partly lodged in that world.

[7]

The familiar world is too confused, at once too fluid and too rigid, too much at odds with itself, to allow it to be treated as final by anyone who would know basic truth, no matter what its guise. Though never entirely abandoned, it is also not closed off at all times and by all men. Again and again everyone moves, not only toward actualities, but toward finalities. No one remains constantly in the daily world; no one should, and no one can entirely escape from it. To stay with it is to take superstition, convention, societal needs, and interpretations as fact; it is to forget that daily life and its reports do not clearly distinguish truth from widely held opinions, nor attend either to the components of what is experienced or to what lies just beyond this and makes it possible. Yet, though it is not as innocent of arbitrary elements as it at first seems to be, and is not as reliable or as irreducible as its philosophic defenders take it to be, no one can avoid being part of the daily world. Nor is it wise to try.

No one seems to be altogether devoid of scientific curiosity or poetic imagination; again and again men exhibit some religious interest, and engage in philosophic thought. They are not thereby transformed into scientists, poets, religious men, or philosophers. These they can become only if they attend steadily to what is outside the reach of daily observation or procedures.

Our quests begin in and with the familiar world. Science, history, poetry, religion, and philosophy are all reached from there. It is not a neat world, easy to know or control. It has many crude divisions and examined items. Superstition and prejudice are there interwoven with hard fact. Little in it is exact, and what is exact is not certain. Much that is there accepted will betray. Its objects are so heterogeneous and disorganized, its values and claims so arbitrary and biased, and its trends so severely geared to practice as to make it undesirable to remain wholly within its confines, if it is truth we seek and not merely consensus. But there, too, evidence is offered that there are realities outside it, not yet well known. The *openness* that goads speculation is already found in the eyes of a child; the *reverence* that leads to worship is felt by the most routine and primitive; the *interest* that unites men to an ideal good is known both to reflective and unreflective men; *humility* allows all to sense the bonds that unite them; *awe* toward existence is exhibited many times during the day. Each man peers a little below the appearances of even that which is met with only casually.

To move steadily beyond the unexamined, familiar world, we must note what is before us and follow its leads. Sustained and critical reflection, speculation, and systematization are needed if what we arrive at is to be made intelligible. The results will require a somewhat new vocabulary, involving translations, tropes, and supplementations not widely used. It is possible that one might still not have freed oneself from all error; new errors might be introduced; good leads provided by daily life might have been overlooked.

Today many are too ready to assume that if they engage in science, or if they accept its theories or results, these difficulties can be avoided. They tacitly suppose that science yields unalloyed, complete, and final truth, because they fail to note that one carries into science some of the unexamined but unreliable suppositions that ordinary men make. To reduce these risks to a minimum one must be willing, in a sympathetic but critical spirit, to cut beneath all that appears, and then try to express the result in an appropriate language. There is little hope for success unless the entire effort is backed by a testing of each part by the others, and by the whole.

Reflection leads to a questioning of the personal, societal, and constant factors in daily experience, in the hope of reaching what is objective and ultimate. Rather than pursue this route, some are tempted to relax. They try to lose themselves in experience in the hope of avoiding the additions which thought, custom, belief, and practice introduce. But it is not possible to reach a state of mere experiencing, undisturbed by any intellectual contribution. Two obstacles stand in the way. To get to a state of mere experiencing, one would have to pass beyond daily knowledge by an act which, like every other, not only takes its start from the daily world, but is affected by it. Secondly, since mere experiencing exists outside the reach of thought, no one can know what it is, that it is, or what it contains, except by reflecting on what is known, and then isolating its supposed experiential core. An experiencing, unreflectingly involved with immediate, sensed content, is something inferred, not immediately had.

Science seeks to present the public world in an organized, intelligible, precise account, where one can in principle understand everything in rational connection with everything else. But its claims sometimes seem to demand the abandonment of the familiar world in favor of a scheme of rationally conceived, inexperienceable elements out of which to construct or to understand the larger familiar objects. Some think that the larger objects of daily life are composed of such elements. Others take them to provide the units in terms of which those objects are to be articulated and understood.

But most seem to suppose that their acknowledgment, particularly if scientific, precludes the acknowledgment of an equal reality to what is known in daily life. Yet the daily known objects remain. Every theory, even those that deny their reality, begins with them. And in the end, all come back to them for instruments, verification, and control. Streaked with error, not well-bounded or well-understood, the daily known objects are more useful, more humanly pertinent, and even more basic than any others. Though the ultimate elements which make up the public world are what they are, whether men come or go, and regardless of what men want or believe, and though the elements are irreducible and present everywhere, they neither replace nor wholly account for the familiar objects with which we daily interplay.

[8]

Despite our immersion in the daily world, we usually are aware every day of a natural world of objectively existing actualities. Each one of us knows that the stone he touches is solid and unyielding, more than what is felt. His touch, though, like his vision, does not penetrate far. Sometimes he moves beyond where these stop. When he does, he uses what he senses as a symbol. This enables him to get from the familiar to what underlies it.

The natural world of actualities is unaffected by human concerns. Outlasting and outreaching the familiar, it is no mathematically defined region, crisscrossed with straight lines at right angles to one another. It is divided, not by mathematics or rulers, but by whatever objects there be. Flat here and curved there, it is irregular, contoured by hills and valleys. Portions of it are empty and others filled.

The natural world can be known. This claim presupposes an answer to a most vexatious problem—how knowledge is possible of what is other than knowledge. Whatever we know seems to be a creature of ours, or at least to be dyed with personal and social colorings. If we eliminate or compensate for these, the residue seems to be equally subject to these or other colorings, traceable to the act of knowing. What lies beyond the conditions of knowledge seems to be nothing other than that which is conditioned in a similar way. How then, could one ever know anything more than what was relative to an individual or a group?

The difficulty is present no matter what the topic or the domain. It faces all claims to know anything in the daily world; it also faces all claims to know anything in the cosmos, or in the common, public, and natural worlds. If it can not be overcome, if the objects in no one of these could be truly known, the distinctions between one type of world and another will be idle, referring to nothing known to be real.

The difficulty has its own difficulties, and in the end removes itself. If all knowing veils the object to be known by interposing between ourselves and it the relativizing and perhaps distortive conditions of knowledge, how could one know this supposed conditioning without introducing still others? The removal of one taint would but introduce another. We would not only not be able to know what is, but would not be able to know what hides this from us. If all knowing involves conditions that prevent one from knowing what is conditioned, the knowing of those conditions will involve conditions that prevent one from knowing the original conditions. There would be nothing then that one could truly know— not even that there was nothing that one could know.

The problem has sometimes been thought to be pertinent only to the knowledge of objects, and not to the knowledge of conditions. To make this out, one must somehow be able to know what objects really are, so as to be able to contrast them with the conditions of knowledge. And one must also somehow be able to know the conditions themselves, and this without thereby subjecting oneself to the conditions of knowledge.

It could be maintained that all knowledge of objects is intermediated by concepts and other conditions, but that conditions can be known immediately for what they are. But why should conditions be so privileged? Perhaps what they condition can also be known immediately? This is in fact the very idea which a pure phenomenology would defend.

[9]

A pure phenomenology tries to look at everything without blinkers and without illusions. It tries to put aside all concepts, all theories, all demands of practice, and to attend to what is before one. Distortions, additions, errors, and qualifications can, it thinks, be avoided if only one would enter into experience in a truly catholic, open-ended, neutral spirit, in innocent honesty.

A genuinely pure phenomenology would be just as receptive to substances as it is to objects of intention, as receptive to daily objects as it is to what lies behind them; it would be open to mathematical forms, sensuous qualities, constant forces, and transient particulars, prejudging nothing. Such a pure phenomenology is hard to find. No one of the three great phenomenologists—Hegel, Husserl, Peirce—at any rate, produced one. All of them confined their investigations to only some of the available material. They were not interested in everything that was confronted.

Hegel occupied himself mainly with large-scaled items, cosmic in range and historically important, but devoid of interiority. His phenomenology traversed the history of Western civilization with brilliance and ingenuity, but rarely stopped to attend to anything encountered by a man in the course of daily life, or even to note what, if anything, was there revealed about man in himself or about whatever else there was. Husserl, instead, occupied himself with what he could separate off from the world of practical affairs. It was his conviction that an ability to consider something in abstraction from existence or without regard for its usefulness was identical with an ability to consider its essence, freed from all relation to these. He skipped over the fact that the abstract is incipiently concretionalized. Peirce, in contrast with the other two, concentrated on the main types of presented content, and then only so far as these could be distinguished formally. His was a rational phenomenology which attended primarily to the possible classes into which encountered content could be placed. Nuanced phenomena in their full concreteness were ignored.

A pure phenomenology aims far beyond the interests of these

great innovators. Ready to accept everything without prejudice, it refuses to impose divisions, to introduce classifications, to set up hierarchies, or to qualify what it faces. It seeks that virgin state where things are taken for what they are, and not for what we would like them to be or do. If the momentary and the persistent intersect or are intertwined, it reports the fact. It does not, for the sake of some theory, place one over against the other. The good, the indifferent and the bad, the hard and the yielding, the rational and the felt, texture and surface, the given and the taken, the recessive and the intrusive, all are acknowledged in the same spirit. But only a few, if any, are stable or enduring, without depth and nuance. All fluctuate and vibrate in countless ways. Most undergo change, and last for but a short time. The true phenomenologist must let what he confronts advance and recede, fade off and pass away without hindrance. Consequently, he can hardly do more than live through what happens; he surely has no time to examine all that appears. Indeed, he has insufficient time to examine more than one or two items with care. Most of what he confronts at any one time will slip away before he can dissect it, and any report that he writes will be presented at a time when what he noted is no longer there in that very guise. He gets his most satisfactory content if he relaxes, simply enjoys, gets into the spirit of play.

Play takes one away from the workday world. When frolicsome, spontaneous, and unconfined by rules, play makes possible the ignoring of the normal uses of things. But even it must take some account of their contours and capacities, and keep in accord with what is intended. To free himself from even these limitations, a man would have to be willing to do no more than remain attentive to the different flavors of things, as they flow past or into himself. An effort would have to be made to avoid subjecting them to qualifications, practical or otherwise. He would then have an aesthetic apprehension of what was sensuously encountered—roughness or smoothness, the dark or the light.

Aesthetic apprehension is bounded on one side by attentive men, and on the other by a continuum of changing appearances. The men pass unreflectingly from the stage of simple *enjoyment* to that of *acceptance;* from there to *participation;* and finally to the stage of *dramatization.* They come closest to items as they appear in enjoyment, for this is least subject to a conceptual framework. In acceptance men go further. Then they make use of a standard in terms of which items are ordered as more or less agreeable, desirable, or interesting. Participation, in addition, requires them to share in the rhythms and tensions of the apprehended, and to unite with it in an intimate way, while remaining in control of themselves and the manner in which they are united with it. Finally, in dramatization, men sharpen and add to the continuities and discontinuities, the accords and disaccords which the different items have with respect to one another, and perhaps to them. These different stages merge so imperceptibly into one another that it is customary to speak of aesthetic apprehension as though it were a simple act in which surfaces were all subjected to an unreflecting acceptance, acceptance was a form of participation, and dramatization a participation intensified. In any event, in all of the stages—even in the simplest "mindless" enjoyment—men are active, and as a consequence introduce qualifications and stresses into what they acknowledge.

Men affect all experienced content, no matter how it is apprehended. What is confronted makes its own contribution to the result, but only when a man gives himself to it, and thereby colors it. The coloring can be distinctively individual, or it can be similar for many. He who has delicate fingers feels differences where another feels none, though both may feel something to be woolly or glassy. While one man will emphasize what another does not, both can enjoy, appreciate, participate in, and dramatize the very same things.

To be able to do nothing but enjoy, and then without introducing anything of one's own, one would have to lose oneself entirely in sensed immediacy. Only he who was completely passive could do this. But even when so immersed that he could distinguish neither himself nor anything else, even where item slides into item without break, he will have made an impression. This will inevitably involve a stress on some items and a comparative neglect of others.

When, as is in fact the case, he goes further and actually attends, he necessarily emphasizes some things and ignores others.

No one can take account of every facet, even of one of the items in which he is most interested. It has endless details and relations. No man has sufficient time and few have a great enough tolerance of boredom to examine many of these. Even he who sets himself to attend to every phase and facet of what was encountered, would have to deal initially with some items rather than with others, and would so far have to neglect those others. There is no escaping some selection, whether one attends only to the universal and constant, or is willing to take account as well of what is neither. But if one selects anything, one inevitably neglects the remainder; inevitably one does more than simply accept something.

To this it might be objected that nothing is so simple or so harmless as the enjoyment of items one after the other without bias. Putting aside the question whether fastening onto something does not give it a role it did not have before, there is the act of *noting* what is undergone or faced. This carries the imprint of past experiences, associations, interests, needs, and desires. The past intrudes upon the present, making the present at once a consequence and a condition. Detached, neutral observations of what is simply present may be possible to a camera. It is beyond the power of a man, unless it be within his power to have a passive eye and no convictions.

The size of some of these difficulties can be reduced. It is possible to attend to the fact that certain kinds of items recur, or that they have a particular degree of unity, distinctness, and vivacity. Or a steady, pervasive dimension of experience might be isolated and studied at leisure. Our three great phenomenologists, Hegel, Husserl, and Peirce, did something like that. So far as they succeeded in focusing on what was constant and common, they became phenomenologists of a part of a dimension of what was before them. No one of them, of course, was a pure phenomenologist to begin with, even of this limited area, since he had to first select out, and therefore to qualify the desirable part or dimension. The assumption that they did not add anything in the course of their attending, and did not compromise the being or the nature of what they neglected, they never did or could justify.

A good phenomenologist is a narrowed one. But restricting the content of his experience does not give him unqualified material. He necessarily modifies whatever he confronts; like the rest of men, he too faces items which are products, mediated immediacies.

No matter what we do, what we know, initially at least, is not precisely what is so. It is picked out, isolated, and bounded, and thereby brought to a state it obviously did not have apart from us. We make a difference to what we acknowledge. A content may sink below consciousness. It can also be a constituent of some more complex whole. In speaking of it in these ways, we tend to treat it as though in itself it were neutral to the different roles. But it is neutral only in abstraction from an actual functioning. If it lay inert beyond the reach of all approaches, it could not be known.

A phenomenologist would like to stay with his items for a considerable time. At once impersonal and open-minded, he tries to report what he sees, and nothing more. If he backs up persistence with forethought, and supports sensitive observations with analysis, he can minimize what he unreflectingly adds. But he will not be able to compensate for all the changes he introduces, for some of them are produced in the very act of attending.

Today some try to arrive at a pure phenomenological position by taking drugs. They do not, with the great phenomenologists, try to attend to what is in fact encountered. Instead, they try to move into another realm where the knower could not be distinguished from the known. But then they could not possibly know what, if anything, had been altered by the knower. Their drugs, they think, might bring them to a position similar to that which mystics some-times reach. Even if that were possible, they would not get the truths that the mystics supposedly know. Mystics are disciplined; they prepare for their experiences. The user of drugs is simply trans-ported. Instead of bringing something into the experience of him-self as merged with what else there be, he subtracts from it all that he had consciously achieved. Mysticism is accumulative, intensive, transcending; it requires one to lose oneself in something bigger than oneself. That position is not reached by simply losing hold of oneself.

To the degree that men relax, they give up control. To that very degree, there is nothing that they can prevent. What occurs will then push, pull, arrest, and redirect without hindrance. It is not a quiet or indifferent world into which we sink once we refuse to take charge. The strange, the obdurate, the alien, the trivial, and the ominous, are not to be greeted in the same way; if they are, we will be manipulated where we might have been effective.

Contemplatives live in deserts and caves, on mountaintops and along silent rivers. They there escape many of the occurrences that affect the rest of us. But they do not avoid them all. Like everyone else, contemplatives are faced with things that affiliate and separate, congregate and interact in a great number of ways, apart from all uses and practices, conventions and classifications. Self-discipline no less than a partially recaptured innocence is needed if one is to see what otherwise would be obscured, neglected, or rejected. One must become self-conscious, critical, and analytic in order to uncover the conditions that are imposed on all that is observed and done.

All of us for moments, and some of us for long periods, can achieve some success in knowing what is so. At every moment different things have different weights for us. Each of us, consequently, is driven to attend only to some and in special ways, and to set the rest aside. Even if we could encounter a world where everything functioned in the same way, or had the same bearing on human hopes and fears, we would, because of our limited time and power, have to give special roles and places to some of them. We are affected differently by different things; in compensation, we impose our own demands on them. If something comes rapidly toward us, we tend to keep it in focus and to ready ourselves to resist its possible intrusion. If something in the forefront seems alien to our interests, we force it to the edge of our consciousness, if we can, and attend to something else.

Demands, reflecting our appetites and concerns, affect what is confronted. There is nothing given, without a meaning or nature of its own, on which the demands are imposed. The demands are part of an act of encountering—but so are the objects. The known is a product of contributions from both. Neither knower nor object works up or lurks behind passive material. They interplay.

The things with which we daily live—even those we encounter suddenly and for the first time—are partly personalized and socialized. They can not be simply accepted as they appear without our thereby missing what is objectively there. Even that common punctuation, which crucial events provide, leaves them too humanized to permit their being simply accepted, if what we seek to know is what is real, no matter what we want or do.

A pure phenomenology can be carried out only with respect to some aspect of things, or with respect to some items. It gets to the immediate by starting from daily life and attending to portions of it. Inevitably it raises the question whether or not there is a desirable method for obtaining knowledge, and what must be done to heal whatever distortions the getting of it introduces.

[10]

Phenomenology has the virtue of being aware of what many thinkers cast aside—features which need not have been. But if we are to account for them, we must leave phenomenology behind and look for the causes or sources of those features.

The move to things in themselves (or to final, transcendent realities) begins with the attempt to account for so-called 'accidents' or appearances—the present shape or size or color of the leaf. These once were different; they may be different again. But all the while the leaf remains, changed perhaps, but still a leaf. We can learn what the leaf is, not by shearing off the 'accidents' and attending to the denuded object that remains, but by using the 'accidents' to enable us to penetrate into it.

Everything whatsoever has 'accidents'. Some of these could conceivably owe their presence to an aspect of a thing, contrasting with another aspect, its 'essence'. Aristotle took them to be due to a matter which, together with the 'essence', constituted the actual object. But there is no need to dichotomize actualities. The 'accidents' sometimes owe their presence to the whole actuality which surfaces, fulgurates, spontaneously comes into the open in a multitude of unpredictable ways. Friedrich Schiller thought that it was even normal for things to exhibit themselves exuberantly, producing items to excess. But then it must be remembered that such products are related to one another and are qualified by the conditions they encounter.

Some 'accidents' are the outcome of the action or presence of other actualities. The hard makes an impression on the soft; from different perspectives things have different dignities, roles, and meanings. We will still be able to learn by means of them if we do not forget that the intruded-on offers stops and supports, and that the result can help us know something about the intruder as well as what was intruded on.

'Accidents' do not float idly above the objects where they are located. These objects make a difference to them. The 'accidents', consequently, testify to the existence of realities beyond them—of themselves in a more intensive guise and of what governs all of them —thereby enabling one to use them as symbols of those realities.

Two doctrines seem to reject these contentions. One takes only appearances to be real, possessed by no one and explained by nothing. But not only do appearances have changing features because of the changing relations they have to others, but all provide evidence of contexts, apart from which they can not even be together. The second doctrine, like the first, defends an atomism, but an atomism of realities, physical or psychical, Democritean or Leibnizian. Those atoms are taken to have no adventitious characters. But were they not related to one another, they, too, would not make a plurality. Yet if there be more than one, they will together necessarily offer evidence of the existence of a single context within which they are together.

Only a strict monism, which acknowledges just one entity, would not lead to something else. But such a monism can not be known, since knowledge requires that there be a difference between knower and known. The only positions that are tenable are pluralisms of some kind. In each of these there is evidence of something besides the items in their severalty. The issue is not avoided by taking a linguistic view.

Every approach we take, linguist philosophers say, is from the perspective of a language. If the language distorts, it will do so unwittingly and beyond our ability to know, since the distortion will affect whatever we say and whatever we acknowledge. In effect, there will, therefore, be no distortion. The thesis, I think, is somewhat incoherent. Those who offer it believe that there are good ways and bad ways to use a language. The bad ways will lead us astray. From what? Apparently from what in fact is the case. Were it not possible to escape the conditions imposed by a particular use of a language, no truth could be stated which holds when one uses it in another way, when one uses another language, or when one leaves all language behind to observe or to make. If there is a proper use of a language it must be to allow us to say what is the case outside the language.

Languages contain conventional distinctions and have conventional vocabularies and grammars. But these limitations can be known. The fact—if fact it was—that we could not know what alterations language introduces into the data we initially accept, would not show that there were no alterations, but that we were trapped inside language, and had to give up hope of knowing anything outside it, including the data on which it operated or to which it referred.

We can not say anything to others without using a language; but, also, we can not use a language without standing outside it. Since we can speak to one another, it is evident that we are not trapped inside a language. We are not kept from what is the case by language any more than we are by the conditions of knowing. To suppose otherwise is fatal to the suppositions themselves. At the very least, a linguistic philosopher must begin where everyone else does, immersed in a commonsense world, before he engages in and while he continues his study.

Language provides evidence of the structure of our thoughts, the distinctions that interest us, the associations that we make. We in turn provide evidence of the language we use in the structure and relationship of our actions, classifications, grammar, and vocabulary.

[11]

How can we know what is apart from us? If this question can not be answered, there will be no knowing how anything can be known. All talk of evidence of actualities and finalities—even of appearances—will then be illegitimate.

2

KNOWLEDGE AND THE KNOWN

~~~~~~

Controlling Summary: Knowledge and the known are distinct; otherwise there would be no knowledge of anything. Knowledge and the known are identical in content. Otherwise, there would be something in the known which escaped knowledge.

Knowledge adds to the confronted. It tears the confronted out of its context in fact, and subjects it to conditions produced by the knower and his community. Knowledge is the known with new functions; the known stands away from knowledge because it is sustained by what is not knowledge. This which sustains it would be forever unknown were it not identical with the known insisting on itself in opposition to knowledge.

The known is selected out of a confronted world of appearances of substantial realities. That contention is opposed in a number of ways. An exposure of their weaknesses makes evident that the known is bounded by us at the limit of what is not knowledge. To arrive at the limit of knowledge is to arrive at that which is maintaining the known in opposition to the knowledge.

~~~~~~

What we know must be of something. If there is no difference between knowledge and its object there is nothing to know. But if the two are different, there apparently is something in the object that is not in the known. If this additional factor is unknown, we cannot warrantedly say that it exists; if it is known, the difference between knowledge and object seems to be lost.

The alternatives are intolerable: known object and real object are identical; known object and real object are incognizably different. Both views have more than one form. The first view has two main cases; the second, considerably more. A review of their difficulties makes possible a better answer than any of them can provide.

1] The 'identity' view of knowledge and reality can be traced back to Pythagoras. He seemed to have held that reality is at once constituted and known by means of geometrical numbers. Over the course of time, the Pythagorean numbers have been replaced by other equally odd candidates. The Platonic idea, the Leibnizian Simple, the Berkeleian Notion, the Humean Impression, the Peircean Third, and the Whiteheadian Feeling differ from one another in origin, range, and career. But all, like the Pythagorean numbers, are taken to be both known and real. It is not clear in some of these cases whether there is supposed to be no difference at all between the known and the real. Perhaps no one has ever held that pure doctrine. Berkeley evidently tried to defend it, but gave it up in accounting for the persistence of objects when they were not perceived. In the end he distinguished what entities were, as perceived by us, and what they were apart from us, as produced by God. Parmenides, in the first part of his famous poem, identified knowledge and being, but in the second part he allowed for a difference between them.

Could the identity be maintained, both the knower and object would be lost, to leave us with what could be indifferently called an idea or a reality. But the idea could be credited with neither truth nor error, and the reality could not be said to be an object of knowledge. Truth and error require that what we have in mind be distinguishable from that to which it is referred. To be an object of knowledge is to be distinct from the knowledge of it.

The best that could be done would be to maintain that there was a single content which was to be designated in different ways. How those ways are to be distinguished, however, would still have to be explained. And in any case, attention would have to be paid to whatever sound ideas there be which have not yet been related to their objects. And it would be hard to see how room could be made for the existence of objects for which there were as yet no ideas.

2] Stronger and more familiar identity theories explicitly hold that only certain known items are in fact real, the others being dismissed as illusory, erroneous, confused, or as defective in some other way.

For Descartes what is known clearly and distinctly is real. But the clearly and the distinctly known is an idea. Since he does not reduce reality to ideas, he must show how the clear and distinct as idea differs from the clear and distinct as real. But this he can not do, since he can acknowledge only ideas. A variant on his position is given by Leibniz, with the result that he is faced with a variant of the same difficulty. For Leibniz the best of possible worlds is realized. But the possible is not identical with the real. Yet he can not tell us how the possible best world is different from the realized best world, for all he ever knows are possibilities.

Absolute idealists and some pragmatists think that the identity view holds in only one case—when the end of inquiry is achieved. The knowledge one then has is taken to be identical with what is real. The ontological argument is thus assumed to be valid with reference to the totality of knowledge. This position avoids supposing that finite ideas are identical with what is ultimately real. But those finite ideas are then assumed to be identical with equally inadequate fragments of the absolute—which is the first form of the identity thesis all over again—or the finite ideas are all taken to be false, and therefore alone to differ from what is real—which is the second form of the identity thesis confined to one idea, the true idea of the absolute.

The second form of the identity thesis argues on behalf of certain special ideas only—which is perhaps all that the first wanted to maintain. The two, in any case, come to the same impasse: some ideas are held to be indistinguishable from realities. But then there could be nothing of which the ideas were true or false.

[2]

The opposing view, dualism, sharply distinguishes knowledge and the known. They are taken by it to differ in nature, being, power, or locus. Nine varieties seem worth distinguishing.

1] Empiricism achieves a classical expression in the writings of Hume. He thought that all knowledge originated with impressions which were to be distinguished by their greater vividness from what we remembered or imagined. To confront the vivid was for him to confront what was reliable, and, in the only allowable sense, external or real. Yet some images, as Peirce observed, are more vivid than some impressions. Nor need there be any loss in vividness when we remember what it was that we once encountered.

If a quality, such as vividness, could constitute the known difference between the real and the merely mental, why could we not think of that quality, and thereby have material enough to overcome the difference? By adding the quality to what we already had in mind we could, just by taking thought, perform the miracle of making something come to be. If the quality could not be thought, it would not be something in mind, but something outside it. Since it would then be unintelligible, it could not then tell us how the mental differed from the real.

If vividness is conceivable it will not be able to distinguish the conceived from the real. What is needed is a real vividness, not merely one that is conceived. But if that real vividness differs from itself as conceived, it will not make intelligible how a thought differs from its object.

2] Some empiricists did not take up the suggestion that vividness made the difference between real occurrences and what was produced solely in the mind. Instead, they said that the difference lay in the fact that one was sensed and the other was not. This is an advance on the previous position, since it does not take the difference to lie in some conceivable quality. Still, it is possible to imagine what was sensed; the sensed, so far, would seem to be on a footing with ideas merely constructed or delusive. And it seems that one can infer—as Hume saw—to something sensible at times, even though it had never been sensed, thereby producing through the mind's action what could supposedly be given to it only from the outside.

The view confines the known universe within the scope of human sensing and, consequently, must either ignore, construct, or reduce to the sensed such diverse realities as space, time, numbers, history, and sport. The sensed world is not the whole real world. Nor is everything sensed real, unless there be nothing like optical illusions.

3] A more sophisticated version of this last position appeals to 'experience', understood to be the outcome of an actual involvement of conscious human beings with other entities. But the experience is either brute and inexplicable, or there are real knowable entities which make it possible. The latter are evidently not constituted by, and are not part of, experience.

Kant avoids the acknowledgment of real entities existing outside the reach of possible experience by supposing that nothing is real unless it is connected with what is in fact encountered in a present experience. His theory pushes the issue back just a step. What is this connection? Is it known? Is it experienced? If there are answers to these questions in Kant's writings, they are not easy to find. What he seems inclined to say is that the experienceable is an indefinitely extendable domain, produced through the union of a manifold with space and time. Since this manifold by itself is not yet spatialized, temporalized, or organized by means of categories (the means by which Kantian knowledge alone is possible) the manifold cannot be known. Could one get past this obstacle, one would still be left with the fact that there are many other kinds of experience besides that which is occupied with occurrences in a Newtonian space and time. Religious experience, aesthetic experience, experiences of obligation, tragedy, and love, all have their own integrity, and presuppose the reality of more than an extended manifold and a set of categories relevant to this.

4] What we truly know, the Aristotelians hold, is the form of things. This is their intelligible, communicable, scientific meaning. The form as known by us is deprived of the 'matter' with which it had been associated in fact. It is its association, perhaps even union, with matter that enables the form to be objective, to be apart from our knowing of it.

The Aristotelian form in our mind is the very essence of the external object. That object is external because in it the essence is involved with a matter not in our minds. That matter has no essence of its own. But then it can not, according to this doctrine, itself be known. One can not say, therefore, that it does or that it does not help constitute a reality apart from thought. Of that of which we know nothing, nothing should be said.

5] A version of Aristotle's view of matter maintains that it is space and time which distinguish the real from the mental. What is independent of our thinking, what exists outside us is, on this view, an occupant of space and time. One is then required to distinguish not only the time through which we live when we think, from the time which characterizes a world external to that thinking, but to take actual space to be different from any space we could have in mind. Also, since the whole of space and the whole of time are neither spatial nor temporal, they should, on this view be treated as unreal. Similar conclusions must be drawn with respect to numbers, ideals, and selves; the view requires that these, too, since they are not spatial and temporal, be denied reality. This can be done, and it often has been done. The fact does not show that the entities have no reality, but only that the view does not accommodate them.

6] A stronger thesis is offered by Thomists. According to them, what is real has an existence of its own. Yet nothing, they hold, is entirely separable from God's existence. Not only is it then true that nothing exists external to God—which is a monistic result rejected by Thomists—but one still has to distinguish forms which are not enabled to exist and which one may have in mind, from forms existing outside the mind. The extramental forms must be united with existence, but for that existence there are no forms by means of which it can be known. If, too, God's idea of Himself is identical with His existence—which is implied in the formula "God's essence is His existence"—we, with our inadequate idea of Him, are unable to know just what His existence, and therefore Existence as such, and our own derived existence, are like. Once again, it will not be possible to say what differentiates the real from the thought one has of it.

7] A related but better scholastic answer is contained in the idea of an 'act.' To exist is to act; a being is real just so far as it is active. Yet, unless one is to deny the reality of whatever is present but passive, one must allow also for the 'potential,' itself just as irreducible as the act. Were a thing real only so far as it was active, it would be unreal just so far as it was merely potential. This entails that God, who is supposed to be without any potentiality, is the most real of beings, and that matter, supposed to be merely potential, is the most unreal. But how could that matter then make a difference to anything? And, in any case, what is other than God, on this view, would have potentialities. Since those potentialities are precisely what are not active, they could not be known, thereby precluding a complete knowledge of anything other than God.

8] Related to, but better than the foregoing, is the theory that a known object is supported by or grounded in something real. This is thought to give the known object a status which the knowledge of it does not have. What is this prop? Since it is beyond all knowing no one can say what it is like. Left in darkness, treated as unknown, and even as inaccessible to knowledge, it can not be known even to exist.

A variant of this view supposes that ideas are themselves sustained by their own distinctive props. But in this way one merely adds another unknown. If both are needed, both also are unavailable.

9] The strongest form of dualism rests on the ability to make predictions. Simply by thinking we often can learn what will be. Before the occurrences take place, they are envisaged possibilities; when they take place they differ in some way from those possibilities. To know how actual occurrences differ from the possibilities we have in mind when we predict, we must know something not predicted. But this knowledge the dualistic position does not allow us to have. It can not tell how what is now predicted differs from what occurs later in fact, or, equivalently, how what now occurs differs from a prediction of it.

Dualism, no matter what the variants, is not a tenable view. In effect it denies that one can have direct access to anything untouched by knowledge. As a consequence, it denies us the right to say that there is something other than knowing, other than the knowledge or the ideas we have, and other than the known, i.e., other than what is encountered in knowing, though these others are exactly what it must insist upon. Dualism asserts that there is something distinct from knowing, knowledge, and the known. It knows that all knowledge is a 'knowledge of,' but it is unable to do more than just claim this. It can not say that any object is known; indeed, it has no warrant for claiming that any object exists at all. Since it defeats itself another answer is evidently required.

[3]

The different forms of the identity and dualistic views are primarily occupied with conceptual knowing. This they misconstrue in a double way: they mistake the relation of idea to object, and they confound conceptual knowing with other ways of apprehending.

Unless *knowing* be distinct from *knowledge*, there is no outcome to the act of knowing. Unless *knowledge* be distinct from the *known*, there is nothing of which it is knowledge. And if the *known* is not distinct from the *object*, there is nothing which is being known.

Knowing, knowledge, and the known are all involved with dualities of some kind, but the dualities do not have two terms or realms in radical opposition. If they did, not only would something escape us, but we would be oblivious of that fact.

A leaf belongs to an open-ended world. It is assertive, insistent on itself at the same time that it is subject to external forces. When we know the leaf, we do not abrogate its place in the open-ended world, its insistence on itself, or the forces that act upon it. We give it new associations and new neighbors; due to our memories, expectations, imaginations, and beliefs it acquires new roles in our economy. More important, we not only hold it away from other entities, but we impose a boundary on it.

Knowledge *adds* to the real, and this without thereby jeopardizing the integrity of that reality. It puts a boundary around content encountered, to make it a separated *known* entity, related in new ways to what else we may have in mind. The vivid, the sensed, the experienced, the material, are ways of referring to an object as independent of the boundary we impose on it.

Were there an omniscient God, He would know the totality of things. In knowing it He, too, would impose a boundary on what He knew. This would make what He knew into a single known object, related then and there to other possible worlds or ideas that He might also have in mind. The Aristotelian God is a thinking on thinking; the Hegelian, a self-consciousness of self-consciousness. Such Gods, if real, must insist on themselves—as every reality does—and at the same time impose a limit on themselves so as to make themselves be possible objects of knowledge. This last the Aristotelian and the Hegelian, to be sure, do not allow, with the consequence that their Gods must know themselves in a manner dissimilar from that by which we know anything. Their Gods' thinking and self-consciousness is not a knowing, if knowing is what men do.

When we know we attend. That to which we attend stands out. It is distinguished, marked off, held away, selected, in the very act of being focused on. The focusing ends in a bounding of it, a limiting of it for us. Because it is we who provide those limits, what we confront is in a sense our product. But since the content is there to be known, it is so far not constituted by us.

[4]

We know what exists outside our knowledge. Though the content of the knowledge is identical with the content of the known, it functions differently in the two places. It has two, not one set of relations and adventures. In our knowledge we give the content a career additional to that which it continues to maintain on its own.

We would be caught up in subjectivism and relativism were it not that knowledge reaches to the object, and yet adds to it to make it known. The contention will meet with resistance, even by some of those who agree that knowledge and the known must be identical in content while differing in function, since they hold that we can have a direct knowledge of some things. These are known, they think, just as they in fact are, immediately and with certainty, so that the known, though distinct from knowledge, is identical with the object known.

Over the course of centuries, philosophers have offered a number of plausible types of content which they took to be known without alteration, addition, or subtraction. They have followers today who also insist that 1] the measurable, 2] the impersonal, 3] the pragmatic, 4] the practical, 5] the humanly significant, 6] the arresting, 7] the substantial, 8] scientific evidence, or 9] the valuable, are bedrock as known and in fact. None of these contentions can withstand criticism. An examination of their implications will make evident that an object not only has a different career from the knowledge we have of it, but that the knowledge involves the imposition of a boundary, thereby at once constituting the known and making it possible to recognize that there is something present not yet known, because not affected by our knowing. There are no completely soft data, simply awaiting moulding and stiffening by knowledge; but there are also no absolutely hard data which the knower passively confronts or receives.

1] After awhile, some men come to know that when they are occupied with items which concern their welfare, or the welfare of those whom they cherish or despise, they do not see as clearly or as steadily as they otherwise can. Some thereupon make a rough division between those things that they observe with some detachment, and those that are affected by the observer. The former they tend to take to be primary and to identify with what is measurable or mathematically expressible—size, shape, number. What is left over they credit to themselves—greens and reds, sweet notes and sour, the precious and the indifferent, the dangerous, the hot, and the pleasant. These are lumped together under the heading "secondary qualities." The practice is at the root of some modern scientific accounts of the course of nature and of the current accepted view of what is subjective.

A distinguishing of primary from secondary qualities is most useful. We tend to adhere to it, even though it can not withstand the scrutiny of a suspicious reason. Two centuries ago Bishop Berkeley made clear how all that we perceive, whether primary or not, is inextricably involved with the limited and personal positions that the perceiver assumes. The color of an object varies with the way it is related to its neighbors, with the nature of the prevailing light, and with the distance it is from the observer. So does its visible shape and its visible size. Like every other quality, from smoothness to roughness, from experienced resistance to experienced insistence, size and shape are inseparable in being and nature from the relation which they have to the perceiving being.

Shape and size are sometimes said to be more objective than color or smell because they can be measured by means of simple, impersonal instruments, and because the results of such efforts can be precisely stated in terms that can be related readily to and compared with others made at different times and from different positions. But measurements can be noted only if the perceivers attend to secondary qualities. And they yield different results, too, when the circumstances and the perceivers' positions are changed. Also, instead of reproducing the size or shape of objects, they substitute abstract transcriptions for them. A size or shape extends, stretches out. Since a measurement is only some numbers, it can never replace the measured without our losing what is in fact present.

One type of quality is not more objective and real than another. To accept one and to dismiss others is to be arbitrary; in the end it is to do violence to what is encountered. If we wish to distinguish kinds of qualities persistently, we must introduce into observations a principle by which they are forced apart, even when they appear to be inextricably bound together. It is good to do this if one wants a communicable measure or would like to lose himself in the sensuous. The division occurs, however, not in fact but in thought, and it takes any one of a number of alternate routes. What is put aside as sensuous for one approach is allowed to cling to the measurement in another.

Both measurement and a submission to the rhythms of things,

dictate a separation of primary from secondary qualities. The result is an achievement, not a datum, and is affected by one's demands and purposes. The separation, even if well sanctioned by practice, does not entail that the first is objective and reliable, and the second subjective or unreliable. For artists, lovers, and bird watchers the reverse is closer to the truth.

When things are measured, an aspect of them is bounded off from the colors with which the aspect is in fact intertwined. When the colors of things are attended to they, instead, are bounded off. The bounding has the same cause in both cases; in both cases, the result is an aspect added to. One of these is not more objective, real, resistant than the other. One or the other will prove to be of more interest or use, depending on what we thereupon seek to know or to do.

2] Sometimes men readily grant that they now and then alter what they deal with. When excitements, angers, and jubilations subside, when they are alerted or are painstaking, some things previously acknowledged seem to have vanished. Distinctions and unions that were once apparently unavoidable are no longer evident. Conceivably, some might continue to exist were all observers removed. All we apparently can be sure of is what is indifferent to our personal likes and dislikes, the impersonal. This is not to be equated with the measurable; a study of color blindness may forego measurement and yet treat colors with magisterial impersonality.

No matter what it is to which individuals attend, they qualify it with their distinctive histories and prejudgments; when they attend to what is supposedly impersonal, they cannot but personalize it. The impersonal is personally noted. If unreality or nonobjectivity are effects of the personal, the impersonal must be unreal or non-objective as well.

Things intrude forcefully. They often go counter to human intent and interests, thereby making it necessary to distinguish what is impersonal from what is not. All of us separate the indifferent from the relevant; we note the relentless movement of nature and hold it apart from what we make and unmake as we will. The distinction between the impersonal and the personal, though, is relative to the attitudes we assume toward ourselves and nature.

Once the dance was thought to have the rain under control. Men believed that they could make it fall when and where they prayed it would. Theirs was a personalized rain, a rain inseparable from human wish and virtue. Today we often think that the rain is indifferent to our plans, and that it can be controlled only so far as we deal with impersonal chemicals which exert their powers no matter what we believe. To be impersonal, it is tempting to say, is to avoid superstitions and to accept instead the reliable, settled knowledge characteristic of the present. But sometimes the impersonal loses for us what sympathy and concern reveal. The impersonal attitude men once assumed toward the sick, the mad, and the poor has fortunately been somewhat replaced by a more personal attitude allowing us to note what before had been ignored.

There is nothing that can not be looked upon with indifference. But indifference inescapably entrains assessment. It, too, is not entirely separated from or unaffected by desire and need.

The great rationalists wanted the impersonal above all. Identifying it with the mathematically clear, and the personal with the emotionally confused, they turned a useful distinction into a fixed principle. This they thought would enable them to separate forever what was true from what was false, what was reliable from what was not. But errors and confusions occur everywhere. Even such simple truths as $1 + 1 = 2$ or that I am I, require the help of a fallible memory stretching over a period of time. To know them, the beginning of the judgment must not be allowed to slip entirely into an unrecoverable past; it must be kept operative in the present. Unless memory is self-contradictorily depersonalized, knowledge, because it involves the retention of what is past, can not be entirely free of all personal factors.

The impersonal is the outcome of a decision. We can take the constant or the variable, the sensuous or the formal to be unaffected by us, and treat the remainder as derivative. But other decisions are also possible, and have in fact been made. What is preferred by the rationalists is dismissed by the romantics. Neither side is privileged, and both of them are opposed by others—idealists, for example, who divide the phenomena in quite another way.

3] One preference, which in the hands of some practitioners

comes very close to the foregoing, contrasts the significant with the idle. Here one asks for what makes a difference in practice. This, according to leading pragmatists, is at once humanly relevant and known through the use of the objective devices of an impersonal science. Pragmatists seem to think that they are able to be on both sides of the division made by the rationalists and their opponents, and there separate off the effective from the useless, the real from the abstract.

Pragmatists take their principle to be applicable to all data whatsoever. They observe that our perceptions anticipatorily mark out the course or terminus of actions; they remark that what we know is forged in the light of what we use as material, and what we change this from or change it into. Whatever the agency— perception, language, or thought—they say, it serves solely to bridge one island of activity and another.

Pragmatism has shown that the verbally different may at times be properly identified because the words have the same practical import. As a consequence, pragmatism has made it possible to avoid a number of nagging puzzles. One example is as good as a dozen: Since no practical difference follows from the supposition that every item in the universe has expanded to twice the size it had a moment before, pragmatism rightly rejects the idea as meaningless for science.

It is not possible to carry out this method in all areas. Not all of the results in higher mathematics have distinguishable practical consequences. Nor does the historic past, particularly as something to be discovered for no other reason than that of satisfying an intellectual curiosity. Private reveries and self-knowledge need have no pragmatic import.

Pragmatism is paralyzed before the prospect of making sense of the being of God as He is by Himself, not wholly involved in human affairs. It lamely identifies art with the heightening of the results of craftsmanship, and denies meaning or existence to the objects of mysticism and speculative knowledge on the question-begging grounds that they can not be made practically relevant.

Pragmatism is most persuasive and powerful in the area of middle-sized facts. The grossly observable, the tangible, and the effective all yield readily to its methods. Powerful when it comes to the present and the future, the public and the social, pragmatism can not handle the problem of the reality of the past, the private, the formally necessary, the ideal, or the transcendent.

If we have room only for a distinction between what makes a practical difference and what makes none we will soon say foolish things. With Peirce we will be inclined to remark that the difference between the Catholic and the Protestant interpretations of the Eucharist must have only a practical meaning or express no difference at all. Suppose that these religions used the very same rituals and prayers, and were outwardly in every way alike; would they not still differ radically, and that in part because they envisaged the Eucharist in different ways? Catholics hold that there is a real, while Protestants claim that there is only a 'symbolic' change in the very being of the water and the wine. Each side insists that a decision to accept one interpretation rather than another has consequences. But those consequences do not necessarily eventuate in this space-time world, the only one with which pragmatism is concerned.

John Dewey made an unusual effort to accommodate the rich variety of occurrences that make up the daily and public worlds. He flawed his work by too quick a reduction of the formal to merely instrumental roles in well-structured pursuits, holding that those who took the formal to be real merely illustrated historical errors somehow kept alive by language or academic tradition. What he could not bring within the orbit of his view he supposed was just mistaken or illusory. The judgments he made about his opponents' selections they, with equal warrant, make of his. Logicians, for example, sometimes insist that whatever is real is fully expressible in technical, formal language, having no necessary bearing on the practical, or even on what exists in this space-time world. That position is as well (and as unsatisfactorily) grounded as any pragmatist's. Both make the very same distinctions, though with opposite stress, for both divide what they confront into what has and what does not have pragmatic import. Each attends to his half only, because for pragmatic and other reasons, such as familiarity and a Western outlook, he prefers this to the other.

4] The pragmatic is not necessarily the practical. What is practical is effective in social life. Even illusions, delusions, superstitions, religious faith, and the like have a practical import. These are not as reasonable or as well sustained by scientific method as the items which a pragmatist would endorse. Whatever pragmatic value they might have is not proportionate to the effect they have on human lives or affairs.

A philosophy of practice, in contrast with a pragmatism, accepts an illusion in the shape in which it appears, particularly if it plays an important role in what men believe or do. A pragmatic philosophy would, instead, ask for the difference that the illusion makes in one's activities, and would reduce its meanings to that difference and what it implied. A philosophy of practice grants errors all the weight they in fact have in life; a pragmatism grants them only the positive value that they can add to something else. Each of these approaches can be backed up with telling instances. The existence and success of both precludes either from rightfully claiming that it provides the only legitimate way to deal with illusion, or that only it is empirically oriented. Both, in fact, fail at crucial places. Neither can deal adequately with what is abstract, necessary, cosmic, or private.

A philosophy of the practical is more catholic than pragmatism, since it accepts much that is not endorsed by science or reflection. In compensation, it is overly social in attitude. Meditation, contemplation, treated as ends in themselves, are beyond its comprehension. Leisure activities, games and sports, a stroll or a swim, are intelligible to it only as aids to relaxation or health. It does not know how to say that they are good in themselves. Yet idleness is sometimes not only pleasurable, but the state which ought to prevail for awhile. Sometimes we are most ourselves when we do nothing at all. Were every good only a good for something, there would be naught but means for means for means without end.

It would not be perverse to turn the philosophy of the practical upside down and maintain that the practical is meaningful only so far as it makes possible what is good for nothing, that which we need not use. He who says this, of course, divides phenomena in the very way in which the philosophy of practice does, but with an insistence on what this dismisses. Once again, we have two positions making the same distinctions, through with opposite emphasis. And once again, both opponents are opposed by men who, with equal justification, operate with other limited principles.

5] Anything assessed by men as being good or bad for them or their concerns is humanly significant. He who is interested in it tries to maintain, even more firmly than others do, the emphases that are in daily use. He puts aside only what is taken to be irrelevant or trivial, or what is not evidently related to what has already been taken to be significant, and this whether or not it be personal, empirically or socially important, or part of a practical enterprise. Yet some personal matters, such as the way one walks, holds one's shoulders, or associates colors with sounds are not, except in quite special cases, of much or any human significance. The debilitating and the boring, in small doses, have none or little bearing on men's claims and interests, and what bearing they have is not proportionate to the time and place they occupy in men's lives. But kept to long enough, they become humanly significant. The nature of the outermost galaxies and the possible life that may exist there, the ocean floor, the speed of an electron, the shape of the world a thousand years hence are, in contrast, fascinating topics for a number of disciplined thinkers. But they are not now, and may never be, humanly significant.

What is ignored today by those concerned with the humanly significant may once have interested men. It may perhaps interest men again at some later time. The fact points up the relativity of the idea. "Human significance" is without a constant meaning; it changes in content and range. Some occurrences—birth, maturation, marriage, and death are of primary interest everywhere and to everyone. A theory which leads us to treat them as not real or as unimportant is surely ill-advised. No view can claim finality which rejects or minimizes these major turning points in the lives of men. Any agency which fastens on them is worth using, and deserves to be extended as far as it can go. But then one will eventually arrive at the point where he will acknowledge what men in another age disdained. In different societies and different times, the very same crucial events have quite different bearings on what men are and do. Nor can these events be altogether sundered from the distinctive myths, institutions, and practices which prevail at different places and in different epochs.

Events, whether they are common to all men, or vary from one group to another, are somewhat blurred at the edges. Each merges imperceptibly into others. No one of them is precisely demarcated or precisely characterizable. The selections we make among them are functions of some interest. This is true even when we allow ourselves or our plans to be guided and corrected by technical devices. Every instrument, both in its structure and its use, is made by us for a purpose and is put to work at special times for specific ends.

Should any agency churn out figures or exhibit phenomena which do not touch upon some human concern, we will usually ignore it. It will then be treated as though it were an idle ear or a roving eye. Yet with a change in the intellectual climate, its products can become important and arouse great interest.

The humanly significant is too time-bound to yield more than a few constant, somewhat loosely bounded pivotal phenomena, whose weight and value shift from place to place and time to time. We must, if we are to do justice to the idea of the humanly significant, allow that items now rejected might have a status equal to that accorded to what is now important. But this, though right, is too vague a concession. If we try to specify what might be humanly significant in the future, we will have to be content with unsupported guesses.

Remote astronomical bodies and those courses of evolution that have split off from the one that led to man are not now and may never be significant to men in fact. Those who attend to these bodies or to the defunct lines of development justify their occupation sometimes by claiming that their discoveries will eventually illuminate man and his activities, his history or his destiny; but no one knows if this promise will be kept. The domains are now studied, and will undoubtedly continue to be, regardless of whether or not they have any import for man.

6] There are at least two kinds of human significance: what makes a difference to the being or welfare of men, and what makes no such difference, but nevertheless interests some men. He who selected something because it conformed to the first of these conditions would ignore the galaxies, the subatomic particles, and similar items that occupied the second.

There are men who raise questions where others find all to be calm, without difficulty or value. Some are perplexed where the rest are undisturbed. Some want to find out what is the case, regardless of how the outcome bears, or whether it bears at all, on human affairs. They turn away from themselves, and devote energy and time to the careful examination of what appears to be interesting, and seek only to understand it. They often, of course, benefit from the understanding, but the benefit usually accrues to them incidentally, and because they are concerned with understanding and not with being benefited.

The difficulties with which dedicated inquirers begin are related to what the child experiences, but modified, sustained, and enriched by a knowledge that has been acquired and refined over the years. What perplexes a biologist may not be remarked by well-trained, carefully observing physicists; perplexity is often a function of what one has already learned. For some men nothing is to be accepted as it initially appears, but only as a source of clues or as a test of what else might be discovered. They see problems which no one else seems to have noted. Whatever insights they have are in part a function of their desire to probe beneath the unexplained. They set themselves in opposition to those who attend only to the humanly significant.

The wondrous arrests attention. It is also propulsive, forcing one away from where one is. To be faced with it is to be driven to attend to something else instead. Any device for keeping the wondrous to the fore is self-abdicating, since the wondrous directs one elsewhere. It leads one to doubt, to inquire, to seek a ground. Such efforts are carried out most boldly and widely by the philosophic mind. But progress toward the explanation or source is hazardous and halting. Nowhere is it backed by more than a few supportive data.

Were the world a single whole of tightly interlocked parts, it is conceivable that we could start from any one of a number of places and in any number of ways eventually come to attend to everything that there might be. But it is made up of islands and continents, with much space in between, uncharted and unknown. We wonder at and we ask after, we know and we consider, only a fraction of the whole.

Philosophy begins in wonder and in the end tries to find what brought the wonder about. Some accounts take it to originate in our confusions and ignorance; others take it to be grounded in a misuse of language. It has also been said that we are perplexed to see that things are what they are, or where they are, or how they are. For some, order and constancy raise questions; others find nothing more puzzling than that there should be anything. But all seek explanations. And all, no matter what they find, leave the wondrous still wondrous. Those who successfully trace the wondrous back to its source, find on their return that the wondrous has a depth and is more widespread than it had been initially acknowledged to be. A philosophy ends with the discovery that everything whatsoever deserves to be looked at with respect and some astonishment.

Aristotle rooted philosophy in wonder; Wittgenstein took it to begin with problems. Both thought that they knew how to make the most insistent questions vanish. But here they surely are in error. The explanation of what initially baffled is broader and more basic than what it is used to explain; it manifests itself there and elsewhere as well, as a power not wholly caught in what is here and now. So far as we are aware of it, it prompts us to raise questions where none had been raised before. We move from the arresting, not in order to make our questions vanish or to kill our curiosity, but to know better. A better knowledge, though, does not preclude continued, even greater, wonder. He who has come to understand why there is something rather than nothing, why things keep pace in time, or why phenomena are affiliated and disaffiliated in multiple ways, finds them to be not less but at least as perplexing as before, if for no other reason than that they continue to exist apart from the explanations.

If we could bring everything within the orbit of a good explanation, we still would not have taken care of everything. Our beginning, moreover, would have been made with items which other men might have rejected, and our end may not satisfy all. What we embrace can be and will be only partly accepted by those who are concerned with the other dimensions we have just looked into; it does not always and in every part excite their interest or ground their inquiries. More important, what explains also needs its explanation. Nothing so explains everything that it need not be explained, perhaps even by what it explains.

To begin anywhere, and therefore also to begin with problems, is already to begin with a narrow selection of phenomena. And even these must be neglected to some extent when we set out on a search for their explanation. Initially only a few items arouse curiosity. Only they seem to be perplexing. But to fasten on these is to ignore much that is now to the forefront. And we pursue them to their source only by wrenching ourselves away from the pressing need to act, to make, and to move.

7] The world in which we live is no play of shadows. We must struggle to maintain ourselves in it in the face of the challenges that others provide. What we confront resists us and insists on itself; it objects, forcing us to make an effort, to use energy, to act, if only in order to remain as we were. We are able to continue for a while with some success so far as we know something of the promise of objects, what might happen when we intrude on them and they on us.

Every day we interplay with things, animals, and men. They and we are substances, powerful and unitary, only aspects of which are manifest at any one time. To speak in this way is to risk the adoption of a view that most philosophers have now more or less abandoned—the traditional idea of substance. New views of the nature of activities—that there are ultimate, unobservable physical particles, that the most basic realities are events, that men impose their own structures on an amorphous world—if not more plausible, are at least more acceptable today. The reason for this shift is not easy to find, unless it be a dissatisfaction with Aristotle's or Locke's account of substance.

According to Aristotle, substances are ultimate realities with intelligible natures over which are laid transient, not altogether intelligible 'accidents' (of which sense-qualities are the current, most conspicuous, and familiar examples). Substances were for him the object of scientific knowledge, and what was 'accidental' was irrelevant. All that was distinctive and unduplicable in a substance was beyond his interest or reach. Since he did not grant that anything transient had a cognitive value, he had no way of crediting intelligibility to the pulsating vitality which is lived with and through by man—and perhaps also by some subhuman beings. Aristotle knew that individual substances could be acted on; if living, that they could be cured, befriended, and habituated. But he could not say how they could be known in their individuality. This serious limitation was not faced until comparatively recent times, in part because attention was directed instead at the issue of whether or not the Aristotelian position could do justice to the needs and thrust of science.

The upsurge of the modern scientific movement, with its stress on the clear and distinct and the mathematical, led to the abandonment of many of the main contentions of the Aristotelian outlook. Much that the Aristotelian had to express in qualitative ways was later quantified, clarified, and modified, where not completely rejected. The Galilean and Daltonian recovery of atomism, supported by observations occasioned by high-powered instruments, made men aware that there were many more types of entity than the Aristotelian had considered, and that the Aristotelian substance most likely contained within its confines other real entities which had quite different natures. With the development of evolutionary theory and its express denial of the "fixity of species," nothing seemed left or worth saving of the doctrine that the world contained substances, particularly if one tied the view to the supposition that species were fixed, with steady essences, decorated in each individual case with irrelevant, unknowable accidents.

Locke granted that there could be a genuine knowledge, but not of the substances. He took them to underlie what was known, but to be themselves outside our reach. He somehow knew them and yet somehow did not. His account paved the way for the acknowledgment of the primary qualities as alone real.

Some contemporaries have thought it desirable to replace substances with events. These, strung together, are supposed to yield a semblance of persistence, continuity, and distinctiveness—the supposed characteristics of substances. But such an account fails to yield anything that might act. Events occur, but it is substances that perform, move, change.

Without knowable substances to act and to be acted upon, or to maintain themselves over a period of time, we would be forced to deny that anything was individual, possessing features in terms of which it could be understood, evaluated, and rationally classified. We would have difficulty in understanding political action or creation in the arts. Both living and nonliving beings persist and react; this no event can do. Events just are; they have no obligations, responsibilities, hopes, or fears.

We need not suppose that substances are hidden substrata or that they are made up of form and matter, or of fixed essences and unintelligible accidents. Nor need we suppose that we know them by agencies which in no way add to their data. The alternative to an Aristotelian or Lockean view of substance need not be a theory of events, momentary or cosmic in span, it can be another account of substance.

Substances are known under conditions which must be counterbalanced if we are to know the substances as they exist apart from those conditions. In the beginning and at the end, one can note a number of basic types. Men, creative, intelligent, complex, and alive, are distinguishable from animals, and both of these from things, even the most complex of them, in bodily composition and in function. The differences are in some cases very small, allowing one to treat men as more or less complex or developed forms of animals, and animals as more or less developed forms of simple organisms, and these in turn of complex molecules, and so on. But continuity in bodily natures and functions does not preclude a difference in kind as well as in degree.

In many respects one type of substance differs from another only in degree. But they can still exhibit differences in kind as well. Only men have ethical standards, inherited languages, arts, sciences, and religions. Only they can express intentions, purposes, and plans.

But whether different in degree alone, or in kind as well, both men and animals are substances, interacting with one another and with substances which lack all life.

These substances are not to be identified with the roughly defined, poorly classified, and conventionally modified objects of commonsense men. Nor are they the substances which the sciences take to be final. Scientific objects are, of course, more intelligible and explanatory than the commonsensical. But unlike the latter, they may not be encounterable, and may have only a distant connection, perhaps through the human mind alone, with what is in fact encountered. Some are reached only after one accepts certain experiential content as data and evidence, as a base from which to operate, and as a check on what is claimed. But then it is evident that the acknowledgment of scientifically certifiable substances follows on a prior selection of the evidencing phenomena and on a rejection of others. He who takes those substances to be his primary realities has made a decision to take them to be so. This decision needs justification. Until it is provided, the decision is not in a better position than is one that takes something else to be primary, be they events, other kinds of substances, or aspects of substances.

8] An empirically oriented science takes daily objects to provide evidence of the existence of subatomic substances. More often than not, those substances are understood to be beyond the reach of observation even when this is aided by mechanical devices. Resort must then be had to theory. Theories affect what is seen; eventually, they are replaced by others which pick out different evidences and probably arrive at other kinds of particles. What we know today in science can not be entirely divorced from an effective set of ideas and instruments.

No one is sure just what the ultimate physical particles are; more likely than not we will never know, for there is no likely end to scientific inquiry. The available evidences lead, not to a knowledge of particular, ultimate, indivisible physical particles, but at best to an undissectible multitude of them. Today we have considerable statistical knowledge of physical particles; we know something about the behavior of swarms of them, but not about their individual natures or behavior. This generalization is not without exceptions. Occasionally one finds good grounds to remark on the nature and action of a dislocated particle. This does not often happen; in any case, we then learn only about a special type of substance.

Most men know how to read the snarl of an animal, the smile of a baby, the vacancy of a stare without being taught. What they conclude is sometimes false. They are easily misled by close limitations, and are too readily prompted by wish and hope, fear or prejudice. As a consequence, they misconstrue what exists in fact. Their failures can be minimized where not eliminated, by attending more carefully to the evidence and proceeding more judiciously to the required conclusions. Although the untrained man cannot make the connections or the predictions possible to those who have scientific knowledge, the evidences on which the scientist relies—photographic plates, light signals, the recordings on precision instruments, are in principle observable by him as well. The untrained man also makes use of evidences which do not interest scientists. He uses the features and actions of men and animals to lead him to what these are in and of themselves. The results are too speculative, imprecise, and individualized for science as it is today.

Scientific evidence is bought at the price of rather arbitrary decisions and rejections. It is always taken out of a wider whole. Some parts of this whole may be quantitative, some qualitative in nature; some may come into prominence in practice, while some may have to be uncovered through analysis. Any principle which leads us to face one kind of evidence is matched by others which point us elsewhere.

At its best, the account science provides is partial. It does not explain singular experiences, aberrant judgments, speculations, or the objects of faith. It does not do full justice to the mystical, the formal, or to what is practically useful or socially desirable. The scientific approach uses only part of the available evidence, and attends only to a part of reality.

9] Every selection carries out some value scheme. All inevitably focus on what answers to an interest. That interest makes use of a standard of what is to be faced and considered. Only those items are fastened on that conform to the standard; it is these that are preferred and chosen.

But values seem evanescent; facts alone appear solid and at hand. The one seems caught inside limited perspectives, the other seems to be neutral and knowable by all. Men are consequently tempted to follow the positivistically minded, and take evaluations to be but expressions of the emotions, to be set over against what is in fact the case. Could this position be maintained, it would be possible to hold that a principle of selection, no matter where and how it drew lines between what is to be accepted and what is to be discarded, would never intrude on its material.

The hypothesis that nothing is done to data when we divide them into various classes in thought and practice makes sense if they are only externally related one to the other, for then we could act on any one without making a difference to anything else. But all items occur in contexts and come in clusters; they contrast, oppose, merge, interlock; sometimes they move toward, and sometimes they move away from one another. He who would deal with all of them severally would ignore the way in which they in fact occur. And if he tried to deal only with those whose severance apparently does not affect the rest, he would still have to ignore others equally prominent and worthy of being acknowledged.

Acknowledgment or acceptance, even of that which is without value, if such a thing be possible, involves evaluations. These are acts of preferring and fixating; they endow both what they embrace and what they reject with the character of being in consonance or dissonance with standards.

Since items are usually accepted or rejected because they promise something desirable or undesirable, evaluations could be said not to bestow anything on them but merely to mesh in with them, adding and subtracting nothing. But an interest selects; it gives the items on which it fastens the status of being representative, important, or reliable—traits the items do not have by themselves. A mode of selection imposes a standard of value on what is encountered, whether or not the encountered has a value apart from the selection, and whether or not the value it has is identical with the value that is imposed on it. We can, therefore, look upon all of the eight previous ways of attending as so many different standards of value. The choice of one over another could be justified if it could be shown that it had an excellence denied to others— in range, in the type of entities favored, in simplicity, or in precision. But then one would have invoked another standard by which the various standards were evaluated.

[5]

Each method leaves out something worth acknowledging; there is no one that must be used, or which is the best in all circumstances. In a spirit of generosity one might therefore be inclined to give a role to each of them. They could be treated as so many different but equally respectable languages, games, or definitions. This is, of course, to suppose that they are all equally valuable, or that no one of them was preferable to another. As a consequence, if we ordered them in terms of their scope, intelligibility, usefulness, or conformity to the needs or procedures of science, speculation, or art, we would be subjecting them to irrelevant demands.

Forcing generosity to the forefront of all the virtues prevents the exercise of criticism or judgment about the desirability of doing anything. It compels one to exclude from consideration such vital questions as the consistency and range, the effectiveness and productivity of the different principles of selection. A better alternative involves a modification of the attitude of generosity, so as to enable one to use a limited number of principles of selection, sharing some such virtue as comprehensiveness or availability. While making use of one of these principles, we would, of course, not use the others. Yet if we used them one after the other, we would ignore all but one at a given time, and would deny the persistent use of all of them over all of the given time.

Though many or most occurrences are encompassed by one who uses a number of approaches, the results are not necessarily identical with what would have been obtained had the principles been used in a different order, or had a different set of principles been employed. Each method requires the passing over of some of the items that others, starting at a different place and following a different route, alight upon. Each demands that what was initially accepted be separated from the rest, and therefore allows for breaks that the other procedures do not permit.

If we are not to use various principles of selection in a sequence, what are we to do? How can we avoid making our data subject to arbitrary decisions and possible errors? Will there not be inevitable omissions?

A satisfactory answer takes into consideration the fact that initial material is always selected in a somewhat arbitrary manner. Even the most familiar objects of daily life provide a beginning for inquiry into what is real or reliable only because they have been focused on. Focusing bounds off items from others; it deprives the chosen objects of whatever features they obtain from being related to others, and from any power which joins them.

We know that we make selections. We learn of many of these by approaching what we think we know from other positions and in other ways. But we will never, in this way, learn what modifications, if any, are introduced equally by every selection. We cannot avoid affecting what we deal with, but this still allows us to know what changes must be made in what we obtain if it is to be a real part of a world existing apart from us. But first we must discover what must be done in order to return the content to the kind of situation in which it initially existed apart from us. If we can do this, we will be able to know what it is as a part of a world existing independently of us.

[6]

This leaf, is it real or is it an appearance? There's life in it; it grows; it is substantial, actual. Evidently it is real. But, surely, it is also caught up in relations, and subject to laws. It is attended to perhaps because it plays some role in our society, and certainly because I have looked in its direction and have seen what my eyes in that light permit me to see. This leaf is a confronted leaf, not free from factors added to it as it is in itself. It is an appearance.

Even when an appearance of the leaf is freed from factors which are personally and socially added to it, we do not yet reach the real leaf as it is in itself. There are forces, laws, and relations intruding on it. The leaf is also related to other leaves, existing at other places, and to other appearances—stones, singers, and tides—which are indifferent to and yet connected with it in space, in time, causally and noncausally. Appearances make a difference to one another's features, positions, roles, opportunities, sometimes by just being with them in a common domain.

A leaf, apart from all knowing, is an objective appearance—objective because its existence does not depend on its being encountered by anyone, and an appearance because externally produced factors have been joined to what the actual, real leaf exhibits of itself.

An objective appearance is a primary appearance, an appearance of first degree. There are higher degrees depending on the extent to which social and personal notes are added to the primary appearance. But no matter what the degree, an appearance varies in the extent to which it is under the control of a context. Without affecting its objectivity, the leaf that appears can be anything from a mere demarcated portion of a single space, for example, to an expression of an actuality in which a spatial extension was a subordinated element.

There is a spectrum of emphases in an appearance, of any degree, in which contexts exercise anywhere from a minimal to a maximal role. Can one reach the leaf as it actually is from any position in that spectrum of emphases? Surely not, if we can know only its appearance. But if we know only its appearance, there is nothing to which we can ascribe that appearance. And, were the real leaf irrelevant to the appearance of the leaf, the real leaf would not be what in fact appears.

An appearance is inseparable from its reality, for it is an exhibition of that reality joined with other alien factors. If we are to reach the reality from the appearance we must pass from the appearance to the contribution which the reality makes to the constitution of that appearance. But first we must know the appearance. But must not the act of knowing, precisely because it yields what is true or false, end with what is distinct from the appearance? The question has already been answered. What we have in mind is inseparable from what is outside the mind; that is why what we have in mind is able to lead us to what in fact appears and, through its agency, to what is real. Because our knowledge of socially and personally modified appearances is distinct from but yet identical in content with those known appearances, and these in turn are constituted by and biased toward the reality which has a dominant role in their constitution, we are able to move from our knowledge of appearances into known appearances, from there into the realities that make the appearances possible.

[7]

We begin perception by focusing on something. But we have first to withdraw from an unquestioned involvement in a larger situation. Initially we withdraw because our rhythms are not in consonance with that which is about, perhaps because we are pulled up sharp by a surge of uncontrolled feeling such as hunger or thirst, or even because we are too relaxed. Only later do we deliberately attend. But, earlier or later, we finally place ourselves in a position where we isolate some content by imposing boundaries on it.

Focusing is an epistemological act. It does not affect the connection that the content, apart from the focusing, has to the rest of the world. Nor does it destroy our presence in that world. While confronting something we continue to be in the very world out of which it was isolated.

Focusing is part of the act of attending. It starts with an involvement with a content and ends with that content caught within the limits of our own devising. A process by means of which some things are pushed aside and others allowed to come to the fore, attention, with its focusing, enables us to get into a position where we can examine, abstract, and even relate what we confront to whatever other items we may have in mind.

Sometimes a focused item is replaced by others or turned into part of the background. Sometimes it just slips back into the background without our getting anything else into focus; we then lose ourselves in reveries or in enjoyment, keeping to ourselves in the one case, or facing a shifting panorama, uncategorized but felt, in the second.

As long as it is focused on, a leaf is held away from all else. Attending to it gives it a role it did not have before. The bounding to which it is then subject is not to be identified with what Husserl calls 'bracketing.' Indeed, bracketing presupposes it. One brackets in order to confront pure essences, mere meanings; the act requires one to put aside all existence, all interaction with anything, practical or unintended. Since it operates on an isolated datum, whose essence is in fact involved with existence, and which has factual relations to other items in the world, bracketing itself evidently depends on a prior bounding.

To know things as they exist apart from us, it is necessary to recompense for the difference which our boundaries make to what is confronted. But the bounding cannot be simply negated so as to allow for a confrontation of what exists apart from consciousness. Removing boundaries brings one back to the situation where one is involved in a world of which one so far has no knowledge.

Bounding a leaf permits us to hold it away from itself as actual, and away from all other items. The bounding adds 'intentionality,' to make the content be something held in mind in this way rather than in that, and available for relating to other content which we also have in mind. But because the content still is part of a real leaf, outside knowledge, it is encountered as brute, resistant, pulled away, and involved in affairs outside us. An actual leaf does not fit entirely inside the limits we set; it resists our encompassment, and absents itself from us. As a reality outside our knowledge, it continues to change and interact, unaffected by the boundaries we imposed.

Can one really know something without in that very act making it be in our minds? Yes. In knowing we face content which is with-drawing from us. To this a rhetorician would perhaps reply: "So far as it has not yet escaped the conditions of knowledge, the object is in the mind; so far as it has escaped, it is not known." But to know is to be involved with what is distinct from what is in mind. There is knowledge only so far as one possesses bounded content at the same time that one faces the content as not controlled by an imposed boundary.

The leaf is outside our boundary at the same time that we make use of it as bounded content. When we deal with it as bounded, we make the content known. The leaf itself is unaffected. It is not subject to the control we are cognitively providing through the agency of the boundary.

The leaf is bounded and thereby known by us. But the presence of the leaf, its status as that which is being bounded, its involvement with other items outside the boundary we impose, is distinct from and not caught in the knowledge we have of it. We know it as that which is withdrawing, because we know that we are knowing. Know-ing has its moment of self-consciousness in which we become aware that we are knowing what is not knowledge. Though we do not then know that we are self-conscious, we can come to know that we are self-conscious in a different act of knowing, having its own moment of self-consciousness. Our rhetorician would not, I think, be quieted by this reply. He would undoubtedly ask, "Do you know the content as it is in retreat from your imposed boundary; do you know where it stops in its retreat? If you do not, you have lost it. If you do know it, you have, on your own theory, bounded it, brought it under conditions imposed by your mind."

These remarks neglect the difference between knowing some-thing and knowing of something. The reach of knowledge extends beyond the constitutive and possessive powers of the mind. When we know something we know that we are also confronted with it as that which is playing a role outside the mind, not confined by our boundaries.

Known by us, the leaf has an appearance and a reality not constituted by us. It is *in* the mind as knowledge, *for* the mind as known, and *outside* the mind as an objective appearance. As known, it is inseparable from knowledge on the one side and from the objective appearance on the other. Since the appearance is itself a qualified exhibition of the actual real leaf, as known the leaf is inseparable from itself, not only as an appearance but as a reality.

3

APPEARANCES

Controlling Summary: Appearances are appearances of realities. Were there no realities which appeared, what was confronted would itself be the real, without depth, without power, without capacities. The appearances are, however, only because they are constituted both by realities to which they are accredited and by realities distinct from these.

Each reality is self-bounded. That is why it is able to maintain itself against all else. It absents itself from the boundary that knowledge imposes, and exhibits itself to others at a boundary which it itself provides.

The exhibitions of actualities are governed by contexts; without such contexts, there would be no connection amongst the exhibitions. The two together, the exhibitions of actualities and the contexts to which they are subject, constitute the appearances of actualities. The contexts are themselves exhibitions of finalities, and are filled out by the exhibitions of actualities. The contexts and their filling together constitute appearances of finalities.

We confront appearances. These are outcomes, available because realities have made an appearance. Appearances are because realities surfaced. Torn away from what produces them, the appearances would be just floating presences, too weak to act, too inert to become, too fragile to be.

Appearances have an integrity of their own. The fact that they are identifiable apart from any reference to their realities seems to warrant the view that they are not products but irreducibles, with which a theory of knowledge and a theory of being must begin and end. They are then supposed to be initial and basic data for knowledge, and even to be ultimate realities. Instead of taking them to be appearances related to realities, one stops with them as so many sense-impressions, atoms of experience, particular colors, shapes, and sizes. The philosophic task is then assumed to be that of identifying data, and the providing of devices by which one can presumably produce something like the complex objects with which one is daily familiar—or at least the knowledge of them.

What is external to and independent of the knower, on such a view, is held to be identical with what he knows when he perceives. To account for the difference between what is initially met with and consequently used in memory and reflection, one then supposes that the latter are faint versions of the former. But the remembered is not always fainter than what is encountered.

Appearances are inert in and of themselves. The view that they are the primary data for knowledge or ultimate realities can make no provision for action. It is a view, therefore, that can not do justice to ordinary practice, to the making of works of art, to politics, or to engineering. Indeed, causal references would be quite irrelevant, since the data one is acknowledging are supposedly atomic, each indifferent to the presence of anything else. The view, moreover, allows for no explanation of the presence or nature of the initial data. They are just assumed to be final, brute, inexplicable. Supposedly they just are, and that is the end of the matter.

There is another difficulty: real men presumably know the presumed data. But real men are not constructions out of them. If they were, the men would not know these data, since constructions have no knowledge.

The integrity of appearances does not stand in the way of a real man, beyond all appearances, coming to know them. And when a man knows them, he finds that he is defied. The defiance is not contained in them, but works through them—a consequence of the fact

that the appearances are outcomes of the interplay of insistent actualities and finalities.

We can detach appearances and deal with them as though they
were ultimate; but we never altogether free them from the realities
that made them possible. No one, consequently, experiences merely
a color or a shape. What is experienced is something colored or
shaped, with many relations to other items, accompanied by an
awareness of a reality absenting itself from the experience.

Appearances owe their presence to actualities and finalities.
They have a status of their own, but not in opposition to the realities
that make that status possible. If they did oppose the realities, the
realities would have other appearances contrasting with the first, and
opposing the realities themselves. And the second round of appearances would require a third, and so on. Appearances have natures and
careers distinct from the realities that constitute them, but this does
not mean that they, therefore, have become realities.

A single actuality has a plurality of distinguishable appearances.
It is large and it is heavy. It could conceivably be reduced in size,
and still remain as heavy as it was before; it could conceivably be
made lighter but kept at the same size. The air in it could be crushed
out; some parts could be removed, but the actuality by itself would
still be a unity. Size and weight there are not distinct units.

Appearances are interrelated in ways that could not be determined by any of the actualities standing by themselves, or even by
their interacting with one another simply as actualities. The view
that substantial actualities are the only source of appearances prevents
one from understanding how a number of appearances, belonging to
different actualities, could be together.

Appearances arise because actualities manifest themselves
through exhibitions which are countered by exhibitions on the part
of finalities. The derogatory sense which tinges the term 'appearances' in part reflects the view that the only fundamental realities
are finalities, external and noble. Only something fixed, absolute, and
grand, it is thought, can be real. For some, the need to refer to
finalities for an explanation of the presence and nature of appearances is in fact so obvious that they even overlook the role played by

actualities in making appearances possible. One then goes on to claim that all appearances exhibit those finalities in limited and distortive ways; as a consequence, substantial actualities are then themselves taken to be appearances, or even to be just fictions which have been arbitrarily assumed and set under the appearances as their supposed supports and sources. The view is congenial to mysticism, monism, and metaphyisical intuitionism. In their different ways, these rightly assert that there is something other than transience and multiplicity. But by taking finalities to be the sole source of appearances, they make the multiplicity inexplicable. No finality could produce a multiplicity having a status of its own without breaking itself asunder. A plurality of actualities is needed if there is to be a plurality of appearances.

Appearances contrast and combine. They clash with and they enhance one another within larger situations. If all appearances were merely exhibitions of finalities, those finalities would not only have to exhibit themselves, but would have to distinguish kinds of appearances—relatively stable relations from relatively unstable terms, and whatever comes between these extremes. But as indivisibly single, a finality has no way of distinguishing these.

One can conceive of an absolute reality overflowing, or spilling itself out over the course of time. But it then must somehow overflow into something, or must somehow have one stage of itself kept distinct from other stages. It has no way of making these distinctions. And if it could make them, it would still not be able to maintain them, for by itself it just is itself. It might conceivably engage in an act of self-alienation, but what was alienated would fall back into it at once, unless it was somehow supported on the outside.

A finality which was the sole source of appearances, would have to divide itself in order to allow its appearances to contrast with itself. But in that dividing, it would have given the appearances a standing of their own. They do have such a standing, but that is because the finality is countered by actualities which insistently make their own distinctive contributions to the presence and nature of appearances. If the appearances accredited to actualities were identified with the appearances accredited to finalities, the finalities would have to impose one set of appearances on another. Once again, the finalities would have had to divide themselves, and thereby cease to be themselves.

The appearances of actualities must, to be appearances, stand away from those actualities. For this to take place, it seems reasonable to say, all one needs is other actualities. Each actuality should be able to appear just so far as there are other actualities able to sustain whatever it might present. No recourse would then have to be made to finalities, or to the domains these provide. And it is a fact that there are appearances which are the joint product of a number of actualities. The wire is bent because it was pressed down by the rock. The shape of the wire is due both to the wire and to the rock. It can be attributed to the wire because it is already distinct from the wire, and is distinct from the wire because it is dependent on the rock. But though the rock is a cause of the bend in the wire, it does not support that bend. A cause is one thing; a support another. The wire remains bent after the rock is removed, with the other circumstances remaining unchanged.

If the bend in a wire needs support, it must get it from what is not another actuality. What must be said, at the very least, is that the bent appearance is sustained by a number of actualities—not necessarily by anything that might have operated on the actual wire—so as to elicit that appearance rather than another. Still unaccounted for are some of the relations that the bent wire has to other appearances. These relations are common conditions, contexts, neutral to a multitude of appearances; they can not be attributed to any set of them, or to all of them together.

The appearances accredited to actualities have a double base, enabling those appearances to be at once members of a sheer multiplicity and to provide filling for various contexts. As the one they occur in their severalty; as the other they are contextualized. The latter state is possible because finalities exhibit themselves.

Instead of a finality being needed to explain the presence of a context, however, one might try to go no further than to man, and particularly to him as making use of an impersonal, universal understanding. That understanding, it might be said, could provide all the contexts that are needed in order to have a single knowable world. But the context governing an objective world is not identical with that which governs an experienced one. That there is a context which governs what is not yet an object of experience means that it is not dependent on the operation of a human understanding.

The understanding needs content to be given to it. That content is either a sheer brute fact or it has a source and explanation. The source and explanation cannot, obviously, be the understanding. If brute, there is no accounting for the content; if it has a source and explanation, it belongs to what is not the understanding.

Appearances are dependent on more basic realities, and have an integrity of their own. Two kinds of reality contribute, though unequally, to their constitution. Each, instead of simply adding to what the other contributes, also infects it and sustains it. An appearance which is to be credited to an actuality is both partly constituted and sustained by a finality. Similarly, an appearance which is to be credited to a finality is in part constituted by an actuality which sustains at the same time that it supplements the dominating contribution of the finality.

Were actualities and finalities merely alongside one another, there is no reason why their contributions should mesh, why they should be compatible, why they should continue to be together. They could separate out at any time and, therefore, for all time. The world of appearances would then only apparently be a distinct world of appearances. Also, were the contributions of the actualities and finalities merely alongside one another, neither would be sustained by the other. Neither would have any role apart from its source; both would be just surfaces inseparable and indistinguishable from the rest of the realities to which they belonged. Appearances depend for their presence on the insistence of both actualities and finalities.

If the difference between actualities and finalities were converted into a spatial distance, the meeting of the two would be arbitrary, and might even be impossible. But where the one is, so is the other. Together, they constitute objective appearances. Here there is a meshing of the terminal and the relational, filling and structure, occasion and demand, fact and prescription.

[2]

Appearances have three degrees of ultimacy. One, the ontologically grounded, exhibits the objective outcome of the interlocking of the exhibitions of independent realities. A second, the empirically available, is what is encounterable by any man. A third is the familiar, what is actually experienced. The first is the direct product of a union of the contributions of actualities and finalities, the one providing contents, the other contexts. The second degree appearances are the occupants of the common world. These appearances are unaffected by particular social conventions or special reference points, but they are relative to man and perhaps to other conscious beings. The third results from the overlaying of common appearances with social and individual notes. The third degree of appearances presupposes the second, and this in turn presupposes the first. There are appearances in the daily world because there is a world of appearances common to mankind; there is a world of appearances common to mankind because there are appearances apart from mankind.

Here is a green leaf. It is an appearance. It is seen under a shifting light, at various distances, by me with eyes with distinctive abilities. I associate the leaf with spring, health, food, in personally significant ways and in some consonance with the associations characteristic of men in my society. Those who fail to see that leaf in somewhat similar circumstances point up a limitation either in themselves or in me. One or the other of us is to be understood to misconstrue a paradigmatic appearance for any man, but which is to be experienced in special guises in special circumstances. It is an appearance of the second degree that some distortive agency may have made me or others experience in a particular way. Were there no such paradigmatic appearance, there would be nothing one ought to see in such and such circumstance; color blindness, colored glasses, twilight and snow, shadow and distance would here have no explanatory role.

Apart from men, it has sometimes been maintained, there is only a swirl of colorless physical units; appearances would then exist only for men and for similar conscious beings. But this is to forget that the green leaf is conditioned in a number of ways, apart from men. It is, for example, spread out in space. The spread is ingredient in it, and also related to spreads beyond, making it possible to locate the leaf in relation to them in a common extended domain. If men were the sole source of appearances, they would produce not only green, or a spread-out green, or a green leaf, but the extended domain within which the leaf is located. The Kantian claims nothing less. Were he right the entire voluminous universe would somehow arise when man—presumably an unextended actuality—came to be. Since the green leaf is related to other appearances in a common extended domain, a man must so divide himself that he can offer to the domain issuing from himself the qualia that are to be related there. But then why and how could anything resist him? How could he himself be located? Somehow, too, he must stand somewhere in between qualia and the context in which they fit, and bring one to bear on the other.

Appearances of the first degree are the products of two distinct kinds of reality, actualities and finalities. Each kind of reality exhibits itself, and is countered by the exhibitions of the other. The result is no simple, detached unit, but a continuum in which an emphasis on one of the contributions gradually gives way to an emphasis on the other. Its nature is best seen by remarking on at least eight points in that continuum.

1] The surface of an actuality is a sheer *quale*, an immediate, individual, presented facticity. The surface of a finality is an indefinite, uniform *presence*. Each is distinguishable from its source only so far as the other meshes with and sustains it. An actuality exhibits itself as a quale. This is the actuality itself, attenuated and not yet affected by finalities. It is, therefore, almost identical with an impression, sense-datum, the quality which empiricists have been inclined to take as bedrock. Still, it is distinct from these, for it is part of an actuality, and is present regardless of whether anyone is aware of it or not.

2] An appearance is a union of exhibitions of actualities and finalities which have more than a minimal effectiveness. The appearance is credited to an actuality, the more its contribution dominates over the contributions made by a finality. The contributions of the finality are fractionated by the actuality, for this not only exhibits itself but counters, as well as it can, the exhibitions of the finality.

The leaf that appears is distended, unique, bounded off, an existent in which an essence is but a minor note. We can encounter it only if we first attend to a more personalized, bounded appearance of the leaf. Later, through a process of analysis and reflection, we can come to know what it is we bounded off.

3] We come upon appearances as together with other appearances. Each has its own distinctiveness, but within a context which it occupies with others. We encounter it because we begin at the context, and pass beyond it to the item as together with other items there. The togetherness of the appearances, of course, is due to no one of them; nor could they bring it about with one another's aid, for that would require that they first be together. Nor is that togetherness innocuous; appearances are relevant to one another, and they are subject to laws and other prescriptions characteristic of the contexts where they interplay.

4] Knowledge begins with an act of attention directed at some appearances. These appearances are almost in equilibrium between the thrusts of actualities and finalities. Normally, there is a bias toward the actualities; common contexts, governing the appearances, serve primarily to enable those appearances to be distinguished from their actualities. When we assume this position we readily take the appearance of an actuality to be the actuality itself; but the appearance is distinct from the actuality, because it is also part of a context. The distended green leaf is in a common space, time, and causal chain; it is subject to forces which control how next it will be related to other appearances. It is also a part of a common intelligible world, having a being and a unity of its own; the leaf is also connected with other appearances in subterranean ways.

5] Hardly distinguishable from the previous position is one where the exhibitions of finalities begin to dominate. They then do not fully control the exhibitions of the actualities, and are in fact punctuated by them. As so punctuated they are so many detached appearances of the actualities just noted. Because the exhibitions are punctuated, it is easy to overlook the fact that finalities are first exhibited as single contexts. One consequence is that it has been comparatively late in the history of civilization before men began to take seriously the fact that the contexts are the finalities, though in a minor key.

Because this position is so close to the other, one readily passes from the appearances of actualities controlled by common contexts to the contexts as punctuated by the appearances, and back again. Were we able to balance the one with the other, the result would be a *phenomenon*. Phenomena are appearances balanced between constitutive forces. As the product of equal and opposed emphases, they have a status denied to appearances. This does not make them more stable than the appearances. They are not inherently stable, any more than appearances are. Indeed, it is questionable whether there are any phenomena at all, except at those rare moments when the continuum of interlocking emphases is fixated at the center, or when oppositely emphasized appearances are merged with one another.

Appearances are without a force of their own. Yet they do not vanish as soon as they come to be; actualities and finalities persistently appear with one another's help. The actualities are to be credited with the joint product of themselves and finalities so far as the contexts enable the exhibitions of the actualities to function as terms; the product is to be credited to finalities, instead, so far as contexts are in control.

The detached appearance of an actuality is held away from its source in that actuality by finalities. The finalities both contribute to the constitution of the appearance of an actuality and serve as carriers of the side of it which the actuality provided. The degree of contribution the finalities make to the constitution of an appearance varies from a minimum, leaving the finality to function primarily as a background, just enabling an actuality to make an appearance, to a maximum, making it questionable to credit the appearance to an actuality.

Distinct appearances are held apart from actualities by finalities; sets of appearances are held on to by actualities. Both come to be and pass away. This is not due to any inherent transience, but because actualities replace one exhibition of themselves by another. Any one appearance or phenomenon could conceivably last as long as any actuality. But it gives way to others sooner or later.

The contributions of actualities and finalities join without seam. This fact, at first glance, seems to allow only for the existence of phenomena. Phenomena, though, because not biased in one direction or the other, might belong to no one and to nothing; they could be sheerly present, with a dignity all their own. Any actualities and finalities that were behind them might be at best preconditions, having nothing to do with the phenomena once these were in existence. Like a grown animal which has no recollection of its parents, the phenomena would lead their own lives. But each contribution is biased toward its source. It is just as much opposed to the contribution of the other as it is in consonance with it. Were the two contributions simply opposed, they would not mesh; were they simply constituents of phenomena, there would be no warranted attribution of them to sources beyond those phenomena. The existence of those sources and therefore the existence of the phenomena would be mysteries.

Phenomena tell us nothing about either actualities or finalities. The very success of joining the factors on which a phenomenon depends prevents us from knowing what those factors are. But appearances are biased either toward actualities or finalities, at the same time that they are constituted by and to that degree are inseparable from the other.

The appearance of an actuality is continuous with both the actuality and a finality. We cannot free it from either without losing a twofold insistence, one of them dominant and the other dominated, originating in the recesses of the actuality and a finality.

An empiricist finds little difficulty in crediting an appearance to an actuality, but the attribution of an appearance to a finality he dismisses as unintelligible or unwarranted. The appearances of finalities can, for him, be only abstractions. Yet while it makes sense to speak of abstracting an aspect of a phenomenon to obtain an appearance, it does not make sense to speak of deriving one kind of appearance from another. Such derivation would nevertheless be involved were it the case that the appearances of finalities were abstracted from the appearances accredited to actualities. Nor would the attempt at a converse derivation be in a better position. One can not get a leaf by itself by abstracting from a leaf which merely has a position in space or time. The one is nonrelational; the other is a term in a relation.

Appearances are the products of contributions from actualities and finalities, biased toward one of these more than toward the other. As so biased they are rightly attributable to the one rather than to the other. The contribution of that other is nevertheless involved with the contribution of the first. Since that involvement would seem to allow for the contribution of the other to hold the first away from its source, it seems to make unnecessary a reference to some supposed carrier for what the first contributes. If so, there then would be no need to maintain that appearances are sustained by realities to which they are not attributed.

The suggestion that is now being considered and found wanting, makes the contribution of a reality do double service, first as a constituent of an appearance, and then as enabling the result to stand away from the source of the other constituent. But a constituent of an appearance exhausts its power in the constituting of that appearance. A source is stronger than the contribution it or another makes to an appearance.

Appearances have sources, and are biased toward those sources. Since appearances are inert, and actualities and finalities exert power, there is evidently a discontinuity between appearances and their realities. Only a miracle or an unjustified leap, it would seem, could get one from those appearances to their supposed sources. The difficulty is based on a confounding of a phenomenon and a reality. The neutrality of a phenomenon makes it opaque to reality. But appearances exist because of, and are continuous with, their realities. We confront those appearances, but from a distance. We come to them from a position which allows us to identify them. If we could not do this, we would be so caught up in them that we could never find either them or ourselves.

6] The encountered appearance of an actuality has its counterbalance in a context with variegated shifting features. The context here is an encountered kaleidoscope of colors, shapes, interchanges, slippages, montages, and transactions. It is what we note when we dim our eyes and try to have a purely aesthetic experience of what is present. One then has something like Peirce's state of musement, where anything is allowed to occur in a single, undivided domain.

The encountered appearance of a finality encompasses qualities. These punctuate it while enjoying careers dictated in part by their actualities. A context is therefore more like Plato's receptacle than it is like anything we actually experience, for what gives it filling evidently has its source elsewhere.

Appearances are known. Knowledge gives them boundaries. These hold the appearances off conceptually, not only from one another, but from the actualities and the finalities which constitute them. Knowledge gives the appearances a role in memory and expectations, in after-images, in associations, and in inference. More important, it sets the appearances in opposition to themselves as continuous with and pulled back into their sources.

7] We come closer to finalities when contexts are seen to have nuances which are entirely within their control. The exhibitions of actualities are now subordinated, controlled notes. Such appearances of finalities are not encountered; rather, they are analytic factors within the encountered appearances of variegated domains. We have here the analogue of the second case, discussed above. But there the exhibitions of actualities successfully defy the demands of a context; here they do not.

8] A finality exhibits itself as a context. Like the exhibitions of actualities, this is midway between its source as it is in itself and that source as minimally affecting the exhibitions of actualities. It, too, is not separately encountered; nor is it to be found by freeing oneself from the contingencies of experience. It is present as a mere exhibition in all the other stages, thereby enabling one to arrive at a finality from any one of them.

[3]

The appearances accredited to actualities are actualities, but weakened and interlocked with the exhibitions of finalities. The appearances accredited to finalities are finalities, but weakened and interlocked with the exhibitions of actualities. Failure to acknowledge the double fact leads to the loss of singular and common truths, and of their bearing on one another.

Take space as an example. As an exhibition of a finality it is almost empty (see point no. 8 above). Newton supposed it was entirely empty; Einstein supposed that it contained many concrete entities. The two are brought close together with the recognition that there is a stable nature to space, not entirely severed from an involvement with what is in it. Its acknowledgment is presupposed by physics.

Space has hills and valleys, short and long stretches, bumps and curves, light and dark areas. It is temporalized, vitalized. This is the space which naturalists know (see point no. 7 above). To account for variation in it, it is necessary to refer to actualities outside the space, whose expressions the space encompasses and interrelates. Space assimilates all spatialized items; they are locatable in the space, but retain the power to diversify it. This is the space a phenomenologist knows.

Space is also a locus of turbulent activity (see point no. 6 above). The Taoist thinks the turbulence is due to us; the Bergsonian attributes it to a basic duration. Neither makes provision for distinct actualities; yet it is these which appear in space.

Space encompasses but does not fully control whatever is in it (see point no. 5 above). Things come and go; once in space they have spatial relations not of their own making. That space is a miscellany of distinct regions connected by powers in space. It is the space of territoriality.

All actualities are related in a common space (see point no. 4 above). That space gives them positions, while leaving them free to be and to act as distinct individuals. Private lives are expressed in public but not fully controlled there.

Each actuality is a distinct reality. It exists apart from all others. Yet it is together with them in space (see point no. 3 above). That they are together is a truth about them all; it does not alter them.

Every actuality is extended, with contours of its own (see point no. 2 above). Its spatialized appearances are here taken in their severalty, not yet located in a single space.

Finally, each actuality yields qualia within which spatiality is a private extendedness in a subordinated role (see point no. 1 above). This is apparently the position which Aristotle took when he treated place as a category subordinate to substance.

We attend to the appearances of actualities only after we have passed from a punctuated domain (see point no. 5 above) to it as relating distinct appearances (see point no. 4 above). Then depending on our interests, we move to the appearance in which the contribution of an actuality has a maximum role (see point no. 1 above). At that point, it makes little difference whether we say that we are occupied with an appearance of an actuality, or with the actuality itself as individually distended in consonance with a space external to it.

[4]

The conditions for knowledge, for experience, or for a world apart from but open to these, are appropriate to particular experiential contents. But then it would seem that there is no need to suppose that those conditions are contexts, belonging to but distinct from finalities. If so, though the appearances of actualities might be traced back to actualities, the contexts, which serve to interrelate those appearances, could not be traced back to appropriate realities. Indeed, if one were to try to trace them back one would apparently move backwards over an endless series of more and more primary conditions.

Contexts have little force of their own; they have no power to subjugate. There is no way for them to unite with content, particularly if that content originates in actualities having an independent career. Nevertheless, they do subjugate, they do unite with content. Because they are attenuated continuations of finalities, they are able to transmit, in limited form, the forceful demands of the finalities.

The movement to finalities is not up a chain of conditions. Such a chain could never arrive at anything but other weak conditions. Metaphysics, the search for what is ultimate, does not attempt to convert relativized conditions into absolute ones. Nor does it start with what is harmless or even useful and then inevitably but vainly try to complete a series of conditions. The initial conditions are themselves already part of what is final. To start with them is to start inward into the finalities, and therefore into what is more intensive.

An exhibition of one reality is present for another; their juncture is distinct from either, though biased primarily toward one of them, its source. So much, seems to be clear. The consequences of this contention, however, look so radical that they tempt one to withdraw. It looks as though we are required to say, for example, that a Roman Catholic not only acknowledges sacramentality as a dimension of baptismal water, but that the water is ingredient in an appearance of God, and there provides a position from which to acknowledge the water as an appearance of an actuality existing apart from God. Yet we obviously can come upon water without paying any attention to God. Few, if any, have an acquaintance with God from which to set out. In any case, it seems odd to say that God has an appearance and that this is in part constituted by finite actualities.

The disturbance we feel depends in good part on a confounding of a personal God with one who is a final reality and who provides one of the contexts where appearances are together with one another. It depends, too, on the failure to distinguish an appearance ascribed to one reality from a constituent of a different appearance. Water is an appearance of an actuality. A sacral factor in that water has only a minimal role. If we could free the water from that factor, the water would not be part of a unified world governed by a context stemming from God, a final Unity. The sacral factor in the appearance of water achieves greater and greater prominence as one comes more and more under the influence of God. The appearance of God contains the constituents that He and actual water contribute to that appearance, He maximally, it minimally. The result is a sacral unity tinged by a fluid contingency owed to actual water.

Even the water—any appearance of an actuality, in fact—which nonreligious men know, contains a sacral factor. This factor is a minor note in the secularly known water, but it is sufficient to allow one to begin a movement toward God, a finality, not necessarily an object of worship. Both baptismal and nonbaptismal water are water, where a beginning with an involvement with God, or Unity, can begin. And, since one can begin such an involvement with any appearance, any could lead one to God. The sacramentality is not peculiar to any one of them; it is a feature shared, a context in which exhibitions of actualities have subordinate roles.

To get to a finality from an actuality, one must ignore the appearance as credited to the actuality to attend instead to a subdued factor in it. This is the finality at its most attenuated. As involved with what the actuality contributes, this factor is a constituent of an appearance of the actuality. The usual appearance of water is biased toward actual water and is interlocked with a contribution by a finality. That contribution has the role of a context governing the way in which the water is related to other appearances. The two contributions, could they be balanced, would constitute phenomena. But the sources of those contributions are too independent, distinctive and effective to permit this, except in special cases. Normally, we face appearances, primarily oriented toward substantial realities, and occasionally toward finalities.

Appearances do not float on top of their realities. They do not constitute a veil or a barrier; they are not obstacles thrown up by the realities to hide themselves from us. To attend to those appearances is already to be beyond them, to have moved in depth toward the sources of one of their factors. The factors are pulled away from the appearances, passing continuously and therefore imperceptibly into the sources. Knowledge of a reality, consequently, is not a knowledge of something radically distinct from its appearances; it is a knowledge of those appearances, purged and intensified. If practice, conventional thought, and speech, if experience and understanding are concerned with the appearances of actualities, then they are necessarily concerned with those actualities, for appearances are realities, perceptually present, qualified, and obtrusive.

We are content, usually, to stop quite quickly in our penetration into realities. For the most part we are content to learn how some rather obvious features follow on one another. But this does not content us always; again and again, we penetrate considerably below the surfaces toward actual things as sources of a multiplicity of exhibitions. We go further, sometimes, with animals, and are able to take some of their appearances as symptoms—evidences of what they are like and what they promise to be and do. Every one of us, now and then, is able to go even further, particularly with reference to those human beings with whom we are emotionally involved. We recognize some of their appearances to be primarily expressions, revelatory of what human beings in fact are.

Despite prejudice and foolishness it is possible at times to grasp what men are like. We converge on them from a number of sides; the appearances with which we begin are so many impure fragments of the reality at which we eventually arrive. But we never get to an individual in his very centrality, not because this is blocked off at some particular point, but because our penetration is resisted, and eventually fades off into a darkness in which we lose our way.

Actualities are limited, palpable, and locatable. And we men are actualities. But Being, God, and other finalities are ineffable and unlocatable. These, it is often said, must be beyond all knowing, experiencing, speaking, and reaching. But, as a matter of fact, we do speak of space and time, of ought and other prescriptions, of nature, laws, God, the future and the past, without having to resort to a new vocabulary, and without having to violate the rules of ordinary grammar. Even if they were to have a meaning for us only because they bore on some empirical occurrence, they would be distinct from those occurrences. They are, in fact, confronted in the form of conditions and contexts, without which appearances of actualities are not possible. To know those conditions and contexts is already to know some finality, for they are continuous with it, attenuations of it.

Our daily language has terms pertinent to finalities and their appearances just as surely as it has terms pertinent to actualities and their appearances. But when we speak of either type of reality we must, of course, not speak as though we were dealing with their appearances. And when we speak of the actualities we must not speak as we do when we speak of finalities. This means that a careful use of daily language will require a distinguishing of two types of referents, one taking us toward actualities, the other toward finalities.

Philosophy is a subject to be pursued, not by abandoning the world of everyday, but by attending to factors which constitute the appearances there. The fact that we speak of those factors every day enables one to begin philosophy, as one does science and art, here where everyone is. The task is one of refining, clarifying, dissecting, penetrating, and systematizing, not one of ignoring the world everyone knows, and postulating another which no one understands.

The contexts operative in experience are finalities thinned out, but occupied by exhibitions of actualities. To stop with those contexts is to cut oneself off at an arbitrary point. But we are then able to attend to the way in which they are interlocked with the content provided by actualities.

Contexts, by their insistence, betray the fact that they are rooted in something more powerful and basic than themselves. They remain part of this even while united with content. Going beyond them to their sources is not going into another world, but simply continuing onward into realities already entered. There is, therefore, no need to occupy oneself with an attempt to somehow total or to come to the end of an endless hierarchy of contexts or domains. There is no need to search for some absolute, last condition. Finalities are already present in the conditions which are constitutive of the appearances of actualities.

4

~~~~~~

SYMBOLS

~~~~~~

Controlling Summary: Appearances are related to their sources by adumbrations and lucidations, the one leading into actualities, and the other into finalities. Symbols are appearances merging into adumbratives and lucidatives, and thereby into realities. Were there no symbols there would be no acquaintance with realities. We would know only appearances, but not know that they were appearances.

All symbols are impure because affected by what sustains them. That is why there is difficulty in isolating and using them. The symbols become purified in becoming used; otherwise they would not function as symbols, merging more and more into the sources which produced them.

The resistance, which symbolization progressively encounters, evidences a more and more self-insistent reality. The symbolization ends with the possession of the symbol by its source. When we know a reality we always know that there is still more to know of it, for we always face the terminus of a symbol as under the control of a power distinct from it, the symbol, and ourselves.

~~~~~~

Philosophy is a distinctive enterprise, concerning itself with what underlies every other. It cuts behind special disciplines to note what all of them take for granted, and what all of them initially accept.

Inevitably it is driven back to consider the first acts in which one must engage in order to obtain knowledge in any situation. There is no other place to begin but where one now is, but there it is desirable to stop and reflect on what it is that one is doing. This is nothing less than engaging in an act of attention.

All attending occurs in a situation where it is dependent on and determined by the insistent presence of men, minds, customs, and language; society, events, things, space, time; the past and the dynamics of nature; a prospective future and the requirements of action. Different studies focus on different items. While one of them starts with space or time, compounds or organs, another accepts sensed objects or behavior; while one begins with commonsense objects, another jumps at once to substances, lying just beyond. What are data for one discipline may be presuppositions for another. The cells fastened on by a biologist are simply accepted by the zoologist.

Attention has a double thrust. It demarcates certain items, bounding them off from others; it also prevents those others from assuming an equally positive role for us at that time. In the ordinary course of affairs, the prevention is guided by prejudgment and habitual discrimination. Vocabulary and grammar, customary beliefs and practice, lead to a neglect of what does not readily fit into our categories, classifications, divisions, combinations, and relations.

Some modes of attending and selecting have fairly short careers. Others are operative for almost the entire length of a life. A passing fancy makes one fasten on an otherwise uninteresting item, and reject everything else. Long-entrenched habits turn us in one direction rather than in another. The thought of a fortune makes the bank stand out from other buildings. An available cigarette raises the smoker's hand and purses his lips. Had some other operation been prominent, what is now kept at a distance might itself be to the fore.

Rarely is a conscious, deliberate choice made to attend to this rather than to that. Usually we do not know how to make such a choice; before we attend there is nothing for us to deliberate about. But choose we do. We fasten on what we might have neglected, and neglect what we might have fastened on.

There are a half-dozen reasons why attention turns where it

does. Some of the reasons we do not fully understand; some of them we are oblivious of until special circumstances make us aware of our hidden motives and desires. Philosophically, it makes little difference why we focus here rather than there. Knowing why we focused on this object rather than on that does not help us know what we now can justifiably say about what is before us. Wherever we attend, and for whatever reason, the same issue arises.

[2]

In attending to anything we isolate it and bound it. When this fact is overlooked we are tempted to maintain that in knowing we contribute nothing at all to what we confront, or to hold that we are the source of all we know. The former, in effect, likens perception to a searchlight which, without addition or subtraction, makes evident what is there. The latter attributes everything intelligible, and perhaps even the entire being of the known, to the knower, to make him a creator of what he knows.

A searchlight takes an object out of darkness and drenches it in light; if knowing contributes nothing to an object, the object either remains in darkness, or the change to light is no change at all. But no one is as passive as the searchlight view requires. All men classify, order, evaluate, connect, and divide according to interests and experience.

Nor is the perceiver ever as powerful as the creation theory requires. All must observe in order to know what is so. All must submit to what is if they are to learn what is—and what will be. All must give some weight to what is not their product if they are to get what they desire. Insistent needs and egos are satisfied only when they make room for what is not themselves.

Knowledge is possible because one has withdrawn not only from a mere interplay with other realities, but also from what is confronted. The withdrawal is usually not deliberate; the knower rarely initiates it. Although made on behalf of knowledge, it is ontological in character, the outcome of an inability to advance because of what is in one's path. As one moves on, denser and denser content is met.

The advance is gradually slowed; finally it is stopped. For a further advance to occur, it is necessary to withdraw and start anew, but with a grasp of what had already been reached. What otherwise would have proven to be an insuperable barrier is thereby overcome, and a further penetration into the object achieved. This process can be repeated any number of times. It has no end, for no matter how far we penetrate content is always being withheld from us.

There are men who are most reluctant to withdraw from anything. Sometimes they think of themselves as vital and concerned. But in fact they are indifferent, men who have only a minimal interest in whatever it be that crosses their path. Others would like to avoid taking up a position. Thinking that they demonstrate laudable cautiousness, they in fact carelessly allow themselves to be subject to whatever happens to be dominant at that time. While the former tend to ignore what would disturb their indifference, the latter tend to ignore the need to make provision for other occurrences. Both, of course, withdraw to some degree. In fact, they exhibit just the attitudes they do, because they have stepped back from an unreflecting penetration into what lies beyond the appearances. Both, however, fail to withdraw when and how they should, if knowledge is to be maximized.

Withdrawal should be controlled in the light of the need to attend and to advance into what is known, to a degree that was not possible initially. To see this better, it is necessary to remain alert to the way signs differ from symbols.

[3]

A sign is anything whose presence prompts attention toward something distinct from itself. There is no sign if attention does not make use of something present to direct us to an object elsewhere, indefinite and ill-defined though this may be. The object might even be the entire world beyond, awesome and frightening.

Words can be signs. So can gestures and grimaces. So can clouds, smoke, shocks, and sneezes. The thought of a friend can be a sign of the picture of someone else that one has on the desk; the picture in turn can be sign of the idea of the friend. Normally, one wants signs to be effective for more than one conscious being—which the private thought of a friend cannot be. And, since one commonly wants the objects of signs to be available to others, there is a tendency to ignore those signs which, like the picture, have ideas as their referents. But these too are signs, just as surely as the others are.

Signs are used deliberately and consciously, as well as accidentally or incidentally. In both cases, the signs must be passed beyond, not attended to. The sign maker, the designer of signs, and the student of signs rightly focus on them. But then they hold up their use of the signs. They treat them, not as functioning signs, but as objects to be produced, examined, sold, and then presumably to be used as signs.

A sign and its referent are distinct. But they can be carried by the same object. A loud noise may prompt one to attend to the quality of its sound. Most signs, though, are used to enable one to attend to what is distant from them. The attending elsewhere has its causes, and proceeds along the lines of established structures in consonance with controlling laws.

Usually it is the prompting object, the object which stimulates the attention, whose appearance is used as a sign. But sometimes one signifies what, through training and conventional practice, one has learned to associate with the sign. The words of daily language rarely direct one to their causes; they are signs of what one has learned to attend to on the occurrence of the words.

As a rule, signs are involved with beliefs. But they are also sometimes freely forged and used. We give a name to the newborn child, and in the beginning use that name with accuracy, not because of any laws or habits or conventions, but because we have decided on that use.

A sign may be natural or artificial; the one makes use of what occurs apart from men, the other uses something that a man made. A cloud is a natural sign of rain; a word is an artificial sign of an object. The sign-role in either case is not native to the items used as signs. The signs are produced by an attentive being; he gives them that status.

A concern for the course of nature leads to the isolation of natural signs—usually, of what is to be. Such natural signs have been in use evidently since the beginning of the human race. It is by means of them that men have been able to take care of their crops, sail the oceans, and act anticipatorily on hearing the growl of an animal. In this respect, men seem to differ from animals only in degree. But men also have the ability to combine signs in constantly new ways in accord with rules, and to produce complex signs having their own distinctive objects. They alone have a complex, expandable language. Many of their initial natural signs are given a place in an organization of artificial signs. Some of them evidently were used apart from a language. Even today not all natural signs are absorbed into a language. A growl and a bear track are good illustrations.

Although enabled to be a sign by man, a natural sign is objectively connected with its referent. It can, therefore, lead one to attend to the referent's nature or presence. Properly speaking, it is then a signal or cue. But it can also provide evidence of the intent of the referent. A growl often has this role; it is then more than a mere sign. An artificial sign, in contrast, need provide no evidence of the nature or presence of its referent. It does, though, tell us something about man—that he is a sign user and may seek to communicate. When it does this, however, it no longer functions as a mere sign.

There could conceivably be natural occurrences which had no bearing on anything else. In a Humean world, where all entities were atomic, externally connected with one another, a cloud, just like the word "cloud," would have no relation to rain, possible or actual. On the other hand, there could be created signs which conceivably had some kind of connection with the objects to which those signs referred. The sound of a word could mimic the sound of what is signified. Though it is usually necessary to be trained in the use of such signs, in certain cases it is possible for one to recognize their referents straightaway.

In order to know if a sign is being used by someone, it must be accompanied by an evident sound or act. If one expects the accompanying sound or act not only to be followed by the act of another but to be relevant to what the first signifies, the first signalizes or (where the signalizing is vocal) calls to that other. When the accompanying signalers are themselves used as signs of what is being signified, there is communication.

[4]

Appearances are constituted by exhibitions of realities. These exhibitions are not distinguished in the appearances, but they also are not confined to them. The exhibitions fringe, and thereby coarsen, the appearances as well as constitute them. The realities do not release their exhibitions, even while they are being allowed to mesh with the counteracting exhibitions of other realities. As a consequence, appearances have *textures* and *roughings*, *grains* and *grits*, and are *possessed* and *grounded*. Textures, grains, and possessions are *adumbratives* which root an appearance in an actuality; roughings, grits and groundings are *lucidatives*, rooting an appearance in a finality.

Adumbratives and lucidatives lead into the recesses of the realities that appear. Those realities prevent the appearances from being subtracted from them. It is because of them that the appearances are able to stand away, not only from one type of reality but also from us and the boundaries that we impose.

A symbol is anything whose presence prompts a movement to a more intensive version of its dominant factor. It is related to its object in ways not explicable by reference to laws of nature, causes, or even volitions. Its object possesses and pulls on it and its user. By affecting both the symbol and its user, the object makes it possible for the user to reach that object by means of that symbol. Unlike a sign, which is always in an external relation to its referent, an appearance can be a symbol of its object because it is intimately related to it. By following the lead of its adumbrative or lucidative we can penetrate into the reality which helps constitute the appearance.

There are also symbols which are parts of languages, giving those languages not only a length but a depth. The depth is not evident when the languages are written, being manifest only in the activities, attitudes, and intentions of those who use the languages in living discourse. Written languages encourage the belief that all reference and communication is the work of signs.

Symbols extend into their objects as these exist apart from the perceiver—a fact made manifest by the absenting obduracy of those objects. Were there no symbols, one would not be able to know that confronted objects exist independently of knowers, except in the guise of a sheer, brute, irrational something.

Because we use symbols almost unconsciously, we penetrate without reflection beyond appearances, but not very far or very effectively. Routine leads to the replacement of many of these symbols by signs. A better understanding of what knowledge presupposes and what it can do would lead instead to a replacement by other symbols, obtained after a withdrawal, and enabling one to penetrate further into the symbolized than was possible initially.

The existence of symbols has not been widely noted in philosophic thought, in part because scientific practices, which make minimum use of symbols, have been taken as paradigms. There is also the fact that symbols are of primary interest to the practitioners of disciplines in little repute, such as graphology and the occult sciences. That symbols are of interest to students of religion and psychoanalysis, instead of lending credence to the claims made on behalf of symbols, has led many today to view these enterprises themselves with suspicion. More important, perhaps, is the fact that the adumbrative and lucidative continuations of appearances have not been noted. Whatever the reason, the role of symbols in perception, practice, and daily communication, has been given insufficient attention by contemporary philosophers. Psychologists, linguists, and sociologists have not made good the deficiency. As a result, a most useful agency for learning about reality has been insufficiently employed.

All men symbolize, though carelessly, to be sure, and without much control. Signs, particularly when well-designed, clearly defined, and conveyed in technical language or in mathematical terms, are used with more precision and mastery than symbols are. But they are not the best and certainly not the only ways by which to convey or to obtain knowledge. Nor do they lead us to realities. Having allowed themselves nothing but the use of signs, many philosophers have found themselves unable to reach, in a professional capacity, what they already had penetrated into.

[5]

A symbol has an integrity of its own. Without compromising this, or the symbol's rootage in its object, it is also involved in a reality other than that object. But the rootage in its object is full-blown and dominant, while its rootage in the other is subordinate, sometimes hardly operative, merely allowing the symbol to be sustained there.

A totem pole is a piece of wood, carrying a symbol of a potent reality. The symbol has clinging to it something of that reality. What carries the symbol, the wood, also keeps the symbol from sinking into depths of what it symbolizes. When the grip of the wood that carries the symbol is loosened, the symbol is able to join up with its appropriate reality; to the degree it does this, to that degree the symbol becomes indistinguishable from the other contributions of the potent reality. The movement is intensive, in depth. We never penetrate all the way into any reality; there are unprobed depths beyond any point arrived at. But what remains over is not absurd; there are, as we shall see, ways of knowing what is then beyond the reach of the symbol used.

A carrying reality prevents a symbol from being a pure symbol of the reality in which it is primarily rooted and which contributes most to it. The wood not only allows one to acknowledge the symbol, and be prepared to use it, but keeps the symbol from having more than a limited penetrative power. That power is increased just so far as the symbol is freed from the influence of its carrier. The use of the symbol purifies it, since, by means of the symbol, one moves into its primary source.

Signs are used more often and more widely than symbols. For ordinary purposes, in logic, mathematics, and science, nothing more is needed to make judgments and to communicate than to link signs together, and then to refer the result to some external but independent reality as its counterpart. The success and the simplicity of the procedure can be a cause, and occasionally a result, of a misconception about the nature of symbols and the way they function.

1] Signs are external to one another and to their objects. When symbols are acknowledged, this characteristic of signs may be superimposed on the symbols, with a resultant misconstrual of what symbols are and what they do. One then turns to the comparative study of the allegories, metaphors, and figures in the history of art as the primary cases of symbol, for these all have an integrity of their own, and are externally related to their objects but in ways quite different from those appropriate to the objects of common sense or scientific discourse. Iconography and comparative art history only rarely start from accepted symbols and proceed to the understanding of what is the case. Instead, they usually offer highly sophisticated ways of dealing with signs that also have a symbolic use. They use symbols only when they use their material vitally in an act of penetration, not when they make it the object of an impersonal inquiry.

Cassirer goes unnecessarily far in supposing that symbols are themselves constitutive of what they order, as though, apart from the symbols, all was chaos and unintelligibility. His symbolic forms are employed as creative conditions. They could have been used to lead him into finalities. Instead, he treats them as though they gave meaning to an otherwise inchoate world of actualities. Were one to assume his position, one would still not have freed oneself from the thrall of a doctrine of signs. One would have merely added to it the claim that the most important signs are those which give structure and meaning to the content they organize, and to which they are to be referred for grounding and determination.

Symbols are involved with what they symbolize, not because they organize these, or produce them, or control them, but because they are appearances, rooted in what they symbolize. If appearances told nothing about what appeared, there would be no symbols of either actualities or finalities. But then the appearances would exist by themselves and in effect be realities and not appearances, or they would simply reside in, be carried by, realities, as purposeless accidents, metaphysical drones. They would be appearances of what never happened.

2] Symbols must be detached from what carries them in order for them to be able to be used in a symbolization. The detachments are never so neat that they leave no trace of those carriers in the symbols. Symbols are relativized by their carriers, and thereby are prevented from functioning free of all limitation. The symbols are then able to be used as signs by means of which one refers to the carriers. When this fact is given undue prominence, we get the denial that there is any possibility of knowing or understanding what actualities or finalities are in themselves.

We make use of symbols to reach individuals and their sympathetic bonds, the being, the intelligibility, the space, time, and process, and the unity governing the exhibitions of those individuals. When those symbols are used simply as signs, one turns in another direction, toward what is indifferent to those symbols. The claims of a part will then be so exaggerated that the rights of the whole are denied. It is one thing to note that symbols are also signs, and another to take them to be signs, and nothing more.

The sign function of a symbol is often what is first noted. We then use the symbol to mark the place where it is in fact encountered. When, instead, we use the symbol in an act of penetrating to the depth of a reality, the sign role falls more and more into the background until, when the symbolized object takes over, the role is no longer identifiable. The symbolic act starts with a symbol, turned away from its carrier, and pulled into a possessive, insistent reality.

All symbols have a sign function; some signs have a symbolic aura. Our language as a whole is a mixture of terms, some of which are primarily signs, some primarily symbols, some primarily signs which also symbolize, and some primarily symbols which also function as signs. It is just as difficult to keep to the surface of the world, to remain just with appearances, as it is to keep below the surface, involved in realities. By convention and practice, we set rough limits to the depths to which we want symbols to descend. We also allow some signs to have a symbolic role, and make some symbols remain external to their objects and, therefore, be in a position to function as signs. It is, consequently, just as true to say that we never can speak adequately of transcendents, as it is that we can never speak adequately of appearances; it is just as true to say that we can never free all discourse about transcendents from empirical references, as it is to say that we can never free all discourse about the empirical from transcendental references.

3] Could symbols be detached from the symbolized, one could reach the symbolized by adding a process of symbolization to the symbols. The symbolization would then yoke together what in fact was externally related. When symbols are separated from their objects, the process of symbolization reduces to a reference of a sign to an object.

Yet, if symbols are continuous with the symbolized, to have a symbol, apparently, would be to have the symbolized, and therefore to have a symbol no longer, and no opportunity or need to symbolize. Symbols are continuous with the symbolized. But not only are they doubly directed, toward actualities and finalities, though with biases in one direction or the other, and not only are they carried by realities which maintain them outside the realities they primarily symbolize, but as so distinguished from the symbolized, they are inseparable from adumbratives and lucidatives. They have textures and roughnesses, grainings and grittings, they are possessed and grounded. One can credit these factors to the symbols or to the symbolized, but one never succeeds in attaching them wholly to the one or the other, for they are consequences of the fact that symbols operate in depth, and are not only produced by but are under the control of a dominating source.

Appearances are grasped as belonging to actualities and finalities. An emotion of wonder carries our bafflement and curiosity, our being faced with something whose explanation lies beyond it. Any quieting that the wonder then obtains is preliminary to a return to what is also wondrous—more than it would have been had we faced in that direction initially. A return to symbolizing appearances, after one had probed in the opposite direction, leads one to deal with a world even more wondrous than before. The range and intensity of wonder increases as a consequence of a penetration into a reality and a subsequent return to the object of the original wonder.

Later, a *concern* for actualities and an *appreciation* of finalities are separated out of the wonder and pursued on their own account.

The concern for actualities achieves a wider range and a greater depth after one has become appreciative of finalities. Conversely, appreciation becomes more intense after one has concerned oneself with actualities. At no time does one of these emotions, or the wonder which is the amalgamation of them, reach to the actualities or the finalities as they are in themselves. There is always more to wonder at; there is no limit to the possible intensity of wonder. What is left over at any moment quiets the wonder directed at it, only to make possible a more intensive wonder leading in the opposite direction. There is no completing of it, but also no fixed barrier beyond which it is antecedently defined as unable to go.

(In my first persistent, systematic inquiry into the various finalities, I clearly distinguished three of them: Meaning [Ideality], Existence [Extension], and God [Unity]—I have placed in brackets the alternative names I sometimes use. But the term 'Actuality,' unknowingly, was used to refer to three other distinct realities: particular entities [actualities], Substance, and Being. The discovery of the distinctive natures of these three realities, hidden from me by my use of the same term, has taken years.

The earlier acknowledgment of four finalities made it possible to distinguish and clarify the nature of such basic enterprises as ethics, politics, art, history, and religion, public and private. The discovery that what had been termed 'Actuality' was in fact divisible into Substance and Being, and that these were to be sharply differentiated from actualities, makes it possible to recognize additional basic enterprises.

The individual occupation with Substance is the concern of mysticism, the becoming one with a finality which permeates all privacies. The public counterpart of this activity is rhetoric; this uses language to lead to a grasp of the power of Substance. Theoretical knowledge is the outcome of the attempt to understand Being. It is matched by an experimental science which is concerned with ultimate, equal, unit beings.

In contrast with the disciplines occupied with finalities, is an ontological phenomenology which attends to and uses symbols of actualities. The counterpart of this is taxonomy, the enterprise of so grouping actualities that they are revealed to be at once defiant of and contributive to a common public result.)

The being of a symbol is continuous with that of an adumbration. The adumbration continues into the reality until it is lost, together with the symbol with which one began. Wherever we cut off the symbol in order to have it as an object to consider, we leave over some of it.

Adumbratives are mediators, and therefore never capable of being encompassed by a symbol, no matter how deeply penetrative this be. But precisely because an adumbrative mediates, it cannot be credited entirely to an actuality either, if this is set in contrast with its appearance. Measuring the distance that had been traversed by an actuality in making an appearance, an adumbrative orients the appearance toward the actuality's center. The nearer an adumbrative is to an appearance, the more receptive is the adumbrative to that appearance—but also the less insistent and vigorous it is. The nearer an adumbrative is to a reality, the more absorptive and denser it becomes.

Adumbratives are experienced. They can be referred to by means of signs; they can be made the objects of articulate judgments; they can be symbolized. Contrasted with actualities they are parts of symbols; contrasted with symbols they are parts of actualities. When symbols are detached from what they symbolize, the adumbratives are denied efficacy, and dangle from each end as useless appendages. Stretching between symbols and actualities, they relate surface and depth, limit and center, thinness and thickness, public and private, the comparatively light and the comparatively dark.

There is a continuity between appearances and actualities, and therefore between appearances and adumbratives, and between adumbratives and actualities. We need acknowledge no adumbratives if appearances just appear. We would not need to acknowledge adumbratives if actualities remained in themselves and did not make themselves present to others. We would not need to acknowledge actualities if adumbratives were not touched upon at the surface, and did not stretch from surface to center. Adumbratives share in the adventures of appearances and still remain distinct from them; they

are integral to actualities and yet relate these to what is held apart
from them. We must acknowledge them so long as we acknowledge
that there are appearances, and realities which these symbolize.

Over thirty years ago I saw the need to acknowledge adumbratives, but since I then paid little attention to finalities, there was no
occasion for attending to lucidatives. Of the adumbrative I remarked
that "it is by means of it we mark the dynamic, singular lilt of a
thing as unfolding itself in time. The adumbrated is the real as just
beyond the grasp of articulate knowledge; a given unity of contemplated and indicated, less relativized and more substantial than
their judged togetherness; the contemplated and indicated as the
specific nature of an object. If we were not aware of it in perception,
we should have no surety that what we then articulately know is less
than what there is to know, and our articulate knowledge would for
us exhaust the being of a thing" (*Reality* [Carbondale: Southern
Illinois University Press, Arcturus Books, 1967], p. 57). What I did
not clearly see then was that adumbration has a dynamics to it, and
does not simply complement articulate knowledge.

Adumbration is an integral part of the elements which make
up knowledge, as well as of symbols which are not used in judgments.
It leads us into the darkness that begins where knowing ends, but it
does this only because the reality that gives rise to symbols continues
to hold on to them, and to pull them toward itself. It is that holding
and pulling which is adumbratively experienced when we symbolize
an actuality.

Much of what is true of adumbratives is also true of lucidatives.
These, too, stretch from symbol to symbolized; these, too, mediate
dynamically. But lucidatives point in the opposite direction from
adumbratives—toward finalities rather than toward actualities. They
are effective, too, with respect to man, who experiences them
emotionally. Humility, awe, reverence, and similar basic emotions,
are not simply turbulences. They are effects which finalities produce
when men themselves are made into symbols of those finalities.
Actualities have no such effect, and men, as a consequence, must
make use of symbols external to themselves in order to arrive at
those actualities.

Because finalities invoke emotions that grip men, the finalities enable them to retrace the path which the finalities took in the course of exhibiting themselves. To get to the finalities, men add their own symbolic import to that of the things they encounter. But, since actualities do not provoke the basic emotions that are elicited by finalities, there is no need for men to add their own symbolic weight to what they encounter, in order to reach into actualities. All they need do is to be submissive to the luring adumbratives which connect the actualities and their appearances.

Lucidatives connect appearances with their finalities in a way that parallels the connection which holds between appearances and their actualities. The lucidatives are modes of concretization of contexts, ways of going from the symbols to the finalities.

Because men help constitute known appearances, the Kantian supposes that there is no need to acknowledge objective conditions, continuous with finalities, which operate directly on what actualities present. Recognizing that there is a world which men never made, materialists, instead, suppose that there is no need to acknowledge any contribution by men in order for there to be known appearances. The one sees that men help constitute known appearances, and the other that there are appearances which men do not help constitute. But the one takes man's mind to be a finality, the other takes man to be simply an effect.

4] Every entity affects others. It has sometimes been held that this is the result of an aboriginal exuberance, an overflowing, a self-multiplication, a fresh, undirected and uncontrolled outpouring, to be subsequently pruned and ordered. The idea is at the root of Darwin's theory of evolution and of Skinner's behaviorism as well as of Schiller's aesthetics and Marx's account of surplus value. It unnecessarily assumes that a limited result is the outcome of a union of a wild chance and a selecting agency. The facts they seek to explain can be accepted without making those assumptions.

Although generosity needs no excuse it does have an explanation. Giving is part of an effort at enrichment. Affecting is a giving, the first of a series of activities in which a reality attempts to subjugate and eventually possess others, and thereby become more complete. The affected object is not passive. It accepts on its own terms the qualifications others impose and may, as a consequence, alter those qualifications to some degree. At the minimum, it simply sustains what qualifies it; at the maximum the object transforms what it receives, to make this hardly distinguishable from what it would exhibit on its own. The greater the acceptance, the greater the accommodation.

The affected object internalizes something of the qualifications which it accepts. The effort at internalization can be so feeble that it leaves the qualification largely untouched, a mere presence. But the qualification is sometimes so completely internalized that it makes a serious difference to the object and what this thereafter does. Whether or not an object internalizes qualifications, it manifests itself in relation to the qualifications to which it is subject. The result is a meshing of the qualifications with exhibitions of the qualified reality.

So far as its own contribution is dominant, a reality offers a comparatively pure symbol for what is within that reality, and a comparatively impure symbol for others. The exhibitions of an actuality allow its symbol to be comparatively pure, with the contextualizing conditions playing only a minor part. Similarly, the exhibitions of finalities allow for comparatively pure symbols where the exhibitions of actualities have only a subordinate role. In either case, pure or impure, surfaces are entrances into depths. A comparatively impure symbol is converted into a comparatively pure one in the course of its use. In the progress toward its dominant source, the symbol is freed more and more from its sustaining reality. It becomes purer and purer, and more and more transformed, the deeper one penetrates into the reality.

Finalities affect actualities severally in one way, and affect them together in another. They arouse them as individuals and make them function together. Exhibiting themselves in opposition to the exhibitions of the actualities, they act on each at the same time that they act on all. If they acted only on them severally, neither actualities nor appearance would be together. Did actualities or their appearances merely function harmoniously together, there would be no reason why they should continue to do so. Both actualities and appearances are governed by laws; they are controlled by contexts; they function as terms for what provides the relations; they introduce variety, punctuation, and stresses in otherwise empty domains.

Once again, sacred objects offer a good illustration. Objects in a context, they are caught in a network of rituals, ceremonies, myths, and traditions. Even if there were only one sacred object, there would be a social context connecting it with men. That social context is a limited form of the context rooted in a finality. Together with the sacred object, the men there sustain a common, imposed sacramentality, symbolizing the finality. At the same time, the men and the supposed single sacred object are sacred independently of one another. It is, therefore, possible to conceive of only one sacred object or man. But if that object or man could not be used together with others as a symbol of the divine, neither would be fully sacred; at best, it would be only an important unit in that society.

5] Symbols take one into the realities that produce them. But not all the way. There is always something left over. This observation, it would seem, is impossible to maintain. If the symbols stop at some point, how can we know that there is something more? How can we know what is there? Are we not back with a theory of signs and the objects exterior to them, which we cannot reach or know?

The fact that any one symbol comes to a rest before one arrives at an actuality or finality as it is in itself, does not preclude the use of further symbols to begin where a previous one ended. There is always something left over, but this which is left over can be dealt with by means of new symbols, on and on as long as we choose. This consideration does not, of course, show that a symbolic knowledge, no matter how often we add symbol to symbol, will ever get to a reality as it is in itself. Indeed, the observation to the effect that all knowledge of actualities and finalities is affected by our starting point in alien carriers would support the view that no multiplicity of symbols will ever get us to those realities in themselves. But then we are left with the question of how we know that there is something still to be reached.

Symbols are inseparable from adumbratives and lucidatives. A symbol stops, but the adumbratives and lucidatives continue on. We know that there is more than what our symbols reach, because there is always a pull on them away from us. The content does not remove itself to a distance; but it is held onto by that which defies, blocks, resists us. We know that there is more to symbolize and that it is desirable to continue symbolizing, because we are aware of the pull of adumbratives and lucidatives before we are able to follow their lead.

More important is the fact that that at which we stop is then and there being filled with details, emphases, insistencies beyond what the symbolizing provides. Realities not only absent themselves from our boundaries, they add to the content we have bounded. They not only intensify what already fringes our symbols, they add material which cannot be accommodated by the symbols. A symbol is not cut off from an alien object; that would make it a sign. It is part of a reality which eventually overwhelms it, and which reveals it to be less than what it is enabling us to reach.

There is a proliferation of insistent details at the point where our symbols stop. Were those symbols used to refer to what was there confronted, the symbols would be used as signs. Symbolism reveals its own incapacity to encompass the fullness of the very reality into which it enables us to penetrate beyond any preassigned degree. But this is only another way of saying that symbols are possessed by the realities which make them possible, that every reality is richer than anything that it might make appear, and that this fact is made evident when we symbolize.

The difficulty of getting to the full reality does not arise at the end of an effort to symbolize. It is faced right at the beginning, and throughout. A symbol is always in the grip of powers beyond its control or mastery. Since symbolization properly begins only after one has held what is sustained away from what sustains it, it properly begins at the very reality into which the symbol is to penetrate. The symbol's main constituent is that reality, attenuated and relativized. By moving along the route of an adumbration or lucidation, the process of symbolization becomes more and more under the dominance of the reality as it is in and of itself. The successful symbolic use of an appearance inevitably ends with its disappearance in an absolutized version of one of its constituents.

The process of symbolizing a finality takes one no further than to the source of a context. That source is identical with the context when this is freed from a reference to content obtained from actualities. It is reached by lucidatively shifting attention from content, subject to contextualizing conditions, toward the content as an integral but transformed part of the context, to the context iself, and then to the finality beyond this. When a man uses himself or a facet of an object as a symbol of a finality, he moves along the route of a dominant factor to end with a penetration into the finality.

5

MANIFESTATIONS AND DISPLAYS

~~~~~~

Controlling Summary: Appearances are junctures of insistent actualities and finalities, distinct from both. Because the appearances are biased toward a dominant reality, they allow one to symbolize this. Because they are fringed by the attenuations of the reality, they enable one to continue into it. By virtue of the factors produced by subordinated realities, the appearance can be distinguished from the reality to which it is to be credited.

At their most attenuated, actualities are qualia, and finalities are presences. Together they constitute manifestations, which are appearances characteristic of things, but also creditable to the living. Those appearances are textured or roughed, depending on whether they are inseparable from adumbratives, leading to actualities, or from lucidatives, leading to finalities. The manifestations, in turn, provide grains and grits for displays.

Manifestations are interrelated within things: displays are interrelated by living beings. The displays are not reducible to manifestations.

~~~~~~

Life is precarious. Competitive and involved with dangers, occupied with necessities and simple continuance, most men have little room or time for any but practical interests and activities. Even after they have managed to find ways to protect themselves and to survive,

they continue to be practical, though mainly for the sake of occupying some position, or of carrying out some role in society. Although
it is usually not as hard for them to maintain themselves as it is for
other living beings, men are consequently almost as much immersed
in practical affairs as these others are.

The young of men and higher animals are not too tightly
caught in practical affairs. They play, they blunder, they are dis-
oriented. Adults must guide them to perform properly, even in the
supposed instinctually dominated areas of sex, food, and security.
The young, of course, are not without all practicality. They have a
strong orientation toward those who are able to feed and protect
them. They differ from their elders, not in having no involvement
in practical affairs, but in the range of their interests, abilities, and
experience. The practicality of the young is in fact so throbbingly,
pathetically persistent, that it provides a fine clue to the nature of
practice. The mature obscure it somewhat by their habits.

To be practical is to pass beyond surfaces, to lay hold of what
is substantial, palpable, and to allow one to be guided by this. There
is here no time given to a contemplation of the nature of what is
confronted. What is confronted is used at once as an agency for
dealing with the source of what is needed and desired. Because
there is no time given to a consideration of the presence or natures
of symbols, or of the way these can be most effectively used to
reach the symbolized, one can be readily led astray and made to
direct oneself to what is not the appropriate terminus of symbolization, and therefore not a proper object of practical need.

The growing animal and the growing human increase in strength
and habituation. Gradually their insistent dependence on the help
of adults is quieted, and their range of practical interests extended.
But only a matured man is able to withhold himself both from a
practical and a playful involvement with what is about. Only he is
able to open himself to the influence of final realities pulling him
toward what is vaguer, larger, and transcendent, almost just beyond
the reach of his consciousness. To be sure, most men pay little attention to what is then made available. But when they do, they are
able to offer a counterbalance to their usual tendency to possess and
use what they confront in the course of practical living.

Some men overbalance a tendency toward actualities with a deep involvement with transcendent finalities. These are mystics, speculative philosophers, mathematicians, artists, the truly religious. No one of these can maintain himself steadily in this position. Just as the ordinary man's tendency toward a practical involvement with objects is challenged and countered by a tendency to attend to transcendents, those with an opposite bent find that their occupation with those transcendents is effectively challenged and countered by a tendency to deal with objects. All men face content that is determined in opposing ways.

[2]

A leaf is an actuality with a substance, being, nature, extension, and unity of its own. Finalities exhibit themselves there, thereby provoking a union of their exhibitions with the exhibitions of the leaf. The result is an objective appearance of the leaf, an appearance of first degree, not yet modified by social or personal notes. There is a point where the exhibition of a finality is so minor that it is impossible to tell whether the leaf is an appearance or an actuality. An appearance is fringed by an adumbrative which roots the exhibition of the leaf in the leaf, and by lucidatives which root the exhibitions of finalities in those finalities. The adumbratives and lucidatives make appearance have the role of a symbol.

The appearance of a leaf passes imperceptibly into an appearance of a finality. This has the very same constituents as the appearance of the leaf, but with an opposite stress. In it the exhibitions of the actual leaf have less and less efficacy, until they seem to vanish altogether. At that point it is impossible to distinguish the presence of the finality from its appearance.

An observed leaf is an appearance; so is its color. These appearances differ in the extent to which the exhibition of the leaf, out of which they are partly constituted, externalizes the actual leaf. A minimal externalization is a *manifestation*, a greater is a *display*. When we come to man, we find that a still greater externalization, an *expression*, is possible. All three have a first degree, unaffected by social or personal notes. All three vary in the extent to which the externalizing exhibition of the actuality is dominant in the appearance. When the exhibition of a finality dominates over that of an actual leaf, what appears is the finality. That finality helps constitute contextualized manifestations, displays, or expressions. Since a greater externalization includes a lesser, expressions are inseparable from displays and manifestations, and displays are inseparable from manifestations. In turn, what is included coarsens that in which it is. Manifestations grain and grit displays; displays possess and ground expressions.

[3]

Manifestations are low grade appearances, constituted of qualia and presences, of what comes from actualities and of what comes from finalities. When the insistencies expressed through qualia and presences are in equilibrium, the manifestations are phenomena; when there is an emphasis on one of the factors, the manifestations are just appearances, textured or roughed.

Nominalists take manifestations to be simply qualia, and idealists take them to be simply contexts, i.e., presences in which qualia can be located. The nominalists isolate the symbols of actualities; the idealists, instead, isolate the symbols of finalities. Neither, because neglectful of what the other fastens on, is able to do justice to what is manifest.

Qualia, immediacies, are felt, undergone, lived through, and lived with. Each is unduplicable, existing only when it is experienced. Somewhat similar to what Peirce called 'Firsts', they are also different, since a number of them can be located in the same place. The presence and the changes of some have a steady and intelligible relation to others. So far, they are linked. Despite this linkage each quale is distinctive, able to be even if there were no others.

Qualia enable us to learn little more than that there is something manifesting itself. They tell us what is true of an actuality, but in abstraction from the fact that it is a thing, an animal, or a man. To stop here, is to know actualities only as realities which put in an appearance. But we know more than this.

A manifestation has a textured side which adumbratively roots a quale in an actuality, and another, a rough side which lucidatively roots a presence in a finality. It is individual and immediate, as well as duplicable and universal, an appearance of one kind of reality sustained by the other.

One moves from a manifestation into an actuality by starting with a quale and then following the lead of its adumbrative texture into the reality inseparable from this. The move into a finality, instead, starts with a presence, and then follows the lead of its roughed lucidation. The first move demands a yielding of oneself to a textured appearance, with the consequence that, along with the texture, one is subject to what is actual beyond the appearance. The other demands an adoption of the roughed appearance, with the consequence that this is made to share in a lucidation characteristic of a man already open to the finality that is responsible for the roughed appearance.

[4]

Actualities insist on themselves. Nothing is thereby detached from them. With decreasing effectiveness, they expand, at the same time that they are blocked by the existence, and suffer the insistent exhibitions of other realities. They appear both because of the way they insist on themselves and the way their insistence is countered. Each manifestation belongs to and remains biased toward an actuality; it is, therefore, not to be equated with the effect of the actuality produced in some other entity. And each manifestation is both partly constituted and carried by another kind of reality; if it were not, the manifestation would be indistinguishable from the actuality and would not, therefore, be a manifestation at all. There is something manifested because there are other kinds of realities which contribute to the result, at the price, though, of diminishing the role of the exhibition of an actuality in the manifestation.

The manifestations of an actuality are kept distinct from the actuality by another kind of reality. But they are also biased toward the actuality. Were this all, it is conceivable that the manifestation might simply be on the surface of the actuality, an execrescence which depended for its presence on the actuality, but which could tell us nothing about it. Symbolization would then be an act by men who, without guidance, tried to retrace the steps by which a biased appearance was produced. But actualities not only insist on themselves; they hold on to what they present, somewhat as someone who lends money still lays claim to its return. The thrust outward is matched by the actuality's proprietary grasp of an exhibition which has a dominant role in the manifested appearance.

Because realities maintain a grip on their exhibitions, there is a path available along which one is able to move from manifestation to source. If such a movement were due solely to the efforts of those who attend to the manifestation, they would in effect be using signs, but along routes which lead them to the producers of these signs. But realities pull on their manifestations; they absent those manifestations from the boundaries which men impose when consciously remarking them. That pull is inseparable from a thrust which affectively brakes it. Were there no brake put upon the pull that realities exert on their manifestations, the symbolic use of those manifestations would be indistinguishable from the pull exerted by those realities. Because of the pull, an entrance into a reality, which the thrust would preclude, is made available; because of the thrust, the pull is unable to provide the limitless access to the reality that would otherwise be possible.

Did thrust and pull exactly equal one another, but with opposite stresses, there would be no going forward or backward. Yet if one of them is dominant, the brake which the other provides must be proportionately ineffective. They must be equal in force, and yet cannot be. This paradox disappears with the recognition that what is thrust forward is not identical with what is pulled inward.

An actuality thrusts itself forward. It is prevented from bursting into innumerable fragments because the pull, which is inseparable from that thrust, turns the entire movement outward into a single, individual exhibition. The pull is prevented from compressing the exhibition to a point and from absorbing the exhibition without a trace, because the thrust, which is inseparable from that pull, slows the entire inward movement. The actuality pulls its exhibition and, therefore, the manifested symbol, more or less freed from its carrier, into a denser and denser inward darkness, where symbolization loses its way.

[5]

Like a manifestation, a *display* can be attended to only with effort. It has a thickness to it, and can be held apart from the actuality that possesses it. Unlike a manifestation, though, it is expressed in relation to other displays, often located elsewhere. In contrast with the manifestation, it is also able to function as a distinct entity together with others, thereby making possible the realization of ends or goals shared by a number. It is not only encompassed within a context, but has a distinctive place in it. Sometimes it makes a difference to the way in which other displays will continue or alter. Most important, it allows one to symbolize living beings.

Living beings, no less than things, appear in the guise of manifested qualia interlocked with the presences contributed by finalities. But only in living beings do manifestations have the role of adumbratives for displays, leading one into the recesses of living individuals.

The displays of others tempt and antagonize, attract and repel. A study of that interplay tells us much about the kinds of communities the living beings form with one another. But they do not tell us what a living being is in itself. To know this, one must avoid responding to a display and must instead follow the lead of its graining back to its source. Though we never get to the living being's absolute center, we can thereby move toward it, beyond any preassigned limit.

A presence provides grit for a display. If the display be faced as a phenomenon, and thus with its grain and grit in balance, it will effectively obscure both the presence of the living being and the finalities which are at the root of the display. One will then, in knowing the nature of a display, not know an individual or anything beyond it. To get to one or the other from a display, we must start with the display as a grained or gritty appearance and, therefore, as merely sustained by a finality or an individual, respectively.

Traditionally, manifestations have been treated as though they were simple entities, without complexity, despite their nuances, their changes, and their modifications by one another. Displays, instead, have rightly been taken to be complex, not only in their observable features, but in their development. They begin and they end, and this not merely in the form of externalizations of what is suffered in private, but in relation to one another.

A living being might conceivably display itself without regard for others. But the development of its display depends on the displays that it is able to observe in the course of its own display. Its own display is an incidental consequence of its symbolic grasp of the display of others; its penetration into them, slight though it is, is accompanied by changes in its own display. A bird usually does not merely sing; it sings to other birds, and then in some accord with the way in which they sing to or with it. A child does not merely cry out; it cries to and with, and alters the cry in the light of the way in which others display themselves. It does not want words of comfort and concern, and is not usually satisfied by them. The child reads these symbolically; if they do not make it aware of a desirable state in another, they often prompt the child to increase its cries.

A child's cry can be attended to. We can note its pitch and timbre, its location and its insistent tone. The cry will then not be used symbolically, but will be dealt with as an occurrence, having its causes and effects, its conditions and consequences. One can stop the cry with a nursing ring or a bottle, and perhaps a slap. A sympathetic response to the cry probes deeper, allowing one to attend to the child, beyond oneself and the cry.

Relieving the child of its pain is usually a necessary condition for a passage beyond its pain and cry, to the stage where adult and child are one. A concentration on the cry as an occurrence will keep one from penetrating into the child; it will also keep one from penetrating into what encompasses its openness and one's own. The desirable practicality of helping the child, in contrast, promotes a penetration into the child, but with a neglect of the finalities which provide contexts for the cry and other displays.

A man can add to an openness to a finality, carried by a display, an openness of his own. He then will not just respond to the cry of a child, but will use it as an occasion for a union with the child's openness to a finality. The result will be a single complex symbol of a transcendent, relevant to both.

[6]

"Symptoms" are displays which come within the purview of medicine. In the course of ordinary living they provide clues and evidences of what one might expect of others in a common social setting. Stigmata, moral fervor, heroism, artistic activity lead not to actualities, but to finalities for which those actualities are places where the finalities are displayed. Displays, though, are most often used as symbols of individual living beings, and not of finalities.

Under the influence of Wittgenstein, and under other headings, displays have recently come into prominence in the discussions of contemporary thinkers. Following his lead they have concentrated on such displays as cries of distress and pain. These are taken to be occasions for the formulation of a public language. Were man only an animal, were language properly understood by seeing how in fact a child acquired it—despite the obvious truth that the result has a different structure and objective from what a full-fledged user requires—and could a human do nothing more than offer public displays of states undergone in private, this approach would have more than a passing value. But finalities not only display themselves; they and men also express themselves, use the expressions of others as symbols, and assess the value of what they confront.

Biological naturalists are quite familiar with displays. But today these biologists have little standing with the rest of the biological fraternity, in part because it is supposed that good science means experimentation and quantification, and in part because the vocabulary of the naturalists tends toward metaphor and anthropomorphisms. But facts have rights that no method and no demand for precision should be allowed to abrogate. After all, a method is justified only if helps one to arrive at facts; precision is desirable only if it helps one know exactly what is the case.

[7]

The manifestations and displays of actualities are unit occurrences; they are appearances of single entities. But these entities, we have learned over the course of scientific history, contain within them a multiplicity of smaller units. The physical units, dealt with separately or in clusters are unlike known appearances; they evidently have energy; they act and react; they are interrelated in a cosmos; they seem to be presupposed by all complex actualities, and they can sometimes be predictably combined to yield observables with their apparently unitary properties.

A sharp and clear reductionism, it might be argued, will eventually lead to the substitution for appearances by the more elementary physical units and their physical and chemical combinations. The difference between the displays and manifestations will then be a minor difference between superficialities which together vanish in an accurate, scientifically substantiated account of the natures and behaviors of more fundamental and truly real elements. But: 1] We do encounter manifestations and displays. Their presence must still be explained. To say that they are just interpretations, confused ways of referring to hordes of particles, is still to be left with the question of how they are able to hide from us what in fact is real. It is also to force one to question the evidences that are supposed to show that there are neutrons and positrons, and similar unexperienced, unencountered particles. Fictions and confusions cannot provide reliable reports of what in fact is real.

2] The elements that concern the sciences are charted on a cosmic scale, where they are related to one another. But those elements are in fact found clustered within the confines of actualities. Each actuality keeps a limited number of elementary particles together. A scientific account that ignored the confining units in which a number of particles are and act together, accepts one part of an actuality and denies another. It is in just as vulnerable position as is a view which, aware that it is men who speak and walk, denies that blood and bones, cells and molecules are to be found within their confines.

A cluster of elements is first here and then there because a complex, confining actuality moved from here to there. If this role of the larger actuality be denied, the swarm which is within it becomes nothing more than a compact group whose members act on one another, in ways similar to that in which they act on the members of another swarm. Yet the members of one move together and act on one another, despite the fact that some of the members of another swarm might be nearer to some of the members of the former than either is to various members of its own swarm, clustered together in some actuality.

Reference must be made to the bonds which clusters the elements. If such reference does not point to encompassing entities, it will tell us merely that certain elements happen to keep together. If H_2O is water, it is wet; if it is just hydrogen and oxygen together, it is gaseous. We blur these facts when we say that there are molecules of oxygen and hydrogen in water but that they are there without the functions that they have in gases, and when we say that the molecules constitute a water but that this is neither fluid nor wet. Water, wet, fluid water, is distinct from molecules, singly or together.

A difference in the degree of complexity of combinations of elements might conceivably account for the production of a manifestation or display, if these were just independent exhibitions. But things manifest themselves in one way now because of the way they had manifested themselves before. Animals do more. They relate their displays to the displays of others, and to what concerns continuance or welfare.

3] It is not possible without serious loss to reduce macroscopic entities to the elements that are within their confines. Nor is it possible to reduce one kind of macroscopic entity to another except by suffering another great loss in material and explanation. There is little to say in favor of those who hold that animals and even men are intelligibly reducible to elementary particles. There is not much more to say in favor of those who hold that they are complicated machines, i.e., things. If they were things, there would be no significant difference between a manifestation and a display, or between either of these and an expression. Every expression, it could then be said, is a complex display, and every display just a manifestation having causes outside the manifesting reality, with which it may interact. We would still remain with observables, but we will have ignored or canceled out many facts—sympathy, communication, preparation, responsiveness.

Men are sensitive, emotional, rational, attentive, self-conscious, and self-controlled. If nature had a place only for insensitive things, men would have to occupy a special area outside nature. But then it is hard to see how they could die from a blow, delivered when they were asleep. Men are in nature as surely as are other actualities. This does not mean that they differ from the others only in degree, that the others have at least a tincture of human feelings and thoughts, or that men have these in their fully developed forms. To suppose that human feelings and thoughts are identical in kind but more fully matured than those characteristic of the subhuman, is merely to be prepared to read out later what one had arbitrarily inserted earlier.

If we use manifestations as symbols, we can get no further than to learn what a man is in a world of things. If we use displays as symbols we will be able to learn nothing more than what a man is in a world of living beings. Only *expressions*, when used symbolically, lead into the recesses of a man as a member of mankind. Those expressions are coarsened by displays, and are thereby enabled to take one along the path of a possession toward the possessors of the expressions and displays. When used emotionally, the manifestations, displays, and expressions function as unit symbols, whose nature is not examined. We just use them, and thereby achieve an immediate acquaintance with the source of their dominant constituents.

Because daily life is by and large stabilized in relation to appearances, we usually find it desirable to attend to those appearances, dissecting and uniting products of the dissection in judgments. The judgments are expressed in *asserta*, which contain what is perceptually known of appearances. True asserta are what we know of appearances when we perceive. They are distinct from yet continuous with the appearances, and therefore with the realities which provide the dominant constituents of those appearances. The appearances are of the third degree, since they are affected by various social and personal additions. Yet they allow us to know actualities, because they are coarsened by the adumbrative presence of those actualities. We confront and know appearances that have had their objective natures somewhat obscured by individual and group interpretations, but without an affect on the coarsening which textures, grains, and possessions give to them. As a consequence, it is possible to use what is daily confronted as a symbol, and thereby reach to the actuality whose exhibition dominates in the constitution of the known appearance.

Asserta can be true or false; they exist *in* the mind as well as out of it. Percepta, instead, are more or less reliable, and exist *for* the mind as well as out of it. In the latter guise they are appearances which exist even if there are none to know them. The asserta and percepta get careers and associations from the knower. They are also in relations of less to more independence of the knower, because they are less or more coarsened, less or more pulled upon by actualities.

6

~~~~~~

THE ASSERTUM

~~~~~~

Controlling Summary: Within the area of the focused, judgment distinguishes a designated and a contemplated. Otherwise articulation would involve a loss of the object. It unites the designated and contemplated to make a single unit. If this is accommodated by the actuality it becomes true of the actuality.

The designated and contemplated introduce boundaries within the focused, and are relative to one another. That is why they can be used in thought, and why their union is not arbitrary. The indicated, contemplated, and their union are symbols, not altogether separable from what is perceptually confronted. The terms and statements of a language into which the designated and contemplated and their judged unity are translated are properly used only when used symbolically. Otherwise what we knew in thought would be lost in discourse.

An assertum is claimed to be true or false of an appearance. If true, it is the beginning of an act of acquaintance with the actuality. If false, its unity continues to be symbolic of the unity of some actuality or other.

~~~~~~

A symbol is used at the beginning of an adumbrative act. At the end of the use, a deeper, more intensive content is encountered. It is the function of a designator to enable us to attend to the presence of that content.

A *designator* is part of, but separable from something designated; a *denotative* is independent of, and stands apart from, something denoted. A *designated object* is the terminus of a specialization of an original act of attending; a *denoted objective* is the counterpart of a denotative.

If we attend solely to words, i.e., to the terms used in discourse, we will overlook designators. Words cannot lead to anything outside language. No words commit one to anything unless it be the use of more words. The fact is not altered if instead of ordinary words we use variables, quantifiers, numbers, and the like.

"This," "here," "there," "this leaf" do not designate, but merely alert others to us, to our acts, or to the objects of our attention. Nor do they denote. Denoting is something that men, not terms, do; though, to be sure, when men denote they sometimes accompany the act with terms.

A designated is attended to; it is an aspect of the focused, standing in contrast with ourselves. Since it is produced by operating within boundaries imposed by us on the focused, a designated is only an aspect of what appears. But it is also more than what is focused on since it is constituted by and is inseparable from a distinctive boundary introduced inside the focused, thereby enabling the designated to be known there. More important, it leads us into an actuality, because like the whole appearance, it, too, is adumbratively connected with the reality.

A designator may symbolically relate us to a *place*, an area limited and given within a larger space and time. It may symbolically relate us to a *position*, a place occupied and contrasted with others. It may symbolically relate us to the *occupant* of a place or position. Or it may mark out a *claimant* for a place or position—even for the very one that is occupied. No one of these functions is entirely cut off from a reference to the others. All require that we refer to something other than ourselves or our terms. Ideally, though, they can be separated and thereupon studied so as to enable one to grasp a little better than otherwise what is initially designatable, and what this imports for knowledge.

A place is designated by means of a *salutation*. Sometimes it is said that a salutation is a term in a language and that it refers to a bare "*x*" about which nothing could be said except that one is to ascribe predicates or descriptions to it. But this is to forget that the salutation and its referent are extended in space and in time. More important is the fact that the "*x*" could not be altogether bare. Otherwise, no predicates would be pertinent to it, and all descriptions would be mistaken.

Salutations help us isolate regions of space and time. What they enable us to separate off is in a position. The position is bounded off from others, and related to them. As so related it has a kind of general meaning; it is what it is only by being connected to what is distinct from it. The terms used to remark it are on a level with such other terms as "black," "wise," "heavy," and are significantly related to them. They are all universals, items in a language or judgment. Capable of endless exemplifications, they retain their meaning even when not exemplified, and are individualized in use.

On some theories every noun denotes something. "Centaur," "the emperor of ice cream," no less than "Paul Weiss" or "the inventor of the radio" are all taken to denote. Others correctly see that these, like all the rest of the terms in a language, are floating universals, pointing to nothing. They may accompany acts of reference, but have no referential force or use of their own. This does not leave over a mere "*x*," an "it" to which these terms refer in different ways. Such an "it" or "*x*" would be unknowable. Not only would it be shorn of every mentionable quality, but there would be no accounting for the fact that this rather than that characteristic was attributed to it. All places would be positions, somehow held away from others.

The recognition that a denotative, which could be a number, a figure, a picture, as well as a term, is a universal is one of the bases for Hegelian idealism. This treats all denotatives as embryonic forms which predicates are to complete. Since there is supposed to be nothing that stands outside the realm of these universals, there is nothing that one has to do, given any idea, term, or facet of an object, but to try to produce a coherent system in which the universals supplement and complete one another, until we arrive at a single complete whole that alone is real. But a denoted objective is part of a spatiotemporal world; it is extended, distinctive, obdurate, individual, and related. To get to an actuality we must give up denotation for designation, for this alone is continuous with the actuality, leading us into it while enabling us to remark on the presence of that actuality, as still beyond us.

The designator of the occupant of a place or a position is a *name* of that occupant. The name marks out a region and has a depth reference. We combine the two in such expressions as "this leaf," "the leaf here." The "this" and the "here" are used to lead us to the region demarcated, the "leaf" to lead us to the appearance to be found there. But the name does not tell us anything more about the appearance than that it is an occupant of a place or a position.

A claimant of a place or a position is designated by means of a *proper name*. That name is intrinsically symbolic, continuous with its object. The object, in turn, is an appearance making a claim to a place or a position. When that appearance itself functions symbolically, it enables the proper name to apply to an actual claimant as well. "Tom" names the man whose appearance makes a claim to a place or a position. "Tom" also names the actual man who occupies the place or the position through his insistent exhibition in that appearance. It does not refer to him in his full concreteness. To make such a reference it is necessary to combine a designator with a contemplated and use the result as though it itself were a proper name. It is then a term of address. "God," for the religious man, is such a term.

The name "God" has a distinctive philology, history, and definition. It also has many different uses. In the dictionary it is a term right below "go-cart." For philosophy it designates a final reality known through speculation, and which may or may not have religious import. For the orthodox Hebrew it is a surrogate, a nickname, a mask for the unpronounceable holiest of holy names which is in fact inseparable from his being. For the ordinary pious man it has the meaning of a focal point for a community of worshippers. What is common to the philosopher, the pious, and the student of symbols is the recognition that the name "God" is a term of address whose use involves a change in attitude and activity from that which is relevant to everyday affairs, or to the proper names that apply there.

A religious man starts from a reverence expressed by the individual or in the community; a philosopher, instead, starts with the appearance of a unity. Some linguistic thinkers are inclined to start with the residua of these usages. Since they do not acknowledge that the addressing of God is part of the naming of Him, in one move they betray an ignorance of religious usage and an inability to understand the nature of certain genuine proper names.

To name a finality is to expose a proper name to specification by what is named. Such a name has a different grammar and logic from those appropriate to mere signs, externally connected with one another and with their referents. The outcome of the use of such proper names is verified, not by looking to an alien world to see if what was in mind somehow had a duplicate there, but by noting how the name gains intensive meaning, depth, and emotional weight when it is in fact used. 'Being' adds meaning to 'Substance' and conversely. The outcome of philosophic inquiry is an intensified set of articulated proper names, all mutually supportive, and supported by the realities to which they belong.

[2]

Language is one of the binders of a community, together with manners, ways of dressing, moving, working, and playing, to be used in a distinctive way if one is to be a member of a community. It does not tell us that any one has a mind; it is not the singular possession of men; it is not indispensable. Men speak without thinking; various animals have languages of their own; the embryo, the autistic, and the senile are human even though they may not be able to use the language of their community.

Austin has made many of us aware of the fact that some expressions are performatives, integral to the very activities in they are used—"Agreed," "I promise you," "I want your attention," "You

are now authorized," "This court of law finds you guilty." These
function as symbols in somewhat the way in which "Tom" does.
Every expression, in fact, can be viewed as a performative, since it
brings the objects and occurrences of which it speaks into relation
with the world of man. A reference to a stone or a leaf, to an event,
a quality, or a place, attaches the expression to them, and thereby
connects them with human values, interests, and organizations.
Since the attachment is more or less uniform in the ordinary course
of daily living, one is inclined to ignore it, and therefore to deal
with the expressions as though, except in special cases, they functioned simply as signs.

If expressions adhere to what is spoken of, and, like appearances,
enable one to penetrate into that to which they adhere, will it still
be possible to turn—as one can with appearances—in the opposite
direction and penetrate into what sustains them? I think so. Some
expressions tell us about their users—"I am unhappy," "I don't
know what to say," "You are a liar," "I want your attention," "I
accept the nomination," "People are not to be trusted." These do not
differ radically from "Today is Tuesday," "Unripe apples are tart,"
"San Francisco is west of Washington." All tell us at least that a
truth is being claimed, that something is being attended to, and that
one is sharing in a language system of a society. Proper names and
terms of address—even salutations and common nouns—all tell
something about their users. What they mean in one direction, of
course, is quite different from what they mean in another, and in
either case what we learn in the course of their use may be so minor
or so familiar that we will tend to take it to be the object of a mere
sign.

Linguistic expressions are not symbolic, however, unless both
the referent and the speaker contribute to their constitution. It
would seem at first that this requirement is never met, since men
make up terms and can use a language ceremonially as a mere part of
the process of binding themselves together in a community, with
no contribution being required of the referents in order to have the
expressions properly used. But even in these cases, as with appearances, one contribution is dominant over another, sometimes over-

whelmingly. The referent of every expression makes a contribution to it. The contribution, though, is only minor, except in those cases where we use proper names and explicit forms of address, or conspicuous performative expressions which enable what they express to exist in fact. Usually we are unable to get the contribution of the referent in a dominant position and, as a consequence, can say nothing more than that it provides an occasion and an objectivity, justifying our reference to it by means of the expression that is claimed to be true.

We do, of course, make references to what is not present; we also use proper names when we just distinguish one item in space from another. These are derivative usages, promissory of historical, transcendental, or eventual confrontations with their referents—at which time the terms can be properly used. The expressions await supplementation by some act which will then allow one to make use of them as genuine terms of address.

[3]

To designate a leaf is not yet to be occupied with the entire leaf. It is, instead, to attend only to an aspect of the leaf, correlative with a contemplated, meaningful aspect.

A dictionary offers a closed system of meanings, in which each item is understood in terms of the others. It presupposes that we already know some meanings; if we did not know any, we could not make use of it. Where do we obtain those meanings? To say that they are taught us is but to push the question back a step to the previous generation, or to society. It is to forget, too, that some meanings are learned without teachers—unless by "teacher" we mean experience, experiment, analysis, and reflection. Some meanings are associated by convention with what is unlike them in nature and function. But the meaning they have, in the end, depends on others, obtained in another way.

A meaning is the outcome of the conceptual transformation of some accepted item. The meaning of "leaf" is "a stem of a plant grown into an appendage"; "growth into an appendage" here is a transformation applied to "stem of a plant"; "stem of a plant," as subject to that operation, is the meaning of "leaf."

"Growth," "stem," "appendage" are all meaningful. To understand them, reference must be made to other entities and other transformations, or "leaf" must be subjected to the converse of the process by which we arrived at its meaning. A transformation need not, like "growth" have a counterpart in some natural change. "Leaf" has as many meanings as there are other items which can be conceivably transformed into it. Some of those items might be finalities. When we refer to the leaf as real or existent and the like, the meaning of it is the result of a conceived transformation of some finality.

Any entity is the meaning of any other into which any conceivable transformation converts it. The meaning of "leaf" is anything else, let us say "cat," when the cat is conceived to be subject to transformations such as being grown on a stem, denied a heart, etc. Similarly, the meaning of "cat" is "leaf" subject to the converse of these transformations. Or, it is some other item, let us say, "mountain," as subject to conceived transformations which turn it into "cat." Given both "leaf" and "cat," the meaning of the transformation from one to the other is provided by operating on one terminus by the other. That act requires a change of fixities into functions, and is reflected in a change of nouns into verbs. "Cat" then operates on "leaf," or conversely, in such a way as to yield the meaning "mountain" as that conceivable transformation which would take us from one to the other.

[4]

The contemplated is approached from slightly different angles at different moments. As a consequence, one is confronted with variations of it. Yet it is accepted as a constant because it has a single meaning. There is an adumbrative side to it, also. This enables it to escape our constituting and bounding, and allows us to symbolize the nature of an actuality.

A contemplated contains less than, is identical with, and contains more than the focused. It contains less, since it is abstract, having been separated out of the focused. As so separated, it lacks power, and vanishes as soon as attention is turned away from it. It is, only so long as we keep it distinct. The contemplated is also identical with the focused, for it is just the focused as a meaning from which various understandable consequences are to be expected. The contemplated, too, is more than the focused, for it has its own imposed boundary. And, unlike the focused, it contrasts with, opposes, subordinates, is subordinated to, and has some independence from merely conceived universals, some of which may not have embodiment anywhere.

Rarely do we get the contemplated in a pure state. Usually, we read into it something of our selves to make it more individualized and biased than it otherwise would be. Consequently, we fail to grasp the clear, full import of what is before us.

Every contemplated, it is sometimes thought, is shorthand for a reference to a plurality of particulars or singulars. If we took care, if we were more interested in each and every item, we would mark each off with a proper name. The name could be used again and again, but that would not mean that it had any generality to it; it would mean merely that we had occasion again and again to remark the same unduplicable reality. On this view, a proper name would be just a sign, a distinct mark. But then, strictly speaking, it could not be a proper name, for this carries with it a part of the respect involved in addressing something. The more surely we take contemplateds to be shorthand for references to a number of distinct particulars or singulars, the more surely we refuse to make use of proper names. But if all we have are just marks, separately or in bundles, they would be equally indifferent to the entities to which they were applied, and equally uninformative. With a faint stab at humor we might call a cat "Sir Walter Archibald Raleigh," or name a couch, "The 96th President of the United States." Were these pure marks, there would be nothing amiss and no one would think there was any humor involved, no matter how feeble.

Every term carries overtones of the criteria, justifications, and practices which permit its use and not others. No one is a pure sign, having nothing to do with its object. The references that they may have been established to have are part of their meaning, and this ties them to their proper objects. The tie is loose, but "loose" is not identical with "nonexistent."

A foreigner and a child have to be taught which names go with which objects, which descriptions apply to which observable features. This learning is not a process of yoking together items that have nothing to do with one another. It is, instead, a way of adjusting the child and the stranger to the use of a language in a society. For most purposes it suffices to point a child or a foreigner to an object of which we are speaking, but such pointing will not teach them how to use the terms properly. Proper use requires some penetration into the objects, with an accompanying involvement of the speaker, as a member of that society. A dog can be made to go toward the door on hearing a word or even a tone, no matter what the word. But the dog will not then understand what is being said any more than a foreigner or a child does, until these have made a type of response part of the term, and thus have made this approximate a symbolizing name.

[5]

A leaf seems to continue to be a leaf though it changes in shape and color. The shape and color seem to make no difference to the leaf, and can apparently be accredited to entities other than the leaf. This is why it seems reasonable to contrast shape and color and similar features with the mere leaf, as though they were adjectives to a noun, predicates for a subject, accidents for a substance, referents to a locus, signs in relation to a signified, or relativized data supported by what is objective and absolute—to note only some of the historic variations of the view that color and shape overlay something alien, but more permanent and real.

A shape and color could remain constant while the leaf was radically altered. The leaf could be cut or mutilated, so that it no longer was the leaf it had been, or even a leaf at all. It does not depend on the shape or color for its role as a leaf; instead, it offers one of many bases where a color and a shape are in fact unseparated. Still, the leaf is no less an appearance than the color or shape.

A contemplated leaf is a universal, specifiable in any one of a number of ways. Were the leaf without any specificity, a pure universal, it would be abstractable from any and every situation, and would be specifiable in an endless number of ways. Every specification of it, no matter how detailed, would, however, leave it still a universal. Individuals cannot be reached by adding determinations or details to a universal, any more than they can by adding universal to universal. If they could, simply by taking thought we could produce a reality apart from us. Moreover, were the leaf a universal, since every universal is conceivably duplicable, it would be possible to have the leaf duplicated perfectly. But if the leaf could be duplicated in this way, so could anything else. It would then be a mystery why there are not two, or any number, of exact repetitions of everything. It would be possible for me some day to meet myself coming toward me.

All leaves have the same nature. When subjected to the same set of conditions, one series of consequences follow from them all. Subjected to another set of conditions, other consequences are produced. But when we predicate an abstract universal of any one we attribute that universal to what is too determinate to have it in just that guise. There are no natures riding on top of indifferent individuals; universals are not to be found in the world, separate and pure.

An abstract universal, the universal in mind, is different from a *nature*. This, too, is a universal, but one that is imbedded in an appearance. The nature is an operative contemplated, making the appearance function in definite, limited ways. Because of it, an appearance has a rationale of its own, precluding it from being just an item hurried about by blind forces or wholly caught up in a web of imposed, unbreakable laws. But a contemplated is not a distinct factor in an appearance. It is we who distinguish it and set it in opposition to the designated.

A contemplated is continuous both with a focused appearance and with a designated. That is why it is so easy to slip from a consideration of a contemplated to a consideration of these others. Like a designated of which it is a correlate, a contemplated also has an adumbrative side. It too is a symbol with an intension as well as an extension. We, in being aware of this, face something other than it and other than ourselves. Through a symbolic use of it we move to the nature of what exists apart from us. That nature is the contemplated transformed, freed from alien additions and not controlled by the boundaries which we imposed when we focused.

A contemplated depends for its distinctiveness on the operation of a mind. Rarely, if ever, does one separate it entirely from the rest of an appearance. As a consequence, it only partially coincides with the nature of an actuality as it exists apart from us. It has a generality, but this is singularized in the course of a symbolization, when it leads us to the actuality with its distinctive career and promise.

By itself, a contemplated enables us to symbolize a locus of tendencies, thereby making it possible to predict what intelligibilities can be discerned later. Together with a designated, it converges on an actuality. We reach into that actuality with the convergent use of both a designated and a contemplated, and thereby come to know it as a singular claimant, here and now, which can exhibit itself in a plurality of ways.

[6]

Designateds and contemplateds are correlatives. What is put into the one is taken from the other. Each offers an opening to be filled out by the other. They match—the result of their being correlatives, derived from the same source—and are therefore able to be united in other than arbitrary ways.

We do not confront a designated or a contemplated separate from one another or from an appearance. They are distinguished in the course of the act of perceptually judging what we confront, and are thereby enabled to have distinctive careers. If we did not distinguish them we would not know an appearance, or the actuality beyond this. To know either, we must be able to hold designated and contemplated apart. Distinguishing them is the first step of an act of judgment. The judgment ends with them united. Joined with a designated, a contemplated allows one to have a perceptual knowledge of a symbolizing appearance. That appearance coarsens their union and thereby enables one to have a symbolizing knowledge of an actuality.

The independence of terms referring to designateds and contemplateds holds only so far as discourse is autonomous. This it is, but only partially. Discourse is also involved with what is happening; language is no more completely cut off from objects than it is from users. What one language distinguishes another does not, what one classifies in this way another classifies in that, because each reflects the habits of a distinct community. But a community is not simply men huddled together, away from a world. It is a group of men interacting with one another and the world around them. The groupings that their language reflects and permits are involved in their practical efforts. And practice has symbolic import.

It is easy to overlook the symbolic role of distinguished designateds and contemplateds. This is due in part to the usual dominant interest in what is seen. It is also in part due to the crediting of a symbolic role only to special items such as blushes, inadvertent errors, and unnoticed gestures. Most men, plain and professional, take these to be singularly revelatory of the characters of men, of their intent and of their dispositions. There is, perhaps, also some predilection toward supposing that only focused objects can be true symbols, and that parts of these lack the requisite efficacy or concreteness.

Did designateds and contemplateds not have any symbolic role, there would be nothing which had such a role in a judgment, or this would be the exclusive privilege of the copula or of relations. "Is" (and its cognates, and the relations which overlay it), not only connects items on a level; it orients them in an actuality. But the items are then not dragged into what is alien to them; they are enabled to converge in the actuality. Apart from that convergence, they would lead us to places and positions having nothing to do with claimants, occupants, and natures.

Designateds and contemplateds are united in judgment. The outcome is a unitary, judged item of knowledge. Since in judgment these do not need some third term to hold them together, there would seem to be no need to suppose that, as objective, apart from us, anything else need be considered in addition to the two. No account would have to be taken of anything which was more than the designated and contemplated together. But just by themselves they do not coalesce. The unity of the two is not their work.

An appearance, in which a designated and contemplated are distinguished and which symbolize it, is more than either and more than both. Otherwise they would not have a common convergence. The attempt to recover appearances by attending solely to the factors which had been analytically derived from them, ends with a dissolution of the appearances; in the supposition that the very tie that one provides in judgment works on the other side of the elements as well, to make them into an objective unity; or in the supposition that there is another tie out there, as invisible as it is powerful.

What is reached through the symbolic use of a designated and contemplated is an appearance through which an actuality insists on itself, and pulls on all three. Its unity points up the fact that these were separated by us and that, though we may relate them in a judgment, they are in fact not separated. If we were to take the indicated and contemplated to be separate items, merely alongside one another, we would have no way of explaining why we do not encounter them as distinct items but have to work on what we confront in order to obtain them. A judged unity of designateds and contemplateds is an achieved result, depending on a prior dissection of an appearance. There, neither stands apart from the other.

Designated and contemplated have one another as suppressed components until they are made into full-fledged correlatives in a judgment. In that judgment, they are equals, reproducing the roles they have as equally significant factors in the objective appearance. Their distinction, and their union in judgment, is the result of our activity. What we then know, though rooted in an appearance and through this in an actuality, has a significance in relation to us, but with consequences which we do not produce.

[7]

By itself an appearance of an actuality is unanalyzed and un-judged, neither true nor false. It is just more or less illuminating, depending on the extent to which the exhibition of an actuality plays a dominant role in it. The judged accretes the character of being true when, through the agency of a claim, the outcome of the judgment is used to symbolize an appearance. The claim relates the outcome to the source of the designated and contemplated, and thereby makes it a knowledge that is true of that source.

The outcome of a perceptual judgment is an *assertum*. Were there no asserta: 1] There would be nothing in common to a number of perceptual judgments. But an individual can make the same judgment of the same object again and again. And different men, in distinct acts, can make the same judgment of the same object. An assertum is the common core of particular perceptual judgments.

2] A perceptual judgment would not be true or false of an appearance. It would connect factors but would not necessarily have the result in relation to anything beyond. An assertum is held away from the act of judging and from the appearance which we bound in our initial act of attention.

3] There would be nothing which was being claimed to be true. But the assertum, while being held away from the source of its factors, is related to that source by a claim. That claim accepts the appearance as a measure of the satisfactoriness of the assertum.

4] There would be no testing of the claim that one knows truly. For such testing to be possible one must be able to pass from what is in the mind to what is outside it. An assertum stands apart from an appearance; but because its elements are in the appearance, it is able to symbolize the appearance and, through this, the actuality. The symbolization is in accord with the claim, and therefore moves into the known, and through this into the actuality which pulls the content of the known away from the boundaries we imposed.

[8]

Like statements, asserta are produced by men; unlike statements, they need not be verbalized. Like propositions, asserta are expressed in many judgments; unlike propositions, they are claimed to be true of appearances in which designated and contemplated are indistinguishably united.

An assertum can be spoken of in different languages and with the use of different vocabularies. "This is a leaf," "This is an appendage of a stem," "This is untreated tobacco" all may express the same truth. Translating these expressions into other languages leaves the assertum unaffected. It is true, of course, that the different expressions are not precisely equivalent, due to the fact that different terms have different associations and implications when taken as just terms. The expressions in which they are, nevertheless are equivalent because they are related to the selfsame assertum.

In the expression, "this is a leaf," "this" and "leaf" are on a footing. The "is" here has two tasks. It refers to the unity of an assertum and to the unity of an appearance. The one unity is subsequent, the other is prior to the elements. The former awaits our distinguishing, but has a role of its own apart from this, since it is a symbol of the latter unity. Were there no distinguished elements in terms of which an assertum was to be forged, there would be no way of saying what it symbolized, for by itself the unity of an assertum symbolizes some unity or other, and that is all.

An assertum can continue to be when that to which it pertains is no longer. It will then, of course, not be possessed by an actuality. But the assertum will still be connected with the actuality through a claim. A claim refers to an actuality, whether this is in the present or has become part of the past.

The fact of error and the passage of the actuality point up the truth that a claim begins with an assertum, assumed on our responsibility, and relates this to an actuality, via its appearance. The assertum is claimed to be true of an appearance, and through the symbolic functioning of this, to be true of an actuality. It could not have been so constructed that it answers to no appearance or actuality, for even the most fanciful assertum requires us to resist the tendency of some appearance, through the power of its unitary actuality, to pull the unity of the assertum into it. By creating an assertum out of imagined elements we make it possible for the assertum not to hold in fact. But because the unity of every assertum is inseparable from a controlling objective unity, even an assertum that we created would be about the world. The symbolic union of the assertum's unity with the unity of an appearance gives the assertum a categorial bias no matter what falsity is produced. Fictions exist only so far as we effectively combat the pull of fact.

On our responsibility we take an assertum to give knowledge of an actuality. We claim the assertum to be true of the known appearance, and through this of the objective appearance, and finally of the actuality. The assertum as true consequently differs from the known appearance, not only in having its elements subject to a subsequent rather than to an antecedent unification, but in not being directly connected with the appearance as it exists apart from us.

We use the assertum as a symbol of the known appearance. Through the mediation of the known appearance, the assertum symbolizes the objective appearance and finally the actuality. Such symbolism depends, not only on our following the lead of a claim but on our yielding to and following the direction of the pull that the actuality exerts on its appearance, and through this on its known appearance, and through this on the assertum.

On behalf of clarity, or on the supposition that they are inviolate, we can try to unite the designated and contemplated in a purely external fashion, to obtain a unity which acts as a sign of an object. But to succeed, we would have to tear the indicated and contemplated away from an appearance. We would then fail to obtain a true assertum, for this internally unites a designated and a contemplated which are objectively one.

The assertum is the known appearance as articulated by us; through the known appearance it brings us to the actuality. Though a true assertum is our product, it is, therefore, in the end inseparable from an actuality. The unity of a true assertum is continuous with the unity of an actuality. It can not be separated from the factors which we distinguished in order to know and judge it.

Designated and contemplated are organically one in an objective appearance. Because that appearance is the locus of whatever elements we distinguish in it, and is not something alongside or alien to them, the symbolizing assertum has an objectivity even while it is being responsibly accepted by us. It is coarsened, and through coarsening is adumbratively united with the appearance.

Treated as distinct from the assertum, the coarsening adumbrative side of it is a vector. Because it begins in a judgment, and never is free of it, that vector is epistemological in nature and function; because it points us away from what we judge and allows us to penetrate into the actuality, it is at the same time ontological. It leads us into an appearance and a reality which we have not made, orienting what we know away from us.

We can symbolize an appearance and an actuality because these maintain a grip on the adumbrated that is inseparable from the assertum. No product of ours, the adumbrated has its own dynamics and status, enabling us to note how the elements we have distinguished are merged and intensified. Without that adumbrated, we would never be able to distinguish the assertum as in relation to us from the assertum as identical in content with what makes it true.

Sometimes we are unsure just what is real and what is not, particularly when we have lost our familiar bearings. We are deceived again and again by the appearances of things. Sometimes we erroneously take something to be hard when it is soft, heavy when it is light, our own when it belongs to someone else. Those errors are occasionally spoken of as though they were the result of mistaking appearances for reality. But, instead, one appearance was incorrectly used to lead to another that was to ensue when position, time, or attitude was changed.

The soft is an appearance and so is the hard. Our judging something to be hard when it is not, is a consequence of our anticipating what will be when we touch it in such and such a way. We say that we were mistaken in holding it to be hard because we take the touched soft to be a standard appearance, or an appearance appropriate in the prevailing circumstances. Such mistakes are also possible to animals. But the power of symbolizing by means of an assertum or its parts is peculiar to man.

The higher primates sometimes calculate, and sometimes shrewdly anticipate what is occurring. Many animals know where to look, how to expect; some know their young, their mates, their enemies. But they do not make a claim to know anything true. They can grasp an object as located, but not as that which is also intelligible. An animal can look at a leaf and treat it as a single entity. But it does not know what the leaf by itself is like; it does not understand the leaf since it does not articulate the leaf via the leaf's designated and contemplated components. It uses no asserta.

Without men there are no asserta. This does not mean that asserta are completely inside men's minds. Apart from a man there is no property, no state, no history, but this is far from denying them a reality outside, distinct from him. To suppose that an assertum is just in the mind is still to leave over the fact that we do attend to appearances of realities, and that these appearances have symbolic roles. Such an assertum would be neither true nor false, but just an occurrence having nothing necessarily to do with anything outside the mind. But because an assertum is related by a claim to what is outside, it can be true or false. An assertum, consequently, cannot be identified with the appearance about which it speaks; this would preclude it from being true of that appearance. And it would most surely preclude it from being false, since falsehood demands that it be other than, indeed, discrepant with its object.

A focused object is an appearance. We start with it as a bounded item separated out of larger situations. It had neighbors with which it interplayed; it was involved with still other appearances. When we articulate it, it continues to be undivided in itself and to be involved with others. When we adumbratively move into it, we deal with it as still bounded from those others. Not until we go on to the appearance itself as it objectively exists do we arrive at what is apart from us and together with other appearances.

An entity is not broken asunder when one distinguishes factors in it; nor are these just facsimiles taken from it and given a new residence in the mind. The factors are in the appearance; but they do not there stand apart from one another or from the appearance. They are distinguishable in the appearance, functioning there, but not as distinct from one another.

The distinguished designated and contemplated are united by us. But, separate or united, they are distinct from the actuality. Separately and together, as distinct symbols and as components of an assertum, they are held away from the appearance and therefore from the actuality. It is also true that they belong to and are inseparable from the appearance and the actuality. That is why, though the presence, distinction, and union of designated and contemplated depend on us, these factors are not entirely in our control.

An assertum is unaffected by what we individually are or do, and remains even when the actuality is no longer. Were the assertum to occupy a domain of its own, it would not be involved with a claim and could not be true or false. It would just be, indifferent to all else. To account for our knowledge of it, for its use, for its relevance to an object, something would have to be done to it. We would have to relate it to ourselves on one side and to an appearance or to an actuality on the other, in order for it to be an assertum for us about something else. In a domain of its own, an assertum would be like a love without a lover or a beloved. There would be no reason to suppose it existed except to answer a need to have something which was not identifiable with either side. But it is also involved with both sides.

An assertum is distinct from an actuality; it is claimed by a knower. It is distinct from a knower; it symbolizes an appearance and through this an actuality. And it is distinct from both knower and actuality; it has its own nature and role. An actuality allows for an assertum but also controls it. The assertum can be held apart from the appearance and an actuality, but it still belongs to these. We can make use of it, but it also challenges and defies us. We can misconstrue it, make it serve purposes other than that of making a claim, but such misconstruction and use presupposes that it has a nature and a role apart from our present occupation with it.

Did we not unite the designated and the contemplated, we would have them just alongside, indifferent to one another. If they did not affect one another, they would not be items in a genuine single assertum. If we could not make a claim which involved them in a unity of our making, we would not at the same time claim anything, or make it be our claim. And, if we did not have the result external to ourselves, we would not have an object known.

7

THINGS

Controlling Summary: An advance is made in going from a claim about a thing to the statement claiming that it is true, or to the assertion that something is the case. The advance entails greater and greater responsibility for what is asserted.

Because everything is together with others, no thing can be perfectly simple, isolated, supreme, presupposed, or dominant. Each thing makes its different manifestations relevant to one another. It is a concrete necessitation uniting its manifestations in a single whole.

What is true of things is true of living beings and of men; but these add to what things are and do.

Facts are the residue of present objects. They are incapable of change and, despite their determinateness, are without concreteness. The finished side of objects, they are inseparable from a present process of coming to be. The passage of time distinguishes facts from a subsequent moment of coming to be, itself united with subsequent facts.

Facts have the same content as truths, but the latter alone depend on us. The facts are aspects of realities outside themselves; the truths are related to those realities. The truths may be interlocked with that to which they relate, but the facts merely coexist with one another in the present and in the past.

136

He who says truthfully "here is a leaf," refers to a fact. At the same time, he refers to what makes the fact be. An actuality justifies many truth claims because the actuality sustains many different facts, each answering to a distinctive truth. When we know symbolically, by means of an appearance, we know an actuality as the base for many facts, and the warrant for many truths.

Pragmatism normally maintains that the meaning of an idea is given in the conceivable consequences which actually ensue upon it. In later and more popular forms, pragmatists assume that the consequences that ensue are merely items which, as a matter of fact, happen to come about in the course of time. What had been and what will be, on such a doctrine, have no connection with one another except so far as they are subject to common laws of nature, or society, or language. But the original thesis, as formulated by C. S. Peirce, attached both the idea and its consequences to an ontological base—thereby exposing the Hegelian bias of the pragmatic view, as was quickly seen by Bradley and Royce. It is not necessary, though, to be an Hegelian in order to say that appearances have sources which account for them, severally and together.

If we are to know things, whether through perception and cognition, or in more complex ways, we must begin by knowing and symbolically using the manifestations of those things. The manifestations are appearances in which the contributions of things dominate over the contributions made by finalities. The appearances, with which the manifestations are continuous, are themselves part of a world of appearances. But we can come to know distinct appearances, and through the symbolic use of these come to know individual things. The things, though they retreat from the boundaries that we introduce when we focus on their appearances, are the realities *of* those bounded appearances and, so far, are located within the limits provided by those boundaries.

Manifestations are relevant to one another. If we know the relevance, we can know how to determine which manifestations in the future are to be related to earlier ones. The later give the pragmatic meaning of what is now faced or accepted, but that meaning cannot be known just by examining the later or the earlier, or even the ways in which they are connected by laws or rules. The relevance of the one to the other depends on an actual thing. Only if we can know the thing can we avoid being driven forever and ever toward the future in order to know the meaning of the reality we now confront.

[2]

A thing is the source of manifestations, and governs their order. Not equatable with any fact or truth, with a unity, or even with a totality of facts, a thing is the explanation for their occurrence in such and such relations. As known, it is distinguishable from itself as standing apart from us. We can then state what the thing is in some such claim as "it is true that this is a stone." It is then acknowledged to be an actuality, in opposition to ourselves who know it.

The expression, "it is true that," introduces us to what is known, at the same time that it keeps what we are claiming inside a world of truths for which we accept responsibility. In discourse, one makes a claim for a truth on behalf of all. As a representative of other men, one offers to them what is theirs by right. In both cases, responsibility is assumed for the claim.

By stating a claimed truth, we make explicit that the truth has a dignity apart from ourselves because it is grounded in what is objective or real. When the truth we assert is released from our possession, but not allowed to be captured in the world of appearances or the world of actualities—a result we achieve in discourse—it is at once ours and not ours. It is ours because we produce it. It is not ours because it is claimed for and made available to other men.

The language we use in daily life is understandable by others because it is largely anonymous, indifferent to the peculiarities of either speaker or listener. Since that language is not indifferent to the peculiarities of the society or the uses to which objects are put, however, it cannot do full justice to what is real. This real is what it is, not only apart from all men, but regardless of what all societies suppose or presuppose.

A neutral, universal language would permit the formulation of claims in trans-social terms. One such language is mathematics; somewhat limited versions of this are used by the sciences. These enable one to speak outside any particular social perspective. But a mathematical language might have no pertinence to anything in this space-time world. Also, it dispenses with penetrative symbols, and therefore cannot help us to advance into actualities. It and scientific languages are too formal, too indifferent to actual things and to their constitutive facts and warrants for truths, to be able to convey what things really are by themselves.

"The fact of this stone" refers to the stone, just as "it is true that this is a stone" does, but solely as part of a world distinct from ourselves. The latter refers to the stone as that which both grounds what is asserted and which relates manifestations—and therefore the facts which exhibit the fixed side of those manifestations. The relation between the manifestations is dynamic, not static, not only linking the items that are being manifested, but transforming one feature into one another. A stone is not only hard and grey, but a power interconverting them, and converting them both into still other items.

The reality of the stone is not postulated; nor is it the result of our thrusting outwards what we know privately. Postulating and thrusting get no further than hopes which have not yet broken from the confines of our minds and suppositions. An actual stone is an independent reality, symbolized by means of what we perceive of it, judge of it, and claim of it. To say what the stone is we must say what is needed to translate one truth into another, to interrelate its manifestations, or to interconvert its different features. The actual translating, the very making available of new manifestations, the work of interconverting, is the work of the stone. Different truths, united with their appropriate facts, are all symbols of it. The stone is the bond that makes those symbols be related to other symbols that had been or are still to be produced.,

We know that there are different actualities because we know truths that are not equivalent. This stone makes the truth that it is grey equivalent with the truth that it is brittle. That stone makes

the truth that it is grey equivalent with the truth that it is hard.
The equivalences hold in each case because the truths report the
very same reality with the same fidelity.

Is the actuality that I know accessible to others? It must be if
they too are able to use a manifestation to symbolize a source of
itself as well as of other manifestations. When symbolized by me
it is, of course, not then discerned to be accessible to others. But if
others do actually know a truth about it, they know the very
reality that I do, for their truths are translated by the thing to say
exactly what mine do.

The known, appearing stone is not cut off from the stone as
available for knowledge. The latter can be symbolized because it
provides textures for its own appearances, thereby enabling these to
lead us into it. This is not yet to arrive at the stone as it exists
without reference to any knowledge, actual or possible. The actual
stone is beyond the known stone, beyond the objective appearance
of the stone, and beyond the known appearance of it.

[3]

"It is true that x is y" expresses a claim; "it is the case that x is
y" expresses the fact that we have released the claim and now face
that which is claimed—an objective appearance in the possession of
an actuality. The stone is properly referred to by "it is the case that
this is a stone" if what we wish to report is what is there, independent
of us.

"It is the case that this is a stone" says more than "it is true
that this is a stone," and "it is true that this is a stone" says more
than "it is a stone." "It is a stone" refers us to some part of the world;
"it is true that this is a stone" tells us, in addition, that our observation or judgment is to be relied upon; "it is the case that this is a
stone" goes further, and tells us that the stone is there, whether it be
known or not. The first presents us with something, reports on observation, and offers a form of introduction. The second communicates to another, and presupposes the assumption of a responsibility for a claim. The third reports a settled fact, also on our
responsibility.

If a man says "x is y," he tells us there is something answering to this. If he adds, "it is true that . . . ," he adds that he knows this by virtue of an acquaintance with it. If he goes on to say "it is the case that . . . ," he adds that there is a reality for which he has evidence.

Let us suppose there were no stone, and that one man says, "this is a stone," another, "it is true this is a stone," and a third, "it is the case that this is a stone." The first has made an error; he is to be held accountable for being improperly adjusted. The second has gone further and made an unjustified claim; he is irresponsible. The third has gone even further and assured us about what stands apart from him and his knowing; he does not merely claim that something is true, but purports to report a reality. If there is no stone, he has spoken as though he had properly represented the community of men in a relation to what is real but in fact failed to do so.

When wrong, he who uses the first is criticizable for carelessness; he who uses the second is criticizable for lack of control; and he who uses the third is criticizable for presumption. The first has shown himself to be a poor guide; the second fails to make good on a promise with an indefinite range; the third betrays a trust. The first we depend on, on that occasion; when we find he misleads us, we make the necessary correction and let that be the end of the matter. The second speaks to a community, each member of which is responsible for maintaining and increasing the store of truths for all; when a man fails here, we see him as having unnecessarily jeopardized the entire store. The third speaks of a world of existents of which all men are also a part; if he is wrong, he has, while assuming a position of a representative, put an obstacle in the way of the rest to know. The first could excuse himself as having expressed only a hypothesis, a belief, or a hope. The other two cannot have recourse to such an excuse, since they have gone out of their way to join those who preserve truth, or who define mankind as contrasting with all else.

What we assert when we say "it is true that . . . ," though offered for all, is known through our agency. It retains a reference to us. That reference we do not remove but try to render harmless by assuming responsibility for it, as something claimed to hold for all men. But the claim falls short of presenting the object as independent of us and our checks. If we intend to refer not only to what, like a truth, is given a boundary by us, but to that which is apart from us, we should say "it is the case that . . . ." This says that the item was subjected to various tests, and reports not merely that there is a stone, but that it is completely immersed in a world apart from us.

What is the case is not only something by itself, but is in effective relationship to other items. Though it has its own boundaries, it is entangled with others and with the possible future. Entangled with others, it exists, functions outside its location, is effective on what is located elsewhere; entangled with the future, it is able to have a career which stretches beyond the present in which it is actual.

[4]

In his poem "Description Without Place" Wallace Stevens writes:

> *It is possible that to seem—it is to be,*
> *As the sun is something seeming and it is.*
>
> *The sun is an example. What it seems*
> *It is and in such seeming all things are.*
>
> *Thus things are like a seeming of the sun*
> *Or like a seeming of the moon or night*
>
> *Or sleep.*

A reality is present in its appearances; by means of the appearances we can symbolize it. The grasp of it by means of its appearances is a symbolizing of it as at once self-contained and yet available. What is symbolized has a different career and meaning from that which the symbolizing appearance possesses. It is more important, more permanent, and more powerful than any symbol of it. After all, it is the symbol itself, but purified and intensified.

The symbolized is present in the symbol of it, but as ever-receding, self-determining. Because it is present it can be known.

Because it is known to recede it is known to have a reality of its own. The knowledge we have of it differs from it, not in content, but in function. The knowledge confines the object within a boundary imposed by us, but the object bounds itself. The one has implications, the other consequences. The consequences can be known. So can the boundaries that we impose. But the consequences are not known until they are produced, and the boundary is not known until it is imposed. What can be known of them in advance lacks detail and specificity; it tells us only of their possibility.

The boundaries we impose on what we confront may be misplaced; we may make them so close together that essential parts are left outside; we may make them so distant that irrelevancies creep in. These mistakes are to be corrected by what is learned in the course of experience, and by attending to what can be learned of the reality from other positions.

Knowing begins with a focusing on some item, with an incidental alteration of the situation in which it is, since the item is then distinguished and bounded off by us. The alteration of the situation is in relation to us; our separating and bounding do not cut into the objects there. When we go on, and not only separate out factors in the focused, but unify them in a claimed assertum adumbratively passing into an actuality, we make contact with the very reality which the process of knowledge presupposes. Knowledge ends with knowing what makes knowledge possible, by facing the known as that which is outside what is distinguished and claimed.

What we claim to know, we would like to have accepted or endorsed by others. If we differ from them on particular claims, we or they will be in error. If we reject what they claim but, nevertheless, try to be part of their community, we are mad, since we then at once deny what they accept and what makes the acceptance acceptable. The judgment that we are in error or are mad is correct just so far as we fail to acknowledge what the others do. This does not mean that there is nothing which we are acknowledging, or that we were wrong to make the acknowledgment. It means only that we have not lived up to the prevalent social norm of what is right, sane, or decent.

Both the remembered and the expected are defined in opposition to what is not now in mind. We learn that we are remembering or that we are expecting when we see how what we have in mind is excluded by what we are now confronting. What we have in mind is known to ground an expectation so far as it yields a consequence which is too general to be able to have a place in what we now confront. We know that we remember so far as what we now confront is not only a consequence of what we have in mind but precludes this which we have in mind from now existing. We have as sure a knowledge of a world outside our minds as we have of the fact that we are remembering or expecting, because the latter is defined— or better—refined when the world outside is acknowledged in an oppositional guise.

We also associate what we have in mind with other items already in mind. The association would result in a merging were it not that, even while being associated, the items diverge in fact. Because in the very act of association we experience a divergency in the items we associate, and because we then are able to follow the process of divergence to end with what is merely alongside and external to us, we are able to know that our judgments are controlled by what is not ourselves. What controls them we do not, of course, then know. All we then know is that what we have in mind is part of an objective world in which it is related to other items.

[5]

'Knowledge' need not exclude confusion or even the occurrence of a common delusion. We often say that we know something even when we grant that we might be mistaken. By 'knowing' we then intend merely to make the claim that what we assert will be accepted or endorsed by others. Unless our claim is justified, what is 'known' will not be objective or true. Apart from such justification, what we 'know' is only what a number agree upon, whether this number be a limited community of users of some language or hypothesis, or whether it be an unlimited community of scientific inquirers.

Each group of people, depending on what its leading members or authoritative figures agree upon, accepts certain claims as unquestionable. Though one group will usually take another's set of indubitables to be interlarded with superstitions, conventions, myths, and errors, it may have no warrant for maintaining that its own set is better, more basic, more surely true, or more reliable. We in the West take seriously the claims of science, law, and politics, but in the East, religion, philosophy, and mysticism have been taken to yield more reliable and basic truths. The two positions are equally strong and equally weak. It is their rejections that must be rejected; what remains in each seems to be compatible with what is the other.

Hume subjectivized what he and all of us symbolize; as a consequence, he lost the relevance of his impressions to one another. To recover that relevance he took himself to be its source. In effect, he reversed the facts, for their source lies on their side, not on ours. The symbolization of the stone roots an assertum in it. The act enables the elements of the assertum, severally and together, to be involved with others, severally and together. Something of the reality of the stone is then grasped as producing and relating what is manifested. Were this not so, there would be nothing of which our knowledge would be true, unless, perhaps, all that we knew were faint versions of floating impressions. In the latter case there would be nothing to which the impressions belonged, and nothing, therefore, to which they could be attributed. There would be nothing to act, nothing to resist, nothing which manifested itself.

At the terminus of a symbolization is an actuality. This is final, finite, and spatiotemporal, a source of the relevance of manifestations to one another. It is something more as well—that which exists with other actualities. It is in itself but also for others. Existing together with other actualities, it nevertheless maintains itself as distinct from them.

[6]

An actuality is powerful and self-maintaining. Its nature is expressed in the relating of its appearances to one another. To express it in communicable terms, we must articulate its appearance in an assertum formulated in terms of factors analyzed out of it, but unified by us. What we know of it, we know through the help of its designated and contemplated, as subject to its controlling unity. It is symbolized by starting with the designated, contemplated, or their union, and then following the adumbrative leads. The deeper we penetrate, the more closely we come to the reality as that which provides a necessary connection for the distinguished factors.

An actuality is a necessitating source, but once its manifestations are sunk into it, all trace of them and the necessities is swallowed up. A logical aside may make this evident. Given any true "a" and "aRb," we have, as Peirce remarked, all that is needed in order to derive "b." The "b" is necessitated by "a" as together with "aRb." The a, aRb, and b may all be ideas in our minds; one, or the other or all may have once existed outside our minds. Not only does the necessity introduce an insistence not found in any of them, but its operation does not depend on the nature of any. Nor is the necessity which relates a and aRb to b our creation; it is prescriptive, forcing us to accept b once we have accepted a and aRb. And it is not limited to a particular situation. The very same necessity that yields b, given a and aRb, yields d, given c and cSd, no matter what these are. Since the necessity operates in every situation, it evidently expresses a state of affairs which relates meanings regardless of where they are, in or outside the mind.

If we unite a with aRb to constitute a single term, there is nothing but necessity left by means of which to obtain b. Formally, this necessity is expressed as the entailing relation which requires b, once we are given a and aRb. That necessity justifies the 'therefore' of inference. The a and aRb together necessitate b. No matter what a is and no matter what R and b are, there is a necessitation which begins with a and aRb and ends with the warranted item, b. That necessitation is provided by the actuality. For us to derive the b, we must therefore provide a dynamic version of an actuality's necessitation.

And "a," "aRb" together require "b." The b is distinct from them. It is available to anyone because it is objectively necessitated. In the stone, the a and aRb are not set in contrast with b; nor do a and b have there the status of entities which are added to aRb.

Instead, *a* and *b* are beginning and ending both *for* and *of* the stone. They are related to things external to R, even while they are one with R.

Necessitation is a single, dynamic power which makes *a*, *aRb*, and *b* into a single whole. The *b* is necessitated by both *a* and *aRb* together, but there is nothing which holds *a* and *aRb* together to allow for the independent operation of the necessity. It is this fact which allows one to see how right Hume was, and how wrong. He could not find a bare necessitation in his experience, for there was none to find. But this does not mean that there is no necessitation and therefore no causality. The causality is a process, and the necessitation is in the process, as beginning from and with *a*, and ending with and for *b*. The *b*, as an effect, is external to the process in the very sense and to the very degree that the *a*, its cause, is external to it.

An actuality provides the necessitation for its appearances. When we know the necessitation via the appearances, we know the actuality as something distinctive. The exhibitions of itself in the appearances come closer and closer together the further we penetrate into its necessitating reality. But the deeper we penetrate the more are the appearances purged and submerged in it.

We progress from a grasp of a mere necessitation, approached from the position of distinctive appearances, to a grasp of a buried necessitation which is their unitary locus and source. An adumbrated bridges the distance between these two necessitations. When we speak of an actuality's appearances we keep toward one end and must, therefore, supplement what we say with an acknowledgment of a necessitation at the other end, capable of producing other appearances and relating them.

We are compelled to return again and again to experience to see how our knowledge is in consonance with what is outside our minds, for what is carried by an independently operating reality and process is subject to conditions not effective with respect to it when it is part of knowledge. We know this because we can see it yield consequences there which are not identical with the consequences demanded by what we have in mind.

The physical resistance encountered when dealing with most actualities seems to have led many to the supposition that the actualities are also beyond the reach of symbolization. Given the lack of interest men have in knowing what physical things are in themselves, given the fact that most of the things known are compounds, and that by symbolization one learns little more of things than that their manifestations have a common necessitating source, the normal supposition that things are impervious to a penetration readily assumes the shape of a dogma. But then it becomes a mystery how singular things could be known, how inanimate beings could be part of the same world as living beings, and how it is that there could be changing appearances relevant to one another and possessed by the selfsame actuality.

No actuality is ever completely expressed in the interconnection of its manifestations, or what we symbolize of it. To know an actuality we must supplement what we learn from a study of its interconnected exhibitions and from what we achieve through symbolization, by what we learn from an acknowledgment of its spontaneous insistencies. These fill out the interconnected items with detail, and add unpredictable features to them. The fact becomes conspicuous in and central to the understanding of living beings, and particularly man.

Though we have a poorer grasp of the nature of living beings and of men than of things, we are better able to penetrate into them. As a consequence, we not only come to know more about what is behind their appearances, but, because those living beings and men are in fact more complex and flexible, come to know something more than there are necessitations at the root of what appears, making them relevant to one another.

A thing—and therefore a living being and a man approached from the position of manifestations rather than from that of displays or expressions—exhibits itself in one way now because of the way it had exhibited itself before. The thing provides the reason why one set of manifestations is followed by another. Given one set, the thing justifies the expectation of the other. Were there no thing, there would be only a sequence of presentations. These would not even be appearances, for appearances require that there be something which appears.

A thing is a categorial base making one set of manifestations relevant to another. Apart from the effective operation of the thing, the connection between one confronted content and another would be dictated solely by practical convenience and conventions, as it is for the most part in legal thinking. But relevance, even in law, is grounded in real things; that is why there is a warrant for opposing some expectations and some legal enactments as arbitrary or foolish. A law which denies all redheaded men the vote fails to isolate what is actually relevant to the right to vote; it would be an unjust law because it had no grounding in the nature of men. The U.S. Constitution is a set of general principles in terms of which the bearing of specific enactments on social living are to be structured and assessed. The enactments are just, to the extent that they relate acts to consequences in ways which the nature of men demands. Since men are more than things, the enactments do more, of course, than provide such conditions. They add to the meaning of relevance (pertinent also to things) considerations stemming from men's distinctive nature and activities. Men's consciousness, language, social order, art, and religion make them require distinctive consequences from antecedent exhibitions.

[7]

It is possible to suppose that there is a single, cosmic dynamism in complete possession of all appearances. This is what Schopenhauer maintained with his doctrine of the Will and Bergson with his élan vital. But this is to deny that particular things have an integrity of their own. Different types of actuality have distinctive ways of manifesting themselves, and have their own ways of relating their manifestations to one another. A stone has one kind, a leaf, a book, a man, others.

A book is put together by stitching and paste; these can not make a genuine unitary entity. But the book is no simple summation of these. Just as ultimate particles join to produce new unities with new properties and powers, in which the energies of those particles are modified and channeled through mutual interplay under the control of the unity in which they are, so the parts of a book are parts limited and controlled. In natural complex objects, the control is exercised by the encompassing being; in the case of a book, it is exercised by the social context which provides the book with an integrity in relationship to other social objects, such as money, libraries, readers, and the like.

Every reality has some degree of determinateness. The completely indeterminate would be determinately what it is and would, therefore, not be completely indeterminate. The determinateness entails that there are at least two entities, each having the character of being 'other than' the other. If they are not to be identical, if they are to be realities in their own right, each reality must possess the common character in a distinctive way. Each will then be a source of a negation, by means of which the other is qualified.

Only because there are separate actualities can there be actualities together with one another. But they always are together. As together, each exhibits the necessary *effects of pluralization:* no reality can be absolutely simple, absolutely alone, absolutely superior, absolutely presupposed, or absolutely dominant.

No reality can be absolutely simple. It is always related to what else there be, by a qualifying negation. Let x be one reality and y a second; "negated y" then expresses the result of subjecting y to x's negating. A leaf is one way of not being a stone, and one way of not being a horse. And the stone and the horse are themselves distinctive qualifying negations of one another, as well as of the leaf.

The x operates on y by means of a distinctive negation. The result, "negated y," would be identical with x, were it not that it is a product of x and y, and is divisible into an operation and a term. Because y is inseparable from x through the agency of the negation, x cannot be absolutely simple. Necessarily articulated as the negating of y, it is dependent on y for the content which it negates.

Nor is any reality ever absolutely alone. Each limits and is limited by the others. Whatever reality any one has precludes the others from being absolutely perfect, for nothing can be absolutely perfect if it lacks some reality. Each one is determinate because there is something distinct from it. Determinateness is one with being together with other realities. To be determinate is to be imperfect, because it is to be a member of a plurality.

Nor is any reality absolutely superior to the others. The others remain outside it, denying it some reality and providing it with content to negate. They condition it, each in its own way. They use it as content for their own negatings, and it faces them as having natures and careers it does not control. A kenotic theory of the universe, which maintains that a primal reality empties itself in order to make something else be, goes only part of the distance that an adequate account demands, for determinateness requires that there always be more than one reality, and therefore that there never be that which could be the source of all, unless it were radically indeterminate and, therefore paradoxically, indescribably unable to act.

No reality is absolutely presupposed by all the others as their explanation. If it were, it could not be accounted for. Everything would be explained by what would itself have to remain inexplicable. But each reality provides a position from which to express what the others are. It is a base, a schema for the rest. In turn, it is to be understood from their position as well. There is a circle here, of course, but it is as large as the universe. It causes no more difficulty than does the largest of dictionaries which defines every word within it by means of words within it.

No reality is absolutely dominant over all the others. That would make the others completely passive, malleable without limit, contributing nothing to any result, and therefore as though they were not there at all. Each reality insists on itself, and as a consequence denies any one reality a completely dominant position over all the rest. Some, to be sure, are stronger, more rigid, harder, bigger, more insistent on this or that mode of activity than others are. But all the while the others make a difference to the final result.

Each reality is also something by itself. Otherwise, it would not be able to act, and it would not offer content to be negated. It is independent of all others; and would be completely indeterminate, did it not, as so independent, possess through its negating what is other than it. It overcomes a possible radical indeterminateness by laying hold of what is external to it.

The *principle of self-determination of the independent* is here operative. It requires that *what is necessarily true of a reality because of others is also true of it because of what it does for itself.* Were the principle to fail, a reality would be constituted from without in a way that could be discrepant with what it is from within. It would then be divided against itself, torn asunder. To be sure, a reality may internalize what it suffers from without. But, instead of this making the principle innocuous, it presupposes that the principle has been carried out. In order to internalize what it receives, a reality must first be. If it is to produce what will be in harmony with what it was by itself, the reality's internalization must be guided and controlled by what the reality is in itself, what it is independently of all else.

Each reality in itself determines itself to be that which is not absolutely simple, alone, superior, presupposed, or dominant. It is able, therefore, to be selfsame as at once independent of and together with others, and is able to benefit from the actions of others without thereby sacrificing its integrity. It can be conquered, subjugated, broken, destroyed as a consequence of the imposition of forces beyond its power to control, but these presuppose that it already is real.

An actuality exhibits itself without making any reference to what is outside it. What it thrusts outward must be held away from it if there is to be an appearance of that actuality. The actuality must at the same time continue to maintain itself in itself. If it did not, it would annihilate itself in the very act of making an appearance. Its thrusting outward is one with the act of making an appearance, an act which comes to an end in a qualified attenuation of itself. The actuality is able to be something reached from that result because it holds on to what it exhibits there—a fact made evident in the coarsening of the appearance.

It is also true, however, that by itself each actuality is simple and alone, and able to be superior to, be presupposed by, and to be dominant over anything else. Each is at once simple and complex, alone and together with others, conditioning and conditioned, presupposed and presupposing, dominant and dominated. If it were not simple, it would not be a unit; if it were not complex, it would not be determinate. If it were not alone, it would not be self-centered; if it were not together with others, it would not be part of a world. If it did not condition, it would affect nothing; if it were not conditioned, it would not be something affected. If it were not presupposed, it would not explain, if it did not presuppose, it could not be explained. If it did not dominate, it would not act; if it were not dominated, it would not be affected. If it were not all of these together it would not be an actuality which appears.

Each actuality is self-contained and undiminshed at the same time that it receives new determinations through the aid of others. The union of its exhibitions with those stemming from finalities yields appearances. The appearances are oriented either toward it or the finalities, depending on which contributes most to its constitution. As so biased the appearances adumbratively or lucidatively terminate in the actuality or the finalities.

Actualities and finalities are not remote from the appearances they jointly produce. Nor are they remote from one another. They are factors of the appearances in a purified, intensified form. The purification and intensification of an appearance begins at the coarsening of the appearance, and adumbratively or lucidatively passes into a reality beyond that appearance.

8

LIVING BEINGS

Controlling Summary: The ultimate particles of the world, which it is one of the objects of science to know, are not simply together in a single cosmic field. Clusters of them are confined within the areas of distinct actualities. Those actualities modify and limit the activities of the particles at the same time that those particles dictate to those actualities. That is why weight is at once a single qualitative character and an aggregated quantity.

Living beings confine and control organs, and these confine and control smaller units. In addition, each living being displays itself and accepts the displays of others as connections for its own displays. We can know what a living being is by knowing how this accepts our displays as connections for its displays.

Since men are living beings, they too connect their own displays by means of the displays which others provide. But they go further as well. What they set aside they also assess, thereby giving a new import to what they accept.

The world of daily life is rather neatly ordered for practical purposes. But for a detached intellect it contains a wild heterogeneity of ill-assorted items. Colors are alongside one another in no order; bodies move and act without apparent reason. It is almost incredible that men could ever have found a way to credit that world with any intelligibility. That the sciences should not only have begun, but that they should actually have made progress in the understanding of the world we encounter every day, is a fact which never loses its wonder, no matter how often it is noted. The price science has had to pay for this is that, for objectivity's sake, it has had to hold itself apart from common experience, language, and practice, and, for clarity's sake, has had to concentrate on only some features of things. That price is not too high, providing others are willing to continue in the age-old task of saving the appearances by relating them to the realities that make them possible.

Starting from perception, science allows us to express the nature of the daily world when this has been purged of irrelevancies and given cosmic importance. It is not the world of things in themselves, but rather a world of manifested things together, as viewed by an omniscience. The world in which science is interested is an aspect of the world as it might be seen by God. From this perspective, science can be said to be a part of theology carried on by other means. As such it is to be studied in order to know something of what God has in mind. If we wish to know what exists, we must supplement this knowledge with what is learned in the course of a symbolizing penetration into actualities and other realities. The conceptual grasp of that result is a grasp of what the realities are in and of themselves—which even God has to mind.

Each actuality provides well-entrenched routes along which energy is expressed, thereby justifying expectations and inferences regarding its future behavior. But some of its energy is more loosely, more aberrantly manifest. The steady course of things is disturbed by the intrusion of uncontrolled forces. The disturbance may produce so small a deviation from what is customary that it would not be improper to say that it is negligible or nonexistent—unless one would rather have his theories be exact and not merely useful. The world which most of us report in our reflections is a social world mapped out by engineers, not merely in the sense that it is triangulated, subdivided, mechanized, and interlocked in accordance with engineering objectives and demands, but in the sense that the engineer's idea of accuracy, theoretical value, clarity, completeness, and truth have come to dominate the minds of modern man. The atomic bomb, the airplane, polio vaccine, add up to the contribution of science in the press. But pure science is a matter of theories, supposition, hypotheses, and creative thinking in a cosmic setting. It is good that a use has been found at times for what science has discovered. But we distort science and its ideas when we suppose that its values, criteria, and constructions are identical with those which characterize the social world.

Science is concerned with idealized states of affairs. The supposedly endless repetitive behavior of falling bodies, moving in strict conformity to implacable laws, has no warrant in fact and little in theory. Bodies could behave in this way only if they were isolated in an absolute vacuum and then operated solely in mechanical reaction to the pressure of indifferent cosmic forces. But there are no isolable systems, no absolute vacua, and no bodies which are purely passive. When energy is expressed within the confines of a structure, form, law, or other pattern, it turns them into dynamic agents, with careers, relations, and consequences they did not have before. To infuse energy is to introduce something not fully specified by the structure thereby quickened. The more carefully experiments are conducted and recorded, the more attention that is given to action, the more alert that one is to the reality of individuals, the more that one accurately records the behavior of microscopic and submicroscopic entities, the more does one become aware of deviations, of unpredictabilities, of spontaneities accompanying the utilization of a structure.

Modern physicists, chemists, and biologists affirm, on the basis of a convergence of evidence, and occasionally as the result of direct observation, that within the area of even microscopic bodies there is a multitude of smaller ones. Some think the smaller alone are real. The view is a development of the atomic doctrine that was given its first clear, modern form by Galileo. The weight of an object for him was a simple numerical sum of the weights of the separate particles in it, each of which fell separately as a single unit. That view contrasts with Aristotle's, who held that weight characterized the object as a whole, and could not properly be divided into a set of unit entities and weights, each of which existed and moved in independence of all the rest. Since a five-foot man who weighs three-hundred pounds is also fat, evidently Galileo and Aristotle are both right.

[2]

All encounterable actualities are complex, encompassing a plurality of smaller elements. Those elements are real, and function in some independence of the complex, with distinctive powers and roles. They may contain still smaller units, which function in some independence of them. A living being may have organs. These encompass cells, and the cells in turn encompass still smaller units, until we come, in principle at least, to ultimate particles. Bodies fall in accord with the activities of the smallest, but these are clustered and interrelated by the more complex units, themselves clustered and interrelated by others, with the consequence that the occasion for a fall will sometimes be found on a level other than that where the ultimate particles exist.

The relation which ultimate particles have to one another inside a massive body is similar to that which physical units have inside a chemical unity; similar to that which chemical units have inside a cell; similar to that which the cells have inside organs; similar to that which organs have inside plants and animals. The complex body of a man is similarly related in his society. In all these cases a number of smaller units are not simply alongside other units of that kind in the world, but function as members of a single cluster. The cluster has its own configuration, rhythm, cause and effect, properties, implications, and career. The crediting of these to the cluster as a single unit is one with the acknowledgment of a higher order unity within which the members of the cluster are confined. The higher order unity may in turn itself function together with a limited number of other similar unities. The result will be a new cluster with its own configuration, tempo, career, and properties. The moving leg determines where the cells, electrons, and ultimate particles will be next, and also how the foot and what it encompasses are to be related to the thigh and what this contains.

It is not necessary to suppose that a cluster is a plenum. A

cluster allows for empty regions. But it adds something. No summation of the actions of independent elements will do justice to what
they do when they are clustered together. The cluster relates the
units in new ways, making some effective toward others that are
remote when measured in flat space. But it is not necessary, with the
emergentists, to suppose that higher order clusters follow the lower
in time. Nor is it necessary, with the vitalists, to suppose that some
new kind of entity enters the world in order to make something be
alive. One can treat a cluster as the product of an interlocking of
elements; one can even identify the kind of relation which the various
members of a cluster have to one another, with a localized, extensionalized form of a law. But, since the cluster lawfully interplays
with other similar clusters, its governed items are at least indirectly
subject to determination by the operation of a more widely applicable law.

   We cannot avoid a reference to realities other than ultimate
particles. This is a possible maneuvre only if a) no higher order
realities exert control over the lower; b) if there are no distinctive
qualities possessed by some higher order realities; c) if they did not
have distinctive modes of action and distinctive careers subject to
laws pertinent to them; and d) if they did not introduce novelties.
None of these suppositions can be persistently maintained.

   a) Complex inanimate objects apparently do not act in any
other way than that dictated by their parts. But this is not the case
with living beings. These have appetites, interests, and engage in
displays which entrain changes in positions, conditions, promises,
and activities, and thereby affect where their parts are and what they
can, are likely to, and in fact, do.

   b) What we observe has distinctive qualities. To be sure, these
are only appearances, constituted by exhibitions stemming from different realities. Still, those appearances are distinct from the constituent exhibitions and from the sources of these. They are reducible
to one of those sources, not by being broken up into smaller units,
but by being freed from what they owe to any other source.

   c) Living beings have wants; they procreate, grow, and decay in
characteristic ways. These activities require the presence and activity

of interlocked units, but this does not deny them their integrity. A sentence might be constructed by putting a noun and a verb together, but the sentence is then related to other sentences as a unit sentence. If it be said to be a combination of a noun or a verb, it is a combination which has a distinctive function and career. What is true of a sentence is at least true of a living being.

d) There are routine activities in which no apparent novelty can be discerned. Other novelties are regularities whose occasion or explanation we have not yet understood. But there are also spontaneities, adventures, acts of creativity, thought, and judgment which do not merely add to whatever an antecedent cause produces, but alter the entire product. Such novelties may well occur on the lowest levels; it may well be the case that the ultimate particles act in essentially unpredictable ways, and that what we take to be regularities are only statistical averages. But this would show neither that the particles were alive, nor that living beings were just aggregates of particles. Living beings introduce their own kind of novelty into whatever it be that their subordinate elements are able to produce.

Encompassed items and, ultimately, the smallest particles, can be credited with latent powers which come to expression when they come together in various ways. The result of their conjoint activity could be said to be nothing more than an aggregation of their individual activities as so interlocked. But we would then merely restate what had already been said. We would not have eliminated the whole with its distinctive control, qualities, career, or novelties. We would still have to acknowledge it, if only to have material to explain in another way.

Idealism and materialism are not as far apart from one another as they take themselves to be. We cannot accept only one of these views. The airiest of fancies has a material base; the most brute of occurrences takes place within a confining whole. Controlling configurations are to be found on the lowest as well as on higher levels.

Life is not a substance which stands outside of, interplays with, is reducible to, or absorbs, inanimate bodies. It is a characteristic of a certain type of actuality whose displays are not bodily in the sense in which inanimate acts are bodily, but are so in the sense in which thinking, desiring, and intending are not. These, also, of course, could be said to be bodily occurrences; if so it must then be said that cooperation, social behavior, and religious ritual are not bodily in the way these others are.

There are different types of activity. If their distinctive natures are preserved, it makes little difference whether we say that everything that occurs in this world is bodily, or that the bodily has to do only with what takes place on some comparatively low level of organization. The decision will be arbitrary; and it will still leave over the question of the relation of actualities to the finalities which continue to be outside the realm of bodily functioning—and, of course, it will still have to account for the control, qualities, activities, and novelties which are peculiar to a particular level.

The structure of an actuality alters the kind of role its confined units would otherwise have. They, as confined within the complex actuality, are where it is; the adventures that it undergoes determines where they are to be, clustered together. The two of them, the structure and the units, are the agencies through which the complex actuality makes itself evident. Since the units are distinguishable in location and act from those inside other actualities, an account which acknowledges nothing but the units must abstract from their distinctive careers in the different actualities where they are diversely confined and conditioned.

A living being not only encompasses a plurality of particles and makes them function as a single cluster without altogether abrogating their capacity to act in some independence of it, but also encompasses unities of these. And, through its displays, it interacts with other living beings. It has a distinctive existence, and a number of crucial spots where injury brings about a cessation of life throughout. The life is not located at those crucial spots, to radiate out or to be transmitted to the other places. A crucial spot is not a source; it need not even be the place where life first ceases. It is only the place where life must be if it is also to be in other parts.

Contained particles, in abstraction from a control by complex actualities, are all members of a 'natural' state of affairs. 'Natural' here can have any one of three senses: the totality of existing particles, the extended cosmic field in which those bodies are locatable, or a combination of these two. If, with some materialists, we acknowledge only particles, we give up all prospect of interrelating them or small complexes to one another, and eventually give up understanding why they are clustered as they are. If, with some cosmologists, we attend only to a field, or to the laws which govern it, we lose all finite referent points and checks. We must acknowledge the existence of fields and particles if we are to do justice to cosmological physics. But this is not yet to acknowledge the complex actualities in which the particles are controlled and clustered. The behavior of those particles is not entirely explicable if we attend to them as merely cosmically connected.

Only actualities are able to act, to move, to rest. Science, however, is not concerned with these in their full being, but with them as purged, universalized, and formalized. This fact will be ignored if one reifies the constants and variables in terms of which scientific expressions are framed. Science seeks a coherent, integrated, formal account of bodies as solely spatiotemporal, and interlocked in a pattern of intelligible causes and effects. As a consequence, it is forced to abstract from the encountered world. It cuts behind experienced features, abandons commonsense meanings of space, time, causation, process, action, and the like, and expresses the result in universals, variables, and laws. It does not thereby produce fictions, for it does not thereby lose all contact with reality.

Science purges the daily world of multiple features, not all of which are conventional. Some are the special topics of other disciplines, and are known from other perspectives. The result is a public world—purified, verifiable, intelligible, coherent, systematic, and abstract, freed from cultural and conventional accretions, and comprehended through the agency of formally expressed laws, but less than the whole of even space-time reality. Qualities, values, and social roles are also there, also dependent on actualities for their presence.

Once we decide to deal with the objects of commonsense under the conditions imposed by mathematics or the exact sciences, the mathematics or the sciences will define the proper way in which expressions are to be formulated. But we have no warrant for supposing the divisions, junctures, and rests which these offer, even when they serve to express the most accurate observations and predictions, have precise counterparts in fact.

As was already observed, it is tempting to mistake technology for science. No one can avoid being impressed by the signal technological achievements of the last decades. When the popular press speaks of science—and often, too, when philosophers do—it is to this that reference is usually made. But technology is not science. It is occupied with ways of manipulating and using commonsense objects under the guidance of science and mathematics. That it should be so successful is an indication of the pertinence that science and mathematics have to our daily world—and also of the relevance that our root commonsense views have to the formulations of a usable science and mathematics.

[3]

Positivists, empiricists, and materialists are inclined to take things as their paradigms, and therefore to speak of animals and men as though they were just complex things. An adequate knowledge of them in such terms, these thinkers confess, is not possible now, but it will be had, we are assured, some day. Prophesy is not difficult for these men.

Colors, shapes, sizes, weights, are not floating qualities. They adhere in beings which are usually more persistent and effective than those features could be. Only unattached items are what they are and nothing more, but it is precisely such items which have, but are not, qualities.

Appearances originate from the depth of realities. As a consequence those realities can be reached by starting with those appearances and pursuing a process of symbolization. If the realities are inanimate actualities, the results are expressed by making use of such abstract and general terms as place, position, occupancy; quality, meaning, nature; and their combinations. The accounts of different things will then distinguish one from the other only relatively to some chosen position, meaning, and the like. Things will be 'individuated' relatively, not as privacies.

Things are self-contained and yet together. Each exists over a period of time; together they occupy a temporal slab of nature. They are also effective. Each transmits something of itself to others. There is a predictable steadiness to the way in which they behave, even though they act independently to bring about concrete results beyond the reach of all predicting. Sometimes they merge, sometimes they subdivide. Often they get in one another's way. But occasionally they support one another, helping one another to continue or to achieve a better equilibrium.

Some actualities are quick to respond, not only to the presence of others, but to changes in them. They exhibit dim flickerings of life. The coming together of a number of them, the building up of complex housings for them together, and the increase in range and power of their sensitivity, has apparently taken millions of years. Their sensitivity is similar to that which is characteristic of the higher living beings, enabling them to be keyed to objects at a distance from their borders. Instead of passively answering pressures when and as they occur, they insist upon themselves, directing themselves in a tensional way toward what lies outside. Their center of gravity is not inside themselves, but at a distance.

An actuality *acts* only so long as it is alive; when it dies it will be *active* or *reactive*, but it will not engage in any act. It is easy to mistake its action for a *response*. But the two are quite different. A response awaits definite elicitation, and brings about a specific result within a structure directed toward some object, whereas action alters the structure of an established situation. The outcome of a response is a possible adjustment; the outcome of an action is another situation. Action creates a situation in which an actuality is an indispensable but not necessarily an adjusted or valuable part. Response brings an actuality into accord with what is beyond it. In action, something is first accepted as coordinate. In response, nothing need be accepted, but only answered, struggled with.

A response has a nature only when it is expressed. An *appetite* has a definite nature before it is expressed. It does not, of course, hide within the recesses of the body, to leap out at an appropriate time. Its nature is defined by a possible objective—some things at a distance from the body are, in relation to it, made into prospective possessions, obstacles, or agencies. Energy is exhibited with reference to these prospects, to turn them into items with which the individual deals in order to satisfy its appetite. Abstract goals and references to signs shared by a number are also capable of awakening appetites; so far as they do, with desired things they make up the future that is pertinent to the actuality.

Scientific predictions refer to future prospects. Each prospect is the terminus of a law govering the functioning of antecedent occurrences. The prospect, consequently, defines an area in which what will subsequently occur will take place, and thereby come to be the predicted outcome. We know of a prospect just so far as we know what is to occur after a given occurrence. Were there no prospects, there would be either no laws, or there would be mysterious forces coming from above and somehow controlling the adventures of particular things. The energy that living beings provide is normally forced along routes dictated by the prospects. But this does not always occur. If it did, appetites would always find satisfactory termini.

Some living beings are able to control their appetites, to subjugate them, and to make them yield to other demands. They do not merely eat to quiet a hunger, but for other reasons as well. And they do not eat just what awakens their hunger, but what is consistent with a satisfaction of a need for water and rest. Without knowing what they are doing, without deliberation or intent, they subordinate their appetites to a single prospect—obedience, food, care—and force their different termini to fall into place as subordinate to this.

Appetites resist overarching directional actions. Sometimes the resistance is very great. Appetites then function too autonomously. When this occurs the body pursues a miscellany of unrelated objectives, and is a creature of what happens to attract it for the moment. A reverse stress is also possible. The individual may be so absorbed in the splendor of some more distant prospect that it neglects the needs of particular appetites. When this occurs it longs rather than seeks, aspires rather than pursues.

As is true of response and action, appetites may follow step by step along the well-demarcated junctures of the structure that its energy quickens. But it also may skip steps; it may fill out the structure so as to make the entire pattern a newly enriched structure which can be subsequently filled out with further energy; or it may overrun the structure entirely, as it does when the living being is gluttonous or compulsive. But when the steps through which the appetite goes are dictated by the prospective objective, it is properly ordered. The steps here are laid out in advance of the energy which goes through them, but only a step or so at a time, each determined by the prospect in reply to the achievements of the organism in the course of its progress toward it. Because the appetitive actuality has made such and such a move toward the prospect, it is required by the prospect to then take another, and another.

A life has no direction; it is a present filling of an anatomy. When a living actuality acts on the world outside, the life in it receives as well as takes, interplays rather than alters or submits. Its action, like its life, fills out a present structure in which different parts are coordinate; but unlike the life the action has a definite direction, issuing as it does from the individual and moving out to some distant point which it then uses so as to constitute a new situation in which the individual is a part.

Were one to follow the lead of some relativistic theorists, and say that *any* two spatially distant entities are necessarily related in an order of earlier and later, or have no relation at all, we would be forced to say that there is no living body in which all the parts coexist and are interdependent. There would be only a sequence of events. Since there would then be no complex actualities existing at a present time, there would be nothing which could act or be acted on; there would be just ongoings and sequences of them, which just came to be and passed away.

The more traditional view takes the opposite tack. It treats the individual as essentially spatial, as one whose activities manifest a static nature. Time here becomes a servant of space, offering a way in which to make evident what was already in the space, but hidden or unapparent. On this view, one never adventures in time; history has no truth of its own; struggle and action never bring about a result that is distinctly new. The view minimizes the role that energy plays in transforming the structures it fills out and uses.

Anatomically viewed, the parts of a living body, and the parts of these parts, have distinct junctures connecting them with other parts. We seem justified, therefore, in speaking of a nerve impulse as going from synapse to synapse rapidly but step by step, something like a fast local which stops at station after station in an unalterable order. But though structure guides and qualifies energy, the energy has an insistence of its own. It will occasionally jump over well-marked-out junctures.

As the surgeon's knife makes evident, the parts of a body can be divided at an endless number of places. But not all the points at which the divisions are made exist before the knife is used. The knife brings them into being; until then they were only possible positions in a continuum stretching over a region of space. We are not, therefore, justified in supposing that the nerves which are of importance for sensing, are triggered in a sequence answering to the divisions that neurological surgeons and anatomists distinguish. Stimuli are related to responses in single extended presents. The result need not exclude, and indeed may even presuppose, a sequential opening and closing of gates, without any use being made of the fact. An express train can be waved at from every local station. But on occasion, energy overruns all junctures. It can also vitalize juncture points which in no way answer to the larger divisions so evident anatomically.

Anatomically viewed, a nerve stretches over a spatial region. Every part of it is coexistent with the rest. When vitalized, charged with energy, the nerve becomes a unit set of triggered occurrences, afferent or efferent, temporal rather than spatial in nature, related as before and after, not as earlier and later. Countermovements and feedbacks turn some of the triggers into the triggered. A stimulated heart makes a difference to the operation of the lungs, and the lungs in turn make demands upon the heart. But this is no mere return trip; the heart and lungs work in unison, triggering one another coordinately.

Energy has its own demands, but this allows it to work inside the present confines of a single, living body. Much of the energy remains unchannelized, a latent power that might be used in other parts of the organic whole, and which may come to expression in the body on other occasions. Though the amount of available energy usually increases as the body matures, there seems to be no fixed ratio between the degree to which the body has matured and the amount of energy that is utilized. But as the body grows in complexity, it provides more and more places through which energy can in fact be expressed.

An adult may sleep as soundly as an infant; he may be as weak as an infant and as relaxed. The infant, though, does not have many available ways in which it can make its energy manifest. It tends, therefore, to expose rather than to express itself. An infant exists hungrily, revealing its singularity through the action of its stomach and its voice; an adult can walk and think and remember and hope and fear while he hungers.

The different parts of the body trap energy within their confines and thereafter operate with some autonomy. It takes time for that autonomy to be acquired. A body is most mature when it has a maximum number of parts which, while under the control of itself as a unity, operate autonomously. A being can be mature in this sense and yet be barely alive, just as it can be immature while very much alive. It is barely alive when it exhibits only a minimum amount of its unitary existence inside its body. This minimum is approached when it sleeps, when it is quiescent, passive, or listless. As a rule, different parts use little of the available energy on these occasions. But there are times when some parts of the body operate at a great rate and sometimes at the expense of other parts and the welfare of the body as a whole. When this occurs we have fits, somnambulism, cancers; despite the vitality then exhibited, the body may be barely alive. Where, on the contrary, the body expresses itself maximally while the parts function minimally, energy is manifest in unordered ways, making the body very much alive, but with the life given a poor articulation.

To pass from sleeping to waking, quiescence to alertness, passivity to responsiveness, reserves must be brought up, charging dif-

ferent parts with a vitality greater than they had before. It is one of
the tasks of physiology to determine the maximum and minimum
degrees of energy that can be expressed in different parts, and to determine the kind of outcomes these then have. But it is not possible
for this or any other science to tell just when or where an individual
will exhibit the minimum or the maximum degree of energy, or
when or where it will be in between. We live by spurts and starts,
advances and retreats, expansions and contractions. Some of these
are autonomously produced; others are elicited in the attempt to
keep diverse factors and operations accordant. Neither is deliberate
nor intended. We can fall asleep all of a sudden; we can awaken like
a lightning bolt breaking through the silence of the night. Without
wanting to, and surely without knowing how or why, we can
become very active, or most quiescent, or get somewhere in between.

[4]

Were a living being to have only a structure, it would not be part
of a transient world. It would be a mere form or idea, an intelligible
unit without location, without date, without meaning. And were it to
have no substructures, it would not be very complex. Any structure
that it has is in part bodily and in part nonbodily. The part that is
bodily includes a portion which has to do with what is outside the
borders of the space and time its body occupies, relating it to an
environing world and desirable goals. The nonbodily part includes a
portion which can be employed by whatever psyche it might achieve.
Some of these structures are stable, others transient; some are unique,
others common.

Different parts of the body are also connected by nonbodily,
transient habits, associations, feelings, and techniques. These connections differ from individual to individual, since they are forged in
the process of living. Though important to the individual, they do
not by nature belong to it. They cannot, as some of the stable structures can, be identified with the essence of the beings in which they
are.

A living being produces some structures in the course of its use of energy. Those structures are intelligible universals. No one has them in just the guise that others do, for it has not made use of energy in the ways they did. An individual leaves some trace of itself inside the structures produced through an interplay with things about.

Each living being has stable and transient structures together. If the transient structures be ignored, it will not be possible to know changing individuals. Nor could we know them if all knowledge were only of stable structures, or nonindividualized essences.

Socrates is an individual *man*, not merely "Socratic" or a "man." He is a Socratic-man, at once an individual and a member of a class. His stable structure is not unified enough to be an essence in fact or function, except so far as it is infused with energy. He, and every other individual, has its own existence, which is to say, his structures control the use of his energies. Some thinkers, though, with Thomas Aquinas, say that all existence is in or from God. Were God to turn away from the world everything, they hold, would sink into nothingness. But this is a most peculiar view to be urged by men who believe that God really created the sun and the moon, the birds and the trees, and above all, each and every man. To create is to make something be, to give it an existence. If Socrates' existence does not belong to him, if it is not truly and fully and indelibly his, then surely he was never created. The most that a Thomistic God could have done for him would be to suffuse him with some of His power, a power which He apparently never abandons but only lends. That power could, of course, keep Socrates from falling back into the presumed native and appropriate nonbeing which is truly his. But since in himself he is still supposed to be nothing, he is not really created, not a genuine reality on his own.

The one thing that believers in a creation ought to affirm is what all men have known since men have known how to think: each being exists in itself, having its own energy which it uses and abuses, keeps latent, and expresses in its own independent, idiosyncratic way. Created or uncreated, every actuality has a distinctive existence. It borrows energy from the surrounding world and is affected by other actualities. Qualified by its structures and expressing itself through them, every actuality has a distinctive rhythm, and distributes its energy differently from the way others do. Its structure is vitalized by its individual use of the energy. There is no deliberation here; there is no one behind the energy pushing it into and through the structure. From the very beginning, some of it is trapped within and some of it passes through the individual's structures.

An individual's energy is part of a single totality of energy. But it is used in individual ways. As a consequence, a living body is subject to the same laws that govern other bodies, and at the same time is able to act distinctively. It can fall from a height both as an individual, terrified and frustrated, and as a thing, plummeting down at the rate at which anything else would move were it dropped from that height and under those conditions. Because it has energy it is able to fall in well-defined, objective ways. Terrified, its energy is uniquely interlocked with bodily and other structures to yield a distinctive fall.

Each living being intrudes and is intruded upon; all act in ways beyond the prevision of those who attend only to structures or to energy. Intruded upon or intruding, keeping close to accustomed grooves or striking out in novel ways, each expresses itself freshly and freely, varying in strength and direction from time to time. Infused with and making use of different amounts of energy, the expression exhibits different degrees of insistency in the course of bringing about some one result.

Does each structure and activity have a distinct amount or kind of energy at its disposal? The matter has been extensively discussed in the literature, particularly by psychologists. A little while ago they were considerably exercised over the problem as to whether or not there were specific energies in man, all keyed to produce particular effects or to operate through specific channels. Some held that this had to be the case; touching, they emphasized, is an activity quite different in pace and quality from, say, hearing, and must have its own energy. Their opponents held that there was only one kind of energy in the universe, manifesting itself now through this opening, now through that. What was local was, for them, either a minor detail or at best a composite of many different lines of force, all of which were identical in nature and operation. Both sides need one another. The energy outside an actuality is not individualized; in the actuality it is.

[5]

A thing manifests itself; a living being both manifests and displays itself. A thing is a subterranean necessitating source and link for its manifestations; a living being, in addition, provides a necessity for its own displays, and for the displays of others with which it is in fact involved.

A living being displays itself in a certain way because of what occurred beyond it, when it made a previous display. This which occurs is adopted by it to constitute a link for its own displays. Where a thing exhibits y because it had exhibited itself as x, a living being accepts z, the display of another, as relating its own x and y.

A living being displays itself in one way in response to what happens when it displays itself in another. It is a necessitating being for its own displays, but only so far as it has linked them by means of a display by another. Though the living being's individual manifestations and displays suffice to enable one to symbolize it, a richer symbolization, and therefore a deeper penetration into the living being, is achieved by taking account of the linkage. One then begins the symbolization with "if x, then y, because of z," where x and y are the appearances of the symbolized, and z is the appearance of another, accepted as that which makes y be required after x.

A living being, in response to different displays by another, follows the display x by different displays at different times. Another's display, z^1, different from z, explains why y is not forthcoming after x. Neither z, nor the z^1 need be provoked by the initial display, x.

Even the most extreme behaviorist operates within this understanding of a living being. Though he would like to occupy himself solely with appearances, he in fact makes use of what he himself identifies as rewards and punishments. But there is nothing like a reward or punishment, except for a being which accepts them as the displays of another. Were it to reject or misconstrue what had been offered to it as a reward, its own subsequent display would be different from what it otherwise would have been.

For the most part, we are content with supposing that every member of a species accepts what the other members do. We take them all to be instances of a kind. As a consequence, we do not learn much more from one of them than we could learn from another. But, occasionally, a trainer or an owner goes further and notes how his particular animal's displays differ in the same circumstances from the displays of similar animals. He then speaks of his animals as being spirited, afraid, cowardly, friendly, intelligent, and the like. The fact that the vocabulary is 'anthropomorphic" and quite general in character need not disturb us any more than it disturbs him.

Living beings differ in how they accept the display of another as a connection between their own displays. In all cases, however, the connection is made to operate in abstraction from its own grain. The acceptance of the connection is one with the allowing of it to share in the graining of the displays it connects. As a consequence, the accepted display functions in the opposite way in which a copula or its counterpart functions with reference to designated and a contemplated. The latter moves on in advance of its related terms; the former does not.

The importance which one living being has for a second is given in the display of the first as providing a connection between the second's displays. If you first smile and then sigh on seeing me, I can understand this to be due to your mood, or to be the result of the way your acceptance of my display functions in you. I either take your mood to express a law of your nature or I take this law to be expressed in your acceptance of me. The two are equivalent in meaning and in value. Both allow me to know you as a being who can so adopt my display that you can connect your own displays in intelligible ways by means of it.

Living beings have features similar to those belonging to things. In addition, they have unified, sensitive bodies, articulated in organs. By attending to these and other facets as well as to its displays, we find good grounds for dividing the realm of the living into more or less impassable subdivisions. At times, it is possible to note what seem to be expressions of pleasure, anger, and frustration, as well as different kind of movement and action, in the members of some of those subdivisions. Without hesitation, we suppose that the beings have feelings corresponding to the expressions, and desires and appetites matching the movements and actions. But it is not really known whether or not they do have these feelings, desires, and appetites. If the supposition be permitted, one would, in any case, deal only with a living being's responsiveness in certain circumstances. If we supposed that the being lived through on the inside what it was exhibiting on the outside, we would take it to be only a quasi-individual, an internal locus of an externally evident and theoretically duplicable responsiveness. We must know more, if we are to know men.

Like a thing, a man makes a difference to the situation he is in. Like any other living being he displays himself in a plurality of ways, interrelating them in a manner which reflects his own being, as well as his acceptance of the displays he confronts. In addition, he assesses whatever there be. Forcing something to the forefront in an act of focusing, is a conspicuous instance of an act of assessment, for what is focused on dictates that everything else in that situation function in the lesser role of a background. Animals, of course, also attend and focus, but what they then neglect has no role for them. Man is the being whose dismissals and ignorings carry a value, contrasting with the value of that which he accepts. Like every other actuality, he makes a difference to a number of items in his environs and thereby constitutes a new situation with them. He starts outside the situation which they together constitute. But he not only makes himself a part of the situation, he makes use of some items—the objects on which he concentrates as being the case—to serve as a base in terms of which the others are to be dealt with.

Every actuality makes a difference to the situation of which it is a part, but it is only man, in the role of assessor, who maintains a relationship to what he has put aside. Even before he knows, through attitudes, reactions, dispositions, beliefs, and efforts, he exhibits a value-scheme which makes him part of all there is. As a consequence, he introduces evaluations throughout his divisions and combinations, on what is inside and what is outside himself.

9

~~~~~~

HUMAN ATTITUDES

~~~~~~

Controlling Summary: To know that animals or men are attentive
is to know not only that they bound appearances which are pulled
away from them, but that they assume a posture in which those appearances are brought into relationship with anything else that will
be focused on. In man that posture encompasses five distinct, not
altogether separable, attitudes. They dictate that experience have an
aesthetic, an aggregational, a rationally coherent, a programmatic,
and a valuational unity. Each attitude epistemologically reinstates
the connection that men in fact have to what is external to them.

At any one time one or the other of the attitudes is prominent,
and attention is directed at only one of many possible appearances.
Each man is criticizable if some other attitude or object should have
been given preference instead. The criticism presupposes an ideal
excellence.

~~~~~~

We already know something about animals in themselves when we
know that they are attentive. What they focus on is bounded by them
and separated off from all else. They face receding content and are
in a position to relate the focused item to others bounded in similar
ways. But we are never certain just how developed an animal's knowledge is, and sometimes we are not sure whether it is really attentive
or merely tensed in a certain direction. We usually have to be content

with learning what animals are through a symbolic use of their manifestations and displays. Of the subhuman we learn only what symbols lead to; of man we know something also of what it is to which the symbols should lead.

Focusing on an appearance bounds it. By means of the boundary, a known appearance is distinguished from that appearance as it stands apart from the attentive actuality. The boundary confines the appearance within limits, but the appearance continues to exist apart from the boundary and, indeed, is pulled away from it by the actuality that appears. The boundary separates the appearance from others, but a connection between them continues to operate at a depth below where the boundary reaches.

If a boundary controlled the content focused on, what we had in focus, and the boundary as well, might be our creation. We would not find ourselves defied by the appearance, and would consequently not know that there had been an appearance for us to know. If the boundary broke up an otherwise connected world, we would lose all hold on what we ignored, the more surely we attended to something else. The attempt to build a theory of knowledge and reality on the basis of sensations is blocked by the first of these considerations; the attempt to build them on the basis of isolated data is blocked by the second. The one has private content but nothing external to which it belongs; the other acknowledges objective units, but has no way of knowing whether or not these could be together with others.

In the act of focusing, we bound content and thereby separate it off from whatever may be outside it. The boundary we impose is inside a larger whole, one part of which is filled out with known content, and the other of which is projected outward, to be filled out and fixated by similar known content. The boundary divides the filled from the unfilled portion. If we did not connect the very parts which were separated, we would not know that further experience was even possible.

In effect we compensate for the boundary that we introduce, by a readiness to accept, in the same spirit as we are accepting what is now before us, whatever else we might subsequently focus on. At one and the same time we attend here and now, and make provision for a focusing on the appearance's neighbors and associates. Conceivably, there might be nothing which will fill out the empty portion and thereby help determine and stabilize it. To know if there is, we must confront content there.

The whole, in which the focused fills out just a part, is faced in an *attitude*. An attitude is appropriate to appearances because it instances the very conditions which govern the world of appearances. There are a number of different kinds, any one of which may be prominent while the others are hardly noticeable. Each incorporates a demand that what now is present and what may be present be united in a distinctive way. That fact makes it possible to provide some general characterizations of experienceable entities before they are in fact encountered. These summary remarks require and will receive elaboration. But now, perhaps, they may suffice to make one alert to some major limitations in a related, widely held Kantian view.

[2]

Kant is so subtle and daring a thinker that it is almost impossible to characterize his position in one way without having to shift the emphasis almost at once, sometimes to such a degree that the apparent opposite of what has been remarked is affirmed instead. But one does not do undue violence to his central theses, I think, in remarking that: 1] Kant identifies appearances with known appearances, and then not only as focused on but as the objects of articulate judgments. According to him, all appearances are produced through the operation of judgments which, mediated through the pure forms of space and time, unite basic categories with raw material. Putting aside the difficulty that the raw material could not be known—since all knowledge involves categories, and the material is precisely that which is presupposed by these as that on which they are to operate— there is the fact that we do make judgments, sometimes mistaken ones, not only about known appearances but about the appearances themselves as they are, apart from all knowing.

By taking the divisions and distinctions that his categories and judgments involve to be integral to the knowable world, Kant in effect denies that we experience a resistance to those divisions, that our attitudes transcend them, that we are aware that we are focusing, and that the awareness is inseparable from an awareness of the absenting of the appearance from the boundaries we impose on them when we make them into attended, encountered objects.

2] Kant speaks at times as though there were a realm of bare categories or concepts, already formed and distinguished, merely awaiting content. But apart from content there is nothing by means of which those categories could be differentiated one from the other. A supposed realm, in which distinct categories are lodged, rigidifies an attitude, and fills it out with distinctions which are in fact made only when content is encountered.

There are conditions that the experienceable must meet. But those conditions depend, at the very least, for their determinateness and diversifications on a focusing on some actual content. As not yet filled out, they impose satisfiable demands on what is to fill them only because they are already operative in a focused region where similar demands have already been met. They are attitudes, not categories.

3] All appearances, according to Kant, are new constructions, quite alien in nature and career to the sources of their material. There is nothing that makes an appearance. But then the knowable world, instead of being a world of appearances, is just a world of fictions somehow floating on top of what is real but unreachable.

4] Possible experience is to be filled out with content and thereby converted into actual experience. But the two are not shown by Kant to have any connection. There is no reason why, on his view, the categories or even the extensions which help constitute what is experienced should have any application to what one subsequently comes upon. There is, to be sure, some warrant for saying that for Kant the categories and the sources of the material on which these operate are outside time and space and therefore could not change; they will always make the same contribution, and what will be experienced will, consequently, be constituted in the same way as what is now experienced. Yet, even if one held that the very conditions governing actual experience governed possible experience as well, it might still be the case that there was great difference between the kind of material which was given now and what was given later, unless the very presence of material now, imposed limits on what could be given later. Also, the contributions of the material, the forms of extension, and the categories must be brought together at each moment of actual experience. Each union is distinct and independent of others; there is, therefore, no reason why they may not subsequently produce an experience altogether different in kind from what had been before.

Possible experience is the correlate of actual experience; one has them together through an attitude. The filling out of the attitude in the future is, of course, a distinct occurrence, independent of the filling out that now takes place; but it is one in which the attitude and filling both have prescribed roles. One undivided attitude, filled out at one time, continues to make similar demands on what is yet to be encountered; one undivided world continues to provide filling for the attitude, now and later.

Possible experience begins where actual experience ends. Despite the boundaries between them, what is in the latter is united to the former. Items are connected, therefore, not because matter is passive or categories eternal, but because the attitude and filling involved in present attention also dictate what is still to be experienced.

5] The known world, Kant holds, is constituted by the Understanding which operates through the pure forms of space and time on given material. That material is supposed to be endlessly malleable. But then it is impossible to determine why it is molded in this way rather than that. Kant is prevented by his theory from recognizing that a knowledge of appearances does not cut them off from realities.

6] Kant speaks occasionally as though the whole of space and time were present all in a piece. It is more in consonance with his main position for him to say, as he also does, that they are progressively produced. Constructions in mathematics are not imposed on space and time but are themselves ways in which space and time are contoured. The Kantian categories themselves are only constructions which are produced together with the time and space over which they are sometimes thought to be stretched. His forms of space and time and the categories are on a footing. All are made determinate in being used.

Possible experience is an indeterminate continuation from actual experience. Before a filling is available for the possible experience, all that can be said of the possible experience is what follows from its continuity with actual experience. Kant also says this, but it is hard to see why he does, except by implicitly presupposing attitudes. The attitudes men assume with reference to a possible experience are the very attitudes that are operative when they attend to what is before them.

7] The pure forms of space and time are taken by Kant to be flat, monotonous stretches, divided by categories and intensified by material. But experienced space and time are not flat. Bare undifferentiated space and time are abstractions from the space and time of a world of objects. The portions of these that are involved in an actual experience are contoured; what is involved in possible experience is not yet spread out and is, therefore, neither flat nor contoured. If space and time were constructed in the course of experiencing, they would be contoured then and there. All the while there would be a space and time apart from the experience, enabling us to locate ourselves and other realities, and to speak intelligibly of an extended world which existed before there were men or acts of knowledge. Both unexperienced space and unexperienced time are continuous with encountered portions of themselves; both are confronted from one indivisible attitude.

8] In his schematism Kant takes his categories to be joined with space and time so as to constitute a single context for whatever is experienceable. How could the union of categories and extensions occur in the absence of filling? Experience is an experience of appearances in which one can distinguish content, space, time, causality, and other categorial determinations, no one of which need be supposed to exist apart from or prior to their joint presence. Kant wants to avoid this result because he thinks that the necessities of a formal mathematics are produced in the absence of all experienceable content. But those necessities are not compromised when they are located in experience, provided that variations in this experienced content are abstracted from. A strict mathematical constructionist cannot allow that mathematical results holding in present experience hold also for possible experience, unless he takes the mathematics to encompass what is common to them. But then he must allow that possible experience is continuous with actual experience, and that the separation which our boundaries introduce does not affect what is true apart from us.

9] Kant says that "though all our knowledge begins with experience, it does not follow that it all arises out of experience." He intends by this to point to his doctrine that the knowledge of appearances depends in part on contributions made by the Sensibility and the Understanding. But this surely does not preclude the possession, on the side of the object, of distinctions and connections that require and match those involved in the use of the Sensibility and Understanding. Kant could allow for this; but he denies that we could make it intelligible. But if it be possible it certainly is intelligible.

10] Kant took experience to be organized in purely conceptualized, spatiotemporal ways. Even if one were to confine oneself to the examination of the presuppositions of knowledge, or more particularly, of scientific knowledge, it would be necessary to acknowledge, if not many other types of organization, at least additions to the Kantian conceptualized spatiotemporal ones. His concepts and extensions do not wholly exhaust the conditions of experience, and can not be completely freed from steady expressions of human interests, common human perspectives, and value schemes. Understanding is impoverished if it must remain inside twelve categories spread out in a Newtonian space and time; it misleads if it introduces human concerns into what it takes to be objective.

11] A theory of knowledge, whether restricted to what is conceptualized or perceived, or expanded to include other forms of organization as well, cuts behind idiosyncratic approaches to expose what is essential in every legitimate claim. If this adventure is treated as though it had no relation to what individual men in fact do, one will have difficulty in getting the general results to have any bearing on what in fact occurs. An experience is unique because it satisfies an individual attitude; but this permits the making of claims on behalf of all.

12] Men do not always cognize or perceive. To begin with these, as Kant does, is to begin in the middle of a story of man's struggle to master the world about him. Cognition and perception result only because we are ready to analyze, discriminate, structure, and unite. But there are other activities equally legitimate and basic. Sometimes we are primarily responsive; at other times we are appreciative, ready to take what we confront on its own terms; at still other times we judge; at still others we plan, have intentions, prepare for action; and at still other times we creatively forge unities out of multiplicities. The attitude we assume has all of these factors intertwined, but usually with one to the fore.

13] Justified in engaging in cognition at a given time, we may nevertheless fail to attend to what is fundamental, and spend our time on the derivative or trivial. A justified sympathetic occupation may stress the accidental rather than the intrinsic; a justified appreciation may pivot about the adventitious rather than the basic; a justified readiness to act may be directed at the instrumental rather than the final; and a justified attempt at construction may get bogged down in the unimportant rather than the important. He who fails in these ways is so far defective. The defects are measured by a standard. If the standard itself can not be justified, criticism will express only the fact that demands, of what might prove to be an unworthy standard, have not been met. To be able to criticize the attitudes and divisions that men make, with the same claim to objectivity that is exhibited in those attitudes and divisions, one must not only assume an attitude, but know what attitudes to emphasize and where to focus.

Kant never asked himself when it was that he should engage in knowledge, and what it was that he should focus on at a given time. He slipped over the ethics of knowing and the right to emphasize one interest rather than another. Nor did he see that cognition was but one of a number of basic attitudes, all equally legitimate.

14] Men are criticizable, not only for the way they approach the

world and to what they attend, but for not acting in such a way as to
overcome whatever defects there be, both in what they confront and
in what they do not. Each individual inevitably deals with different
items; each might justify a persistence in some particular attitude.
But he will still be subject to the judgment as to whether he has
done all that should be done in order for maximum excellence to be
achieved. A standard is presupposed which requires that men attend
in the right direction. The failure to tie up action with cognition
prevented Kant from judging whether or not cognition was appropriate at a particular time, whether or not attention had been directed
where it should have been, and whether or not enough was being
done in order to make all the appearances together be maximally
coherent.

[3]

When men attend, they exhibit a number of interests toward
the world. These are not entirely sunderable from one another. But
any one of them can play such a dominant role that the others make
little difference, and can be ignored for all practical purposes. The
different interests are encompassed in a single *posture*; this, men
diversely express by insisting on the different interests in different
degrees. A life style is a special case of posture; sentiments, roles,
programs or rules, dispositions, habits, and temperaments sustain different interests. One man might be interested in birds while another
is interested in money. These interests may come and go, and need
do nothing more than govern the direction of attention.

At least five basic attitudes can be distinguished in a posture.
Each attitude, like the posture, governs experience now and later;
each, like the posture, is colored by different interests at different
times. The attitudes dictate the kind of experienced object with
which one then has to be occupied with. Different attitudes can be
expressed at the same time, but with different stresses, or they all
can be amalgamated to constitute a single complex attitude, articulating the posture.

1] Men do not simply wait for the world to impinge on them.
They go out to meet it, approaching it as that to which they will

sympathetically respond, which they would like to accept, and which they would like to be in consonance with. They can try to form a bond with what they confront, answering display with display, expression with expression. Though the responsiveness is not elicited by the object to which they respond—for the object is what that responsiveness helps them to confront in a distinctive way—it is not the independent production of men. Men are responsive to the distinctive way in which they and what is outside them are together.

2] There are times when men try to retreat from the world. They then give tacit preference to whatever is most insistent, and follow this with an effort to make it remote from themselves through rebuff, negation, or escape. Sympathetic response does not have a primary position for them; priority, instead, is given to an appreciation of the intrusive. This is attended to, and then the boundary is displaced, to surround whatever of oneself is to the fore of attention.

Appreciation approaches content as having a status of its own. Where responsiveness exhibited a power to which both men and the rest of the world were subject, appreciation exhibits both to be subordinated instances of some central reality. As a consequence, we adopt toward what we confront an attitude which insists that it is coordinate with us. To one devoid of all appreciativeness, a receding content would be merely beyond control. Appreciation faces content as having a reality equal to ours, as that which will in fact recede from any boundaries which we impose.

3] We are not always thinking, as Descartes and Kant supposed; nor are we forced to think only when in difficulty, as the pragmatists maintain. Some mental activity seems to be going on most of the time, but it is not always conceptual. And when thinking is to the fore it is not necessarily because we are confronted by what we find disagreeable. Indeed, did we not approach the world in an attitude which is carried out in discrimination, analysis, judgment, and claims to truth, we might well act at random, ignore the entire matter, or just enjoy the situation. Pragmatists tacitly assume that one's primary attitude is appreciation; when this cannot be fully exhibited, they suppose that one reluctantly replaces it with cognition, itself to be replaced, as soon as possible, with a readiness to act.

We sometimes try to deal with what we confront through the

agency of rational judgments instead of through responsiveness or appreciation—or, to anticipate, through a readiness to act, or by an effort at creative construction. When we adopt as our own the rationale that governs both us and what we confront, we do not begin with a knowledge of what that rationale is or even that it exists. Our attitude is appropriate to what already is the case; were this not so, rational efforts would not necessarily result in making contact with anything that could be known.

4] Sometimes we intend, plan, organize ourselves, ready ourselves to act. Our preparation would be futile did we not incorporate in our readiness the very kind of relation which in fact has to be traversed in order for us to reach and utilize what will be confronted.

There are some who claim that preparation for action is the dominant attitude of men, and that even sympathy, appreciation, and thinking are only limited forms of it. Others have taken preparation for action to be but the making explicit what sympathy, appreciation, and thinking already implicitly demand. But preparations to act might be largely habitual, and might require little more than feelings of depletion, tension, and a need to control. Sympathy, appreciation, and thinking could well be idle, or they might have no other function than that of providing ways in which what is confronted is to be privately acknowledged.

5] Judgments of value are themselves open for judgment. The nature of men's interests, the rights of their needs, the reasonableness of their desires, and the standards they invoke can all be questioned. Such questioning makes use of a transpersonal standard. Since even the evaluations of a society can be similarly questioned, evidently recourse is being had to a standard that is trans-social as well. This is incorporated in a value-attitude. This represents the way in which men and the rest of the world support and oppose one another and, thereby, together constitute a single whole which is excellent to the degree that its elements are mutually supportive and enhancing.

Men are prompted by their own internal economy, by external circumstances, by their experiences, by their estimates of possible success and failure, and by the success of past and present efforts, to insist now on this attitude and then on that within the total context of a single posture assumed toward whatever content is confronted. Ideally, all the attitudes are equally and always effective, but the finitude of man's energies and his inadequate control over his own impulses and what he needs in order to persist and to prosper evidently preclude this, without altogether denying some role to every one of them in the posture.

[4]

The boundaries instituted in attending might keep us from ever attending to anything else, were they not imposed within a larger region. At the very same time that we are attending and therefore are in contact with what is other than ourselves but within the boundaries we provide, we are also outside the boundaries as well, making possible an experience of what is not yet confronted. At the same time that an attitude serves to bring us in contact with what is beyond us it overrides the boundaries we instituted.

Both what is now and what might subsequently be focused on are already interconnected in five ways, matching the five attitudes already distinguished.

1] The spirit of sympathetic responsiveness is actualized but not exhausted in an actual act of attention. It continues to provide the manner in which confronted material is acknowledged. Since that to which one attends in sympathetic responsiveness may not be human, it may not, in turn, respond sympathetically to men or to anything else. But it is responsive to others as an item in a single aesthetic totality with them. Clashing, contrasting, supplementing, and intersecting one another, all contribute to that single qualitative whole. Sympathetic responsiveness brings the possibility of such a whole to bear both on what is and on what is to be encountered. Depending on the extent to which the various items enhance one another, the result will have any one of an indefinite number of degrees of aesthetic excellence.

2] Appreciation would be misconceived if what was confronted did not have a dignity, a status of its own, apart from its relation to an attentive man—or anything else. It grasps the fact that what is confronted is together with others, without compromising the irreducible independence of any of them. Their contribution to an aesthetic totality is abstracted from; to know them in that guise it is necessary to change to the previously examined attitude. The reverse is also true; to experience the aesthetically united, one must replace appreciation by sympathetic responsiveness. And what is true of these is true of the other attitudes. Each is the counterpart of the way in which appearances are in fact joined together. To know one kind of totality in which the appearances are in fact, it is necessary to adopt the attitude that is appropriate to that totality. Conversely, the attitude is appropriate because it operates on the appearances as together in a distinctive manner.

3] Understanding requires a focusing on what is confronted in such a way as to distinguish a designated and a contemplated, preparatory to the forging of a judgment whose outcome is claimed to be true. It is conceivable that nothing but what one had already faced can be so treated; everything subsequent could conceivably be brute, irrational, not capable of being understood. That subsequent content will then not be approached in the same manner as present judged content is. If it is defiant of all intellectual comprehension, an attempt to deal with it conceptually will not reach to it. Thought is not opposed by what is irrational; it makes no contact with it whatsoever, and does not therefore know that it is there. What is intelligible, what can be approached as that which is to be understood, is related through an intellectual attitude to what had already been understood.

The adoption of an intellectual attitude to what is confronted, demands of it, and what else is confronted in the same way, that they cohere with one another. If they did not in fact cohere, we could not understand them both as rationally together; the understanding we had of one would be disconnected from the understanding we had of the other. Such a disconnection would be quite different from one that occurs when we change our attitude in between times, or when an interval passes before we engage in a second act of judgment. It would be a disconnection that denies the bearing of the attitude on anything not present. Were there such a disconnection, we would not impose boundaries in the course of understanding something now, since that requires us to stand outside the boundaries at the same time, if only to hold the intellectual consideration of anything else in abeyance. Or we would ourselves be caught inside those boundaries, and there would be no way in which we could compare our present understanding with a subsequent one to see if they were similar or dissimilar in nature. Attention to what is to be understood now is inseparable from a conceptual approach to what still might be confronted. Refusal to attend to anything else in order to concentrate on what is before one does not destroy this position; it is insisted on as having a possible application which we then do not actualize.

The attempt to understand demands that what is now understood cohere with what is still to be understood. That coherence is two-directional; it does not favor the present over the absent. Coherence of the two could require a subordination of the present to what was understood later; it could require a subordination of what was known later to what was known earlier; or it could demand alterations in both in order to obtain a result where each item clarified the other. All that is now known is that they must now cohere apart from us, and that we will be satisfied only when they cohere maximally, i.e., in such a way as to make the most comprehensive whole in which each part sustains the others.

4] What is confronted is spread out in space and exists over a time. It is also pulsating with activity. We grasp it in this guise when we attend to it in a state of readiness for action. That readiness stretches not only from oneself to what is confronted but over the item itself. If it stopped there, we would have something to act on, but there would not be room in which the result of the action could occur. Readiness to act on what is now focused on is inseparable from a possible readiness to act in some related region of space, time, or causality.

The readiness to act connects us epistemologically with extended items already here, and makes them into a part of one experience where they are connected with whatever else is to be encountered, despite the boundary which attention introduces. What lies beyond that boundary is now also faced in the readiness to act, for that readiness was not wholly spent in the present, but just given determinations there.

When we focus on this or that item, readiness is made determinate in the form of a particular tension toward it as part of a particular way of bounding it. The readiness is directed beyond that item in the form of an indeterminate readiness to act on something else or at some other occasion. There is here no production of space, or time, or causality. Not only do appearances have their own extensions, but they are spatiotemporally and dynamically related, whether or not they are attended to.

5] We are able to confront something because it is compatible with us. When approached as an object of value, we bridge the gap between ourselves and it by making epistemological use of that compatibility through an evaluation of it as having some degree of importance. The evaluation expresses a standard of value that is applicable to anything that we might confront. The evaluative attention we direct toward what is now before us, because it actualizes a possible evaluation of whatever is confronted, subjects both what is present and what is absent to the same standard. Encompassable within the same value scheme, they are at least minimally in harmony with one another. For there to be a greater harmony, one or the other, and usually both, have to be altered. But as approached from the standpoint of a valuational attitude they are faced as items whose values necessarily have at least minimal compatibility.

In each of these cases, a single attitude is assumed toward whatever is and might be confronted. The confronted is not itself affected by the boundary we introduce; the attitude assumed defines a range of experience, only part of which is actualized and made determinate at a given time. That attitude achieves a maximum enrichment when the various items are integrated with it. From moment to moment we vary the insistence we put behind the attitudes that we assume, allowing them to function anywhere between the extremes of a mere frame in which all experienced items are simply encompassed, and a demand that the items contribute to the making of a single excellent experienced whole.

[5]

We know that what we have not yet experienced will, when attended to, be bounded, that it will depart from our boundaries, that it will be connected with what we will subsequently bound, that it can be simply accepted, and that it can be measured in relation to all others in terms of its contribution to a final excellence of a special kind. This is a priori knowledge, obtained, not by attending to the conditions of judgment or by sharing in some absolute dialectic, but by drawing out the implications of an act of attention. It is a priori knowledge rooted in what has been experienced, in somewhat the same way that a prediction of a far-off event is rooted in the present and yet anticipates what is going to be. A prediction, though, builds either on the coherence of intelligible items or on the continuity of the extensions of existent ones, and is evidently a special case of the use of a cognitional attitude or an attitude of readiness.

An excellent world requires that all items be maximally responsive to one another, function as primary pivots for all the others, contribute to the production of an all-inclusive rationale, make a maximal difference to one another while maintaining their own positions, and add to one another's value so as to produce an unsurpassable single totality of value. Each attitude provides a measure of a particular limited form of that excellence.

In a final excellent world, men will attend at different times to different things and in different ways. What those things and ways are no one can tell in advance. But it is possible to measure one type of approach against another, and an attention here against an attention there, to see which brings one closer to what excellence demands. The result is to be judged in terms of the measures incorporated in all the attitudes. Normally, though, we are satisfied to rest with the measures that are incorporated in society's practices and edicts. But when we come to pass judgment on the society, we are forced to move on to a trans-social judgment of what is in fact needed in order that excellence be attained.

10

~~~~~~

THE ASSESSMENT OF MEN

~~~~~~

Controlling Summary: Man differs from other living beings in a number of ways. He makes claims on behalf of all men; he asserts and assesses as their representative; he assumes a posture governing the way in which appearances are to be experienced in relation to one another, and insists on that posture as a measure determining what must be done in order that the world of appearances be as excellent as possible.

A man is not only responsible for what he does, but he is identified with this as a man more or less defective. It is his task to be perfected in consonance with the rest by his realization of what ought to be through action. Some of his actions serve to enhance actualities and appearances, while others make him aware of even higher values not capable of being realized by men, even at their best in the world. One can rightly say of each that he is obligated to realize what he cannot, that he ought yet cannot be a full, perfected man, and that he is allied with other men in a world where appearances and actualities should be better related in ways not possible for men to bring about.

~~~~~~

A man exists together with other limited beings. He, and the others, also maintain themselves apart from the rest. None would be distinct or have a specific nature were this not so. Normal functioning humans remember, imagine, believe, and know; they also suppose that there are others who can do these, too. Implicitly, at least, all assume that there are others like themselves. But no one has such a firm grasp of human nature that he is always certain just which beings are human and which are not. Abortion would not be such a heart-rending problem if one could be absolutely sure that a malformed embryo was or was not human. Our prejudices, cruelties, and wars verge on the edge of defining and perhaps supposing that others, who otherwise might be thought to be men, are in fact somewhat less than this.

In the beginning, many kinds of beings are treated as though they were human. Experience, teaching, and training soon lead to a restriction of the kinds which are taken to be on a footing with oneself. The few that are accepted are used as ready and quick checks on what is to be accepted as human and what is to be taken to be true and reliable.

Each man looks at the world in the light of what he had been taught. What is known reverberates with what he remembers of his past, his parents, his fears and hopes. He projects something of himself into what he confronts. No one else really knows just how he feels; no one knows his secret thoughts or the emphasis he places on what he observes. But the acceptance of him as a man means that he is accepted as one able to transcend his personal bias, to know what every other man can also acknowledge.

One soon learns that there are some who are not highly gifted, or who are handicapped, denied a full opportunity to know and do. These are, nevertheless, taken to be men, part of a single human realm, if what they claim is accepted by the rest. Even when others are approached as aliens, strangers, or enemies, they are treated as though they face objects and situations in ways similar to the way we do. Despite our antagonism, we take them to stand with us, against all else.

Some living beings seem able to act on behalf of others. Some serve as messengers; most feed their young; a few herd, control, and discipline their weaker fellows; quite a few cooperate with one another to obtain what they need severally and together. But they offer no evidence that they envisage what is before them in terms which express what this is for anyone else. A bee might show others where the honey is; an ant might act as though it were a replaceable unit; a bird might snatch up a worm for its young; the mammals, at least, seem to be able to respond to warnings, sexual demands, and the threats of others. But no one of these occupies a standpoint as that which others could also occupy; none takes itself to be a representative of the rest. This is in part because no one of them has a language of neutral expressions with which to convey to everyone what is there for anyone.

The recognition that another is able to claim as we do is the recognition of him as one of us. The recognition of him as one who can speak on our behalf is the recognition of him as our representative, and therefore as having a responsibility at least as great as ours. If he cannot represent us, we may still represent him; he is then only a ward, not a full functioning human. To stand alongside us he must be able to make the kind of claims that we make.

As a consequence of the way in which an infant interplays with its mother, or a substitute, it acquires a perspective that encompasses its mother as well as itself. In the absence of its mother, it continues to maintain that perspective. Its awareness of this is one with its awareness of how its kind of display connects its mother's displays. As the infant grows up and grows away, it continues to maintain the perspective, but in a modified form. Eventually it comes to see how others accept its displays to connect their own.

The child soon learns that its initial attitude has to be refined if it is to be in accord with what is not its mother. The doll does not answer when spoken to; it does not react to cries or smiles; it does not relieve pain or irritation; nor does it quiet hunger or thirst. An initial alliance with the doll quickly becomes limited in form. By trial and error the child learns that it is not accepted by and cannot ally itself with some things, except by denying itself in important ways. More effective alliances are achieved with what it later learns are animals and men. Over the course of time it discovers that it can be effective with only some of these. These help it to satisfy its needs and desires, and to deal with what is around in more effective ways.

From the first, the infant tries to ally itself with something in every situation. The failure to become fully in accord with what it tries to ally with, ends with a reduction of itself to the level where it can be in accord; in an effort to make itself be in accord; or in the maintenance of an established attitude of alliance. A reduction of itself to the level of others, particularly of inanimate beings, is the result of excessive caution, a way of preventing hurt and protecting privacy. Were the infant fully in accord with inanimate things, however, it would not be able to satisfy pressing needs and appetites, though it might thereby be able to escape stress and the need to function as part of a community standing over against the rest of the world. The infant makes an effort to be in accord with other humans so as to become powerful and self-sufficient. The effort to make itself in accord with those others, evidently, is a special case of an attempt to live up to an evaluation, since it involves the raising of itself to the better position, where it can be in some consonance with what had been acknowledged to be superior to it.

The importance of an object is usually one with its position in a society. If most central, men act and react in terms of it; if it is least central, peripheral, their activities are often guided by something else which it serves. Most objects are at neither extreme, and most of them shift in their role from time to time, sometimes even from hour to hour.

[2]

The alliance of humans is promoted and cemented by language. From the start, the language is used not so much to make possible a transmission of knowledge or to evidence what is felt, but to complete an alliance and to solidify it. The mother's cooing and lullabys, the repetitions and imitations of the infant, are agencies which enable it to ally itself with her. Subsequently, when the infant speaks for the sake of communicating knowledge or feeling, the language rides on a previous use, expressing the sharing of situations with others. What is thereafter said, even if it be only to report what it is feeling, continues and modifies an initial accord.

A language has its own grammar and vocabulary. That grammar has a structure not in perfect consonance with the structure of the society. The vocabulary does not coincide with the distinctions which are of basic importance to the infant's welfare or continuance. The language may include references to privacies and transcendents with which that society or any combination of men in it may not explicitly note. But whether it does or not, the language helps to equalize men.

Even a language that primarily serves to transmit orders from authorities to subordinates, or which is subdivided into subsets allocated to different classes arranged in an hierarchy, requires that the recipient grasp what is meant by the speaker, and that the speaker grasp what the recipient understands by it. We communicate by taking up the position of another, even though the intent may be to have that other thereupon submit himself to us.

When men ally themselves, they modify their initial ways of approaching common objects. Through trial and error, through punishment and reward, by a series of adjustments, they learn to live in a common world. Instead of attending to what any man might know, they then live in terms of what they, as members of a particular group, take to be the case.

The child allies itself too loosely, while the social man allies himself too firmly, to be able to report exactly what is there. To know truly, the alliance must be loose enough to enable each to speak for any man, and tight enough to enable each to be one with all men, in contrast with everything else that there is. Then each man can confidently accept his displays as the connection others use for their own displays and can use theirs as objective presentations of the means by which he links his own displays.

The child moves directly, not to the position of one who knows on behalf of all, though this position is a tacit component all the while, but to that of a full-fledged member of a given society, and, therefore, of one who approaches the world in societal terms. Through imitation, control, admonition, and habituation, it is forced to restrain activities and to act on, with, and toward different things in various established ways. From the first, it learns through acts of dissuasion and encouragement to recognize where others take its rights to stop and theirs to begin.

Having achieved the position of being together in a single society with other men, the child is in a position to deal with the world in similar terms, even when it is alone. Its attitudes and acts involve a reference to the way in which it had been together with the others, and to the way it must be together with them if it is to continue to be with them with a minimum of friction and personal distress.

Depending on the role they play or what the dominant social demands may be at the moment, men fasten on something in the situation which they confront. This on which they fasten can become the object of perceptual knowledge, ending eventually with a symbolization of what lies beyond the confronted. But that to which they attend can also be accepted as it is, conventionalized though it be, and it can be recognized to have a role in relation to other perceived items. It will then be dealt with as the counterpart of reasonable, i.e., fully adjusted, social men, who know what it imports in that society.

For a society, at a given moment, this or that item is central. When men concentrate on one object they necessarily neglect others, but without affecting their status in a social context. There may be items of central social importance which a man might decide to neglect or slight; if so, he has made himself, so far, deviant from the norm.

Agencies for socialization are many. If language be used in a broad enough way, to include not only what is spoken and written, but gestures, actions, signals, and other instruments of communication, it is evidently the most prominent. It can then even be identified with the very structure of society. The values and the expectations appropriate to the members of a society can then be said to be embodied in the grammar and use of their language.

Language is a bond uniting men in one way, and uniting them with things and animals in another. Though used by individuals, it is produced by no one of them, expressing, not what men undergo in privacy, but what things mean to them as interplaying beings. We classify and organize what we confront in terms of the social, neutral distinctions and connections which language provides. But it is also true that language is only one dimension of society, contrasting with other binding societal powers. Authoritative figures, central institutions and their representatives, the habits of eating, working, and resting, the customs, beliefs, feelings of amity and antagonism, enemies within and without, also help bind the members of a society together and allow them to face all else as alien.

Social beings use what they perceive as guides or agencies for mastering objects considered as having social significance. He who would be social without also perceiving, would be one who lived in accordance with plans or myths formulated and followed, regardless of what was then being confronted; while he who would perceive without allowing any social factor to intrude would have a knowledge which had no necessary bearing on what others in a community believe or do.

It is the hope of civilization that men, without losing their places and roles in society, can recognize that they are allied in principle with men everywhere. Until they do, their assertions are shorthand for what is acceptable in their limited groups. But criticism of societies by their members does occur, and rejections of social acceptances and values are not uncommon. Some of these are based on no principle, expressing only a reaction to the prevailing controls; others involve judgment and principles of evaluation, pointing up the fact that men are able to look at the world and the society in which they live in terms that the society itself does not provide.

A society consists of men who, while independent, are so linked with one another that they work together to produce commonly approved results, as a consequence of an effort to realize common goals. Those goals are rarely focused on explicitly; few of the members of a society could state just what these are. Nevertheless, they are available in the common folk lore, stories, songs, judgments, in heroic exploits, in the traditions and beliefs which define what is good and what is bad in that society. When given expression in these forms, they are often captured in myths—dramatic ways of presenting the ideal as pertinent to the men in that society.

A society is a community with a common ideology. Its ideology is its myth become a guide for social action. Not necessarily made explicit or expressed by any member of the society, the ideology is nevertheless effective in dictating the direction in which expenditures and energy will be there employed. At its best, a society is a communion where men are directly related one to the other in such a way as to enhance what they were and what they accomplished. Such a communion is today partially realized by that small segment of society which is occupied with some trans-societal objective or some trans-empirical reality.

In language, structured activities, ideology, and communion, a limited part of society heightens the nature of the whole, and thereby allows one to see what the society would be at its best. All offer contexts which are binding on what they encompass, thereby effectively controlling and directing the members of the society who are involved with those limited situations.

Without society men would at best be together in disconnected ways, each with limited and perhaps opposing purposes. Society interlocks them for limited ends. Apart from it the men might be alongside one another, but would not stand together in contrast with everything else.

In work and in games, one usually enters into a subdivision of a society, and there attends to more limited rhythms, spaces, times, values, objectives, beginnings, and endings. A smaller group is thereby formed, a society in miniature, contrasting with and sometimes opposing the larger. The larger society has rules to which men must learn to conform; the smaller societies within it, constituted by work and game, have rules they come to accept. Game and work are cut off from the society as a whole by virtue of their rules and rhythms. In work and game men produce a nonlaboratory gathering of individuals who are interlocked in accord with commonly accepted rules and conditions, somewhat independent of those that characterize the group into which they were born. When men use a language there, it is a specialized one, with its own vocabulary and grammar, but related to that characteristic of the larger society which encompasses the game and the work.

[3]

The social situation, in the small or in the large, is not altogether satisfactory for man. What he is and what he faces there are not substantial entities, but appearances. It is the awareness that there is more to the individual and what he confronts than what both are socially which leads a man to move to a deeper level of himself, and thereupon to be in a position to encounter entities more basic and independent than any social ones can be. His movement there is usually prompted not by a desire to achieve such a deeper level but by the resistance of social objects, defying the limitations imposed by the social being who apprehends, selects, lives in terms of it. A man moves into himself so as to be in a position to overcome that resistance.

The kinds of conventions that are imposed, the roles that are given to various objects frequently have some regard for the nature and capacities of those objects. This, while making it difficult to separate off the conventional from the nonconventional, does allow one to see that conventions often tell us something about objects. He who says rain is a reward for virtue has already begun to attend to a symbol of a process in nature which is of importance to man. He will, of course, not know what rain or water is in itself, until he allows the encountered rain to carry him and his interpretation outside the scope or interest of his society.

A social object makes a difference to various items in that society. Taking account of that on which it is making a difference, and using the present perceptions of it as a guide, it is possible to converge on the object as their common source. To grasp it as it is outside society, we must get to it as able to affect others, even those having a nonsocial role.

[4]

Perception is never entirely free of evaluational factors. Men are brought up in families and societies, and what they perceive partly reflects the nature of their upbringing, their inherited categories, their unquestioned beliefs, and their acceptance of certain places, objects, times, and acts as central and conditional for all others. The Eskimo discriminates different types of snow and wind, where another, coming from the forests, would not. We can and do distinguish chairs, stools, perches, and seats, where a man from another culture would see nothing worth differentiating. And we take some things to be important and others not, some to be most precious and others to be dangerous or bad, in terms of traditionalized categories and evaluations. This does not mean that the objects have no values or even rights apart from us. Human schemes of value often fail to do justice to what is not human.

From the beginning, an elementary use is made of a principle which is more expressly employed when one later speaks of something being the truth or being the case. "It is true that x is y" and "it is the case that x is y" are complex expressions whose proper usage is mastered after considerable reflection, but the principle that they embody was in operation at more elementary levels. In using the expressions "it is true that . . . ," "it is the case that . . . ," a man acts as a representative of all the others, in the sense that he takes upon himself the responsibility of presenting, maintaining, and warranting something for any man. The "any man" on whose behalf he speaks is instanced by himself in the same way that he takes others to instance it. But long before he is in a position to assume responsibility for what he claims, he looks out on the world in terms which are appropriate to the approaches of others as well.

From the very beginning, but made explicit only much later, all of us approach the world in terms of a limited form of a final Ideal, embodied in customs, traditions, and rituals. Preferential status is given to some items for which others are taken to be means, obstacles, background, and lesser forms. Initially, it is assumed that our particular evaluations are shared by others. When it is discovered that this is not so, the others are taken to be superior or inferior beings to be imitated, reformed, corrected, admired, loved, dismissed, despised, hated, or adjusted to. Eventually, each of us must learn to assess what he confronts on behalf of both acknowledged and un-acknowledged men. When we look at other men as objects to know— since they, too, are parts of situations whose members we assess— we then look at them as beings with whom we are already in principle allied. Consequently, we come to learn much about them which we could never have discovered had we seen them only as things, or as merely living beings.

Sooner or later we arrive at the stage where we accept some other men as beings with whom to ally ourselves. Once this stage has been attained, it is no longer possible for us to see them as though they were simply things. Even when engaged in the most savage of cruelties, even when we are at our most bestial toward those with whom we were most intimate, our acts are directed at what has already been taken to be like ourselves. We do, to be sure, turn against those we suppose pervert the values all share. The very fact that we turn against those others as perverse *men* reveals that those others are assumed to have approached the world from a common human position, but with different emphases. The others are recognized to be men too, but men who, perhaps because of circumstance, race, gene, or vice, are dealing with what all men deal—values—but with a different valuational stress. We may see others as strangers and dangers; they may seem to be gods or devils, outside the usual order of things; we may enslave and humiliate them and use them as though they were things; we may give greater value to animals and even to property and money; or we may work for some hoped-for outcome in such a way that we have little compunction in destroying other men. The others, even those we are intent on destroying, are taken to be realities who, like us, evaluate what they confront on the basis of a common standard, used perhaps with consequences which we abhor.

Each man represents all. The position is assumed to some degree when one uses the established language properly. Here claims are expressed that others can accept as though they had been checked by themselves. Those who are not yet developed, who are malformed or perverted cannot, of course, properly represent the rest. That is why we treat them as only incipient or partly obscured humans. And that is why what we claim is qualified so that it accords with what they can in fact grasp and confront. Our qualifications may be so numerous that what we say will be relevant to only one man, but what is said will be objective to him, in the very way in which less qualified claims refer to what is objective for others. We can see that what another confronts might be there only for him, and what we confront might have to be stated in terms limited to what is appropriate to him alone. But we treat him as a human, even if only in promise, so far as we take account of what is objective both for him and ourselves.

[5]

Most men are able to use the snarl and teeth of a tiger and the hiss and coils of a snake as testifying to tendencies to be deplored. Experience has taught them how to use the appearances of such beings as symbols of the tendencies. A somewhat similar adventure is carried out with dogs and cats and, occasionally, with horses. Some who have spent their lives living with and training them, seem to know how to carry the adventure a little further. But no one can penetrate all the way; and the further down in the scale of living things that one goes the more difficult the penetration seems to be. When we come to the nonliving, we are almost completely baffled— but not entirely.

A man who persists in speaking badly of his friends is malicious; he who persistently steals is a thief. If you have a fever or blotches on your skin, you may be in poor health in body and perhaps in spirit. But if this be admitted, we verge on the view that there are as many powers in a being as there are actions, or kinds of actions, and that the one perfectly matches the other. As Molière's joke has it, we will be tempted to say that since opium puts one to sleep it must have a dormative virtue or power. If we say this, we will, of course, be right; opium does have a dormative virtue. But to know that is to know little beyond the fact that it will put one to sleep. What one wants is not such "safe and stupid" answers, but more daring and illuminating ones, a knowledge, we would say today, of the pharmacological character of it.

Yet if we suppose that we can begin to penetrate to the nature of a man on the basis of what we know of him from without, must we not be able to learn what he is by noting the color of his skin, the shape of his nose, the deformations of his skull, the way he walks, chews, or breathes? Will we not then open ourselves to the follies of racism, phrenology, palmistry, and typologies of almost

any kind? Not necessarily, for a number of reasons. These enterprises stress rigidities, qualities, and structures, and minimize actions.
Secondly, they attend to only some of the traits of a man, neglecting
others which are in fact organically intertwined with them, and which
would require serious qualifications of the traits initially fastened
upon. Skin, hands, ears, nose and eyes, eating, breathing, chewing,
sleeping are vitally interconnected. Not only can these not be dealt
with in complete separation one from another, but what is learned
from one needs correction by what is learned from the others.
Thirdly, the suspect enterprises apparently suppose that things are
completely exteriorized in their manifest traits or acts, and thus that
there can be an exhaustive knowledge of individuals obtained from a
study of these alone. Fourthly, they forget that the features and acts
are necessarily connected with one another in the actuality to which
they belong, that a man's displays relate the displays of others and
are in turn related by their displays, and that his expressions involve
assessment of what he confronts and are not therefore to be reduced
to just exteriorizations of what he is within himself, independent of
all else.

The position at the opposite extreme, instead of supposing that
every manifestation can be read back into the individual, takes some
or all traits, features, or acts to be completely adventitious, non-
essential, unpredictable, nonrational. They are said to be underivable,
idiosyncratic, contrasting with what is law-abiding and rational. That
position is as unsatisfactory as the other.

The adventitious is in part due to the presence or action of something other than that in which it is. It is something which the object
does not entirely control. When it is taken to be a function of "matter," that matter, though part of a unitary actuality, is not part of
the actuality's meaning. The actuality then betrays, by means of the
adventitious, the fact that there is more to it than what it essentially
is or what it is apart from all else. Yet, though it is determined by
something else, the adventitious is not able to be sloughed off, to
leave the object as it really and essentially is. Though it owes part of
its being to what is external, the adventitious is in fact not im-
pertinent to the actuality in which it is. It, too, is an exhibition of it,
made determinate by what lies outside what appears.

When Galileo and Descartes decided to take quantity and, in general, mathematical form seriously, they also accepted the traditional position in part, since they accepted the thesis that qualities were unrevelatory, adventitious elements. But quantities, too, like qualities, are appearances with coarsening textures which can lead to what sustains them. Actualities give them the role of antecedents or consequents, necessarily related to others as consequents or antecedents.

From the standpoint of the designation "this," as expressing the fact that there is an object, every characterization is adventitious. From the perspective of such a "this," even "leaf" is adventitious, but less determined from without than "brown" is. Consequently, we can unify the "this" with the "leaf" to get "this-leaf" and then take the "brown" to characterize both of them. Because of the unification of the "this" with the "leaf," however, the "brown" is relatively less pertinent than "leaf" is to "this-leaf," when "this-leaf" functions as a symbol of the object.

[6]

An exhibited resistance and acceleration tell us something about an object's mass and energy. Similarly a size, a comparative matter, allows for a movement to the magnitude of the object in and of itself. The taller in relation to this may have the same magnitude that the smaller has to that. To smile is to express pleasure or a desire to seem pleased. When one speaks in these ways, one makes effective use of the refined language of common sense. Scientific discourse, precisely because it is concerned with conceived relations connecting conceived entities, needs other terms. For it a smile is but a play of muscles and eventually, like the others, of molecules or smaller particles intelligibly interrelated in formally expressible ways. The smile thereby becomes an effete particular, a focal point for a dissolution into conceived elements which are just together under the aegis of a cosmic law.

When a man smiles his face changes in contour, but his smile is more than an alteration in the shape of his mouth and cheeks. It is more than a movement of various muscles; it is more than something expressed. If all we saw was a change in a man's face we would not have seen him smile. Not only is his smile inseparable from a larger surface, but it is inseparable from his being. A smiling man is at once joyous and muscular.

A smile reveals. Even an infant occasionally knows how to read it accurately as testifying to pleasure or the desire to please. The infant, no less than we, while confronting another's altered features, moves beyond these into that other, as one who is able to express himself in this way. The infant doesn't conceptualize, but it does make symbolic use of the smile. Since the smile also has other roles, it is possible for the infant and for us to misread it. The smiling man, on his side, may be unaware that he is smiling. A man may smile without knowing that he does. But whether he knows it or not, he reveals something of himself, some value he has assumed and ascribed. It is in terms of this knowledge of him that we act, speak, love, or hate. We know what he is by symbolizing him as one who is mainly responsible for making the smile appear.

Sometimes our reference to a man twists and turns to allow us to know him as one who is quite other than what he is apparently showing himself to be. The rogue smiles; so does the hypocrite. The dupe misreads the smile, relating it to a wrong antecedent and consequent. The result is that he misreads the character of the rogue and what in fact will ensue. He fails to see that the rogue is not using the smile as a representative man would.

The assumption that oneself and others all instance "any man" is implicit in the infant's earliest reachings out and cherishings. Through its acts and babblings, the infant forms a bond with its mother or mother substitute. It allies itself with her, reaching to her rather than knowing her, responding and yielding, insisting and resisting, adjusting and withdrawing so as to maintain itself at the very same time that it keeps in accord with her. As a consequence, together with her it forms a front in opposition to everything else. Similar bonds are forged by the higher primates and by other animals. But the human child, through the help of gestures, artifacts, siblings, and adults, is offered occasions to which it, because of its complexity and malleability, is able to respond and act in ways not possible to lower beings.

Men enter into situations, assessing whatever is there, implicitly or explicitly. They make a difference to other existents, as every actuality does. But, unlike other types of actuality, they are able to bring in a standard of value, expressing in their acts and accomplishments what that standard means for them in fact. We criticize them for ineptitude, and honor them for acts of heroism, sacrifice, and devotion. We rightly view them in terms of what they accomplish, attributing to them the excellencies and failures they produce, despite the fact that these in part are a function of circumstances beyond their control.

Men are not to be disconnected from the world where they move, act, and accomplish. This would deny them accountability and responsibility. They enhance or mar other things external to themselves; for this they are rightly praised or blamed.

[7]

Attention should be directed where and when it yields more good than attention elsewhere would. The attitude which at a given time would make more likely that excellence will ensue, should be adopted, and it should be supported with an insistence that the excellence be realized. It is man's task to restructure appearances so as to bring about what excellence requires. To do this he must act to make actualities have maximal value by themselves and in relation to one another, to make appearances be maximized together, and to make actualities and appearances be maximized in relation to one another. But men attend to this rather than to that, though it may be better for them and for the excellence of the outcome for them to attend elsewhere instead. They give preference to different attitudes at certain times when the assumption of other attitudes would have yielded better results. They insist on their attitudes in various degrees and, therefore, not only assess what is confronted but constantly vary the intensity of their demand that everything be part of a final excellent totality.

At its best, action so affects actualities that these persistently make their appearances be in the state that excellence demands. Such action provides a mode of penetration superior to that which the use of an actuality's manifestations, displays, or even expressions would allow. Since the value of an action depends on the contribution that it makes to the production of a perfect whole of actualities, sustaining a perfect whole of appearances, we can measure the degree to which a man falls short of what he ought to be by the degree to which he fails to do what must be done to bring excellence about.

An artist and a scientist produce works which awaken in others an awareness of final realities as not yet being fully dominant over the appearances or actualities now existent. As a consequence, they enable men to use a higher standard of what ought to be realized than had been utilized before. The acknowledgment of this as not yet exhibited in a connection among appearances, is the acknowledgment of an ideal demand which the actualities and the appearances ought to satisfy.

Where action alters actualities directly to make them better, adaptation makes men aware of better possibilities. The first requires an acceptance of the contexts in which things in fact are, and an effort to alter them so that they are maximized there. The second demands that a better context be acknowledged. That better context might not be realizable because of the recalcitrance of what actually exists. In that case, action would be required to make it possible for the better context to be realized.

By using the changes which a man produced in actualities to symbolize him, we can come to know him as one who imposed boundaries, who preferred certain attitudes, who insisted on a posture, and who restructured appearances. Accepting the outcome of his actions as having a certain value in an ideal state of affairs, we evaluate him. That outcome came about because of the way he attended, the attitudes he assumed, his insistence on these, and the nature of his actions. The world, to be sure, did not sustain him enough; it frustrated and baffled him. But those hindrances should have been calculated in his efforts. His failures to master mark him as so far less than he ought to be. He has shown himself to be one who has failed to bring about what ideally should be. To excuse him as one who has been defeated by circumstance, is to say of him that he could not help but be the defective being that he is.

One who makes evident the nature of ideal excellence enables men to insist on a posture demanding that actualities and appearances be altered so as to be absolutely maximized. This result it is impossible for men to achieve, but its conceivability enables them to recognize that a world maximally transformed is still a defective one. The best of men in such a world would know that, though he remedied it as much as possible, he could not in fact produce all that ought to be. He might be all a man ought to be in a world in which he in fact exists, but he would also be one who would have to be different in a world that was perfect.

A man normally exhibits a posture and pays attention without exercising much control over his body or environment. What is done is mainly the contribution of unsupervised bodily movements in circumstances not understood or mastered. He must learn how better to attend, and how better to insist on a posture. He is mature when he has learned to ally himself with other men, aware of the finalities and the actualities which lie beyond the appearances. This result is promoted by the production of and participation in creative work, and the symbolic use of appearances along the path of adumbratives and lucidatives.

External stimuli, intrusive forces, acquired habits, and inadvertent actions help determine what a man is called upon to do at a given time, and thereby make himself be in fact the man he ought to be, one who represents for all the rest, man at his best. Though what is done is at least in part conditioned by circumstances beyond his control, the import of what he does is nevertheless to be attributed to him. No one, of course, can rightly be identified with movements, for some of these are compelled, unknown, or unsupervised. But the actions and adaptations are his.

Actions and adaptations incorporate a number of movements into a single unit whose beginning is relevant to what is to be at the end. When a man clenches his fist he makes a move; when he hits he incorporates the clenched fist within an action for which he is responsible. Much more is attributable to him. He acts in a world, and what happens there helps determine the meaning of what he does. After all, it is one thing for him to hit this at such and such a time, and to hit that at another. The one might be a punching bag, but not his to use; the other might be a man with whom he is boxing.

No man can be entirely disassociated from what is accomplished as a consequence of his actions and adaptations. Yet there is too much that is the product of accident and contingency to make all that is accomplished with his help be meaningfully attributable to him without qualification. All that he brings about can properly be credited to him, but not without it first being translated into a proper part of him. And this often requires that it be altered in import in the course of being made integral.

<h1 style="text-align:center">[8]</h1>

To be perfect is to be complete, to lack nothing, to be all there is. But there are many different realities in the universe. The existence of the others marks the extent to which each necessarily falls short of perfection. Whatever there be is necessarily imperfect.

To be is not to be the others; not to be the others is to be related to those others by negation. Each entity is related to all the others as that with which it must become one in order to be perfect, and yet which it must negate in order to be the incomplete reality that it now is. Its negations evidently connect it to that which would complete it. To become complete, it must therefore possess what is not it, and make this an integral part of itself. That could be done in one of three ways: The first is by absorption. But nothing can absorb all others; there always are realities independent of it. But it can encompass them through the agency of knowledge. Knowledge has an unlimited extent; it allows one to possess all there is. The objects that are known, however, still remain outside the knower and his knowledge.

The second way of becoming complete is by fulfilling a responsibility to all there is. One then assumes the position of an agent whose task it is to realize that for which he has accepted responsibility. The fulfillment of the obligation—since the prospect is thereby made into a part of oneself—is the perfecting of oneself. But this is only to say that the doing what one is responsible for is also the perfecting of oneself. No one, though, can work directly on behalf of everything. The best that one can do is to act so that a finality is effective in actualities, thereby enriching it by them, and they by it. The task of serving one finality in this way is so great, however, that it precludes fully serving others.

A man utilizes finalities in his attending; he utilizes them by insisting on his attitudes; and he utilizes them in his creative efforts as well as in his maintenance of himself in opposition to them. To the degree that the finalities are not used to transform actualities, to that degree he, even at his best in this world at its best, will be less than he ought to be.

The third way is to work together with those who are occupied with other finalities and other particulars. If each man takes as his task not only the enabling of a finality to be completed by actualities, and conversely, but also presents the result to others at the same time that he accepts their achievements, each will act not merely as an agent but as a representative in a single community of men. He will be an agent amongst agents, all of whom together complete the finalities and actualities by one another and for all men.

What an individual aims at is an ideal excellence as capable of completing and of being completed by all the finalities and actualities together. In describing that prospect he must refer to the realities, not as they are by themselves, but as they might be harmonized. Since the realization is in relation to a community of men, it can be indifferently described as an excellence for a community of men or as an excellence which each man must become by acting representatively for all that is, in an ideal world.

Each representative man, through his acts, contributes to a world of human accomplishments at the same time that the rest of that world is shared in by him. What each accomplishes is part of a common reservoir to be tapped by everyone. Obligated to realize what ought to be, a man must maximize other realities until they are without defect. Required to maximize other realities, he is so far inseparable from them. Evaluated from the position of what he ought to bring about, his character is to be assessed in terms of the degree to which he has made himself responsible for their actual enhancement. But he is in fact good only to the extent that he enhances others, contributes to the realization of a final excellence, and is identical with what he does, where this is identical with what ought to be done.

[9]

He who is a kind father may also be a ruthless banker, an unfaithful husband, and a conscientious scout leader. In these different roles he links his expressions by means of the ideal excellence he is obligated to realize and, in this sense, with which he has inescapably, though rarely consciously, identified himself. By measuring what he does by the excellence, he necessarily measures his own worth.

Having done this a man ought to do that. This which he ought to do he may or may not do; what he in fact does will then be more or less right. If he does what he ought to do, he is so far as he ought to be; depending on how close his own acts are to what they ought to be, he will be more or less excellent. So far as his actions affect another, that other helps define what he ought next to do, for what he does to that other is linked by that other with what he ought thereupon to do to him. The better a man, the more surely he subsequently does what he ought to do, because of what he has already done. Because of what a has done to b—let us say, injure him—a ought subsequently so act that a good is done that overbalances whatever losses were involved. Because b's enhancement is a responsibility of a, this requirement measures the rightness or wrongness of what a subsequently does. A is responsible for the enhancement of b because he is responsible for the realization of an ideal excellence which requires an enhanced b. The desirable result is a unified dynamic world where each builds upon and adds to what others achieve.

A man's accomplishments more or less realize what he is obligated to realize. He is identical with what he ought to realize to the extent that he brings about what ought to be done. His accomplishments, assessed from the position of the final end, therefore, tells us what his merit is.

The attainment of excellence requires some detachment from

what a society demands. In order to be able to immerse himself most effectively in the production of maximum value, each man must therefore operate in abstraction from what a full participation in the society at that time requires. If he supports and promotes whatever supplementary goods others produce, he will benefit himself and others more than he could have, had he kept himself confined to realizing only socially approved or socially relevant goals.

[10]

Sometimes men function in the way inanimate beings do. Every human movement is in fact classifiable in terms appropriate to what is not alive. Together with a few other beings each also has a sensitive body, a flickering consciousness, and an episodically used mind. But unlike any of the others, he is one who is not what he is obliged to be. Other beings, also, are deficient, but no one of them has an obligation to perfect others and thereby itself. Only men, consequently, are characterizable as having failed to meet their obligations.

We can and do acknowledge excellent specimens, and even sometimes signalize certain dogs, cats, horses, and other domesticated and semidomesticated beings as superior animals. Their superiority is to be credited to the contingent fact that these animals happen to have desirable and effective powers, or happen to have achieved desirable results. Their accomplishments are not identifiable with them; the measure of their accomplishments is not an inseparable part of them. Animals are not required to realize excellence. This is man's privilege.

Men are defective as men just so far as they fail to meet their obligation to realize an ideal excellence. That obligation is not consciously assumed; it is not even known to most. When we praise or blame animals we extend this acknowledgment beyond its rightful limits, either because we humanize the animals, or because we confound a praise or blame of a causal power with a praise or blame for one whose nature it is to assume an obligation to realize excellence maximally. We criticize lazy dogs, praise dauntless horses, admire adroit foxes. We say that a dog should not be lazy, and that it is good that a horse is dauntless or a fox adroit. But no one of these animals is at fault for not having done better or other than it has done; they have not accepted, even implicitly, that they are less than they ought to be. Consequently, unlike men, they deserve no praise for having achieved or done what others of the same kind did not or could not do.

If we condemn a dog for "not being a dog" we take it not to have the degree of bravery or persistence, or whatever, that it is normal for dogs to have. If we condemn a man for "not being a man" we do not judge him simply for failing to have the degree of bravery or persistence or other virtue it is normal for men to have; we condemn him for not having lived up to what a man ought to be. We can condemn every single man for having fallen short of this ideal, but it makes no sense to condemn every dog for falling short of being an ideal dog with virtues no dog ever had. We can ask of a dog that it do only what dogs can do. But men are not fully men unless they are the men they ought to be, even though this be more than men can do.

There is no ideal dog for every dog to realize; but there is an ideal man which every man ought to realize. We condemn dogs for not being the dogs that they can be; we condemn men for not being the men they could not possibly be. And we are right to do so. Man's dignity consists in the fact that he alone of all beings has to fulfill an obligation to realize an ideal excellence. To say to him that he ought to do only what he can is to make his obligations match his incapacities. The weaker he was the less he would have to be and do. Or, if we set before him an ideal which, though difficult, could conceivably be realized, an ideal man would be a flawed one—perhaps one who will break a promise, lie, be self-indulgent. But a man with any of these defects would not be the man he ought to be. The ideal man we each ought to be, no one of us can ever be.

[11]

Men's different gifts and handicaps, opportunities and disadvantages reveal them to be subject to different conditions and, therefore, to be able to accomplish different things with the same dedication and effort. Usually a higher value is given to one who under greater handicaps accomplishes the same result as another, on the supposition that he would have accomplished more were he not subject to these, or on the supposition that ordinary men would, under those limitations, have produced less than he had. Similarly, a lower value usually is given to one who accomplishes the same result as another but who has special advantages, such as gifts and luck, on the supposition that he would have accomplished less were he not so privileged, or on the supposition that ordinary men would, given those advantages, have produced more than he had. But none of these suppositions is warranted. Disadvantaged men may be spurred to greater efforts because of their disadvantages; they might relax were those limitations removed. Advantaged men may be prompted to relax because of the ease with which they can achieve desirable results, and might be spurred to greater effort were they subject to limitations.

A reference to intentions and similar private insistencies relates to the incompleteness of actions. Intentions are the outward, incipient and anticipated. A man who does nothing to actualize possibilities does not intend; he only wishes. But whether he intends or only wishes, if he, with the same effort, accomplishes more than another, he is so far a man superior to that other. The conclusion can be avoided by separating a man off from his accomplishments, or by denying that men are to be evaluated comparatively.

[12]

Though existentialists exaggerate the importance of man, and though they distinguish him so sharply from the rest of the world as to preclude an understanding of him as one who has come into the world at a rather late date, they are surely right to revive the Aristotelian and scholastic insight into man as a distinctive kind of being. To use any aspect of him—and particularly an expression—as a symbol is to begin a process which arrives at him as distinct in kind from things, and even from the highest and most subtle of animals.

We discern this when we move to him as a self-bounding responsible individual.

Men are expressive, self-centered, self-controlled beings. Anger, hatred, fear, ignorance, superstition, prejudice may obscure this awareness, and even lead at times to an explicit denial of it in statement and in act. Only later is one in a position to discover that, with the first acceptance of a gesture or a work, one has an awareness of another as a person whose public performances have values which express the degree to which he realizes the obligating ideal.

Such an approach as this goes beyond the usual interpretations of men in terms of character, for these usually reflect only the way men face issues in terms of right and wrong. A man's perfection has to do with other matters as well—the functioning of his body, the pursuit of the arts and sciences, occupation with the machinery of politics, and even an engagement in commerce. These are so many different areas which together constitute a civilized mankind. Not all these areas are of equal worth, of course, and a man may warrantedly occupy himself in only one of them at a certain period of his career, and neglect the others. But what he does is to be assessed in the light of the way it supports and adds to the continuance and promotion of other men who, with him, are obligated to enhance all.

The inadvertent acts of men are revelatory of them. They tell us what men would do in circumstances alternative to those that are now dominant. These acts, just as those that are controlled, determine outcomes for which the men are responsible. And the contingencies to which they are subject offer occasions for them to make evident who they are. An accidental push, a lightning flash, may suddenly change a picnic into a stark tragedy. The result we would not want to attribute to any man. But they provide conditions in terms of which a man is to act. The value of his action and the degree of his merit are determined by the result.

Psychoanalysis, with its unconscious and subconscious, refers to what has occurred in an individual's experience, to how well or ill he is adjusted to others in his society. But we do not then know whether or not it would be good to be so adjusted there. One moves closer to the conventional way of interpreting men, by taking the subconscious and the unconscious to be conditions to which their actions are subject. What is needed is a use of these conditions so as to achieve excellence. Were probing through to the unconscious a means for discovering conditions imposed on the expression of an activity on its way into the open, where it is subject to further conditions, therapy could serve to make one not only aware of the fact that one is not living a life of full significance, but show what has to be done if one is to move toward becoming the man he ought to be.

Consciousness often masks the degree of one's acceptance of the end one ought to realize; dreams often seem to make manifest in imagined situations the nature of one's primary interests. There is warrant, therefore, in Jung's claim that dreams tell one about oneself, or, more particularly, about some compensatory or complementary factor balancing an exaggeration in conscious life. But it seems more promising to take such dreams to exhibit the degree of one's acceptance of the ideal as realized in a merely imagined world. Those dreams, it could be said, tell us who we are, only so far as we can translate the degree of our acceptance of the ideal in them into the degree of our acceptance of the ideal in fact. They will then be something like predictions of what one might expect, were the envisaged situation to occur in fact.

[13]

Men are mature and reasonable if they adjust themselves properly in the situations in which they are; they are representative so far as what they do should be done by all; they are fulfilled so far as they succeed in perfecting every dimension of their beings in a world where others are also perfected.

A man expresses, through the avenue of his body, the degree of his identification with an ideal excellence that he and all other men are obligated to realize maximally. He is not only a responsible being equal to other men, sharing with them an inescapable obligation to realize the same ideal, but he represents them as well. Deny him his representativeness and you deny him not only the right to be judged in terms that are applicable to every man, but

the right to make claims, to say "it is true or it is the case that . . . ."
To be a man is to be able to stand for any, while standing alongside
all.

To get to an individual man we use his actions and other expressions as symbols. He is then known as one who having done so
and so, therefore rightly or wrongly does something else, whether
he intends this or not. Since a number of men might do right to the
same extent, a number of distinct men will, so far, be characterizable
in the same way. But each starts from his own center and therefore
faces a different set of objects from any other, not because he occupies a unique position at a moment, but because he can, while
others cannot, move from his center to those objects. He may assess
in the same way they do, but the assessing is his own. This points
up the fact that the individuality of a man cannot be separated from
his freedom.

Men in their actions freely add determinations to any prospects
they face. They freely prefer and choose. They freely reform and
change their directions. They freely increase or decrease the degree
of dedication they have to the Ideal. But they are not loose marbles
rattling around some fixed box, able to go in this direction or that
without effect or import. Any decision they make, even one to act
with more thought or effort or effectiveness, is but a wish until it is
brought into the open, and there makes evident what they in fact
there mean, telling us how much men are involved in the realization
of an excellent world in which all enrich one another.

Every actuality—not only man—acts freely in the sense that
there is something in its acts which can not be known in its concreteness until the act occurs. Things, living beings, and men are all
free in this sense; man alone, though, is able to express himself in
order to realize what ideally ought to be. But we never come to
know what he actually is, as just that individual, until he provides
us with expressions. By means of these we symbolize him.

These observations are sharpened in part three of this book,
where particular attention is paid to man's individuality, rights,
mind, identity, and immortality. But it is now desirable to turn to
the problem of how we can come to know finalities and what they

are like, for such knowledge is presupposed in an adequate account of man. He is so involved with them, in fact, that he makes use of them even when he denies that they exist. His denial is offered by him as an individual, who claims this as his right, backs it with reasons, maintains it while he changes in other ways, and takes it to hold forever—all of which is possible because he has made use of whatever finalities there be.

PART 2

TOWARD FINALITIES

11

EVIDENCES

Controlling Summary: What one knows is distinct from the known, and this is distinct from the objects that are known. In knowing, one imposes boundaries on what an object makes available, and thereby converts this into the known. The known is, therefore, more than the object, since it possesses boundaries which the object does not have; it is also less than the object, since it lacks the object's independence, intensity, and depth. What one knows in turn is more than the known, since it involves the known in associations and inferences; it is also less than the known, since it is not continuous with the object as the known is.

The boundaries introduced by the knower are not essential to the known. The known is pulled on by its source, and is enabled to stand away from the boundaries. It evidences its source just so far as it is distinguishable from the source by being related to and thereby sustained by the knower.

All effects evidence the presence of realities other than those in which the effects occur. Those of them which both connect all actualities or all their appearances and govern them in distinctive ways are symbols of finalities.

Knowledge requires: a) An individual who functions in some independence of what he knows. b) A focusing on some items rather than others that also could have been known. c) A claim that something is true of what remains indifferent to that claim.

a) A man is a living being, active, practical, sensitive. His knowing is only one of many activities in which he engages. Were the object that he knows constituted by his act of knowing, that object would still not function in the same way that he does. The object would, at the very least, be that which had been constituted by him, and would consequently depend on him, and not conversely. Whether constituted by him or not, the object of knowledge must be distinct from the knower.

The powers of the knower that are not exercised in knowing are affected by the knowing, for they are rejected, suppressed, or neglected in relation to what is then to the fore. But the distinctive powers of the object, because not caught up in knowledge, are not affected by the fact that the object is known. It is conceivable that what is known or our knowledge might be constitutive of the object as known, but it will fall short of the entire object unless there be nothing that is still to be known about the object, and no relations which it has to others.

Knower and object are distinct. It is possible, of course, for a knower to know himself at some other time, or for him to attend to some aspect or phase of himself as an object to be known. This will still leave a difference between knower and known. Even if what is known owed its presence or being to him who knows it, there would still be a difference between the knower and what he knew, and a difference between his knowledge and that which made his knowledge true.

b) There is no knowledge without selection. Because something must be attended to, something else must be set aside. Were nothing selected, there would be nothing distinguished and accepted, and, therefore, nothing which could be reflected on or inferred from. This distinction between the selected and what is left behind is independent of the distinction between knower and object. The one is epistemic, the other ontologic.

c) What is known refers to an object that is known. Without an object referred to, there would be no truth made with respect to it. Were the object not known, what was said about it would not be known to be true. But whatever object is known is distinct from the object as it exists in fact, since the latter is involved with a multiplicity of items that are ignored in making the object known.

Truth bridges differences; it unites what must always in some respects be different. Because it adheres to the known, truth warrants the substitution of the known object for the object. Inferences make use of these substitutes to enable one to understand absent stages, causes, and effects.

In all these cases what is selected and distinguished for and in knowledge continues to be united, apart from the act of knowing, both with the knower and with other realities.

[2]

A knower—whether this be understood to be a person or just an organism—might re-present what was outside him; the object might alter in accord with the way in which he ordered his thoughts; or the two might mirror one another. Were any of these to occur, knowledge and its object could conceivably have every feature in common. Knowledge and the known object, and the known object and the object itself, would nevertheless still be distinct, differing in function, rhythm, associations, relations, and neighbors. That is why knowledge can be of the known object, and the known object can be distinguished from the object. The known object is correlative with knowledge, i.e., what is known. It is also sustained by and is distinct from the object that is known. The known object is the objective of knowing; the object that is known is what the known object is apart from the knowing of it. Beyond that object is the object in a nonepistemic guise.

Objects remain distinct from what is known of them and of the knowledge we have of them, even when those objects are not realities, but dreams, fictions, imaginings. Dreams differ from dreams, perceptions from perceptions, fictions from fictions, and facts from facts. Each type is within a distinct domain. A particular dream is together with other dreams, and is separated from what is merely imagined, perceived, etc. A perceived object is together with others, and separated from what is remembered, dreamt, etc., though sometimes the distinction between items of the different kinds is not evident. Occasionally it is hard to distinguish a perception from what is merely imagined.

[3]

Knowing always makes a difference. It does so even when it does nothing more than accept distinctions between different role-bearers or between different beings. It might conceivably add no element or factor to the items that it selects, but its very act of selection bounds the known object off from what else might then be known. At the same time, knowledge loses something, for it necessarily ignores or obscures the state of affairs that exists apart from the act of knowing.

The known object, though external to the knower and distinct from his knowledge, has boundaries due to him. These boundaries make the known object, even when this is identical in content and location with the object, have a different role from it. Otherwise there would be nothing which was known. Knowledge is always knowledge *of*; the known is always bounded in being known. But knowledge, too, while adding to the object in making it known, also falls short of it, since the object continues to exist and function whether or not it is being known.

The difference made by the knower, to obtain something known, is countered by the object. This retreats and maintains itself, independent of the boundaries which the knower introduces. If this did not occur, there would be no object which was to be known.

Knowledge imposes boundaries, thereby transforming confronted objects into objects known. Those objects are held apart from other items. They can be related to what the knowing being has in mind, and may even be related to other things, apart from all knowing. The boundaries are alien to the known; this is indifferent to the presence of those boundaries because it is integral to the object outside those boundaries.

The acknowledgement that something is known involves a passing beyond the control of the very boundaries that knowing introduced in order to obtain the known. Still, it is the boundaries that enable the known to be distinguished from the object that is known. The known is hemmed in by boundaries; the object known occurs inside those boundaries; the object itself is outside those boundaries.

All content, when known, is distinct from something that is not then known; this in turn, when known, leaves over something not known, and so on without end. When we place confining boundaries around that which is escaping, we find that there is still something escaping the control of those boundaries. The imagined endless process of placing boundaries around content is harmless, for no step in the process actually occurs until one makes a deliberate effort to know what escapes control of particular boundaries. In the normal course of perception and inquiry we impose boundaries only once, and thereupon face content which is confined by us, but whose texture and being are not then confined. Knowledge can never absorb all there is. But there is nothing—even the retreat of the content from the confining boundaries—which cannot be known.

If we could not experience the act of knowing, we would not be able to sense the difference between an interaction with something and an attending to it, between a facing of it and a judging of it. If we could not experience what is beyond our knowing, we could not even experience the act of knowing, for the latter requires a distinction between what it controls through the agency of imposed boundaries, and what is inside the boundaries but not controlled by them.

If an object is perceived—an appearance with its appropriate coarsening—it will occur within, but be uncontrolled by the boundaries that knowing introduces. It will be an object known. This provides evidence of the object itself. And by its possession of contextual traits it will, in addition, provide evidence of final realities. Those realities are outside our boundaries. But when known, they, like any other known objects, will also be inside but not controlled by our boundaries. What is known will, though, be controlled by those boundaries just so far as what is known is an item in knowledge, related to other knowns by inference, association, contrast, opposition, and the like.

A known object, although within boundaries that we introduce, is continuous with itself as apart from knowledge and therefore as beyond the reach of those boundaries. What is known, instead, is controlled by the boundaries we introduce; but as continuous with the known object, it is only within and not controlled by those boundaries. What is known evidences a known object, and this in turn evidences the object itself.

Evidences have different degrees of clarity. Despite this, and despite their differences in kind, they are all equally evidences. This is not due to some common 'evidentiality' which they share, but to the fact that they have a status of their own. They enjoy that status, though, only so far as they are both sustained and referential. Evidences are able to point away from where they are because they are intrusions there; they are separable, not essential, the effects of what is now absent. A complete isolation of evidence from that to which it referred would make it vanish.

Nothing is entirely cut off from all commerce with other entities. Each provides evidence of others; each has been affected by them and therefore can refer us to the source of the effects. Almost every thinker has affirmed this, the atomists being the only apparent exceptions. Whether physical, or the supposed initial data of knowledge, their atoms are supposed to be self-contained, untainted by anything other than themselves. But were this possible, each would be a universe by itself and would not be a member of a plurality of atoms. Were one to take the atoms one by one, each would be an absolute. It would be unaffected by anything else only because there would be nothing else in the same universe with it. One might envisage one of these absolutes separating off limited fragments of itself, but so far as those fragments had any being whatsoever they would be limited by one another and by the source from which they came.

A plurality is possible only if items are sufficiently related to make a single set. But then each must at least be other than the others, prevented from occupying the same place they do, restricted by them in its acts, and therefore evidencing their presence. We, therefore, properly move to the evidenced, not by passing from one side of a limit to another, but by beginning on that other side where the evidence is being produced.

Evidence is already on the side of what is being evidenced. Though it seems to be at rest, it is not an idle adjective adhering to the alien body where it is; it is imposed there, and there resists being so imposed. Evidence is dynamic, part of an evidencing. That evidencing differs from the evidence itself, and from the evidenced. And, of course, it must be distinguished from the knowledge that one has of it. Since the evidenced denies control of itself and of the evidencing by the boundaries which our knowledge imposes, the evidence must be related to the evidenced as a known object is to the object to be known.

Epistemic evidencing bridges the separation of what is known and the known object. Ontological evidencing bridges the separation of the known object and the object itself. The two types of evidencing are embraced in a single symbolization. By conceptualizing the process of evidencing, we are able to characterize it, to specify where it starts from, the direction in which it moves, and where it is to end. The concept we use is static, but this does not make it inappropriate. When the dynamic is conceptualized, our concept of it is not thereby made to undergo change, not because the concept fails to catch some truth about it, but because concepts are not caught up in the careers of their objects. Even a number, inert, formal, and abstract though it is, devoid of all materiality and commerce with the spatiotemporal world, stands away from the concept of it. If it did not, our knowledge would not be true of it.

The knower must follow the dynamic pull on evidences if he is to reach the source of those evidences. Sometimes he must withdraw into himself to find what is evidential of realities beyond. In the one case he immediately symbolizes, and in the other he himself becomes a symbol. In either case, as he moves on toward the evidenced, he finds his progress more and more resisted.

Evidencing is a process, with a beginning distant from its ending. It would break up into smaller and smaller fragments, each with its own beginning and ending, were it not that the process in which evidence and evidenced are indissolubly linked is indivisible as well. There would be no evidencing if a beginning with evidence were not relevant to and therefore inseparable from an ending with the evidenced. But there also would be no evidencing if there were no interval separating a beginning with the evidence from an ending with the evidenced. If the process of evidencing were ascribed to the evidence alone, this would have to have an indefinite depth inside the object it evidences; if it were ascribed only to the evidenced, this would have to engage in an indefinite surfacing toward the presence of the evidence.

Evidence exists only because it has been produced by that of which it is the evidence. But this which produces it does not release it. Evidence is and remains continuous with that which it evidences. But to be seen to have the status of evidence it must be distinguished both from what sustains it and from the source which it evidences. Each functions in a distinctive way. And, though the evidence adheres in what is alien to it and is continuous with what is evidenced, and though it lacks power and ultimacy, it has a status of its own. This is sufficient to enable it to avoid being swallowed up into the being and career either of its carrier or its source.

[4]

Appearances defy our encompassing boundaries. But appearances are inert. They defy us, evidently, with powers not their own. They are pulled away from us by forces greater than we can match. Because we cannot overcome these forces, we cannot denude actualities of their appearances. Evidence that there are actualities is given in the irreducible objectivity of their appearances, expressed through a defiance originating from beyond those appearances. To know what a particular actuality is like we must pass beyond its appearance, to the pull of it away from us, and then to it as not yet having put in an appearance.

A second type of evidence of actualities is available in the coarsening to which an appearance is subject. Even when we bound an appearance, it continues to have a density. If this were an integral part of the appearance, the appearance would be a substantial reality able to exercise power of its own. But the coarsening and the appearance, though continuous, are distinct in nature and role. The presence of the coarsening is evidence of a reality other than the appearance; the resistance of the coarsening to the appearance is an evidencing of the reality which provides that coarsening.

A third kind of evidence of actualities is obtained by attending to the relationship which holds between limited numbers of appearances. The relation that this tartness has to that green is distinct from the relation it has to another tartness and to another green. There is a reason why this tartness and that green are together, and why they both give way together to sweetness and red. That reason is an actual apple, which makes the tartness and green not merely be together or to contrast with one another but to belong together. As so interrelated, they provide evidence that there is an apple; they converge on it as their common source.

Because actions are stopped by what lies beyond appearances, they provide a fourth set of evidences, directing us to the actualities which terminate them. Were there no appearances, we would not know where to direct our actions; but were there nothing more than appearances, there would be nothing on which to act. Action is efficacious but incompletely so, because it reaches to actualities which insist on themselves. We know what the actualities are so far as we know how our actions are terminated.

Known appearances yield a fifth kind of evidences of actualities by means of their adumbrations. An adumbrative is the coarsening of an appearance, approached from the position of the appearance. We know that there are actualities because we know that what we know is not all there is to be known; beyond anything we know, there is always an adumbrative, promising more to know. We come to know an actuality by symbolizing along the route of an adumbration.

By being known, an appearance also offers evidence pointing in the opposite direction from an adumbration. The boundary it acquires on being known evidences an act of attention, and beyond this a claiming, and then a perceiver who is a unity and locus of perceptual factors. And, instead of using appearances as evidences for an act of attention or claiming, and going on from there to the perceiver, we can take it to be a term in a relation. The shift makes it possible to deal with it, not as something limited by consciousness, but as related to other content. The result is a contextualized item with a limit which belongs equally to the term and to the relation. Taking the limit to be part of the term allows one to symbolize an actuality. But taking the limit to be part of the relation allows one to symbolize a finality, of which the relation is an integral part; in this way one bypasses the knower, but at the same time loses the opportunity to use the relation as a symbol of actualities in interplay.

[5]

Because we are primarily practical, we are mainly occupied with the appearances of actualities. These tell us where to act. We are secondarily occupied with actualities on which we act, moving to them through their appearances. In order to arrive at finalities from appearances, we must inhibit tendencies to turn in the direction of actualities, and must, instead, force to the fore what are only subordinate contributions to the appearances that we credit to the actualities, and allow these contributions to lead us to their sources. Or we must start with appearances in which the exhibitions of actualities have in fact only a minor role, and trace the major contributions to their sources. Or we must take account of the ways in which appearances are conditioned together in common contexts. In the first two ways, evidence of finalities can be obtained from single appearances. But the most conspicuous evidence of finalities is provided by a plurality of appearances, not by single ones. Appearances are together in ways they themselves cannot prescribe. All of them are part of a single aesthetic whole, where they resonate in relation to one another. They are also on a footing, with the same degree of reality no matter what their source. They conform to laws which are applicable to them all indifferently. They belong in one common time, in one common space, and in one common causality.

And they, as distinct units, together point to a common, harmonizing unity. These states of affairs are the outcome of the imposition by finalities of contexts controlling the appearances.

Contexts are finalities at their outermost limits. There is a coarsening to all the contexts; they cannot be neatly cut off from the finalities that make them possible. But, filled in here and there with minor contributions from actualities, the contexts constitute appearances of those finalities.

[6]

The appearances of finalities are known in ways that are both like and unlike those involved in knowing the appearances of actualities. Both kinds of appearances are bounded by us; both kinds are pulled away from those boundaries. But the boundaries and pull pertinent to filled-in contexts are different from those pertinent to the appearances of actualities.

The boundaries we impose when we know contexts are specifications of them, expressing what we are as individuals occupied wth such and such transcendent content; the pull that the finalities impose on the contexts has the form of an insistence, below the level of our specifications. To attend to the contexts, we start at one end of the relationship we have to them and try to reach to the other. For us to arrive at the other end in consonance with the relationship which in fact holds between us and them, we first incorporate within ourselves, in the form of a power of increasing specifications, the relation that connects us and them. The specifications that we finally impose on a context is undifferentiatedly included in the specifications which a finality has apart from us. Our bounding provides a specification cut off from deeper specifications, but the finality has the lesser integrally caught up in the greater. When producing the specifications, we know that they are part of a richer, more deeply grounded specification produced on the side of the context. Consequently, when experiencing the context as specified by us, we are also receptive to the presence of the context as available for further specification by us.

These preliminary observations can be expressed as a series of conditions that must be met if there is to be a justified movement from evidences to finalities.

1] *The required evidence is present everywhere in fact or in principle.*

A finality is not a particular, but what could have bearing on all particulars. To get to a finality we must start from where we now are in the world and move to that which is applicable to anything in it. The start is the evidence of a finality.

2] *Evidence constrains.*

What does not constrain and yet is present is adventitious, telling nothing about that in which it is or from which it comes.

3] *Constraints are intrusive.*

Evidence is produced by something not then present; it is insistently added to something else from outside this.

4] *Removal of evidence in fact or in theory leaves a residue.*

Were there no residue, there would be nothing in which the evidences could be found. The datum would be irreducible, not evidencing.

5] *Constraints do not originate with the evidence.*

If constraints originated with the evidence, there would be nothing which was evidenced. Evidence transmits constraints not of its own making.

6] *Evidencing is the converse of the relation of constraining.*

To arrive at that which is evidenced it is necessary to traverse the route by which the evidence was produced.

These conditions are satisfied in two distinct ways:

a) *There are five different kinds of experienceable common constraints:* affiliation, coordination, prescription, compulsion, and harmonizing unification are experienced as characterizing all appearances together, and all actualities together.

b) *There are five different kinds of evidence of finalities to be found in each actuality:* substantiality, being, structure, extension, and unity characterize each actuality. They are the outcome of imposed qualifications by Substance, Being, Possibility, Existence, and Unity, modified by acts of subjectification, possession, articulation, occupation, and diversification.

12

EVIDENCES OF FINALITIES

Controlling Summary: Lucidation can begin with what is in the mind or with what is outside. If it begins with the former, it can take one to the latter, and from the latter into the object which is its source.

Content focused on is outside the mind. The focusing, and therefore the knowledge that presupposes this, is inseparable from a neglect of some items, and of constraints governing both the focused and the neglected.

Common constraints provide evidence of five distinct finalities: Substance, Being, Possibility, Existence, and Unity. The first makes items relevant to one another; the second orients them all; the third subjects them to controlling laws; the fourth brings them within common extensions; and the fifth provides them with a single, evaluating unifier.

Finalities are irreducible permanent realities. One or more of them has been noted by many eminent thinkers. Schopenhauer and Bergson acknowledged a primary inwardness open only to a distinctive noncognitive mode of apprehension. Leibniz spoke of a supreme monad which gave equal being to a host of others. According to Plato there is a finality which grounds the natures that are common to a multitude. Newton said that all things are caught inside a dynamic extended cosmos. Hegel recognized an ultimate self-diremptive unity, partial knowledge of which yielded the aberrational and paradoxical. Each of these men attended to what most others neglect, but none made provision for all the finalities.

Kant in contrast, maintained that an acknowledgment of finalities makes no sense to us. He would not, as he knew he could not, deny that they had any reality. Indeed, it would have been rash for him to claim to know that there were no finalities, for this would have required the examination of a domain for which his philosophy was self-confessedly not equipped. He held that the finalities were not knowable. And they are so for him, for his philosophy does not permit such knowledge. He rested his case on the supposition that all knowledge is mediated by categories introduced into a content devoid of them. They were functions of an Understanding, helping to constitute the only world that could be scientifically known. Post-Kantians offer relativistic interpretations of that position. But this is not to make an advance on Kant; in fact, it loses the Kantian Understanding, and thereby its scientifically known, objective world.

Finalities can be known from a number of positions. Each allows for the recognition that a plurality of actualities is subject to constraints of various kinds—affiliation, coordination, prescription, force, and unification—not accountable by attending to those entities themselves. The finalities dictate what is possible to the actualities together, and how they will be able to act with and on one another. The constraints are due to the finalities; they are, though, not equatable with them. To find out what finalities are, one must move through contexts to the constraints, and then beyond the constraints to their origins. Recourse does not have to be had to intuition. Nor does it require a special revelation which is perhaps not available to others. The knowledge is distinctive, but within the reach of all. It uses symbols, not signs, but the symbols are available even to one who simply perceives.

[2]

A few great philosophers not only have claimed to know absolute finalities, but have tried to say what they were like. It is a common complaint today that such men spoke so obscurely that their accounts of finalities were at best gibberish. The complaint is warranted if what makes sense are only the terms and methods which are pertinent to contingent, limited objects, or their appearances.

No one asks a mathematician to frame his truths in the language of science or common sense, before he is allowed to speak in the company of respectable scholars. Why is he so privileged? Is it because what he says is useful or readily proved? That surely is not the case. One of the oddities of our day is that we are proud of our ignorance of what was once well known: a sound knowledge of finalities results from an effort taxing the genius of man, built though it is on knowledge available to all. In any case, references to finalities are not produced by stumbling over elementary rules of grammar, or by supposing that every noun has an object—the charge usually made by those who hold that no knowledge of finalities is possible.

Because it is known through and is not altogether separate from agencies alien to it, a known finality must be distinct from the finality as it is in itself. The enterprise of getting to finalities, consequently, seems doomed to unintelligibility. But this is true only if one supposes that there are no significant terms of discourse, or intelligible concepts, except those employed by empiricists, logicians, or experimental scientists. Terms such as 'goodness', 'beauty', 'unity', 'substance', the 'self', 'ideals', are not only not arcane, but are used by ordinary men in ways not entirely foreign to the requirement of the most developed metaphysics. To be sure, they are often used as though they answered to images, mirroring something encountered in daily experience. And they are rarely well defined or used consistently. But even then they are helpful, since they are still inseparable from lucidations, unnoticed in purely empirical or formal endeavors.

One of the tasks of a philosophy is to speak of finalities with an appropriate clarity. From the perspective of other enterprises, the discourse seems faulty, uniting what should, it is thought, have quite disparate, empirical references. But, of course, from the position of a metaphysics occupied with finalities, expressions appropriate to contingencies are incomplete, needing supplementation and modification. Finalities are altogether unlike familiar objects or the actualities these objects partly exhibit. They are not larger or nobler forms of these. Not palpable, each is more like an atmosphere than a thing. At once individual and universal, accessible and recessive, each is at once omnipresent and all-pervasive. An approach to them justifies exclamation rather than simple affirmation, admiration rather than formalization.

[3]

In logic, it is common to distinguish between syntax, the study of structures or grammar, and semantics, the study of the relation between what is verbally formulated and that to which it refers. The syntax is normally occupied with but a special type of structure, which it selects, combines, and separates in only some of the ways that are possible. Other types of selection are usually neglected. Similarly, semantics is usually confined to only one or a few of the possible ways of relating focused items to what lies beyond them, and does this only with the units of language. And the two enterprises are treated as though they were independent of one another. But this they could be only if it were possible to have a purely formal language without any referents, and a set of referents having no structural connection with one another.

The syntax and semantics which interest linguistic philosophers are delimited instances of a much more general syntax and semantics. These are not confined to language; nor are they altogether independent of one another. They allow us to conceptually recover the world with which we begin, and out of which we obtain the objects of our initial attention, provided that we take account of the way in which objects actually function in the world, subject to controls stemming from other realities.

[4]

Focusing has three stages: discrimination, separation, and penetration.

Discrimination holds content apart from all else, without affecting the qualifications to which it is subjected by others, or by the context in which they all are. It sets aside what else there is, in an act of intellectual concentration. What affected the discriminated still operates on it, but is not acknowledged.

Intellectual analysis and discrimination are distinct. Analysis begins with what is not distinguished and, under the guidance of an external power, arrives at what is in fact distinct. Discrimination, instead, treats items that are objectively together as though they existed in complete independence. Rationalism mistakenly takes the outcome of a discrimination to be analytically arrived at realities. Idealism, instead, mistakenly takes the results of intellectual analysis to be objects merely discriminated. The conclusions of each are arrived at by methods endorsed by the other.

Separation holds an appearance away from other appearances at the same time that, without tearing it away, it sets it in opposition to its actuality and finality. The appearance is able to function as a symbol of the actuality or finality if use is then made of an adumbrative or lucidative.

Penetration goes further. It moves into the reality itself. Since it in fact begins at the outermost limit of the reality, penetration actively continues what is begun in discrimination and separation.

What we focus on in the world of appearances, as a consequence of our going through these three stages, offers evidence about what is actual and what is final. Both types of reality stand on their own bottoms, holding appearances away from us even while we continue to keep the appearances confined within boundaries that we provide.

[5]

What we have in mind is not something subtracted from what is confronted, but the confronted item given a new career in knowledge, through the agency of boundaries we impose on it. Realities ignore those boundaries. They are not a promise that further content for knowledge will be forthcoming—the idealistic thesis of phenomenologists. Realities have powers and careers of their own, to be known by matching their retreat from our confining by a symbolizing use of what we have focused on.

The encountered leaf is within the boundaries that consciousness provides. It also is pulled away from us, where it has a different career, oblivious of our associatings. The absenting of the encountered leaf is a retreat in depth, not a shrinkage in magnitude, and evidences itself as freed from the control of the imposed boundaries.

For one to be at the present position of knowing the leaf, there had to be a position where one was together with it as not known, and from which one in fact moved. The leaf with which one was then involved was part of a larger world, not affected by the knower. The movement from that world was an act by which the leaf, through discrimination, was detached from its neighbors and bounded. To know that larger world from which one set out, it is necessary to begin here, where one has now arrived, facing the focused leaf. One can recover the world from which one moved conceptually only, not in fact, for the past cannot be undone or be made present. The antecedents of knowledge are conclusions reached from the base of what those antecedents made possible.

The problem we here face is not different in principle from that involved in beginning any activity, be it only a walk or a drive. To go for a walk it is necessary to push aside a host of obtrusive things, so as to be able to attend instead to the hardly noticed steps before us, the street stretching beyond, the corner we are soon to come to, the crossings, the traffic lights, and the other pedestrians. Had it been our desire to dance, we would have had to attend to the floor, our partners, the music, and other dancers. Similarly, had we wanted to begin with some idea, some fact, or some belief, we would, in order to get inquiry going, have had to turn from other possible intellectual adventures. Whatever the route and means of traversal, in all these cases we would set out from where we were, put aside much of what was available, and attend to the remainder. The big difference is that in knowledge one tries to know the object answering to what one has in mind.

One is able to attend to the leaf because one has moved from a position occupied in the past. There the leaf was confronted as a part of a larger world. A good deal of that world escapes present understanding. Whatever one knows of it is altered somewhat from the guise it had when it was present. It is now given new associates; details slip away; some biases are added, others are overcome, and it is faced as that which is separated out of a larger whole. If one is to continue to look at that leaf, a hundred items must be kept from intruding on the vision or hearing. Focusing holds the leaf away from other appearances with which it is in fact connected, and from those common contexts which provide the connections between the various appearances. In compensation, focusing does not disturb the confronted leaf's rootage in an actual leaf and in finalities. It is possible, therefore, to learn something about these realities which lie beyond the confronted leaf.

The past with which one began can never be begun with again. It is different from what is now in mind, precisely because it is remembered, for to remember is to have in mind that which points to what is at a time different from the now of the remembering. The past, as it was, is not the past as now known. Before it was a beginning; now it is arrived at. Before it had been confronted; now it is remembered. It cannot be made completely present without being denied its position as past, outside the present. To know the details of it in a sense that would satisfy an historian one must start with data in the present and, by a process of convergence, terminate in it. That terminating is an intellectual matter; it does not lay hold of the past as in fact excluded by and excluding what is present.

The act of looking at a leaf now is inseparable from an act by which one kept and still keeps a good part of a larger, familiar world at bay. Some of the items in that larger world may have been attended to, or may eventually be focused on, with an effort and a success that one cannot now attain with the leaf. But most of the items in it were never and will never be noted. Other items are taken account of by exclusion. One blocks out the table, the pictures on the wall, the noises in the room, the feel of the chair, and a host of other things. They thereby acquire a negative but effective role with respect to whatever is attended to. The attention is achieved through a deliberate self-blinding and a self-imposed deafness. By disinterest or neglect one cancels much of what else there is in order to attend. Unattended, not allowed to intrude, these items nevertheless provide a background, an environment for oneself and the leaf one focuses on.

To attend to and to perceive the leaf is to isolate it, to bound it off from its neighbors. The focused-on leaf and the judged leaf, dissected and united in an articulate claim, are in the mind through the help of the boundaries attention imposes. But they are never entirely confined within our boundaries; the real leaf pulls them away from the boundaries we impose and toward itself. We move from what is in mind to this very same content as outside the mind by following the route of an adumbration; we move from what is adumbratively reached outside the mind to its source in an independent actuality by continuing along the route of the adumbration.

A known leaf is a selected leaf which can be used as a frame within which factors can be distinguished and then united to constitute such judgments as "this is a large leaf," "this leaf is brown," "this is brittle." The known leaf is evidently rich and complex enough to warrant remaining with it for an indefinite time. Much is to be learned by carefully studying it. But it is also true that a great deal more is neglected. At best, every man is a part-time specialist, for there are only a comparatively few things to which he can attend. Then, under the pressure of appetite, duties, needs, or fatigue, he releases his selected items into the larger world where they, rooted in actualities, in fact exist together with what he neglected. The release does not heal the breach between what had been selected and what had been neglected. The selected item is simply let go, to become subject to conditions of which nothing is then known. That is one reason why those whose focused objects are allowed to be in a larger world do not appear to be any wiser, any better controlled, or more adroit than those who continue to concentrate solely on what had been focused on.

When something is focused on, what is then neglected does not vanish. It continues to accompany the isolated; it may even affect and be affected by it. A return to the neglected, which sought nothing more than to acknowledge it as that which is also present would, therefore, seem to be a most innocuous and proper way to undo the separation produced by attending. But a return to the neglected is far from innocuous; the focused has been wrenched away and thereby distorted; essential relations that it had to others have been ignored. Placing the focused alongside the neglected yields a situation quite distinct from that with which one began.

Despite the boundaries we impose, a focused item is related to and not merely alongside what had not been focused on. Since that with which it is related is also an appearance, the focused cannot control or possess it, any more than the appearance which is related to it can possess or control the focused. What governs them both as objectively together is independent of them—and of us as having attended to only one of them. We ignore that governing power in the act of focusing.

[6]

Evidences are adventitious features, 'accidents' whose presence is due to something else. Thrusting them aside is like wiping a dagger so as to have a clean weapon to show the court. The evidences provided by the connections governing the appearances of actualities are of five kinds: 1] a determinant of relevance; 2] a point of orientation; 3] a prescriptive structure; 4] a compulsive force; and 5] an all-comprehensive unifier.

The first makes contents into intensively connected appearances, which have an affinity with one another despite differences in sensory modality. The smell of lilac is like the taste of strawberries, not like that of onions. The second makes content into appearances of the same dignity and status, no matter how different in role and activity their sources be. The appearance of a man is no more and no less an appearance than that of a worm. The third exhibits a law in the guise of a variable for which the contents offer mere stopping points and no specifications; a single law ingrediently controls this appearance here and that one there. The fourth provides spatial, temporal, and dynamic extensional connections for filled-out positions; appearances are extended in extended fields. The fifth functions as a valuational unity enriched by contents encompassed.

1] When contents are conditioned substantially, which is to say from within, their intensities are intimately related in various degrees and ways, enabling one to cross over lines ordinarily thought to keep qualities in separate unrelated classes. There is a music that goes with this dancing and not with that. A primary inwardness not only gives an inescapable objectivity to the contents, but interrelates them as relevant, necessarily connected intensively. Were there no constraining conditions originating from a single inwardness, the appearances could be altogether indifferent to one another.

A number of explanations can be offered for this situation. The ways in which the different appearances clash and oppose one another, intensify and diminish, recoil and advance, accommodate and repel, could be credited to man's sensitivity, habits, and customs. White, we know, has one value for the Chinese and another for Anglo-Saxons. But we also know that there is protective coloration in insects and in animals, whether there are men in existence or not. The same appearances evoke the same unreflective appetites, sexual urges, and responses, again and again.

Resonances are a consequence of the fact that a common inwardness affects actualities and, consequently, appearances, to make them pertinent to one another in various degrees. Were it not operative and compelling, we would not have a different common world from what now is, but none at all.

A focused appearance and what is set aside are rooted in individual actualities. Those actualities, despite their unfathomable privacies, are affected by a single inwardness—a 'matter' it was once called—and their appearances are unavoidably affected by it as well. We become aware of this inwardness when we become aware of the ground of the resonances that occur among the appearances. A blush is an appearance resonating to other appearances; it offers one instance of the way in which an individual's appearances are relevant to others.

2] The focused and what is set aside are part of the very same world, and to the same extent. For the sake of knowledge, we may give a special import to one, and hold it against the other. No recovery of the original state of affairs is possible unless, regardless of what we do to the one, it is subjected to a power that enables it to be no more and no less real than what had been put aside. To be aware that what is focused on and what was neglected are equally real is one with the acknowledgment of their common orientation to what is beyond them both.

The real, it is sometimes said, is what is, regardless of what we imagine or think. But the contrast is too sharp. What we imagine also has some kind of reality, and what we think about may be what in fact is the case. It would be better to grant that any item in experience is real. In the end one will have to abandon this lead too, for we experience illusions and delusions, the distorted and the conventionalized which we would not want to call 'real'. And, since realities, as wholly in themselves, are not experienced, we must not let ourselves, in our account of the real, be limited just to what experience accommodates. We can also say, odd though it may at first sound, that all objective appearances are real, inseparable as they are from more ultimate realities, and able as they are to function independently of these. The real is any distinctive entity which is coordinated with other distinctive entities by the same power. The real, too, is any single entity, so far as it is qualified by that power.

I am a reality, with a complex body, who thinks, feels, speaks, and understands. It may be that the blood and cells in me and the elements that they encompass have realities of their own. Or, what is less likely, that they are only discriminated divisions in me, ceasing to be truly part of me when they are distinct and separate from one another. No matter what view we take, it will not affect the fact that I am surely real. And anything in space and time on which I am able to act and which can act on me must be no less real than I; otherwise it would not be able to interplay with me effectively.

I do not allow that the color and the shape of this leaf are as real as I, because, though I am aware of them and bring them into relationship with other things of which I had been, am now, and will be aware, and though they in turn affect me, at least sufficiently to make me want to attend to them, neither the color nor the shape can act on me or I on them. Only those entities are real in the same sense I am, which resist me, insist on themselves, persist in being for a while, and are able to act through the use of an independent power. It would be an error to deny all reality to other entities, of course. Appearances have reality. Even when not altogether separable from me and my perceiving, they are sustained by and belong to realities other than myself. But even though sustained by and belonging to these realities, they have properties and relations, neighbors and adventures of their own. This precludes them from being equated with fictions, figments, or dreams. But even a fiction has some reality, and could be made the object of thought or memory. It is real, though, only when maintained by the thought of it.

If some exercise of the mind produces an entity, say an image or a concept, the image or concept is real just so far as the imagining or the conceptualization is. But it has no reality apart from these. We normally take something to be real only if it is not constituted or sustained by our minds, in our imaginings or conceivings. This still leaves the appearances of actualities, which are in part what they are because produced and sustained by the actualities, with reality; while figments do not have even that much. The appearances, though, are jointly real only because they are coordinated by a power operating through a context for them all. They do not have power of their own to crowd out room for themselves in space, to act or react, or to exert or withstand force. This is what actualities do. These are all equally real because they are directly coordinated by a final power. They have that reality, though, only contingently, precariously, thereby evidencing a finality to which they owe their coordinate reality. There are other evidenced finalities; these are permanently coordinated by that finality. Both the actualities and the finalities are real beings also, each by itself, by virtue of the qualifications each suffers from the same finality, the actualities precariously, the finalities permanently.

Descartes thought that he was real. But since he treated his body as though it were a physical thing—a point which La Mettrie exploited—he had to find the human side of himself in his mind. We make no advance in principle on Descartes when we take man to be an animal body, for then, to see a man as distinctive, we would have to deal with him as one who acts in special ways, or who acquires special traits through action or by his associating with others.

We can identify a man with his body only if, with Merleau-Ponty, we suppose that body to be distinctive, a human body. But for that we will pay the price of ignoring other dimensions of him, such as his mind and imagination. Setting these aside for the moment, we can take a man to be real as a body. But the fact that his body was distinctive would not mean that he was more or less real than other bodies. A man can be said to be distinctive as a body, or distinctive as more than a body, but in either case he has the very same degree of reality that is possessed by any body—a stone, a leaf, an electron.

Nor is the appearance of a man more or less real than the appearance of anything else. We may put a higher value on it; it may be more interesting; it may lead us to him, with incomparable, satisfying results. Despite this, his appearance is on a footing with the appearance of the least valuable or interesting of realities. How is this possible? Unless there be a power that is able to give all appearances the same degree of reality, they could well be entirely incomparable, or related only in a hierarchy of more or less reality. The coordinate status of all appearances is evidence of a constraining force which keeps them on a level, one no more nor less real than any other. For the actualities and finalities, which constitute those appearances, to be equatable as realities, a greater leveling force, continuous with the other, is required, for those realities are more resistant and more valuationally diverse than the appearances.

Though some appearances are more basic, others more agreeable, still others more important, all are equally appearances. Those which were capable of the most resonance, those which were basic to other appearances, those which were better understood, those which occupy larger regions, or which were more unified, could be credited with having a higher status as appearances than the others. Those appearances which had the least amount of importance, or which were most remote from those which had any, would presumably enable one to get to actualities or finalities only with difficulty, if at all. But one appearance is as opaque as another; one appearance is as adumbratively and lucidatively rooted as deeply and as firmly as any other. Their degree of importance is not matched by a degree of reality. Were this not so, we would have to follow the lead of the classical rationalists, and attend only to some appearances in order to get a firm purchase on what was most real. But all appearances, outside our minds, are inert and pulled upon; all are less real than actualities and finalities, but real enough to stand in contrast with both. All appearances evidence a finality which keeps them on a footing, no matter what their value or use.

3] Appearances issue from distinct actualities in their severalty. Yet they are rationally related to one another. Sometimes called "relations of reason," products of human thinking, those relations nevertheless exist apart from men and their knowing.

The common world is not altogether unintelligible. Some logical and mathematical inferences anticipate the course of the world. There are groupings, organizations, concordances, repetitions, patterns everywhere. But the common world, also, is not altogether intelligible. There are too many disconnected items, too many novelties, spontaneities, accidents, variations, and sports in it to make a single intelligible account possible. To find our way around such a world we must be content with inductions, probabilities, guesses, which we smooth out and make useful—or at least harmless—by living within a selected portion of the world. This decision is backed by multiple checks and contrivances, and a readiness to adjust to the more signal events.

The contingencies and accidents that make the common world seem beyond the reach of reason, are intersected by necessities and rationalities which make it seem to be a mind incarnate. Those who insist on the one rightly challenge and are rightly challenged by an insistence on the other. The existentialists, who object to both approaches—though perhaps more vigorously to the second—abandon an interest in the common world to concentrate instead on what they can obtain in a direct encounter with other actualities and, most particularly, man. They think this is beyond rational grasp, because they suppose that whatever is intelligible must so far not be real. But this is to dismiss the achievements of science rather cavalierly.

No philosopher, reflecting in his study on the contextualizing conditions for a conceivable world, can know what the common world is like. Even if he had a perfect knowledge of the contexts governing it, he would not yet know what happens to those contexts when they are occupied by the content provided by actualities. Nor could he find out what happens to the contexts by just adding to them the contributions which the actualities provide. Treated without regard for one another, content and contexts are different from what they are as together. The contexts give a necessitating objectivity to the content, and the content gives the contexts contingent data. If a context is prescriptive, structural, the result is appearances interrelated in intelligible ways.

Might not the content so overwhelm a context as to preclude all semblance of rationality in the result? Or, alternatively, might not their context so overwhelm the content that it is turned into a set of counters in a transparent, purely rational whole? The negative answers have both an a priori and an empirical form.

There must always be some intelligibility to whatever common world there is, because a finality makes a structural context apply to it. Appearances may be subject to perturbations; the structure will always lack the power to control the coming and passing away of the content that it is to connect, but this will not affect the applicability of the context, or its prescriptiveness. There is a rational necessity operative in the common world, though how it will function in the future and what it will then do we can not now know. Just as certainly, content will always subject contexts to limitations originating with actualities. The difference these factors make to one another cannot be known in advance. The nature of the combination, the course of the common world, must be empirically discovered; it cannot be deduced. But we can know in advance that there will always be rationality in the result, because this result is an outcome of a manifestation of a permanent final meaning.

The common world is discontinuously intelligible. It is intelligible because contents are connected in a common context which has a distinctive rationale. It is discontinuously so, because the contents are continuous with distinct actualities outside the common world. The contextualizing rational structure, which provides the intelligibility, is at once external to the common world and inseparable from it. Mathematicians, theoretical scientists, and some philosophers recognize its externality, and look to it for their basic principles and ideal possibilities. Its inseparability from the common world guarantees that intelligibility everywhere.

What is now experienced and what will be experienced are both subordinate to the same structures, gaining intelligibility from them. A law is a governing rule to which appearances submit; it is the subordinating structure in a perscriptive role. Contextualizing the appearances, it sets a limit to what can be in the future because of what has been achieved in the past. When stated in formulae, abstraction is made of the fact that the law is operative only so far as it is in fact tied to present appearances, and involves a future that is relevant to these.

A law is doubly prescriptive of appearances. It subjugates the appearances, converting them from separate units into related terms, and it relates them within a single whole in such a way that the state of one appearance is inseparable from a distinctive state of another. But a law, a mere structure, has no power of its own; it can subjugate appearances and dictate what is to be consequent on something else only because there is a power beyond it, which expresses inescapable demands on the appearances through the agency of those laws. The rationality of appearances in relation to one another provides evidence of a finality which, in the guise of a law, interrelates the appearances and makes them relevant to one another. Were there no power which governed appearances through the agency of intelligible laws, the world of appearances would lack rationality and the future would be unpredictable. The focused and the neglected would be just together, inexplicably and unintelligibly.

Because a source of final intelligibility affects men, their minds have an unlimited range. Guided by it, and adding their natures to the natures of appearances they confront, men can move closer and closer to that finality. But like all other finalities, it is too self-contained for men to be able to penetrate it completely. Of that fact they can be aware at every stage of their progress. No matter how far they penetrate, an absolute intelligibility is a goal still to be realized.

4] Appearances in the present exclude and are excluded by the past. Those that are here exclude and are excluded by those that are elsewhere. What happens here is maintained in opposition to what happens there, and in a different way. All of them, also, are extended in a common extended world. Their extensions there are to be distinguished from those characteristic of actualities, severally or together. Each actuality is privately stretched out. It has a spatial configuration, a private periodicity, and an internal dynamism. Each also is extensionally related to other actualities. It is smaller or larger than others more or less distant from it; it comes to be and passes away in relation to others earlier and later; it is affected by some and affects others. The extensions in actualities are continuous with extensions connecting them; both extensions are endlessly divisible by thought into parts which are like the extensions themselves. The extensions are universals individualized throughout; they do not, though, have real subdivisions. There is only an indivisible space, time, and dynamics which, by connecting the contributions of actualities, makes these into extended appearances in a common extended world.

Men live through private times at a pace having no necessary accord with what is happening outside; they are internally distended in the form of unitary contoured spaces; they causally interconnect distinguishable parts of themselves. Despite their private extensions, they are caught up in a common world. Through their appearances they and other actualities are subject to the structures and demands of the common extensions. They are able to remain temporally concordant with observable other men and other actualities, are able to be located in a single space, and are able to act and be acted on through the use of a single reservoir of energy, because of the subjection of their exhibitions by the exhibitions of a finality.

We all live in a common space in which we distinguish an up and a down, a front and a back, a right and a left. Everyone occupies a short-spanned time, lasting as long as a state of consciousness does. All also live in a longer time which starts at birth and which we sometimes hope never ends, and in a space that reaches beyond or at least as far as the horizon. All share too, in the space and time of a society; that time accelerates and slows, buckles and straightens as the society's interests change. None lives in a scientifically measured space or time, except so far as he can keep pace with his watch or with the movements of the heavenly bodies which his watch is calibrated to match. And all act within common causal chains to which each adds his impetus and to which each is subject.

Were it not for its punctuation, one could readily overlook or deny that the extended world of appearances was a product. The common extensions, of themselves, are placid; they make no demands of their own, but merely provide common extended domains. But they are punctuated by qualia. These also are without power; they merely occupy the extensions. Were it not for their extensions which they owe to the actualities with which they are continuous, they would be merely intensive entities instead of being, as they are, constituents of appearances inside an extended world.

What is focused on and what is set aside occur within a common space, a common time, and a common causal process. These mediate a power which precludes the focused items from being without location in relation to what had been neglected. Epistemological atomists, who acknowledge only single items, have no warrant for supposing that what they will eventually come upon will belong to the same spatiotemporal dynamic world as that which they had initially acknowledged. What has been focused on belongs, together with what is being neglected, within single extensions; there is a common constraint imposed on both by a power which is manifested through those extensions.

Were there no extensions embracing all appearances, the appearances would not be close or distant; they would not be contemporaries, or be in the relation of past to present, or present to future; and they would not be part of operative causes or effects. The focused and the neglected are extensionally joined by the power of a finality beyond them, manifested as their common context. We are acquainted with that power just so far as we are acquainted with the context. When we release what we had focused on, we face both the focused and the region embracing the neglected, in a single attitude. That attitude matches the extensional relation that in fact connects them.

There is no necessity that there be an extended world. Both actualities and appearances could have had their extensions totally internal to themselves. And in any case, the extensions of the actualities or the appearances need not have been interconnected spatially, temporally, or causally. But if there be a union of content (stemming from actualities) and of contexts (provided by final extensions), there will be punctuated extensions continuous with extensions beyond them. A common extension makes limited, extended contents necessarily connected over distances, thereby giving those contents an objectivity they otherwise would not have, and allowing entities to be located in relation to one another.

Once it be recognized that men and other actualities have extended stretches of their own, which are at once continuous with and yet different from those characteristic of the appearances of those actualities, or of the common world for which the actualities provide one of the constituents, it is possible to make philosophic sense of biography. This takes what occurs in the familiar world as the beginning of a process which leads, through the occurrences of the common world, to the beings of some of the actualities; these actualities not only make the occurrences possible, and are responsible for some of them, but reveal and betray themselves through these occurrences.

5] The focused and the neglected, we have seen, are joined in distinctive ways, through the agencies of a common inwardness, a common coordinator, a common rationale, and common extensionalized power. They are also joined as items sharing in a single unity even when they have nothing intrinsically to do with one another. Despite their distances from one another, their practical roles, their sustaining actualities, or the different other ways in which they are joined, and regardless of whether or not they have any values of their own, they are subject to a single unity which defines their worth relative to one another. Without this they would be incomparable.

The unity that encompasses different appearances has a minimal expression in the form of an aesthetic whole which gives each of the appearances an aesthetic value relative to others; there the different appearances are modified so as to be harmonized parts of it. The unity has another expression as a scale in which appearances are graded according to the degree to which they can be absorbed within the unity. At its most effective, the unity defines each appearance as an instance of itself; it then meshes with all exhibitions of actualities to produce a set of distinct, harmonized unit appearances.

A final unity, meshing with all exhibitions of actualities, is sometimes identified with the divine. Again and again men try to reach this by taking their start with the common world. Knowing that they can move to it only if that world is connected to it, some have supposed that the world was as excellent as a world could be. But, as Thomas Aquinas long ago observed, the distance between a finite created world and God allows for an endless number of finite worlds better than our own. Thomas could not adequately explain why one of those better worlds had not been created. His failure was obviously not due to a lack of philosophic ability; it was the inevitable consequence of his supposition that the world was created, for this required him to look at the universe from the standpoint of a perfect being. From that perspective there cannot be a best of all worlds. Any created world is necessarily imperfect, at an infinite distance from a supposed creating perfect God. Had any other world been produced by such a God there would still be an endless number of better worlds that could have been created instead. The problem vanishes with the rejection of the idea that the world was created.

The world is not the divine, but it does bear the marks of the divine; it does have a unity imposed on it. To move to the divine one must attend to that imposed unity. With this as a guide, it is possible, by adding oneself as subject to that unity and to other subjected unities, to achieve a beginning of a progress toward the divine as a final unity able to maximize whatever else there be.

It is possible for there to be a world in which a multiplicity of qualia failed to be fully subject to that unity. The qualia would not be units, able to be distinct from one another, but just amorphous fulgurations; they would be continuous with their respective actualities, but would not have an ability to be distinct from one another. But if there is a common world, it contains unit appearances. Each of these is given a unit status by a single unitary context to which all are subject. The result is a world of distinguished appearances.

There are three challenges that can be offered against any discourse claiming to be about a finality, and particularly unity. One we have already noted. It claims that all such discourse is bad grammar, and therefore strictly speaking, nonsense. The second is that metaphysics, or more particularly a religion concerned with unity as a divine and even personal reality, is but one of many languages, no one of which need be pursued. The third maintains that a language relating to any finality is at best quasi-fictional, and has no necessary bearing on anything outside that language. The first challenge is met with the recognition that all terms relating to finalities are transcendental terms of address. Their use is not to be compared to or tested by the use of expressions which employ different kinds of terms. The second is met with the recognition that a language, though one of many, may also have occasion to function as basic to the others. The third is met with the recognition of the symbolic character of metaphysical and religious discourse. Since a final Unity provides only one of a number of conditions, all of which are equally comprehensive and rooted in finalities, the answers to the challenges made to it also have bearing on the other finalities and the contexts these provide.

[7]

We start with an experienceable world in which we separate items off from others with which they are together in various ways. The focused and what is set aside, however, are only a limited selection from all there is; the constraints to which both are subject are applicable to all other appearances as well. Those constraints issue from beyond the common contexts. To reach this which is beyond, it is necessary to move along the route of lucidations. Unless we do this we will be unable to account for the fact that appearances are effectively united, even while we hold some of them off from the rest.

There is no necessity that contexts and qualia should have anything to do with one another, and there is, therefore, no necessity that there be a world of appearances. It is conceivable that the contexts might have no filling at all; they would then just be the finalities at their most attenuated. And it is conceivable that the actualities might not provide anything that was interconnected. The actualities, though they might affect one another, would then not exhibit themselves in the same world. These possibilities are taken to be facts by transcendentalists and empiricists. Transcendentalists deny that their finalities relate the exhibitions of actualities; consequently, they dismiss all appearances as illusions. Empiricists take all contexts to be merely human contrivances; they, therefore, are unable to affirm that the appearances of actualities are objective.

Qualia and contexts are thrust toward one another, with the consequence that the one is subject to constraints and the other is filled out with punctuating, transient material. Because of the content provided by the actualities, the contexts are able to operate; because of the contexts, the qualia are able to be connected. Together they constitute appearances distinct from the actualities and finalities which make them possible. Dehumanized, the result is the public world. This the sciences explore with the aid of well-designed apparatus, and under the guidance of well-formulated theories and hypotheses. At their best, they so understand appearances that one can explain any item in terms that are variants of those appropriate to all the others. What they claim, is most satisfactory when it is checked in encounters which had been anticipated in predictions. Their success over the centuries is astonishing. But, as was remarked, it is bought at the cost of confining interest to only some aspects of experience and to only some of the conditions to which these are subject. The sciences do not concern themselves with the question as to just what objects are in themselves, or what the contexts are which make it possible for the appearances of actualities to be together. They abstract from values, ignore what is not but ought to be, and ask no questions about their own methods, or about the familiar world they presuppose.

The familiar world of daily experience adds local, personal, and social notes to the public world. It is there that one begins investigations; it is there, in the familiar world, that all investigations end. The public world is hidden by it. And it remains hidden, except to one who has sufficiently freed himself from human qualifications to attend detachedly and impersonally to what remains.

The public world is also a topic for philosophy. Philosophy's task is to characterize this world as a whole, to analyze it into its constituents, to assess it, and see what all these imply. In the past, philosophers have been content to take that world to reflect, with more or less fidelity, the nature of actualities, their expressions, the common conditions, or a juncture of the latter two. The logic of their thinking, codified by Aristotle and extended by logicians even until the present day, externally conjoined factors, leaving them visible in and unaffected by their product. There were some— mystics, intuitionists, organicists—who firmly opposed this common trend, but their lack of precision and their inability to explain, gave them little weight in the intellectual community. Their position, nevertheless, was less vulnerable than the position of those who opted for atomic hard data, omnivorous scientific categories, or junctures of the two.

There are those who suppose that men know only dirtied or distorted versions of what is found in direct encounters, or what might be supposed to exist apart from all human involvement. They take experienced content to be subjected to relations which tell us only about our theories, interpretations, or habits. The view leads to the denial that there are cosmic laws and cosmic extensions. The relentless course of nature, and the ability to predict are then seriously jeopardized. This is a high price to pay for the privilege of reducing the conditions of the public world to the status of acts of a fallible mind.

The Kantian, unquestionably accepting the existence of a single, experienceable world, rightly insists that conditions and the content need one another, but he fails to see that the world of experience need not be at all. He supposes that the conditions for the common and public worlds are imposed on passive, dead material having no effect on the operation of those conditions, and making no difference to the result. He has no place for contingencies. Kant's "Copernican revolution" keeps everything as it had been before in the pre-Copernican days of the rationalists, merely shifting the center of gravity from data to categories, matter to form, experience to the judging mind. Both positions turn men into gods who provide the essential factors of the common and public worlds. But content depends on actualities, contexts depend on finalities, and the two come together apart from men.

[8]

It is as correct to say that one knows actualities before one knows finalities, as it is to say that one knows finalities before one knows actualities. Knowledge of both presupposes attention; knowledge of both presupposes felt controls. A lucidative intimation of a finality precedes a knowledge of it; an adumbrative intimation of an actuality precedes the knowledge of it. The realities at which one arrives have already been encountered in the form of evidences for them.

Metaphysics is the art of taking observations seriously. Among other things, it gives each reality its full weight, and gives full weight to what connects it with others. The connections between actualities are not in some separated, remote domain; they are no further away than where one particular is in fact related to others.

To reach a finality one neither adds part to part, nor produces parts from parts. Putting part alongside part yields only an aggregate; a generation of parts from parts may have no stopping point. What must be done is to trace to their sources the evidence provided by separate or joined appearances. The latter takes us first to contextualizing relations, and then to the finalities.

[9]

Actualities exhibit the import of the finalities for them, and the finalities counter that exhibition with one of their own. The result is overrun with contingency but streaked with necessity, changing and persistent, punctuated throughout yet uniform, rooted in actualities but subject to common conditions.

We know that there is content because we confront it. But whether it remains or gives way to others, it is caught in common contexts. Because of these, the appearances they help constitute are necessarily associated, coordinated, made intelligible, extensionalized in larger extensions, and subject to a single unitary control.

Each context has an indefinite range. Each operates no matter how many items there be or how these alter. Whatever the content, the contexts are uniform in their operation, because they are expressions of singular, permanent finalities, operating on all contents at the same time.

Because actualities contribute contents to the common world, the conditions governing that world cannot be as powerful as Kant took the Understanding to be, or as Hegel assumed that Reason was. Incapable of interlocking with genuine, independent, intelligible material, their Understanding and Reason had to give any knowable world all the meaning and being that it could have. By attending to these powers, Kant and Hegel therefore thought that they could know what was the case. Their worlds, after all, were just their categories somehow externalized. But because actualities contribute to the common world, it is not possible to know that world solely by attending to categories.

[10]

When it is said that the world is entirely alien, that we come to it as strangers, an emphasis is placed on contexts. These subject content to demands which do not answer to what actualities are in themselves. They are conditions, therefore, which are not pertinent to us as we know ourselves from within, to ourselves as wanting to know one another as persons, or to ourselves as existing together with other actualities, animate and inanimate, but only to presented qualia in a world of similarly presented content.

Common contexts obtain differentiation from the contents that actualities provide. They exist because finalities do, since they are those finalities at their limits. But as actually filled, those contexts are themselves appearances, roughed, cross-grained, and grounded, and lucidatively leading us into the finalities.

Though the contributions of actualities come to be and pass away, the contexts remain steadfast because they are inseparable from finalities. Yet they are able to function apart from the finalities, for they are interlocked with content. Together with the content, they constitute connected appearances, beyond which there are actualities and finalities.

Common contexts are the finalities as diminished and filled in by the contributions of actualities. Universals without power, the contexts are partial replicas of the finalities. They provide the content with undivided domains, and the content in turn provides the contexts with differentiations. As continuous with finalities, the contexts have no distinctive function. It is only as operative conditions, and thus as constituents of appearances, that they are external to their finalities, while remaining continuous with them.

Though contents are transitory and different at different times, predictions, anticipations, and planning are possible. Most things exhibit themselves monotonously, or in ways which have some bearing on what they have exhibited or will. Also, what an actuality is and does is not without effect on others, with the consequence that their exhibitions are not altogether without pertinence to one another. Lastly, men subject objective appearances to human and social limitations, thereby producing a familiar world in which the perturbations of the common world are partly compensated or overridden. And, not least, the finalities introduce constraints governing all contents in the same way.

The common world is and is not. It is, only when and so far as there are appearances; it is not, where and when there are none. Since appearances are not everywhere, the common world cannot be said to be everywhere. It is equally correct to say that the common world exists always, but is filled out only in patches. It has content here but not there, there but not here, and the "heres" and the "theres" are related, though changing all the time.

The common world has no necessary existence. Still, it cannot cease to exist as long as there are actualities and finalities. Though it is true that the actualities themselves come to be and pass away, it is also true that the passing away of one is the coming to be of others produced in the act of the passing away of the first. Empty here or there, no context is empty everywhere; the emptiness of parts of the common world is due to the failure of actualities to fill up the entire world with their exhibitions. Because there always are finalities, exhibitions of actualities, contexts are internally differentiated, but contingently.

13

~~~~~~

TRANSCENDENCE

~~~~~~

Controlling Summary: Finalities are present at all actualities, but are not noticed until one is able to wonder appreciatively. This is at the beginning of a lucidative move into the finality as it is by itself.

The more one penetrates into a finality the richer and richer is the content, the freer and purer become the lucidatives, and the greater the resistance encountered. The process has no predetermined first or last stage: wherever one begins is later than where one could have begun; wherever one ends is earlier than where one could have ended. Wherever we end can be conceptualized at the same time that we experience a pull and become aware of details not envisaged in the concept.

There are five dialectical symbolizations. These are ordered and rational, but not confined to the mind. All require a beginning with appearances at actualities and in conditions. They lead to a primary Inwardness grounding sympathetic responses, to a Being which coordinates all entities, to a Possibility which provides the basis for intelligibility, to an Existence which enables items to be in extended fields, and to a Unity which harmonizes them maximally. Various logical operations are ineffective with respect to each of these processes.

~~~~~~

Phenomena are neutral to both actualities and finalities. When an appearance biased in one direction is added to one biased in the other, the result is a mental equivalent of a phenomenon. But it is not identical with one, since it does not have an objective status as a single entity. A positioned leaf, if biased toward a leaf, has the appearance of an isolated extended leaf; if biased toward Existence, it has the appearance of a delimited leafish region. The two can be added together by us. But that will not produce a phenomenal object in an extended world of phenomena. Only an objective, balanced union of extended leaf and encompassing extension will yield a phenomenal, positioned leaf, having its own integrity.

What is attributable to actualities or to finalities are appearances. Those appearances are symbols, leading into the source of the dominant factor in them. To make use of those symbols a number of requirements must be met.

1] What men confront in the course of experience is so thoroughly dyed by social conventions, traditional practices, and personal and common needs as to make almost impossible the isolation of symbols leading into actualities or finalities. Men must detach themselves from daily concerns if they are to be able to symbolize what lies beyond these. An escape from these limitations can be deliberately sought, but most men achieve it in the ordinary course of a relaxation of attention, or when surprise, perplexity, or crises dislodge them from their accustomed ways.

2] The individual must free himself from an immersion in appearances and practical affairs; he can then be responsive to the enticements of actualities or finalities. Those enticements are always present, but they become more noticeable and effective when the individual is not attentive elsewhere.

3] Actualities and finalities act on men, attracting them toward those realities. The men respond emotionally with wonder. That wonder is initially quite complex; within it, it is possible to distinguish a *concern* for actualities and an *appreciation* of finalities. The latter is in turn divisible into strands of *openness, humility, interest, awe,* and *reverence,* each with a distinct terminus.

[2]

Appreciation has an empirical grounding in an appearance of a finality in the role of a symbol. This is possible because the appearance is supported by an actuality and, so far, is not controlled by the finality. The appearance would be swallowed up by its finality were it not that an actuality gives independent lodgement to it.

Finalities act on every actuality, turning them into bearers of appearances of those finalities. The Gods, to speak with Heraclitus, are everywhere, in the kitchen as well as in the fields, and we can start anywhere to reach them.

By joining himself with the appearance of a finality which he appreciatively accepts, a man is able to follow the guidance of that appearance into the recesses of the finality. The joining of the appreciation with the appearance of a finality produces a more complete symbol of the finality than the appearance itself provides. It is possible to miss the presence of a symbol of a finality, not only by becoming too much involved in practical affairs, or with actualities and their appearances, but by being insufficiently appreciative or, when appreciative, by not properly utilizing the symbols that actualities sustain.

Appreciation terminates in an all-enveloping presence, without evident division or a fixed and clear nature. Openness, humility, interest, awe, and reverence are basic, emotional vectors, specializing the appreciation. Each specification touches and penetrates into a distinctive finality. This is its proper object with which it can be wholly involved only so far as a man is able to free himself from an absorption in what is daily confronted.

Metaphysics would be a kind of fiction or delusion did the basic emotions specifying appreciation have no objects. But they have objects just as surely as sight and anger do. Those objects metaphysics seek to understand in a systematic intelligible account.

We sense the presence of something at the edge of what we daily confront. This environs what we daily know, surrounding it with an as yet unprobed mystery. No one is persistently aware of this, though it is always present. Nor is it perpetually dominant, or faced free from all admixture or limitation. Not everyone, consequently, is concerned with knowing if there are realities which impinge upon and stand apart from that to which one daily attends. But, also, no one is altogether unaware of something just beyond the familiar world. Inevitably each is involved in a movement toward a more intensified form of this which is beyond. The movement is experienced, lived in, and knowable. At every step of the way richer and richer content is encountered. But it is not an experience that one readily undergoes, since it takes one away from the familiar, the practical, and the palpable. Most men, therefore, are content to note occasionally that there is something awesome or sacred, and let it go at that. Others persist. They try to reach what arouses and lures them and they, therefore, tend to move further and further into it. The more they depart from their starting points, the more resistant they find their content to be. No one could ever reach a final reality as it exists in and of itself without losing himself. Nor is there a specifiable place where the movement must come to a rest. There is only an indefinite depth into which one imperceptibly passes at the same time that one loses all distinction within it or from it.

An emotional movement in depth is begun at the edge of what is daily confronted. It is accepted as that which is qualified by a transcendent power beyond our control and outside the confines of practical concerns. Strictly speaking, it is therefore not correct to say that one is interested in or is awed by this or that. Rather it should be said that this or that is accepted as being of interest or as awesome.

Beyond any assignable limit, the symbolizing appearance is more and more freed from the daily occurrences where it is first found, at the same time that it is purified by the finality. When completely purified, the symbol becomes indistinguishable from the symbolized. And since its user functions as a part of the symbol, he too becomes purified and absorbed in the symbolized, not of course as an actual man, but as a symbolizer.

The symbols accepted at the beginning, during, and at the end of a penetrative movement are less and less affected, but never wholly unaffected, by the items that initially sustained them. But because so affected, their termini can never be more than relatively transcendent, unavoidably involved with the actualities that hold the evidencing symbols apart from their evidenced sources in finalities until we arrive at the point where the sources take over to such a degree that it is not possible to hold symbols and symbolized apart.

An emotional penetration can be stopped at any point to provide a fixated, bounded, attended to, experienced terminus, inseparable from the symbolizing, evidencing, penetrative movement which it terminates. A concept of any one of these termini bounds and articulates it, thereby enabling one to reflect on it. Since an experienced terminus, referred to by a concept, is in the control of a final reality beyond that terminus, when conceptualizing an experienced terminus one is subject to a tug, and confronts details not envisaged in the concept. This result requires the rejection of a long maintained supposition that all significant terms are necessarily oriented toward the contingent and the finite. It also requires the rejection of a less well-intrenched supposition that whatever is beyond the appearances must be an actuality or like an actuality, only bigger and grander. Finalities are not to be dealt with in the same way that actualities are. So far one can be in accord with the former position. Getting rid of the limitations, characteristic of empirical terms, does not, though, produce nonsense or fictions. This would occur only if the result had to be referred to actualities or to their appearances. But there is no necessity that all terms have this orientation. The view that finalities are just actualities, absolutized or ennobled, denies that finalities are realities, distinct in kind and function, to be referred to in distinctive ways. Were one to suppose this, one could with equal propriety say that actualities were finalities relativized and limited. This way of speaking is no better or worse than the other; both deny the integrity of one or the other type of reality, and allow for the use of terms appropriate only to the preferred type.

There is no warrant for maintaining that all discourse about finalities is metaphorical, unless one can justify the supposition that only what one says of actualities is literal. Once again, the reverse could be maintained with equal warrant: what one says of finalities alone is literal, making all reference to actualities metaphorical.

Terms and discourse referring to finalities can be as literal as those referring to actualities. 'Being' is literal, and so is 'beings'. It is when terms referring to actualities and terms referring to finalities are involved with and qualified by one another that each acquires something like a metaphorical import.

Finalities are faced initially as so many different contexts which, with the exhibitions of actualities, constitute appearances. When it is said that one context makes possible contrasts amongst appearances, another gives them equal ontological weights, a third brings them together intelligibly, a fourth enables them to be related extensionally, and a fifth harmonizes them, one speaks literally of those contexts. Since the contexts are continuous with finalities, one is also able to continue speaking literally when referring to those finalities. There is no need to abandon the literalness when one goes on to deal with the finalities as affecting, orienting, ordering, adjusting to, and unifying the actualities.

An initial wonder at what there is offers evidence that there are finalities from whose position one initially approached actualities. If the wonder is pursued back to the finalities, and if one then reapproaches actualities, one once again finds them wondrous, but more than they were before. Their appearances are then faced as in more insistent contexts. Such contexts are appropriate to actualities which have a richer privacy, a greater integrity, and are more interesting, awesome, and deserving of respect than they could have been acknowledged to be before we had emotionally experienced a finality, and then returned actualities.

Contexts themselves are also initially faced in an attitude of wonder. Approaching them from the position of actualities, we wonder at their pervasive presence. If we move back to the actualities and then approach the contexts once more, these contexts will be found to be even more wondrous than they had been, because more radically diversified, despite their indivisible singularity. After an emotional experience with a context or finality, one is also able to return to the world of appearances as one who had been affected by what had been encountered. Appearances are then faced as enveloped in a new aura provided by what had been emotionally experienced.

Concepts derived from an encounter with actualities enable one to understand the determinations and reactivities of finalities. The concepts replace a wonder at those actualities by an intelligible account of the way in which the actualities make their presence finally effective in those finalities. Conversely, concepts derived from an encounter with finalities, enable one to check the correctness of one's understanding of actualities. Speculative ideas can do justice to emotionally experienced contexts and finalities, because those ideas are abstract formulations of those contexts and finalities. But to know what those ideas imply, what they include and exclude, they must be subjected to the critical scrutiny of a systematic, speculative account.

Full knowledge is wisdom when it is twofold, alert to what is and is not, here and now. It is the reward of one who floods what he daily confronts with an appreciation of finalities and a concern with actualities. While recognizing the integrity of both actualities and finalities, he takes each to be an occasion for symbolically moving into the other. The process of symbolization can be repeated. And one can sometimes add oneself to a number of symbols, thereby uniting them, and, through their aid, moving from many points into a finality or actuality. In all cases one turns from confronted entities in order to move to and into what is being evidenced there.

Nothing less than endless encounters will enable one to get to the actualities and finalities at their most intensive. But one can know then beyond any preassignable depth after they have made themselves evident in the unpredictable details and spontaneities which fill out the concepts and symbols by which they are faced and penetrated. To know this is to know that one can never know all that can be known.

[3]

The more alert we are to the independent reality of actualities, the more we are aware that our symbols of finalities were partly constituted and thereby sustained by those actualities. There is then no proper beginning for the symbolization of a finality; any stage where we begin it could have been preceded by another, where the symbol is more deeply involved in the actuality. Nor has the symbolization of a finality a proper ending. We make an end by accepting some terminus as more satisfactory than that provided before. There the symbol is more deeply involved in the finality. If we want to get to the finality itself we would have to jump outside the symbolizing process into the finality as it is in itself. But a finality is too strong and too attractive; if we could ever reach it as it is in itself, we could never return to our world.

Yet there is a sense in which we are always at the end of symbolization, for the symbol is always subject to the symbolized. When we symbolize a finality we are already involved with it and feel its influence. To be sure, previous experiences with symbolization may enable us to move more expeditiously into a finality, but there always has to be a governance by the finality if there is to be any advance into it. The movement to the finality is one with the transformation of the initial content and oneself by the terminus to be arrived at. (In Chapter 4 of *Modes of Being* [Carbondale: Southern Illinois University Press, Arcturus Books, 1968], pp. 324–27 [4.56 ff.] attention was paid to the logic which governs movements to finalities. The final step, it was said, requires the help of the desired terminus.

What in *Modes of Being* was seen to occur at the last stage of a logical process occurs in symbolism from beginning to end. Symbolically, one moves into a terminus as it stands away from the place where its influence was initially felt.)

Movements to a finality can begin with the affect of the finality on distinct actualities, or with what governs a multiplicity of them. These two main branches can be further subdivided. (In *The God We Seek* [Carbondale: Southern Illinois University Press, Arcturus Books, 1973], pp. 5–6, fifteen routes were distinguished and discussed in their bearing on a movement to God. Counterparts of these bear on the movements to the other finalities.) The movements from a multiplicity are more evident than those from single actualities, since finalities are experientially encountered in the form of common constraints on a number of actualities.

To move from a single actuality to a finality, one first attends to the way a finality's qualifications are modified by the actuality, not completely, to be sure, and then tries to get the result in a purified form.

1] Each actuality is substantial, standing away from all else as an irreducible reality. An individual with a center of its own, it is always a subject and never a predicate, as Aristotle long ago observed. Yet every actuality comes to be and passes away. The substantiality of each is maintained only for a limited time against the persistent insistence of a constant, final Substance. Each is involved in an act of subjectifying the affect of the Substance on it, but never reaches the point where it is just a subject. Its substantiality is impure, more a process toward, than the enjoyment of, a state. Its substantiality must be purified if it is to be a true substantiality. But then its substantiality will be made identical with what is final and forever.

2] Each actuality has a being, but is not identifiable with Being. Being is ultimate, that which forever is and never will not be. The being which an actuality has is held on to precariously, and then is subject to limitation by the substantiality of the actuality and by any other qualification it may have obtained from other finalities. The being which an actuality has is tainted; to have being in its purity one must move away from the limitations to which it is subject by the actuality, to it as it is by itself.

3] Every actuality has a structure, a meaning, an essence, in terms of which it can be understood. As ingredient in that actuality, the structure is overparticularized; it is the structure *of* that actuality. To know that structure as a mere intelligible unit having intelligible relations to other equally intelligible units one must free it from the articulated specifications to which the actuality subjects it. This is the move which Aristotle made in his definitions. Aristotle was content to stop with a species character—a genus united with differentia. Whether one stops there or, as I think we must, moves on to what is sheer meaning, the intelligible in and of itself, single, final, and forever, one moves from the articulated and over-specialized intelligible to that which is free from these limitations.

4] Every actuality is extended. The extension is part of it. But the extension is also continuous with an extension beyond it. The boundary which an actuality imposes on the extension which it fills out is a boundary from which the extension must be freed if it is to be extension in its full integrity, for this has no boundaries, no limits, and surely none that owe their presence to something other than itself. The acknowledgment of the extension of an actuality begins with it as subject to limitations due to the actuality. To get to the extension itself one must pull away from the actuality's modifications of it.

5] The unity of an actuality is diversified because it is involved with a plurality of entities within that actuality's confines. Those entities make their presence felt; they prevent the unity from being a mere unity; or, what is the same thing, they show that that unity is not all-powerful, not in complete control, and therefore not Unity itself, that which brooks no multiplicity. We move from the unity of an actuality to Unity itself in the effort to get from a diversified, not altogether effective unity to Unity itself, that which is the master of all that it encompasses.

All five movements to finalities take one from the impure to the pure, from the delimited to the unlimited, from the thin to the thick, from an instance to what it instances. This is similar to the movement that is required in order to go from a context or a common condition to a finality. But a common condition is initially encountered as constraining a number of actualities together; its acknowledgment is forced on one in experience when one first comes upon a number of actualities functioning together despite their independence. The move from single actualities to finalities via the presence of qualifications of the finalities lacks that experiential beginning; we do not have an experience of an actuality being qualified by intruding finalities, and modifying the result. Because the move from a plurality of conditioned actualities to a finality begins with what is obtrusive and experienceable, it seems better grounded and more acceptable than does a move which takes its start from a single actuality's modifications of the qualifications which a finality produced.

Adopted qualifications and the experience of constraints governing a number of actualities provide occasions for the acknowledgment of evidences of finalities. The evidences are the finalities in the guise of symbols of themselves. The movement to those finalities is essentially "an argument by contraction" from attenuations to the self-centered. Equally it is a form of purgation, from the impure to the pure.

[4]

Expectations are grounded in what has been learned in the past. Unless men constitute what they know, their expectations must be geared to the tendency of things to function as they had. The habits of expectation that are engendered in the course of experience reinstate the structures of the dispositions and laws which govern what is known.

The thrust of expectation is horizontal, from past to future. If its object is something which is also to be subsequently, the expectation should accord with the way this object is readied to realize certain prospects rather than others. But finalities are not future objects. We can expect to arrive at a finality at some later time, but what is then arrived at is not an object which exists just at that time, nor is it some prospect realized by finality then; it is oneself and one's symbols in a changed state because of one's changed relation to the finality. Expectation is here satisfied horizontally as the outcome of a vertical move.

It is possible to conceive of an object of expectation as a possibility at whose realization one arrives eventually in a transformed state. The horizontal expectation would then be reduced to a vertical. Conversely, one can view the vertical movement as a form of the horizontal, by supposing an independent path placed between a symbol and the symbolized which, if followed, allows one to arrive at the same outcome at which a symbolization can. But symbol and symbolized are not related by governing laws, whereas present and future occurrences are. Moreover, expectations are in consonance with an objective situation when one proceeds horizontally; in symbolization, an individual becomes part of the process by which the symbol reaches and is absorbed into its terminus. Symbolization alters the symbol; an expectation of what is to occur merely anticipates and awaits.

The absence of any habits or laws relating a symbol to a symbolized finality does not mean that we must reach a finality by a single, uncontrolled leap. This would preclude learning and improvement. We can move to the symbolized in rational, though not necessarily intellectual, formal ways. This is what happens when we are dialectical.

[5]

Over the course of centuries the term *dialectic* has been given a number of distinct applications. A core meaning refers one to a process by which items are to be rationally completed by bringing in what was initially lacking. The Platonist wants to have complete knowledge; his dialectic moves from the obscure and minor to a source which is perfectly good, and which makes all else true just so far as this is in consonance with it. The Kantian refers to an endless series of conditions which would have to be completed if one is to get to a final condition which alone would enable what is known to be objectively real in itself. Since, on his theory, he cannot do this, he takes an involvement in dialectic to offer evidence of methodological error. The Hegelian wants to complete both thought and object. He brings them closer together by supposing that what excludes, both needs and is identified with its other over a series of necessary stages. The Marxist seeks to perfect society; his dialectic operates through economic history, to provide a remedy for the incompleteness in both dominant and dominated social classes.

These meanings of dialectic point up different dimensions of it, having to do with distinctive finalities. (The following expressions in parentheses are those used in *Modes of Being*.) Kant was concerned with an ontological dialectic toward an Absolute (Actuality); Plato occupied himself with a rational dialectic toward an ultimate explanatory reality (Ideality); Marx was interested in an existential dialectic in time (Existence); and Hegel concerned himself with an absorptive dialectic of a conserving reality (God). Each ignored considerations rightly noted by the others; none could possibly reach the finalities available to those others. All, too, need to be supplemented by a dialectic geared to reach into a Substantial Inwardness which underlies all privacies. This mode of being was not distinguished in *Modes of Being*. What was there termed 'Actuality' bundled together this Substantial Inwardness and Being. The Kantian dialectic has to do with Being, but confessedly can not reach this; a different dialectic leads us to the Substantial Inwardness.

A dialectic of finalities starts with a symbol of a finality and, by means of an appreciative use of this, comes to know by entering further into the finality. It forges a concept of the content at which one stops, while lucidatively continuing beyond that point. Because the dialectic begins with a symbol and ends in the symbolized, it is self-contained, occurring solely within these limits. But it is also incomplete, for it is in fact begun and ended inside a more inclusive activity which takes some account of the actual carrier of the symbol and is alert to the presence of a finality beyond the point where one in fact arrives through symbolization.

Because it always has a presupposed prior position and a possible subsequent stage, dialectic always begins too late and ends too soon. It begins with the acceptance of a symbol, and therefore at a distance from an actuality; it is entered into at an arbitrary point, before which there could have been others. And it stops short of the finality as it is in itself, thereby leaving room for still further positions, beyond the point where one stopped, at which one could still arrive.

Though there is no necessary, specific beginning or ending to dialectic, a proper beginning is always made *at* an empirical item and *with* a symbol biased toward a finality. Dialectic, too, always goes through a number of distinguishable steps, and properly ends in a finality. Though it has no earlier beginning than at something empirical, nor any later ending than somewhere in a finality, short of the finality as it is in itself, one always can conceivably start with thinner content than one had begun with, and one always can conceivably end with richer content than one had terminated with.

We can never free the symbols of finalities from the impurities they accrete from the actualities in which they are imbedded. Symbolization, consequently, will not enable us to arrive at the finalities as they are in themselves, pure, eternal, irreducible, and independent. To understand what they are in themselves, it is necessary to give up the actual act of penetrating into the finalities, and instead speculate on what it is like for them to be completely freed from alien influences. The endeavor requires one to take up a particular position in relation to all the finalities; the finalities are then envisaged in abstraction from themselves in their full concreteness (see *Modes of Being*, chap. II). The errors that one might reasonably expect, because one has abandoned symbolization with its inevitable correction by the symbolized the more one penetrates into it, need not arise, and this for a triple reason: The systematic results can be continuations of the outcomes of symbolizations; the results can be encompassed within a single, self-critical system where each outcome supports and is supported by the others; and the categories and principles which the system justifies can ground and be tested by such basic disciplines as art, history, religion, ethics, politics, and education.

[6]

Each actuality has a distinctive privacy. Yet it is not insensitive to the presence and activity of some actualities considerably removed from it. There is a common substantial inwardness touched upon when one probes toward actualities as resonantly together. Even while remaining self-centered each is open to the influence of that substantial inwardness. But there is no precise point where one leaves individuals to be at this, even in its most available form. Nor is there ever an arrival at the substantial inwardness as it is in itself. We are always in between the place where the substantial inwardness affects the individual, and where that inwardness is entirely by itself.

To obtain a symbol for the substantial inwardness, it is necessary first to sympathetically open oneself to the effective presence of that inwardness at some item. The result is essentially one of denying the legitimacy of the ordinary use of logical law of substitution. Such a law requires that what is true of the substituted must be true of the entity for which it substituted. But in the case of symbolization of a final substance, one fails to substitute a single final privacy for a conjunction of limited individual privacies. The symbolization be-

gins at a point which could have been earlier, since there are endless
degrees of greater intrusion that could have been initially acknowledged. And it ends at a point which could have later stages, since
there are endless degrees of immersion in a final inwardness that
might still be attained. What is accepted as a beginning is not
definitive enough to be an object for a substitution; what is accepted
as an ending is not definitive enough to be a proper replacement
for that with which one began. A satisfactory substitution begins
with what is clearly marked off from others, and ends with a replacement which fully preserves the value of that which one began. But
in symbolization one begins with what in fact merges with others,
and falls short of doing all that could be done to preserve the value
of that with which one began.

A symbol used to reach the inwardness is an appearance of it.
Though it results from a meeting of the exhibition of Substance with
that of an individual, it is primarily biased toward the Substance, and
carried by the individual. To obtain the symbol, one must first confront that carrier and then, by assuming an attitude of openness,
attend not to the carrier but to the symbol that is carried. The
openness, awakened by Substance, enables the individual to contribute to and identify himself with the symbol and, therefore, to
follow it as it is pulled inward toward the Substance which made it
possible.

Structuralists have emphasized the ubiquity of the influence of
the final Substance in human affairs. It is their inclination, though,
to take 'openness' to reach to individuals or groups, rather than to be
the agency by which one makes contact with the final inwardness for
which individuals and groups provide filling and diversity. Because
they over-individualize and over-socialize it, they do not see that it
has a bearing on everything. They have made contemporaries alert
to symbols of Substance, particularly those symbols that are lodged
in men, severally and together, but have neglected those symbols that
are available everywhere else.

Humans open themselves to one another. The mother makes
contact with her child, apparently oblivious to any basic inwardness
beyond it and herself. Still, she is not altogether in disaccord with

other children and other humans. It is tempting to suppose that the mother generalizes her involvement with her child so as to become sympathetic with the others, but such a supposed generalization will tend to make her abstract from herself as well, to leave her subject to something irrelevant to herself and them. More important, her sympathies with others are as direct and sometimes even more intense than those expressed toward her child.

While sympathetic with her child, the mother is open to a reality beyond them both. Her sympathy for her child, where it is not an openness to the effect that the substantial inwardness has on the child, is an act of penetration into that child from the vantage point of the child's manifestations, displays, or expressions. These contribute to the appearance which she uses to symbolize either the final inwardness or the child. Her penetration into either makes use of the same symbol, with different emphases.

The observable content of the symbol which the mother uses is provided by the child. She responds to the child's coloring, grimace, and cry. She is able to penetrate into the Substance beyond herself and the child by attending, not to these, but to their affective relationships. It is her acceptance of these relationships that enables her to become acquainted with the final inwardness which keeps a multiplicity of diversely located appearances in accord.

[7]

Are things, animals, and men all on a footing? No answer is possible if items are dealt with in their severalty, for we then lose the possibility of having a way of comparing them. To be judged to be equally or unequally real, they must be approached from a common position outside them all. They could conceivably be compared in terms of their durations, organizations, intelligibility, usefulness, or value. But these will not tell us whether or not they are all equally real, despite their differences in duration, organization, intelligibility, use, or value.

To be is to be coordinate with other entities. That reality, which coordinates them all, is Being. Whatever is, is subject to Being to the same extent and in the same way. Different entities are equalized realities because Being coordinates them. From the position of Being, other finalities, actualities, and appearances all are. No one is more real, more a being, than any other. They do differ, and radically, but this is by virtue of other considerations. As beings they are equal. Being is too remote and too contentless to differentiate them according to type.

'Being' is the emptiest of notions, since it is devoid of all the specifications and determinations characteristic of particulars. But it is not identical with nothing. Its emptiness would reduce it to nothingness if it were without any determinations whatsoever, without any content or meaning. But it is empty only in the sense that it is not pluralized, not made determinate internally by parts opposing one another. A supposed One, beyond that Being, as well as all actualities, appearances, and other entities, would be equivalent with nothing at all. Being, though, contrasts with the beings which refer to it.

From the position of beings, Being acquires all its content from them. It is as if they were trying to produce a premiss by coming together at a common point. But the bringing together of them is an act which already presupposes that the result to be achieved has at least the role of a guiding force. It is Being that coordinates the different entities, no matter how diverse they be, no matter what their source or value, no matter how self-possessed they are, how they function, where they act. It has no effect on them, simply giving them all the same significance as beings in relation to itself, while they continue to be as they were. Being is at once the most innocuous and the most powerful of finalities.

The coordination of beings that one initially acknowledges, abstracts from the items coordinated. That abstraction has endless degrees. Whatever the degree of coordination with which one starts, there is always something of the actualities clinging to it. There could conceivably have been more, and the process of symbolization could, therefore, have been begun earlier with more concrete material. The beings, as coordinated, are already integral to Being itself. Yet Being continues to remain beyond them. No matter how far one advances in the effort to reach that which is effective in the coordination of the items with which one begins, one always has Being still beyond him. A symbolization of Being always ends too soon.

[8]

The philosophical preoccupation with knowledge, particularly when pursued into Possibility itself, has led to the identification of wonder with one strand in it, that of interest in the intelligible. We do wonder about the explanation of things. But we can also wonder about what makes them sensitively responsive to one another, what keeps them in accord, what makes them coexistent, and what gives them value in relation to one another, not to speak of the wonder which is directed at the fact that some particular thing is at all.

The interest in what is intelligible is awakened when something gets in the way of the ordinary course of daily living. This fact Dewey has made conspicuously clear. But he did not make clear that it need not preclude men interesting themselves in the intelligible for its own sake. Once men have detached themselves from daily affairs, even if it be in order to discover just how best to continue there, they are already in a position to interest themselves in Possibility itself. Their detachment allows for an acknowledgment of the effective presence of Possibility in them, and in what they confront.

When wonder attaches itself to the linkages that connect the natures of what is before us, we are at the periphery of Possibility. Natures and their linkages are all affected by the actualities and the situation in which they are. Wherever we enter into the domain of Possibility has possible earlier stages which are more affected by the actualities and the situations than that stage at which we began. When we end our probe into Possibility, we end with natures and linkages not yet entirely uniform with one another. That the linkages could have had other natures as terms, that the natures could have had other kinds of linkages, and that wherever we end the linkages are always more general than the natures they connect, means that we never come to the last stage in our effort to reach Possibility itself.

Any isolated nature has a more specific one which entails it, and from which it can be derived. This, for a double reason. Every nature is a universal indeterminate, and capable of being embodied in many different actualities. It is too general to be restricted to only one particular item. And it is the logical consequence of other universals, more specific than itself, which in turn are consequences of still other universals, back and back without end. As together with all the rest, they defy the law of excluded middle, for what is general is neither this determinate x nor its opposite.

The nature of an actuality is a meaning. When this is distinguished, together with others, in an interconnected intelligible whole, what is left over is not intrinsically unintelligible. What is left over is a source of logically deducible and particular unpredictable consequences. It is an actuality, that which they together help explicate.

The nature of an actuality is no idle adjective, but the actuality itself connected with others in an intelligible way. The natures to which we initially attend are only part of all the meanings there are. But, also, no nature is so inclusive, so final, that no more comprehensive universal is entailed by it. We can, of course, imagine a final tautological consequence of universals, produced by disjoining them all in oppositioned sets, but this consequence does not express a nature.

Distinguished natures constitute a logical chain in which there is neither beginning nor ending. Whatever the nature be with which one begins, there are others from which it follows; whatever the nature be at which one ends, there are others which follow on it. Wherever we are in the chain is a place that has further items linked to it.

[9]

Existence is spatial, temporal, and dynamic. These three types of extension are divisible into smaller, similar extensions. Actualities occupy some of those subdivisions. Those subdivisions, nevertheless, continue to be integral, undistinguished parts of single total extensions. The demarcation of a portion of extension by an actuality occurs at the same time that the extension is kept continuous with the rest of the extension. As separate, the extensions are biased toward actualities; as continuous with one another, related geometrically, serially, and causally, they are parts of symbols of Existence. Existence is symbolized by taking account of the fact that the extensions attributed to different actualities are in fact indissolubly together.

By itself space is spatiality, an abstract stretch without definite structure. One part of it is like every other part. It could never be imposed on unextended content and still yield the variegated hills and valleys, swirls and planes that characterize the world. By itself, time is a mere monotonous sequence of uniform moments, having no bearing on what realities do, undergo, or are. Imposed on nontemporal entities it would produce a single homogeneous whole, arbitrarily punctuated. And causality, by itself, is only an unbroken dynamism, without a purchase on anything that might act or be acted on. The common world has a more variegated space, time, and causality than could be achieved by the imposition of space, time, and causality on nonextended entities.

To reach the source of all-encompassing extensions, one begins at some actuality and moves dialectically toward Existence itself. Any point where we begin the dialectic is an extended region which could conceivably have been more intensive and smaller in magnitude; any point at which we might leave it, is an extended region beyond which there are still further regions, more intimately involved with Existence. We could conceivably have entered the dialectic from the position of more limited extensions, more intimately involved with actualities than is the case with the extension with which we in fact begin; we could conceivably have ended the dialectic at extensions more indissolubly one, and more deeply sunk in Existence than those with which we in fact end.

We enter the dialectic through the avenue of distinguished extensions. We end it when we have made those extensions sufficiently part of single existent extensions to satisfy our curiosity or our desires. But we will not then have begun with pure extensions, nor will we have succeeded in bringing the distinguished extensions wholly inside larger, more firmly grounded ones. Each distinguished

extension will continue to be related to actualities and will, therefore, never be entirely caught within a final Existence. Each distinguished extension is continuous with extensions beyond it and
cannot be maintained apart from it. Existence and its distinguishable
subdivisions preclude the operation of the law of identity with its
demand that each thing be what it is and not anything else.

[10]

For many men, there is only one possible end of speculation or
symbolization. They proceed to that end uncritically, supposing that
they neither begin nor stop at arbitrary points. They begin at a
position for which there can be, they think, no conceivable or useful
earlier position—a sacred object, a revelation, a miracle, an inspired
book, a relic, a sacrament, an outstanding occurrence, or an unusual
man—and, through a religious act, end with what they take to be
the only finality. They are interested in transcendence, but only so
far as it provides a means for arriving at a God, often said to be
unconceptualizable. He, they hold, alone is the proper end of any
move away from actualities.

God is distinct from all actualities and from all other finalities.
The evidences for Him are as sound and as available—though not
more so—as those pointing to the other finalities. The great interest
men have shown in proofs of His existence, and the strong tempta-
tion to place Unity (a less loaded but metaphysically equivalent
term) above all other finalities makes it desirable, however, to give
more attention to the evidence for it and to its associated problems
than has been given to the other finalities.

A God who is everywhere can obviously be arrived at not only
from a position endorsed by some religion but from any other position as well. That fact has been tacitly recognized in part in two of
the traditional arguments advanced by philosophers to prove the
existence of God. They note that one might start the proof with
the acknowledgment of any item, without making reference to the
religious value it might have. That item, if taken to be good or
desirable, is used to provide a beginning of a 'teleological' argument;

if the assumption is abandoned, and a start is made with any item simply as an existent, the item is used to provide a beginning of a 'cosmological' argument for God.

Those who make a teleological beginning for a move to God assert that there is some order, design, purpose, or meaning in the world, as a whole or in some special part, such as humankind, which could not be accounted for except by making reference to an intelligent or well-intentioned source of it. But it is questionable whether any order, no matter how strange or noble, ever requires a reference to a source outside the universe. What warrant is there for supposing that whatever intelligibility or goodness there be owes its presence to God? And should one not, then, with equal justification, attribute the disorder and evil that is also present to the act or existence of an anti-God? But even if it were granted that intelligibility or goodness depends for its presence or operation on some transcendent power, it is not necessary to conclude that power itself is intelligent, purposive, or interested in men and their affairs.

It is wiser to begin with what is more evident, and to proceed more cautiously than do those who take a teleological approach. This is done by adopting the second alternative. The 'cosmological' argument or proof of God starts from any existent or set of existents whatsoever, good or bad, ordered or disordered, separate or together. The argument, then, by a process of remotion, goes back to a supposed aboriginal source beyond which there can be nothing. The outlines of this approach were sketched by Plato and Aristotle; it is accepted by such great theologian-philosophers as Thomas Aquinas, as well as by others who have no religious affiliations or interests. They take as an absolute beginning the presence or existence of something, and maintain that it need not have been. One could conceive of it, they remark, as not being at all; there is no logical contradiction in supposing that it not be. No occurrence or object seems to have been always. But even if it had always been, it could conceivably not have been, and conceivably might not always be.

Some of the defenders of the argument deny that there can be an infinite number of intermediaries between what is accepted as a beginning and the God with which they would end. But this is exactly what one should expect since the beginning is finite and the God is infinite. Of course, if there were an infinite number of inter-mediaries through which one had to pass, one could not arrive at their God, for one would not have time enough to pass through all of them.

Were there no intermediaries at all, one would have to take but a single step from the finite beginning to the final God. In a single move one would cover an infinite distance. But that is an act pos-sible only to God Himself, the supposed infinite being, or to whatever He empowers. Evidently, if we are to prove the existence of God without His help, at least one intermediary must be allowed between our beginning and our hoped-for end. That intermediary, since it is not the necessary being to be arrived at finally, must be a contingent reality, though one that is unlike the contingent reality with which one began. Where the latter is an empirical object, the former is something beyond it, perhaps a condition for it, but in any case transcending it. But then it is either in some intermediate domain between the initial item and God, or it is already in the domain of the divine. If it be in some intermediate domain, it will not bring one to God, but will have to be supplemented by a move to God Himself or, once again, by a move to something within His domain. To go from the finite to God we must make use of an intermediary distinct from both. But this is the unity of an actuality as under the governance of Unity itself. To see this most readily it is necessary to clarify the nature of the unities characteristic of complexities of any kind.

Every complexity in this world has a unity encompassing a multiplicity of entities. Whatever ultimate particles there be are grouped together within distinctive unities characteristic of particular complexities. When the particles are considered apart from the com-plexes, they are all grouped together within the compass of a single unitary, natural world studied in cosmological physics.

No unity in this world is ever pure. Four cases are worth distin-guishing: variables, kinds, natures, and conditions. Each is diversified by the items it includes. The first is articulated by a disjunction of those items; the second is filled out by a conjunction of them; the third is sustained by their interplay; and the fourth is combined with them. The first yields an aggregate, the second a whole, the third a living being, and the fourth a human. The fourth allows a place for the third, the third for the second, and the second for the first.

Because of the diversity which infects it, no one of these unities can be a pure unity, Unity itself. In each case, the unity is affected by the plurality; in the first by articulating members; in the second by sustaining parts; in the third by a filling; and in the fourth by possessions. The result in each case is a unit within which the unity is one factor.

No unity is Unity itself, precisely because it is diversified; but because each unity is inseparable from Unity itself, it is prevented from being completely possessed by what it encompasses. Freed from Unity, it would not be able to have the status of a unity *for* a plurality; freed from the plurality, it would be indistinguishable from Unity itself, no longer a unity *of* a unit. Because each unity is involved with a plurality, it is possible to acknowledge the presence of the unity; because each unity is inseparable from Unity itself, each offers evidence of that Unity. As the one it is oriented away from but held on to by Unity; as the other it is held away from Unity by the plurality, but is at the periphery of Unity itself.

The evidence that there is a Unity in itself is given by any diversified unity. The diversity allows it to *be* evidence; the unity allows it to evidence Unity itself, a unity undiversified. To move from the evidence to Unity, one must free the particular unity from all reference to what diversifies it. That freeing occurs in the process of a symbolization of the Unity.

The unity of each actuality is other *than* Unity itself. Aggregates are logical others of Unity; wholes are its localized others; animals are its vitalized others. Men, because they accept their unities and make them integral to their beings as well as to their substances, existence, and natures, are, in addition, others *for* Unity. What is not human holds on to a unity which it has not made its own, leaving it with a generality that prevents the actuality from standing in itself in opposition to other similar items. Two pigs are equally pigs with distinctive lives, but two men are not only two distinctive living men, but are in themselves others for one another, as unities as well as multiplicities. Men are unique others of Unity, but the non-human are only limited specializations of the unity which they share. Each man *is* a distinctive diversified unity; each non-human *has* only a shared unity for which it provides a diversification. Men, as a consequence, are themselves evidences of Unity; the others merely enable evidence of Unity to be sustained as a qualification, or (in the case of higher animals) as an aspect of a substantial reality which has not yet attained the state of standing in radical contrast with Being.

All actualities are other than one another; each is a term in a relation of separation. Since there are different actualities at different times, each is a term which varies in content and referents. Man, in addition, because he incorporates his unity, makes himself into an other for whatever else there be. He is so far like Unity itself, for this too is an other for all else. No matter what there be, both stand away from it; the coming and going, changes and movements of anything else make no difference to a man's or to God's identity. But whereas Unity is intrinsically other for, a man must achieve that status by a utilization of the unity that qualifies him. The movement from man to Unity, consequently, is a movement from a unity for, which is intrinsically diversified, to a unity for, which is completely self-contained.

Unity is that finality in which all content finds a place. There the law of contradiction lacks application, for there all entities are merged together. As Peirce observed, such a failure of the law of contradiction is characteristic of the vague. Logically, Unity is the vague. All else, from its perspective, is but an integral part of it which can be held apart from it only by what is outside Unity.

Each actuality has a unity. One can move from that unity—and not only from the unity of an actual man—back to Unity itself. Each unity evidences Unity because, though it lacks power of its own, it nevertheless carries sufficient power to impose a single limit on the extent and (in the case of living beings) functioning of the plurality which it encompasses. The tracing back of that imposed unitary power to Unity is a movement to what has a power of its own, Unity by itself.

By taking account of the presence of unities in a plurality of actualities, it is also possible to symbolize the intrinsically undivided unity, Unity in itself. A plurality of unities is unity in a state of self-discrepancy. Each is a one, but each lacks the essence of Unity, since that would require it alone to be one. The movement from a plurality of ones, which deny to one another the status of being unity without restriction, is a movement to Unity as brooking no divisions.

The argument from a diversified unity or from a plurality of unities to Unity itself is an 'argument by contraction'. Strictly speaking, it is not cosmological, because it does not begin with this world or anything in it, though there is where one must look to obtain the evidence that is used. It is not teleological, for it does not claim that the unities with which one starts are desirable, though it is alert to the controlling presence of the finality one is seeking to reach. Nor is it ontological, for it does not argue from essence to existence, though it does remain within the orbit of the reality it is seeking to make evident. It is an argument to a correlate, an argument from a fragment or a dispersion to a single origin, from periphery to center, the impure to the pure.

The limited power of unification, to which particular actualities are subject is the correlate of limited powers to substantialize, orient, structure, and extensionalize those actualities, as well. And the limited power of unification, to which all the actualities are together subject, is the correlate of limited powers to make them affiliate, to be on a footing, to be law-abiding, and be in the same space, time, and process of causality. These limited powers, too, provide evidences which lead, by a purgational contraction, to the sources of those evidences—finalities correlate with Unity itself.

The contention might be opposed on six grounds. Attending, for simplicity's sake, only to the problem of unity, one might claim a) that no actualities have unities; b) that there is no power exerted on what the unities encompass; c) that the power is not a unifier; d) that the unities themselves are the sources of the power of unification; e) that the tracing back of the empowered unities does not lead to Unity; and f) that Unity is the only finality.

a) If actualities did not have unities, they would not be single entities, but solely multiplicities. But multiplicities are distinct from one another. At the very least, they fall into distinct sets, each having a unity of its own. This set of three objects is one set; that set of three is another.

b) If there were no power exerted on the pluralities encompassed by unities, there would be only aggregated sets, and no localized things, no living beings, and no men. Not only are the items in each plurality together in contrast with and in opposition to other items, but the way they function together is partly dependent on the kind of entity in which they are and, therefore, on the kind of unity that encompasses them. The way men act partly determines where their molecules and other subordinate entities are; fish subject theirs to a different career.

c) The power which is exhibited through a particular unity does not affiliate, coordinate, structure, or locate; it keeps a plurality of subordinate items together, makes it a one. The power may be minimal, as in an aggregated set, which encompasses the members within a unity that can be defined as the disjunctive totality of their diverse natures. The items there are together, due to the act of a mind; but the unity that supervenes has a nature, transmits a power, and goes through a career outside of that mind, allowing one to compare the set with others, and to subject it to various mathematical and logical operations. The unity of a set governs the members of the set as surely as the unities of other complex entities govern their pluralities.

d) One could suppose that the unities of different actualities had quanta powers that were sufficient to control, but were not enough to enable them to absorb the pluralities within their confines. When an individual died, or more sharply, when an entire type was no longer in existence, one would then have to suppose that the unities continued to be, but were somehow unable to get a grip on any plurality. They would self-contradictorily be impotent powers, or would have inexplicably lost their powers. In either case, one would have supposed that there was a multiplicity of idle unities for which no evidence could be found. If it be said, instead, that something in a complexity empowers a unity, or at least enables the unity to be effective with respect to a plurality, one would not only once again have given up the supposition that a unity itself produced the power controlling the encompassed plurality, but would have to suppose that there is something in aggregates, in things, and the lower living beings which could somehow make use of the unities. This would turn them into variants of the higher living, or of men.

e) Every unity is diversified and opposed by other unities. For a double reason, therefore, it cannot be identified with Unity, the undiversified and absolutely single, allowing no second. Since the power that is exhibited in each complex entity is a unifier, the source of it must be strong enough to enable a unity to control a plurality but not strong enough to enable it to absorb the plurality or even to deny it considerable independence. The resistance which a plurality presents to a unity is effective—the rate at which the unified entities will fall, for example, is dictated by the items in the plurality, not by the unity—because the unity is both imposed on it and held away from it. That unity exhibits only part of the power that a unity could. The tracing back of the exhibited power to a source of it, is a tracing back to what is purer, more self-contained, Unity itself.

It is conceivable that the power of the unity of an aggregate might be given to it by the mind that conceives it. But that mind itself will have its power traceable back to the unity of man, and eventually to Unity itself. In any case, its operation is not a prerequisite for the existence of living beings. These not only exist apart from minds, with unities of their own, but their unities exert a power on the encompassed pluralities, no matter what one thinks.

f) Unity allows for no other Unities. But it does not preclude other finalities—Being, for example. Unity is a being because of Being and, in turn, Being has a unity because of Unity. Each is at once that to which everything, including other finalities, is subject, and is subject to all the other finalities.

If the items making up a plurality did not resist a unity, the actions of the complex actuality, embracing both the unity and the plurality, would not be conditioned by their number, nature, and functioning. If a unity was not imposed on a plurality, there would be no unified complex objects, but just a copresence of independent items. If a unity was not endowed with power by a more powerful

Unity, it would, if it were not impotent, be an idle unknown power when not encompassing a plurality.

A unifying power varies in accord with the need to have a unity be in consonance with an independent plurality of items. Because the unifying power is imposed on a plurality, that plurality can be part of a single complexity; because a unifying power is imposed through a unity and is not native to it, a particular type of unity can cease to be operative with the passing of a particular type of actuality.

Atomists give pluralities too much power; rationalists give them too little; monists do not allow unities to stand apart from Unity; Platonists endow each unity with a power of its own. Each view puts a needed brake on the excesses of the others; the result allows for the acknowledgment of complexities where unities transmit powers which are partly resisted by a plurality of entities, each with a power of its own.

Whether we start with the unity of a man, with the unity of some other actuality, or with a plurality of unities, we make use of a symbol leading to Unity. The proper use of that symbol requires the assumption of an attitude of reverence toward Unity. When, because of that attitude, Unity is identified with God, the symbol is accepted as sacred. The sacred is the unity of an actuality so far as this is governed by and is continuous with God.

The sacred is so potent that it transforms whatever confronts it. But it is not accepted as sacred except by those who are reverential, and thus who are themselves sacralized. Totems and their objects are sacred only for those who have already acquired the proper spirit from the final Unity to which they are referred with reverence. Some religious symbols though seem to be effective, at least in a destructive way, when one comes to them in a profane spirit. The Bible tells the story of Uzzah, a truck driver who was transporting the Torah; in the attempt to stop it from falling, he touched it, and was immediately struck dead by God. Apparently, he who comes with the wrong attitude to a work, qualified by the divine, dislocates it, and is therefore injured by it. A secular symbol has no such power, though it, too, moves by an emotionally sustained intensification from exterior to interior, surface to depth.

Each entity is internally harmonious to the extent that it is valuable, and is internally discrepant so far as it is evil; each, as a unity, is within Unity, together with the others, with the least amount of loss. In unity all are merged with one another; items otherwise incompatible are there reconciled maximally, for Unity mutes them to make them all compatible, preserving what is internally harmonious, and overcoming what is internally in disaccord.

When an individual symbolizes Unity, he takes his stand with Unity, where he is together with whatever unities he might encounter. From the position of Unity he is distinct from it, and so is what he encounters. But as symbolizing Unity, a man and what he encounters are identified by Unity as belonging to it. Both are part of it, due to its acceptance of them. There is no proper beginning for the movement to Unity, because no unity is just a unity, unaffected by the rest of an actuality; one could have begun earlier with a more concrete unity. But there is no proper end either, because no totality of unities is equal to the entire final Unity. One is caught up in the Unity but is never identical with it; there is always more of it not yet reached.

[11]

In symbolization, because the outcome is present from the start, though in an indeterminate form, there is verification and confrontation at every stage and moment. And because symbolization moves toward what is its source, something is learned through symbolization which could not be known before the process of symbolization was carried out. It is this fact about symbolization which apparently led Plato to say that philosophy is not to be written. Writing it fixates it, places the terms all on a plane where, though read one after the other, they stand alongside one another. In symbolization one moves away from that plane, in depth.

The vocabulary and the grammar of philosophy are not unusual, though some of its terms are used in technical ways, and others are more precise than is necessary for ordinary use. When a reference is made to Substance, eternity, space, God, Being, and the like, the meaning is conveyed in speaking the language, rather than in what is encountered on the printed page. Written discourse is a condensed line which different individuals break up in distinctive ways to allow them all to arrive at the same end result. Their speaking is a penetration, and inevitably involves the symbolic use of words, a fact which we make evident in attention, actions, and other accompaniments of speech.

A symbolization of either actualities or finalities comes to an end short of these realities in themselves. The greater the penetration the greater the resistance to a further advance. At last one comes to a position where no further advance can be made with the symbols with which one began. It is then possible to form a concept of the situation in which one finds oneself. When we think of what it is into which we penetrate it is such concepts that we use.

We come to know what it is at which we symbolically arrive by formulating a concept of what it is. The concept of a reality, because it is an abstract rendering at which a symbol arrives, provides material which can be communicated. Philosophical words refer to the objects of such concepts and therefore to penetrated realities. They are *totalizing* terms, if they apply to actualities, and *global* if they apply to finalities. Neither type can convey all the richness of the content at which the penetration stops. 'Privacy', 'being', 'essence', 'extension', 'unity', as well as 'truth', 'goodness', 'value', 'beauty', are totalizing terms. 'Substance', 'Being', 'Possibility', 'Meaning', 'Existence', 'God', as well as 'Finality', and 'Unity', are global terms.

Totalizing terms fall short of the actualities they are intended to deal with in not referring to anything beyond the point the concepts do. But we discern something of the actualities beyond that point. Each actuality insists, resists, recedes. As a consequence, on using a concept or a totalizing term we are driven to use it again, or to form another in order to deal with what had not yet been reached. The repeated or new concept and the repeated or new term have defects similar to the old. In the effort to deal with the actuality, we will be tempted to try to add concept to concept, term to term, endlessly. But totalizing terms, used together with symbolization, terminate at content beyond which other content is discerned. To say of a symbolized individual that it is substantial, a being, intelligible, existent, or a unity, is to face that individual as fecund, a source of further conceptualizable content about which we can speak, as we had before, but with more feeling.

Global terms are proper names of finalities, attaching themselves to the finalities they name. They, too, stop short of the position at which symbolization ends. Used together with a symbolization, they, too, are filled out with freely produced content, not acknowledged in the use of the terms. They address the finality, but await its answer. 'Substance', 'Being', 'Meaning', 'Existence', 'Unity', are proper names of what is conceptualized of a finality into which we have partly entered. Because they are global terms of address, they invite supplementation by the finality. When we use them, we are always aware of more than what we have conceived or said.

A trace of this use is to be found in the ordinary use of proper names. "Tom Brown" does not refer simply to what is indicated, nor simply to an individual as present here and now, or as appearing in just this or that guise. It makes a general reference to a man who gives concrete meaning to the name, usually with an unpredictability beyond the anticipatory reach of any logic or use of terms. It is prehensile, referring to him as one who stands beyond it as a source of acts, details, meanings. The name is, therefore, not to be reduced to the status of an ordinary noun, nor replaced by a description. A common noun refers to what we mean to describe; descriptions purport to tell about what is encountered. But a proper name tells us that we await content from a source beyond our terms and our ideas, and towards which we are probing by means of symbols.

From Tom Brown we await supplements to what is referred to by his name or by such totalizing general terms as 'substance', or 'person', whereas in the case of finalities, what we await are supplements to what is referred to by such unique global terms of address as 'Existence', and 'God'.

14

~~~~~~

THE COSMOS

~~~~~~

Controlling Summary: Actualities and finalities affect one another to produce a law-abiding cosmos. That cosmos is not experienced, and is forever incomplete because the actualities and finalities continue to remain outside it. Each benefits the other by qualifying it. Actualities differ in status depending on whether, in addition to their ability to internalize the qualifications of a final Substance or Inwardness, they can internalize the qualifications of Being, Possibility, Existence, and Unity. Only man is able to internalize them all; physical things can internalize only the Inwardness; plants, internalize Possibility as well; the lower living beings also internalize Being; the higher living beings add an internalization of Existence. Apart from the internalizations, all are interconnected cosmically, where they function as units governed by prescriptive laws.

~~~~~~

Actualities make a difference to finalities. Since the actualities are diverse, act in independence of one another, and have little power, they impose only minor qualifications on the finalities. Those qualifications need to be altered on being internalized, in order to become integral to those finalities.

Because actualities and finalities internalize the qualifications to which they are subject, and because what they internalize they bring into play in relationship to one another, they fit one another, the one

292

in the form of units, the other in the form of laws. But at their limits they offer filling on the one side, and contexts on the other. Together these constitute the empirically available appearances.

Actualities and finalities also directly affect one another to produce a single, cosmic plurality of interrelated units. The result is distinct from the world of appearances, though this too is dependent for its existence on the functioning of actualities and finalities in relation to one another. While appearances are constituted of content provided by actualities and by contexts provided by finalities, in the cosmos, units and relations are joined together by actualities and finalities in active interplay. The appearances are experienceable, but the cosmic items are not. We encounter appearances, but we can know the cosmos only by understanding what is entailed by the active interinvolvement of actualities and finalities.

Because the different finalities function together, the cosmos contains actualities governed by a number of types of relations. The world of appearances contains contents which are diversely contextualized. An actual man is a unit in a law-abiding cosmos at the same time that he is contextualized.

[2]

An actuality limits all others, actively and passively, both where it now is and where they are. The others, by intruding on it, actively qualify it, subjecting it to their demands. Were the other actualities absent, the actuality would lose those features which it owes to their presence—its weight, visible color, pliability. It also would explode. But the resulting fragments would then limit one another.

No actuality is strong enough to overcome all the others; each is imperfect, with only a limited range and power. The cosmos of transient, law-abiding, finite units which the actualities constitute in interaction with finalities is imperfect in another way as well, because the actualities in themselves, and the finalities, too, continue to be outside it, making it be less than all that is real.

While remaining finite and incomplete, some realities, men, can attain a completeness not possible to other actualities, for they can adopt the positions of others as their own. When a man speaks a natural language, holds himself responsible, claims to express a truth, summarizes history in custom and ritual, or lays down rules or laws, he functions as a representative of other men. But it is not enough to represent men alone. Only if he can grasp the nature of all realities, and exhibit this in a communicable mastery, can he be as broadly representative as a man need be. But he will then not yet be in control of the others, or benefit them maximally. Nor will he necessarily gain anything from them. To be completed he has to carry out what he intends. He must act. And he needs to be rewarded by acts which benefit him in return.

In an ideal community of inquirers, each discovers and asserts on behalf of all; there each accepts, sustains, and enhances what the rest claim and achieve. Were such a community to embrace all mankind, and were it to be backed by cooperative enterprises in which each acts in the light of what others are, do, have done, will do, and ought to be, and in such a way as to benefit them maximally, we would have a civilized world of men at their best. But that world would still be only a fragment of what there is; outside it there would still be a multitude of objects, not only not well represented or controlled, but incapable of acting properly all the time in return. More important, every object there would be subject to controls, to the very degree it was part of that world. Actualities are together in the cosmos, not as they are in themselves, but as units subject to laws.

Each actuality also has a privacy, maintained against the rest of the world. Most men recognize that they exist by themselves, apart from all else, secret, inaccessible, selfsame. They speak of being self-conscious and reflective, of not having altogether manifested themselves in public. Since they are unable to speak satisfactorily of their private side in any other terms but those used in public discourse, and therefore in terms which are inadequate to themselves as unique and forever secret, an occasional philosopher will raise a doubt as to whether there is any privacy. Some maintain that it is nothing but a mere logical point from which one sets out but to which no one can return. All the while the rest of men think of themselves as not fully manifest, not only at some particular time, but over the entire span of their existence. They take themselves to be responsible for what they did years before; they make promises, sometimes just to themselves, to be fulfilled years later; they insist on their uniqueness; they criticize and discipline themselves; they take a stand at a center to which all they do is to be referred for origin, explanation, and responsibility.

Much in this common contention requires analysis and sorting. But there is enough sense in it to permit one to say that a denial of privacy to man is a confession of the inadequacy of one's understanding of oneself and other humans. Even a child knows that it cannot meet itself coming toward itself, that it feels pains and pleasures all its own, that it thinks its own thoughts, persists in its own intent, and remembers what no one else observed. Why deny that this is so? The child, to be sure, is incapable of stating how it knows these; it cannot tell us why it is so sure of them, or exactly what it is maintaining when it insists on them. But we need not remain with its incapacity to explain.

The contention that a man has a privacy cannot be just dismissed. It makes sense to treat it at least as a question worthy of a philosopher. But many thinkers would hesitate to go this far with animals. Animals seem to have no power of reflection; they assume no responsibility; they do not criticize themselves; they do not discipline themselves; they do not have secrets. Great progress has been made in our understanding of animals, a progress certified by sound predictions, illuminating theories, and fine training programs based on experiments which relate the public features or acts of animals to one another; but these make no reference to any center, and surely none to what is beyond the reach of any scientific inquiry. And, of course, we can never know if an animal has a privacy by consulting it. The best we can do is to infer from man's privacy, and from the continuity of the organized world, that animals have a privacy too, unless we can show—as I think we can—that all actualities must have privacies.

Most westerners think it ridiculous to say that an inanimate being has a nonpublic side. Here the common man joins with the leading thinkers; only a primitive, a superstitious man, an anthropomorphizing one, they think, would credit an inanimate thing with a privacy. Things are known to us only as they appear, or as they function in relation to one another or to ourselves. The view that there is no other way for them to be gains considerable strength when we attend to some of the cleverer contrivances which men have made. Automobiles, airplanes, and computers are assembled, and yet they function as single entities. Still, strictly speaking, the assembled is only an aggregate of parts; there is no genuine individuality to it; no inner nature which it exhibits. But its components, or at the very least, the smallest of entities which are components of everything—positrons, electrons, molecules, chemical elements, or whatever—must be something in themselves, if there is something to be joined without itself first having to be put together out of something else.

No matter how small the ultimate particles are, they are complex in the sense that they are extended and, therefore, have distinguishable portions external to one another. They will, nevertheless, have to have privacies of their own in order to be able to keep themselves in opposition to other realities alongside or encompassing them. We cannot avoid the acknowledgement of privacy even to a thing, and consequently, to every actuality, without denying them an ability to be, and therefore to provide substantial, indispensable terms for relations.

By itself, each actuality—thing, animal, or man—is through and through unique; it needs to interplay with a final Inwardness if it is to be part of one cosmos with others. That final Inwardness is substantial, individual. It affects all actualities, and so far is an Inwardness that universalizes itself. Each actuality is qualified by that Inwardness and is thereby able to resonate to others. But each internalizes the qualification differently, giving the final Inwardness a distinctive import.

In considerable accord with the traditions of both the East and the West, the final Inwardness can be termed divine, for God, too, is a reality all internal, without surface, present everywhere, imposing qualifications on all actualities, and, with them, constituting appearances. But, though they have these common traits, God and the Inwardness are distinct finalities. God is a final Unity to which every unity belongs; the Inwardness is a final Substance which maintains itself in opposition to every individual substance.

By internalizing the qualifications that Substance imposes on them, actualities make themselves into individuals which oppose while they instance that Substance. They interplay with the Substance in a cosmos. Men sometimes speak of that cosmos as though it were governed by a world-soul or spirit. But there is no reason to suppose that there is any consciousness, life, purpose, to the cosmos or to the Substance. All that the facts vouchsafe is that the Substance governs the actualities with which it interplays to constitute a cosmos in which each actuality maintains its integrity while it is immediately responsive to others, some of which are at a considerable distance from it.

[3]

Only Being is, said Parmenides. What is other than this is not. He is right. From the position of Being all is being—except the resistances which it suffers and which cannot then be understood. But from a position outside of Being, from the position of other finalities, or from the position of actualities, that Being is itself merely a limit, that toward which they all are oriented.

The idea of Being is the richest of all ideas, expressing what is present everywhere. It is also the emptiest of ideas, lacking as it does all internal differentiation. The identification of Being with nothing simply repeats the fact that Being lacks the determinate features which characterize other realities. But since Being abides, acts, is acted on, and has an individuality inseparable from its universality, it is forever what is not nothing.

An actuality is something in itself, a reality independent of all else at the same time that it is related to them; otherwise it could not be qualified or acted on; nor could it act, defy, and maintain itself. It always is qualified by Being. The envisagement of an actuality, as untouched by Being, is an exercise of the imagination, involving the subtraction of a necessary factor in the cosmological scene. There never was a time when the actuality was in that state. By itself, freed from all connection with Being, it would be sunk into itself. It and its expressions could indifferently be said to be or not to be, for their beings then would consist in their vanishing and their vanishing would consist in their coming together to constitute something that is. Each would be just a turbulence manifesting itself in a multiplicity of expressions at the same time that it was engaged in a process of pulling them all into itself.

Each actuality is a being, but no one of them is Being itself. Together with other beings, it is related to Being; this makes the actuality be on a footing with all the others. Because they have beings but are not Being, they can act, but can not abide forever. Being provides each of them with the same degree of being. But only some actualities are able to internalize the beings that they have in relation to Being, and therefore to be self-enclosed beings. This result is not within the capacity of physical things or of the lowest forms of living beings to achieve. But since each provides a beginning of a lucidation leading into Being, each can function as a symbol for Being. It takes a man, though, to use the symbol. This he does by adding his own internalized being to it, as the first step in a process of following the lead of the lucidation beginning at that symbol.

Because of Being, the cosmic union of beings and Being has a persistence to it. There is stability in the way in which an actuality is at once affected by and affects Being; it interacts with Being as an independent unit or as a member of a collection of units, in a constant way. But because the actualities that are available for a union with Being are different at different times, and because some actualities, by internalizing the beings they have because of Being are thereby altered, the cosmos is always changing in content.

Were the cosmos to consist solely of Being and beings, it would not yet be like Leibniz's universe, with monads which are open to and controlled by a final, primal Being. The cosmos is the scene of their interaction. And there other finalities also interplay with actualities. A cosmos of beings interacting only with Being is an abstraction from the cosmos as it is in fact.

[4]

No actuality by itself is fully intelligible, and this for a number of reasons: a) An actuality is the explanation of whatever it shows itself to be. It itself is unique. To come to it is to be reduced to silence, or to be forced to explain it in terms of other ideas, and thereby make evident that its intelligibility is partly to be understood in terms alien to it.

b) Various exhibitions of an actuality not only occur together but belong together. They are united by it. Yet they remain distinct. To refer to what unites them is at once to leave them behind and to speak in terms too general for that particular actuality.

c) Every intelligible entity has antecedents from which it is derivable. Every one has consequences that can be derived from it. Since its full meaning lies outside it, no actuality is wholly intelligible as long as we keep within its confines. Nothing less than an endless chain of antecedents and consequences, logically involved with it, is needed in order to understand what its nature is.

The nature of an actuality stops at its borders. That nature has only a restricted intelligibility, for it is denied the role of a true universal, capable of being repeated an endless number of times. And if we separate off its nature so as to allow it to a true universal, the actuality will no longer have a nature of its own. Nor would there be any accounting, in terms of that nature, for the fact that the nature was ingredient in the actuality. Yet there is nothing surd to an actuality. Every aspect of it, and it as a whole, can be understood. It has consequences which are entailed by what it now is, and others which, though produced freely, can, after they have occurred, be seen to be rationally related to what had gone before.

Still, an individual reality has a nature which is not yet linked to any other. The actuality becomes the more intelligible the more this limitation is overcome; it is most completely intelligible when its nature is linked with all others. This is possible because a final universal, Possibility, impinges on the actuality, and thereby relates its nature with the natures of other actualities. In connecting the actuality's nature with other natures, Possibility lifts up those natures into the realm where necessity holds sway. Possibility turns the natures into terms for itself, and the natures in turn enable Possibility to be articulated.

Possibility obtains specificity from the natures of actualities. That fact distinguishes Possibility from the Absolute of the idealists. The nature of an actuality fills out a portion of Possibility and, thereby, is enabled to make use of Possibility's linking structures. But Possibility continues to be outside the actualities. To reach it in its full reality, one would have to encompass the natures of all actualities. This can never be done, but one can adopt a rational attitude and, under the aegis of Possibility itself, transcend the limitations to which the actualities have subjected their natures. When a man in a lucidative process of intensification moves into Possibility, he makes more and more natures subject to it. He does not deal with all natures, but there is no limit to the number which he can encompass. The more distinct natures that he provides, the more controlling the Possibility becomes. Since he never attends to all the natures, he and the natures with which he deals fail to obtain what they need to complete themselves. Universality and individuality fall short of being fully united when one does not have all the natures there are, purged of all reference to actualities, including man.

A cosmos constituted of actualities, linked through the medium of their natures, is a rational totality in which there are different terms available at different times. If the actualities have also internalized the qualifications to which Possibility subjects them, they are intelligible units in an intelligible cosmos.

[5]

Every actuality is extended. It spreads out spatially, with a distinctive contour. It stretches out temporally, with a rhythm and a duration of its own. And it has effects as well as causes. Each of its extensions has a limited span; there are empty stretches beyond it as well as stretches which are ingredient in other actualities.

The extension of an actuality is its own, giving it a distinctive pace, geometry, and power. But it is also subject to Existence. As a consequence, the extensions of an actuality are distinguished from and made continuous with stretches connecting it with the stretches in other actualities.

Cosmic extensions are universals in that they permit of an endless number of delimitations. Each portion of space is spatial; each portion of time is temporal; each portion of a causal process is causal. But there is in fact no smaller subdivision than that constituted by some process or actuality. Apart from these, space, time, and causality, though endlessly divisible in thought, and imagined to have beginnings and endings, have neither unity nor limits. It is no less true that cosmic extensions are unique, having no duplicates. They remain undivided even when they are occupied and therefore subdivided by actualities. The whole of space is indivisible; the subdivisions of it are demarcated, not divided off from it into islands of their own. The whole of time abides; only filled moments of it pass away. The whole of causality stretches backward and forward without end; actualities and their activities merely have an occasional footing in it.

By itself, Existence is uniform, monotonous, undifferentiated; the self-extended actualities that occupy it variegate and divide it. Actualities enable Existence to extend over and not merely be extended, to have distinguishable stretches and not to be simply indivisible. By itself an actuality's extensions are idiosyncratic, and do not necessarily cohere with the extensions characteristic of other actualities. Actualities need an encompassing extensionality, if they are to be extended together. They are independent, internally distended realities in their own right, which, by interplaying with Existence, attain the status of extended units in an extensional cosmos, whose occupants punctuate single extensions. Existence is benefited by the actualities, since these provide it with diversifications. Because the actualities give it so many different locations, Existence is multiply located.

Those actualities which do not internalize the extensions that impinge on them interplay with Existence as unit extensions; the others, in addition, acquire individualized rhythms, contours, and paces. Both yield symbols which lucidatively lead into Existence itself. Men make use of those symbols by adding their own internalized extensions to the extensions of objects; symbolization of Existence is enriched by the vital distension of the men who engage in it.

[6]

Each actuality is a unity. Its unity does not depend on its acknowledgement by any man. The unities that are acknowledged in particular religions are no more divinely qualified than others are, though the impact may be greater, and the kind of object selected may be thought to be more appropriate to the kinds of adventures which the divine is thought to have in the world.

A man becomes alert to the unity of an actuality by accepting it, thereby producing a single unity of himself and the object as lucidatively entrenching on the Unity that is beyond them both. This is not possible except so far as he has moved away from himself, as part of the world, into himself as also qualified by the Unity. By adding his own reverential attitude to the object's unity, he is able to move forward to Unity in a process of intensification controlled by the reality at which he is to arrive. Nothing that a man can do, of course, will increase or decrease the unity of an actuality; this is an affair solely between the actuality and the final Unity. The actuality accepts the Unity at the same time that this finality holds on to the actuality through a qualification of it.

From the position of Unity, the various actualities on which it impinges are so many replications of itself. These it possesses, distinguished by and from itself, but not freed from its control. The result, if internalized, becomes intertwined with other facets of an actuality and can then be exhibited in a cosmos. From the position of actualities, Unity accepts them so as to constitute a single, pluralized maximal unit where the actualities are preserved together so far as they are harmonious.

The result of the interplay of Unity with actualities is a cosmos in which the actualities are harmonized in any one of a number of degrees, depending on the extent to which those actualities are already themselves unified and are in harmony with one another. The actualities make a contribution to the constitution of that cosmos as surely as Unity does. Neither is in full possession of the other. As a consequence, the unity of the cosmos is less than perfect. It is a diversified harmony where a plurality of actualities function as units that supplement one another to constitute a single totality.

[7]

Only men set out on a quest of finalities. It is not due to them, though, that these finalities qualify actualities. The finalities do not arrive so late in the world, nor are they so impotent that they must await man's act before they can manifest themselves anywhere. Since the men, too, are actualities, they, too, are affected by the finalities. When they internalize the qualifications to which those finalities subject them they become internally altered, in consciousness, disposition, and attitude. As a consequence, the men are able to begin a movement into those finalities.

Every actuality has been qualified by finalities, and this whether or not men exist or attend to those qualifications. And men could, and sometimes do, progress toward finalities without attending to anything else but the effects of the finalities on themselves. But they usually start a movement to the finalities from the qualifications of other actualities. By adding themselves to these actualities and their qualifications, they provide a better, more intensive beginning than they could were they to start only with the actualities themselves.

Movements into finalities are under the control of those finalities. At every step the actualities are accommodated, thereby enabling them to benefit from the universality of those finalities. At every step, too, the finalities benefit from the differences among the actualities; the finalities become internally differentiated by what they accommodate.

The cosmos is not static. Actualities not only act on one another in different ways at different times, but they come to be and pass away. Each new actuality makes a distinctive difference to other actualities; each presents a new challenge to the different finalities.

The finalities, in turn, provide qualifications for the new actualities, and incorporate within themselves the distinctive differences that those new actualities make to them. As a consequence of its interplay with actualities, a finality presents the other finalities with new opportunities and demands.

Transcendence takes us in the direction either of actualities, or of one of the five finalities. It can be brought to a halt sooner than it need be, which is what Kant does when he stops with a manifold and conditions. It then yields nothing more than factors for experience, to be tightened so as to constitute it, or a pair of contrastive, abstract, empty factors which can never be unified. Kant does not show that transcendence is impossible or futile or foolish, subjective, or avoidable. It would be one of these if its moves did not start with what occurs in fact, if it did not have degrees, if realities did not put in an appearance, and if there were no symbolic penetrations which begin at the finalities and evidence thicker versions of themselves. Because transcendence is possible, we are able to use appearances, and are able to see how there can be a cosmos.

One can agree with Kant that categories appropriate to the items in experience are not to be applied to finalities, and that the kind of "totality" or necessity which is appropriate to a finality is not to be applied to experienced objects. The conditions governing the appearances of actualities are not conditions governing finalities; the characterizations of finalities are not entirely appropriate to actualities or their appearances.

It is just as necessary to modify present content in order to make it be in consonance with categories as it is to modify categories to make them be in consonance with such content. The one modification Kant presented in his schematism, the other in his transcendental deduction. These should have been matched by a schematism of intelligibility which altered the categories to make them consonant with the transcendental unity of apperception, and by a "deduction" which modified the unity of apperception so that it was in consonance with the categories and thereby allowed one to know by means of them.

Kant's categories needed a double schematism and a double

deduction. But just as surely as inexplicable content is necessary for one schematism and deduction, inexplicable power is necessary for the other schematism and deduction. If his schematized time and categories have to receive a filling enabling them to be constituents of what is known, his unity of apperception and categories have to be alloted a power enabling one to know. Neither the content nor the power, however, is really inexplicable once one leaves the Kantian frame; both can be accounted for by reference to the realities of which they are attenuated continuations.

PART 3

~~~~~~

THE OUGHT TO BE THAT IS

~~~~~~

15

Controlling Summary: All the actualities are qualified by all the finalities. Man alone internalizes the qualifications originating with every finality. Only he, therefore, is able to make himself an instance of all of them. As a consequence of his internalizations he is a substance enriched with a being, nature, existence, and unity. In himself he is an individual with rights, a trued self, an identity, and an immortality, each of which reflects the result of his involvement with a distinct finality.

[1. INDIVIDUALITY]

Animal breeders have long known what genetics has amply confirmed, explained, and expanded: various features are inherited. The color of the skin and the eyes, size, hairiness, even deficiencies in clavicles, hearts, and brains can be predicted. Biologists speak with confidence of the discovery of the essential chemical constituents of life. Today even schoolboys know that many new living beings originate with the union of sperm and egg, or analogous pairs. But this is not yet to know anything about the nature or origin of a man's individuality, and particularly his singular privacy. Does it come to be by annihilating one or the other of the privacies of the sperm and egg? Or does it develop out of one of them, with a suppression of the other? How could there be a privacy built up out of or from other privacies? Or should we deny that sperm and egg have privacies? If we do, we will deny that they are substances, and will still leave unanswered the question of the origin of a grown man's distinctive privacy.

Biology cannot tell how or why each plant and animal is unduplicable, or how and why every inanimate object is distinct from every other; these questions are not open to experiment or answerable by observation. They deal with what is not public. Nor is an advance made when one tries to make use of some presumed general principle of individuation. A principle of individuation works uniformally in all cases and therefore fails to individuate, or it is itself individuated, though it is without privacy. How could it be individuated? A general principle can not individuate it, and a supposed individual act begs the question. The problem is not met by crediting regions or points in space, time, or causal chains with individuality. They, too, are without substantiality and privacy; they, too, would first have to be individuated before they could provide individuations for whatever occupies them.

Different kinds of actualities are individuals in different degrees. These kinds and degrees can be conveniently divided into five, in consonance with the five finalities. They approximate roughly to the familiar divisions of actualities into physical things, plants, the lower animals, the higher animals, and men. There are times when we cannot tell whether an actuality is a higher or lower animal, an animal or a plant, a living or a nonliving being; they differ then apparently only in degree, and that degree is often very slight. But at the extremes in each class, the differences are great and persistent enough to mark them off as different in kind.

Whatever is other than an actuality defines the actuality to be so far incomplete, lacking the reality of that other. The actuality tries to internalize what is other than it, consistent with itself continuing to be selfsame. It must, therefore, avoid being overcome by that which it internalizes; while internalizing another it must stand apart from it. To the extent that it succeeds in maintaining itself while benefiting from its internalizations, to that extent it completes itself.

To internalize the qualifications produced by a finality is to instance it; to instance a finality is to internalize the qualifications it introduces. All the instances of a finality are interconnected; they also function in independence of it. The lower the degree of individuality, the less able is an actuality to function independently of all the finalities. Physical realities instance and act independently only of Substance; men, instead, instance and are able to act independently of all the other finalities as well.

Finalities need actualities as surely as actualities need finalities. By accommodating the actualities, the finalities achieve an articulation otherwise denied to them. The extent to which finalities can be articulated, and can harmonize that fact with their own undifferentiated continuations, is the extent to which they are able to complete themselves with the help of actualities.

Physical realities are unique substances under the control of Being which equalizes them, of Possibility which subjects them to laws, of Existence which limits their activities, and of Unity which keeps them harmonized. Plants internalize qualifications stemming from Possibility as well as from Substance and, therefore, give themselves a richer content than physical realities can. They have substantialized natures. Group-dominated, the lower animals internalize qualifications produced by Unity as well as Substance and Possibility. The higher animals internalize qualifications produced by Existence as well; they are territorial and social realities. Men, finally, internalize qualifications produced by all the finalities. Their consequent independence from all enables them to face Substance with a richer content than that available to any of the other types of actuality.

All actualities are independent of one another. Can we simply claim that every actuality is also an individual? If so, individuality seems to have been assumed but not explained. If not, individuality would apparently have to be explained by what is not an individual. The difficulty arises when it is supposed that individuality is altogether present or absent, regardless of anything else. Individuality is possessed in relation to Substance by an actuality which, by internalizing the qualifications to which Substance subjects it, is able to instance that Substance and to maintain itself in opposition to it.

Since the individuality of an actuality depends on its internalization of the qualification, the individuality could be said to be the result of an act of self-individuation. But one might just as well say simply that every actuality is a private, self-maintained substance. An actuality instances Substance; it is a distinct substance; it stands in oppositional independence of Substance, and of any other instance of Substance; it is an individual, irreducibly private and unique.

Individuality is not to be equated with the fact that this or that aspect has no duplicates anywhere. Lack of duplication is quite different from unduplicability. The former means that in fact there is no duplicate, the latter says that there cannot be one. The latter requires the former, but not conversely. Each actuality is unduplicable. Fingerprints could conceivably be duplicated, but an individual's fingers and their whorls cannot be. To move from the unduplicated fingerprints to what is unduplicable, reference has to be made to an individual owner of the fingers who places a unique signature on what he publicly displays. Like the eyes and their color, they are inseparable from an individual privacy. Like them, too, they are textured, able to lead one toward their unduplicable, individual, and individuating source. If fingerprints are considered apart from the fingers, if they are merely classified according to their ridges and depressions, possible duplicates cannot be ruled out.

A man is an individual in a way no other kind of reality can be, because he alone internalizes the qualifications and is therefore independent of all the finalities. His oppositional content is richer than any other actuality's, for he alone confronts Substance in the guise of an independent being, nature, existence, and unity. His individuality permeates him. His bodily features, which we account for by genes and other agents of heredity, consequently are also unique. His eyes, even their very color, are unique, because they are rooted in and qualified by his substance.

If it be supposed that man's individuality has to do solely or originally with his body, one can also affirm that he is in the same world with inanimate beings, plants, and animals. That is desirable. But one will, as a consequence, also have to suppose that his self, mind, and consciousness are functions of his body, or are not individualized at all.

Both men and higher animals have emotions which are expressed in and through mind and body. Those emotions have a depth to them; below what is expressed is an untapped energy that occasionally comes out into the open to supplement, rectify, or replace what had originally been expressed. In animals, and apparently in the unborn, there is no distinguishing of the unexpressed from the expressed emotions. Neither possesses, assesses, or controls its emotions. But this is what normal men do. The unexpressed is contrasted with, but not separated from, all expressions and possessions; it is the man in himself, his inner, his self, or "I." There is no substantial reality hiding behind the scenes; there is just the individual substance stretching from psyche to adoptive organic body, or, alternatively, there is just a man possessing what is exterior.

A man achieves the status of a self most readily with the acceptance of his emotional expressions, and through these of that which is then qualified and possessed. His self is one with the maintenance of himself as an inner in control of an outer. In that act he takes himself to be an "I" contrasting with all else. That I is the locus of the internalizations and diversifications of the qualifications of the finalities, beyond the possibility of an animal to match. Over the course of his life, his I is filled out more and more, absorbing within and reducing to itself whatever it can retain of the encountered. This result is promoted by the use of language, and by participation in common human enterprises, enriching his opposition to all the finalities.

An unborn human has no language, assumes no responsibility. There is no reason to believe that it has distinguished an I. It is not yet a being by itself, or an other for whatever there be. And what is true of the unborn is also true of the newly born. Yet the latter is accepted by its family and others as a distinct human; the former is usually accepted by the mother on quickening. These acceptances could be said to be anticipatory, but it would be just as legitimate to say that the acceptances then and there momentarily distinguish the I, the possessing inner, in the unborn and in the infant. Still, it is only when there is some grasp of language, some awareness of others, or an assumption of responsibility that the I is maintained whether or not anyone acknowledges it.

The self is an achievement, and is enriched over the course of its career. It is the outcome of internalizations of qualifications originating with Being, Possibility, Existence, and Unity, all serving to enrich a substantial privacy. With the cessation of an effort to reduce whatever is encountered to the selfsame constancy, there is a cessation of the self-maintained I. But just as the mother and the family, by their acceptances, enable the unborn and the infant to be credited with selves before they may have distinguished them, so Unity, by its acceptance of every unity, enables the unity of a man to continue even after death, when he is no longer able to integrate the unity with an encompassed plurality.

A unity is distinct from Unity just so far as it is diversified, and opposed by other unities. As diversified, each unity is necessarily exterior to Unity itself; as just a unity, each is inseparable from Unity itself. It is correct, therefore, to say that Unity itself allows a place for each unity on an indefinite number of levels, depending on the extent to which the unity has been able to overcome its diversifications and, to that degree, has made itself indistinguishable from other unities. It is no less correct to say that each unity, precisely because it is at once diversified and one of many unities, remains forever outside Unity itself, and as such must perish with the loss of its diversification and its distinction from other unities.

Recognition of Unity's effective imposition of unities on externally existing pluralities, justifies a third position between the previous two. Each of the imposed unities is distinguishable from others by means of the plurality with which it is involved. It is preserved in that attenuated form together with all other unities. Just so far as they have been unable to control and thereby free themselves from external diversification and opposition, the unities can be brought more intimately together in Unity only by being reorganized and thereby by becoming more and more indistinguishable from other unities and, therefore, from Unity itself.

Short of a complete merger with all other unities, a unity is diversified. In the case of man, that diversification is due to the multiple items that a self integrates with the unity. When, on death, the self is no longer operative, the diversified unity is preserved in Unity, but altered, just so far as the diversification had not been fully mastered.

Each man has an individualized body because his self possesses and quickens it. That self is independent of all the finalities, while continuing to be interrelated and even affected by them. Were it not independent of all the finalities, a man could have an individuality no greater than that of an animal. At the very least, his being would be unable to interplay with Being; he, therefore, could be no more than a sheer unit which Being governs and coordinates with other units.

Layer upon layer of complexity, each a set of individual bodies, are finally overarched by the body of a human. It is possible in principle—as is now possible in fact—for that body to allow for the separation of any of the contained bodies, as it now allows for the separation of the sperm and egg. The released sperm and egg are, of course, not those out of which the complex body originated; each is produced by a single human body and is partly affected by it. The movement of each, and its achievement of an independent status, does not involve a loss to the initial encompassing body's power to function independently of Substance. But there is nothing inconceivable in the idea that there might be ways of dividing men's bodies so that these were destroyed while distinct bodies were produced, each with an individual life of its own. Some of the lower living beings can now be divided into fully functioning individuals, leaving over nothing of the individual in which they were parts.

A self is a *psyche* so far as it not only opposes Substance but appreciatively opens itself up to the operation of Substance on confronted objects. The psyche is thus the self functioning in a restricted area. As so functioning it adds to the individuality characteristic of the self. The results of its operations accumulate. To the constant individuality which is his because he is a substance, a man is therefore able to add a progressively enriched psyche. That psyche reflects the result of his self's adventures at withdrawing from and opening to the presence of Substance, and the use of this Substance to govern and relate the objects of awareness.

Reason is the self involved with Being. Like the psyche, it not only shares in the individuality of the self but intensively adds to it. Man's self is withdrawn from Being in a constant way, but it withdraws as a reason only in the course of a particular act. The results of those acts add to one another, with the consequence that he benefits his individuality more and more. A man's individuality, therefore, has a richness greater than that which is possible to a substantial physical thing. There are times when he makes little or no use of his reason; his speech and acts may reveal the increasing dominance of other facets of the self. But nothing will take away the accumulations his individuality has achieved, since this is one with the actuality he is, with just that past and experience.

The *mind*, like the psyche and reason, is individualized. Instancing and opposing Possibility, it is involved in a man's attempt to become one with Possibility. The more the mind is used, the more it becomes vitalized; the result is a man facing Substance with richer and richer content. To be used, the mind internalizes the qualifications produced by Possibility and thereby enables Possibility to have a role in it, controlling and connecting distinguished meanings. The mind of a man is the unique mind he had as a child, but benefited from the numerous uses it made of what Possibility provides.

It is also true that the more rational a man is the more is his thinking like that of another—and men are usually more rational than children. As one grows older, it would appear, therefore, that a man's mind becomes less and less distinctive. But this is to neglect the fact that the increase in the richness of his individuality, obtained through the adoption of meaningful content, is precisely that which makes it possible for him to make better use of Possibility. The richer the substantial self, the better is it able to accommodate, without distortion, the Possibility which is to govern and connect distinguished meanings. Since a man may neglect to use his mind, or may allow other finalities to crowd out a use of Possibility, there is no assurance that he will progressively become more and more mentally enriched as time goes on. It is possible, too, for him to open himself up to Possibility and, instead of making use of it, merely allow it to order the meanings he has distinguished. His continuance in rational thought consequently is not necessarily accompanied by an individualized use of the result. Though his mind then becomes more and more significant, he makes less and less use of the rationality to which he is subject. He thinks like a machine. It is never enough to know what is objectively and necessarily the case; the knowledge must be individualized.

Sensibility is the outcome of an instancing which is directed toward Existence. Functioning in independence of the larger extension in which the body is, the sensibility makes use of Existence as an agency for prescriptively ordering particular felt existents. Like a psyche, reason, and mind, the more often sensibility uses what it obtains from its finality, the more it enriches the individual. The discriminations men make by means of feelings are few and rough; practice and care, though, make it possible for the discriminations to be increased and refined. The use of Existence is distinct each time, and as a consequence men come to grasp something of it as a single, objective, overwhelming reality, while feeling parts of it in individual ways.

Spirit, finally, attends to Unity, bringing it to bear on intimations of particular unities. When, as is common, Unity is identified with God, a man is seen to be more and more of an individual, the more he makes provision for God to act on the unities of which he is aware.

Psyche, reason, mind, sensibility, and spirit are distinct expressions of the self. Any one of them can be stressed while the others are minimized or neglected. One of them can be emphasized for a while and then ignored. One man, therefore, can be quite commonplace in his sensibility but have a remarkable spirit; another may begin to exercise his mind after a long period of comparative neglect. Ideally, all should be expressed maximally in all possible ways. This desirable result is not often realized because men favor some types of expression over others, in part because of their dominant interests, in part because of habit, in part because they have, due to circumstance and disposition, focused on the objects of awareness appropriate to those expressions.

It is the actuality in its full concreteness, single and final, that is individual. But the individuality is not identical with the actuality; nor is it a fixity in place or content. An actuality is an individual because it instances Substance. As a body it acts as an individual unit in relation to other bodies and under the control of Substance. As a privacy, it is independent of Substance, and may be independent of other finalities as well. The higher up in the scale it is, the richer is its privacy, since it then also instantiates other finalities.

To answer the question, "what is being individuated?" one must refer to an actuality as related to finalities other than Substance. To answer the question, "what individuates?" one must refer to Substance. To answer the question, "what is an individual?" one must refer to the actuality as it confronts Substance in the guise of an independent reality. Questions relating to the being of an actuality are to be answered in similar ways, but with reference to the appropriate finality. A being is opposed to Being, and therefore possesses distinctive rights. If it also internalizes being and thereby instances it, it has still other rights. These are exercised independently but hopefully in harmony with one another, both by each man and by all of them together.

[2. NATIVE AND ACQUIRED RIGHTS]

Each actuality has the right to be just the being that it is. That right can be understood statically as well as dynamically. Statically, it means that a being is justified in standing in opposition to all other beings as well as to Being itself. Dynamically, it means that the being justifiably seeks to complete itself through the overcoming of oppositions between itself and all others. The static form of that right characterizes the being as self-bounded; the dynamic, instead, characterizes it as involved with what is not itself. The static leads to no conflict, but the dynamic, since it has a moment where the being reaches toward and endeavors to make use of others—themselves engaged in similar efforts with respect to it—necessarily leads to conflict except where, as in the case of knowledge, the self-completion of one being does not preclude and may in fact promote the self-completion of others.

The right to be self-complete is native to every being. Men, though, have a richer form of that right than other beings have, because men alone are beings who are also substances, with natures, existences, and unities. Other kinds of beings, though beings as surely as men are, are beings only as qualified by Being. They do not internalize the qualification. Consequently, they are beings only as together with others.

A man's right to be self-complete is an insistent claim made by himself as a substantial reality. It has special forms when credited, not to him as a substance, but to him as a nature, an existent, or a unity. When the right is credited to his nature, it is a root justification for him, as a particular good, to be what he is and to do what he does. When ascribed to his existence, the right to be self-complete is a grounded demand to act on all else. Attributed to his unity, the right to be self-complete is expressed as a warranted persistent effort at self-definition. The self-same right of a being is expressed in all the cases. Since a man opposes all the finalities with the same degree of success, the right can be characterized in all the foregoing ways at the same time.

The right of the being of a man to be self-complete is at once an insistent claim to function as a substance, a root justification exhibited by a particular good, a grounded demand to determine himself, and a warranted effort at self-definition. Consequently, it is correct to say of a man that he always makes a claim to life, that he always has a justifying nature, that there always is ground for his determining himself, and that there is always a warrant for a self-defining act by which he makes himself be a distinctive unity. For analytic and practical purposes, though, any one of the characterizations can be used apart from the others.

Murder, debasement, enslavement, and corruption are wrong because they deny to a human being, with a substance, nature, existence, and unity, the right to be self-complete. Murder denies him individual life, a precondition for being complete; debasement denies him humanity, the level on which he is to be completed; enslavement denies him self-expression, by means of which he is to become complete; and corruption denies him integrity, the status of being complete.

This schema of native rights is but one of the many that are possible. The others, though, to be well rooted, will also have to be grounded in an account of the nature of man. Like the present, they, too, must be supported by a clarification of other topics, such as individuality, truth, identity, and immortality. They, too, will have to take account of the fact that men are involved with other actualities and all the finalities.

The right to be self-complete does not depend on consciousness for its existence. Nor does it depend on the acknowledgment of others, or on the ability to defend it. If it did, we would have no basis for objecting to an ignoring, restricting, abrogating, or violating of the right. Just the opposite—the protection and support of the right to be self-complete measures the value of states and men. We condemn states, other men, and sometimes ourselves when we find that the right has been overridden.

Men's native rights are specific forms of the right to be self-complete. It is not these rights, but acquired or bestowed rights that are of primary significance for men existing together in a well-ordered society. The history of civilization cannot be separated from the history of man's struggle to achieve and maintain these. Some of them express the positions which men have in relation to others, and sometimes in relation to the subhuman. Others are rights against the state itself. Both types have been slowly and painfully won. Sometimes they have been lost; almost always they are hard to maintain; rarely are they insisted upon as fully as they should be.

Lawyers and judges know no rights but those which the state is willing to sustain with sanctions. The state gives and the state takes away the rights that are legally viable. A tyranny differs from other forms of political organization by granting none or only minimal rights against the state. Still, the most democratic of states denies men rights which it once bestowed, and bestows rights it once denied. Habeas corpus has been denied in wartime; amendments to the United States Constitution are needed to assure to minorities rights already enjoyed by the majority. The state, on this view, is the final arbiter; if it refuses to bestow the right to speak, or associate, or worship, the men in that state do not have those rights at all.

Lawyers sometimes argue on behalf of rights not explicitly

formulated in any official document. Their arguments finally rest on what the state, in practice or in formula, has already accepted as man's rights. But were this all to the matter, it would be hard to see why or how new rights are urged, or what objections could be significantly advanced to the consistent practices of any state, no matter how men are treated.

The issue of native rights becomes of paramount importance when one stands away from the state and asks about *its* justice and *its* rights. A state could be unjust in a number of ways. It could contradict itself, denying rights that it had explicitly or tacitly granted. Its injustice would then be directed against its own integrity. The state could also be unreliable, disappointing those who had come to rely on its support in the exercise of their rights. Its injustice here would be against itself so far as its task was to support the expression of native rights; it would be against men so far as their rights needed this support. The state also might deny rights to some men even though the rights were intended to apply to them as well as to others. Once again its injustice would be against itself in that it would go against its own intent; it would also be against the men whose rights were denied, because it would treat them as less than or other than those with whom they were equal. It might also deny rights to certain men whom it had chosen for special consideration. Its discriminations would then unjustly preclude the exercise of various native rights on the part of some.

The failure to allow or to further the exercise of some or all men's native rights interests reformers and ethicists, and is appealed to by those who wish to change the state for reasons other than that of promoting its efficacy, power, or continuation. That failure is known so far as one has a knowledge of native rights; it can be remedied so far as one knows how to translate those rights into sanctioned, bestowed rights. Were there no native rights, there would be no nonpolitical grounds for criticizing the state, no matter what it did, providing its decisions and actions were consistent and successful in promoting the state's existence. Nor would one know just what rights the state should guarantee in order to do justice to what men are and ought to be.

Anarchists deny that a state has rights of its own. They deny that it is anything more than a summation of individuals; or they take it to be a mere instrument for the satisfaction of human wants, or for the protection and enhancement of men's native rights. But no summation of individuals is able to make war and peace, to have a history, traditions, or a constitution. No mere instrument can of itself control, dictate to the men who use it. One could produce a machine with a program which involved a particular use, if someone had already lent the machine the guidance of a human mind. There are those who speak of the state as though it were such a machine, used by men as an agency for subjugating or even helping other men. But it has a history of its own, making it difficult to deny it native rights, expressive of the fact that it has a reality, maintained over a considerable stretch of time, controlling and changing men, and dictating just which of their rights are to be expressed, and how. Did states not have any native rights, there would be no justification for them, in order to continue or prosper, to add, extend, and curtail the publicly expressed rights of men.

The rights that a state possesses are not bestowed by men in an Hobbsean contract. Such a contract either presupposes an existent state with rights which are to be respected, or it produces such a state in the very act of making a contract. In the one case there are rights that are not bestowed by the contracting men; in the other, there is nothing with which to make a contract.

By giving a state a constitution or a law-making body, and at the same time accepting what is then proposed, men produce a quasi-Hobbsean legal state. Having bestowed on it various rights which time and circumstances show must be exercised if the right to be a state is to be protected and promoted, they would be unjust if they then denied those rights to it. But, of course, not all bestowed rights are the rights that should be bestowed.

A state is neither absolute in its rights, nor justified in making decrees which disregard what men natively are or publicly need. Its right is correlative with men's native rights; to violate either is to do wrong. Both types must be translated into publicly exercised rights relevant to the other, whose exercise will enable them to flourish together.

If a state is given rights to act toward other states it is made into a member of a civilized world; if it is given rights to act toward its members it is empowered; if it exercises rights against its members it is authoritative. A state which bestows on its members the rights that enable them to satisfy their native rights in harmony is just; if it bestows rights on members to control its exercise of the rights which they bestowed on it, it is benign.

A just state bestows rights on men; these are to be exercised in relation to one another under its control and with its sanctions. Some of these rights seem arbitrary, such as the right to marry within such and such limits of consanguinity. But what is in fact arbitrary is usually the place where the limits are set, not the setting of the limits. Different societies and states prefer different limits; these are not altogether detachable from the people as governed by myths and established practices. As the society changes, these limits change as well. But unless they are simply willful commands, they respect the native rights of men.

At their best, the laws of a state affirm the viability of the right of each man to be the equal of others, and therefore to be justified in activities promoting self-completion. The public arena provides but a limited area and limited resources, precluding the fulfillment of all men at the same time and in the same way. There is also an exaggeration of some needs at one time, or a stress on one of them at the expense of others. Usually, too, men do not know their responsibilities, do not care to fulfill them, do not know how to fulfill them, or are in fact involved in courses which entail the denial of some rights. Consequently, the exercise of rights by one man may bring him into conflict with others; the exercise by one, some, or all, may bring about a conflict between the state and men.

A duty is a requirement that the right of another be respected. Answering to the single right to be self-complete, is the single duty to respect that right, and therefore, at the minimum, not to stand in its way. The minimal form of the duty to respect the right to be self-complete is the limit below which men cannot be significantly joined together. Men, of course, do and should belong together more intimately than is possible in a family, a community, and eventually in one mankind.

It could be well argued that all men have a duty to promote the welfare of all. Without such a duty, it could be said, there would be no genuine support of the right to be self-complete. But a duty is correlative with a right, and the duty that is to be carried out is the correlate of the right that is expressed. If no one seeks to improve himself in publicly expressible ways, no one has a duty to make him do so, or to produce the improvement on his behalf. For ethical and religious reasons, for reasons of politics and good will one may, of course, go beyond this point, but then one has also moved to where duties are no longer correlative with rights.

Answering to the specific forms of the basic right to be complete are the specific forms of the correlative duty. Since there are rights which the state has with reference to other states and with reference to its members, and rights which men have with reference to other men and with reference to the state itself, there are evidently also duties that the state has toward other states and toward its members, and duties which the members have toward one another and toward the state. Since the failure to fulfill a duty is an injustice, there are evidently injustices attributable to a state in its dealings with other states and with its members, and injustices attributable to its members in their dealings with one another and with the state.

Man has the right to be complete, on a footing with all other men. Any exercise of that right by one of them in such a way as to hobble the expression of it by others, or even by himself at other times, is an expression which has not yet found its proper vehicle. A right improperly expressed is to be referred back to its ground where it is to be granted its proper vehicle. The issue is decided legislatively on the basis of the capacity of the vehicle to make the right viable with a minimal challenge to the exercise of other rights. There is no a priori way of determining just what the answer will be. The history of mankind is in part the history of men seeking ways to express their rights together, and within the orbit of a state. The best of states supports their efforts to be complete together, consistent with its own continuance and enhancement.

Marxists see the state as an instrument at the service of a dominant economic class. In a perfect economic and equitable world, they hold, there would be need perhaps for minimal police activity, but no genuine need for a state. But since the police themselves must be regulated, and since men's rights need to be formulated, protected, and promoted, if only against ignorance and ineptitude, evidently some form of state must remain. The state cannot "wither away" without men losing thereby. What should be corrected is the tendency of a state to defend the privileges of the economically advantaged. But this is only to say that the state should be just toward all its members, taking them all to be equally deserving of its support.

Injustice is done to a member of a state if he is denied the exercise of his native basic right to be self-complete, and is denied the exercise of publicly acceptable authoritative expressions of this right. Injustice is done to him, too, if the state makes demands on him which are not mutually compatible. These injustices have a brute finality to them; they characterize the state, and that is the end of the matter, unless the fact arouses men to change that state or its laws. But a state, no less than men, has rights, and justice requires that changes be made in consonance with them.

[3. TRUTH]

Truth characterizes a surrogate. It accrues to the surrogate if at different stages in the careers of both the surrogate and the original they have the same relations to one another that they initially had. If their careers are mainly in accord, we are usually content to accept the surrogate as sustaining a truth. But it could thereafter independently diverge from the path it had taken until then. Since it is conceivable that any surrogate and what it represents may at some time no longer be related in the same way they had been initially, we can never be sure that what is now taken to be a truthful surrogate will remain one.

But if we have already made contact with what justifies the ascription of truth, why should we abandon it for something else? How could a surrogate, unless it be the very double of what it replaces, be concordant with what it replaces; yet if it be an exact double, why deal with it rather than with the original? The first question is met by noting that statements, thoughts, and the like are more available, more readily manipulatable, and more easily analyzed than the items they replace. The second and third questions are met by noting that a surrogate need not duplicate what it replaces, and could in fact have stages and consequences which are not matched by anything in the original. All that one need find is something that has a number of discriminable stages in a constant relationship to discriminable stages of the original.

Attitudes, thoughts, practices, judgments, and statements can all be credited with truth. They are then to be depended on never to lead one to what is false. The false is that which misrepresents, that whose stages are in disaccord with the stages of that which it replaces, that which can not be relied upon to keep us in a constant relation to that which it replaces.

In logic, it is usually sufficient to provide a surrogate having only a formally expressed antecedent and consequent which are in accord with an initial and final stage of some occurrence. In science, it is sometimes desirable to use mathematical formulae in order to permit a relating of formal derivations to later observable occurrences in the very same way in which the initial formulae are related to the initial facts. The relations could be quite complex, and be in part constituted of unexpressed attitudes and qualifications which make it possible for the formulae to be connected with what is observed. Formulae, having to do with the attraction and repulsion of masses, find application to falling bodies only by being modified and complicated so as to take account of the fact that the observed does not occur in a vacuum, closed off from the influence of other forces.

Difficulties arise when one attends first, not to what occurs, but to ideas, beliefs, or language. If a start is made with these, how could one find their match except in other ideas, beliefs, or language? Can an idea (belief, word) be in accord with anything but an idea (belief, word)? Are we not caught within the world of ideas? Can anything make an idea true, can there be anything of which it could be true, but another idea? Do not ideas tell us what could possibly be? If we use the idea of the possible to determine what ideas to accept, will we not be caught in a vicious circle?

The difficulties have prompted a number of replies: 1] Ideas, language, etc., are not true when they conform to something other than themselves, but only when they meet certain criteria—clarity, distinctness, completeness, the demands of logic, science, etc. 2] Ideas, words, etc., are at best thin versions of facts and are true only so far as they become identified with those facts. 3] Neither ideas nor facts are final, but only their correlation or adjustment to one another. Truth belongs to neither side, but to their relationship. 4] Truth is something to live by; its ultimate ground is in the individual. What satisfies him is true, and what does not satisfy him is false. 5] Truth is what the community sustains. That community may be made up only of commonsense men; it may be mankind at its ideal best; or it may be the totality of scientists all pursuing the selfsame method relentlessly, and over an indefinite period. 6] Truth is an ultimate ideal which men can approach but can never actually attain. What we take to be truth is only what is tolerated or approved of for the time being.

1] A formalist does not look at the external world in order to know whether of not what he thinks, or asserts, or says is true. Amongst the items which he possesses apart from the world, he distinguishes those that have some special character—formal correctness, purity, and the like. This assures him that there is something which answers to what he maintains. Evidently he supposes that the external world is identical with what he acknowledges; the world for him is an exterior version of what he has in mind. But he has no way of knowing that there is such an exterior version unless he can distinguish it from what he has in mind. That act demands that there be something that holds of one of them that does not hold of the other. What could this be? Could it be known? Does it not make a difference to what it adds to or subtracts from? It must. But then it precludes an identity of the entertained and an exteriorized form of it.

2] The empiricist would like to submit to the facts, no matter where they lead. Any idea he may entertain is for him a summary, an abstraction, or an anticipation of what he might encounter. The true, for him, is but fact in a new context, thinned out perhaps but not appreciably altered. He does not, though, accept every item of experience as the equal of others. Some are taken to be more fundamental, more reliable, more acceptable. If this is not done by virtue of some justified principle, his selection will be arbitrary. And, since the facts must first measure up to his principle before he is in a position to use them to measure what else he might have in mind, instead of simply submitting to the facts, he will allow only for those that make his principle true.

3] There are ideas, sensations, assertions, and there are facts, objects, occurrences. To accept one as the basis for deciding which of the others is to be acceptable is to measure triangles by ocean waves, horses by sunbeams. The one has nothing to do with the other, and can provide it with no criteria. The honest thing to do, the third alternative suggests, is to accept both of them, but to seek rules by which they are to be correlated. Find the spectral lines which answer to the color red, and then take either to be the measure of the other. Where does one stand to make the correlation? Is the correlation like the sensation or like the facts, or is it something unlike either? If it be like the sensation or the facts it will not serve to bridge the gap between them; if it is unlike either, it will have to be known in some third way, and its role with respect to the other two will still have to be justified.

4] Truth is no indifferent, idle adjective. What is to pass for truth is what satisfies. The satisfaction could conceivably be one of mere aesthetic pleasure; it could result from the creating of something neat, determinate, and formal; or it could follow on one's having brought doubt to an end, on having made life pleasanter or easier, or something similar. But men find satisfaction in much that eventually palls, fails, betrays, or deceives. Nor need the true have any bearing on what men want or need. The truths offered in mathematics and logic, abstract science and ancient history may have little import for men. They may even prove to be disagreeable or unwanted.

Truth characterizes a surrogate whose presence or career may give men satisfaction at times. It is not identical with the satisfying, for even when it fails to satisfy, it belongs to a surrogate that should be adopted if one is to think congruently with the natures and functionings of appearances and realities. Decisions and acceptances are wise or unwise, good or bad; they do or do not accord with what can be known to be true, apart from our desires, needs, appetites, or interests.

5] We should look, it might be urged, not to individual satisfaction, but to the satisfaction of a group, and then not of a narrow-minded group, a group bent on its own improvement, but of a group concerned with discovery, learning, and with becoming civilized. This should provide the basis for the ascription of truth. What the community eventually settles on and remains with, that which it eventually comes to accept, or that which it is willing to accept without question is alone the truth, and the proper measure of all claims. On this alternative, everything that falls short of winning community support is so far not altogether true. It is not clear whether or not it is also being claimed that what is endorsed now is supposed now to be part of what is ultimately true, or to merely lead us to that truth. But why believe that community acceptance, now or later, is a proper surrogate for what in fact occurs? Communities are often cruel, blind, inconsistent, unmethodical. If they are not as they ought to be in the areas of morals and control, why take them to be the proper measure of truth? Communities also sustain superstitions, fictionalized histories, unsupported rumors, and false judgments of what in fact occurs; not all that they endorse is true.

6] Truth, it could be said, no one can ever in fact attain. It is an ideal, a perfection in the realm of knowledge. Like absolute beauty or perfect goodness, it is never fully embodied anywhere. We may never arrive at it; we may never come any closer to it than we now are; but it is always a beacon in terms of which we can measure claims as more or less defective. But if we are able to know this, its truth will have to be determined in some other way; such truth is precisely what is not provided for by making reference to an unattainable ideal truth.

These various alternatives neglect the role that Possibility plays in man, and therefore the role man is enabled to adopt both with respect to what he maintains and to what opposes him. It is his use of Possibility that enables him to be *trued*, and therefore to be a reality that dictates which ideas should be accepted and which facts deserve to be taken as basic. Possibility enables him to evaluate ideas and facts independently of one another (as the first two alternatives observe) as well as in relation to one another (as is remarked in the third). And it grounds the acknowledgments of the fifth and sixth alternatives once it be recognized that it is men, as possessed of trued selves, who alone can constitute a proper community, where the particular achievements of all mesh with one another.

A trued self is the self as it should be. It is trued *by* Possibility so as to be true *to* Possibility, and thereby to be able to do justice to Possibility's demands. As both together, the self is a true or authentic self. The fact brings one up against the problem of error. Could a true self make, accept, support, or pursue a false claim? If it could, it could maintain what is not true and be divided against itself. If not, it could never be in error.

What is false has consequences. Some of those consequences may be true, others false. There is no way of knowing in advance which they are. But we need not know which they are to know that, since the false has both kinds of consequences, it does not have a steady relation to that for which it is a surrogate. Once we accept a falsehood, we open ourselves to having to make unexpected maladjustments to the world which that falsehood claimed to match.

False claims, to be sure, cannot be made by a trued self. But no one has a completely trued self. No one has maximally incorporated Possibility. Every self is only partially trued, a fact which is manifested by error. We can not, therefore, know whether or not a claim is true by looking to the self, for at any given time the self is only partially trued and can not, therefore, decisively reject all that is false by seeing if it is in disaccord with itself. Yet if we do not refer to the trued self, we will leave the determination of the truth of what we claim to the arbitrary acceptance of some occurrence as being beyond question or questioning.

Nothing is gained by substituting a supposed uncriticizable fact for a supposed unerring self. Yet this is essentially what is done by those who maintain that the true is what is certified by an immediate intuition. A better answer is obtained by attending to the psyche, reason, mind, sensitivity, and spirit. These are roles which the self assumes. In each role it benefits from the presence of Possibility in a distinctive way; in each it makes a distinctive kind of entity be true; in each it attends to distinctive ways of producing certified truths; and in each it is geared to a distinctive finality.

The psyche that has been trued to and by Possibility legitimatizes an initial set of beliefs and objects because they are in accord with it, and uses these as determinants of what is to be accepted subsequently. When that psyche is maintained in the presence of Possibility it provides a test of the legitimacy of a particular belief, and of what is to be accepted as a genuine actuality. Some objects are accepted as actualities and some beliefs are accepted as legitimate because they are in accord with the psyche. The accepted actualities and beliefs in turn provide tests for the acceptability of other actualities and beliefs.

When the reason is benefited by Possibility it legitimatizes various attitudes and demands. Some attitudes are accepted as primary and some demands are accepted as right because they are so certified by the reason. What is initially accepted becomes thereafter a test of what is to be accepted later. It is the reason which provides the initial standard, so far as it is enriched by Possibility.

Possibility enables the mind to define which affirmations and abstractions are to be received as correct. These in turn determine what is to be taken to be an affirmation or an abstraction. We assess affirmations from the position of abstractions derived from the world, assess the abstractions from the position of affirmations, assess affirmations from the position of received affirmations, and assess abstractions from the position of other abstractions.

The sensibility provides criteria for the acceptability of feelings. Some of these are allowed initially because of their ready concurrence with the sensibility. Thereafter they are able to function in place of the sensibility, dictating which further feelings are reputable.

Finally, the spirit dictates that whatever is accepted as true must contribute to a single valuable totality in which everything else is true. Each item in the totality tests and is tested by the others. An attained totality is the locus of known truths, and evaluates all new

claimants to truth. It may be forced to give way to a new totality
where it may have to be altered so as to be in harmony with what is
newly accepted. Though the old totality is never simply abandoned,
it also does not simply remain. It is incorporated in the new totality;
the truth of this requires the old to give up some of its claim to
truth, or to change the import of what is claimed there. Einstein's
physical system neither assimilates nor replaces Newton's; it joins it
in a larger whole of truth where the one is occupied with astronomical
and the other with terrestrial matters. Even the Ptolemaic astronomy
is preserved, though as true only for calculations which do not assume
the movement of the earth. Sometimes, of course, a view is abandoned because it is incompatible with some large body of well-
certified truths. It could have been retained, but at the price of
modifying that larger body.

Naming and describing finalities depends on a prior assumption
of the position of Substance; taking up a position in opposition to
finalities depends on the prior assumption of the position of Being;
conceptualization presupposes the position of Possibility; dialectic
presupposes the position of Existence; and symbolization presupposes
the position of Unity. Naming and describing are faced with the
need to provide accuracy and usefulness; a position of opposition is
faced with a need for detachment and attachment; conceptualization
is faced with a need for clarity and distinctness; dialectic is faced
with a need to provide direction and effectiveness, and symbolization
is faced with the need to be pure and intensive. Each is acceptable
only so far as it is in accord with a trued expression of the self. Each
provides a method for reaching a finality.

The different roles the self assumes are independent of one
another; one can be emphasized and the others neglected. Each can
provide a test for the acceptability of the others. It is because this
is so that it is possible to hold some version of fallibilism with its
denial of final truths. To claim that no statement is final, though,
one must have already adopted the role, say of a psyche, and accepted
the position that no statement is fully in consonance with what has
already been adopted by it. Fallibilists in any one realm are dog-
matists in some other; conversely, those who insist on one of the

roles in preference to others inevitably question the basicality of those others and are so far fallibilists with respect to these.

Whatever the role assumed, it must be maintained against others. So far as it successfully avoids distortion by what is not itself, so far is it able to dictate to others what is to be true of them. A man, to be sure, may obstinately hold on to some idea or statement in the face of the demands of the world about. What he then does is to insist on an error, when as a matter of fact he is overruled and precluded from functioning properly in certain areas. Only what is true is persistently maintained by a trued self against the demands of that of which it is true.

[4. IDENTITY]

Over the course of their careers, men change in body and shape, in mental content, in expression, in self-assessment, in what they do, in how they react, and in their relations to other men and other realities, particular and final. Despite that fact, each is selfsame over an entire life. Responsibility for an evil done cannot be voided by one changing his body or mind, by his forgetting, or by his telling lies. It is the same individual who is born, lives, and dies.

Because he changes, a man cannot be simply self-identical. A simple self-identity might characterize an isolated segment of him. But then we would have the problem of relating this to the changes which also characterize him. His identity is not some item alongside others, but is involved with his changing life and adventures. It is not a thing or a structure fixed in advance, but a persistent outcome, the residuum of a process of identification by means of which he holds on to his past and reaches into his future.

A man makes his identity. He holds on to what had been and what will be, and relates these to what he now is at the same time that he makes what he now is pertain to them. There need be nothing conscious here, no reliance on memory, no expectation or knowledge. What he had been is now in him in his habits and character, and occasionally in his memory. What he will be is in him in his attitudes, his dedications, his hopes, and his expectations. The reduction of the different contents that he takes in from past and future he makes come to the same result. Were there no such identity, there would be no one who acted, no one who could be praised or blamed.

A man's identity can be confronted as a datum in the very act of acknowledging him. His identity is exhibited now because his present radiates out toward his past and the future at the same time that it turns them into its antecedent and consequent. He is self-identical because his present always has the selfsame import for what had been and what will be, changing its relations to them and possessing them differently at different moments in order to have them sum to the same present result.

Despite his changes, a man is confronted as a constant, for his present is faced not as an isolated moment but as affecting what he had been and what he can be. Did we not confront him as owning a past and a future which he sums to the same value throughout his life, we could know him only as present, with an indifferent past and an open future. Other actualities also internalize their pasts and are directed toward relevant futures, but no one of them has a self-same present, because no one of them adopts its past and future so as to make good the losses produced in the past and to satisfy the demands of an ideal in the future. Only man has the ability to reduce what had been and what can be to one constant present value. His identity operates on whatever he is involved with. He leaves his mark on everything, a signature which is always the same in import since it varies with the different places in which it is inscribed. His identity has a different content from moment to moment, always reduced to the same result.

Who is the "he" who reduces the different items to the same result? If he is already self-identical the question of identity evidently has not been faced. The difficulty is unavoidable unless we recognize the complex reality of a man, within which his career and ultimately his identity is to be found. Though a man changes in activity to keep abreast of changes in content, he remains self-identical because he answers those changes with new ways of equating the new with the old. He acts on all else in many ways and with many results; the use he makes of what he confronts depends on whether he is functioning as a psyche, reason, mind, sensibility, or spirit. These are independent expressions of him and, as a consequence, he can be self-identical in one of these guises and not in the others. The absolute self-identical man is one who is not only identical in all, but who has reduced them all to the selfsame result. One can credit that identity solely to the self, provided only that it be understood that the self is no self-contained nucleus, but that which assumes these different roles, and brings their contents to one selfsame result.

An individual, to be sure, grows and decays in the course of time. His knowledge increases; he remembers and forgets; he adventures with his body and bears the scars of past encounters. He sleeps. He may lose consciousness and sanity. But he still continues to be identical because of what he does to what he deals with.

Each action on and by a psyche offers a challenge to one's identity. For the identity to be maintained, the psyche must recover its independence at the same time that it reduces all changes to subordinated notes within itself. This requires it to hold on to what has already occurred to it, and to give a present weight to what is now possible to it. The psyche existentializes itself in relation to Existence, to make the psyche a present background on which memories and anticipations are embedded. It thereby makes relevant the past and future which continue to extend beyond it. Did this not occur, the psyche would have a purely private memory and anticipation whose contents were entirely located in the present or referred to what was alien to them.

By maintaining itself against Existence, a man's reason obtains a past and a future which are distinct from but are as real as its present. There is a genuine external past which history tries to know, and there are genuine future possibilities which function as lures and guides for men who plan and intend. Were this not to take place, every occurrence would vanish with the passing moment, and there would be occurrences in the present which had not been possible.

Past and future for the psyche have a projective character to them; past and future for the reason merely abut the present. For the mind, past and the future have a nature somewhat between these two. Each is directed away from and toward the present, thereby giving the present, despite its unit nature, an internal directionality. Otherwise, past and future would be simply areas without temporal natures of their own.

For the sensibility, past and future are attenuations of the present, fringing it on opposing sides. Whatever is located in the past is then just a fact, a present denied vitality but able to exclude and be excluded by what is now taking place. Whatever is located in the future is then only a possibility, a present not yet determinate but able to lure and control what is happening. Past and future are thereby distinguished from the present but not set at another time.

For the spirit, past, present, and future constitute a single whole of time. This is neither present nor not present; the present, like the past and the future, are distinctions within it. The spirit reduces what will be and what has been to what now is; it makes the past and future always have the same meaning for it, in itself as a single unit. For it, divisions of time are just distinctions made in the whole of time. The spirit is selfsame precisely because their differentiation is not relevant to it. It is of this that Augustine evidently spoke when he referred to time as a "distension of the soul." What he did not see is that there are not only other dimensions of the individual, but presents, pasts, and futures apart from the "soul."

Time is a dimension of Existence. So are space and causality. When the self enriches itself by means of Existence it makes use of these dimensions as well. But the space is utilized only so far as the self is occupied with bodies, and the causality is utilized only so far as the self, through intent, initiates and controls actions. Both presuppose the identity which persistently subordinates and redefines what occurs in time.

[5. IMMORTALITY]

Some men claim to experience God in the course of their religious practices, in ritual and in prayer, in genuine solitude, when they accept various objects as sacramental, or when they achieve a mystical insight. These could conceivably bolster, supplement, criticize, or guide the arguments that have been made to prove there is a God. But there appear to be no independent sources of evidence for immortality to sustain arguments advanced on its behalf. To be sure, we do have reports which purport to be from those who have died. These, however, can be accounted for in other ways with little difficulty. Moreover, if the reports were accurate, they would tell us no more than that some men continue to exist after death, and then perhaps only for a little while.

Immortality, too, seems to pertain only to a segment or a fragment of a man. When he dies, his body remains behind, unquickened, decaying, soon crumbling into dust. If a man is immortal, it must be with respect to some other aspect of him. But if we take this to be some hard core, separate and detached from the rest of him, it will be what does not die because it never in fact was part of his bodily life. It will not assure the immortality of an individual who actually lives through and bears the effects of a particular career in this space-time-dynamic world of interplay, sufferings, and effective action.

If, for simplicity's sake, we take a man to be constituted of a self and a body, each with a controlling unity and a diversity of content, we can say that when he is alive the content of his body overrides the content of his self at the same time that the unity of his self overrides the unity of his body, with the result that the content of the self is submerged beneath the content of the body, and the unity of the body is submerged beneath the unity of the self. As a consequence, a man seems to have just the unity that his self provides and just the content that his body provides. On death, the overriding ceases. The body, therefore, recovers its own unity to become just a body alongside other bodies; the unity of that body is then only the unity of a mere aggregate of parts, no longer functioning under the governance of a self. By taking away the overriding content of the body, death, at the same time, allows the self to have its own content together with its own unity.

This account leaves over a number of questions. How could self and body be related? What does it mean for the self to exist? Why should not the body, once it has been freed from the overriding unity of the self, continue to be a single unity controlling bodily content, and that forever? These questions remain open as long as we fail to distinguish the different ways in which a man, through the agency of his self, is enriched by Unity.

Held apart from a body, there could conceivably be a substantial self, but that would demand, as Aquinas clearly saw, a resurrection of an incorruptible body which must be joined to it if the immortality is to be that of a man. Not only does the position allow the self to exist for a while apart from the body and, therefore, to be substantial enough to exist without a body, but the final result depends on the performance of a divine act not known by philosophic reason. Also, the self is then supposed to be so self-centered that it precludes comparison or relationship with other realities; so individual that it is without intelligibility; so fixed that it is unaffected by the course of life; and so substantial that it is incapable of being a genuine constituent of a complex unitary man, now or later.

The self benefits from all the finalities. Substance enables it to be an individual privacy; Being, instead, contrasts with the self, to make it a being rightly claiming to be on a footing with others. Possibility is accepted by the self as a context in which the self's nature becomes intelligible. Existence is adjusted to by the self, and the self thereby acquires a past and future. Faced with Unity, the self reorganizes itself so as to have a unity of its own.

The reorganization of the self requires the transmutation of the items within it, just so far as they are disparate, irrelevant, or in conflict with one another. The more incomplete its own reorganization, the more must it be reorganized. If the result of its reorganization is not altogether in consonance with other unities, it and the others must be reorganized if they, in turn, are to be encompassed within a more comprehensive unity.

A good guide to the nature of the preservation and transformation that is characteristic of the unity of the self is provided by a painting. The colors on a painter's brush are the very colors that he introduces into his painting; his act of painting is their transformation. The resultant work, if a work of art, is a single whole in which the weights of the various colors are determined by the way they interlock with one another. The colors together are the colors in their severalty, transformed by and within the unity that they help constitute. To get to the colors in their severalty again, one must abstract them from the colors as together.

Immortality accrues to the self in the form of a diversified unity, so far as this in turn is compatible with the diversified unity that other actualities provide. What eventually passes away is the incompatibility; what is preserved is what has been made coherent. At one conceivable extreme are just contents so disparate as to require radical alteration; at the other conceivable extreme are unities which require no change in order for these to be perfectly harmonized.

The psyche is immortal just so far as it is a functioning center for a plurality of individual stresses, promising expression and action in different directions. From the standpoint of Unity, the psyche is preserved by Unity; its center, and what this unites are continuations of Unity. Unity accepts the center as a constituent of its own articulate but coherent content.

Reason has a plurality of contents. These, in contrast with the stresses of the psyche, are so many different standpoints expressing in equivalent ways the being of the self. These are altered so as to be unified in a single unitary outlook. As a consequence of its unification of its standpoints within a single outlook, reason becomes maximally compatible with Unity itself. That Unity finds a place for the outlook and its encompassed standpoints so far as they can be made compatible with the outlooks of other men and with the perspectives of other beings. Since the immortality which reason thereby achieves is independent of that acquired by the psyche, it is possible for a man to be maximally preserved as the one and minimally preserved as the other, depending on how much alteration is required to enable them to be together with other related unities.

Mind, too, is a one and a many. It has a plurality of foci, all encompassed within a single category of intelligibility. The foci are not always compatible, and where compatible are not always relevant to one another. Possibility acts on them to make them constitute a single unified whole. Unity adopts the intelligible unified foci so far as these can be made compatible with other intelligible unities. As a consequence, the mind is immortalized. This immortalization occurs in partial independence of the immortalization of the psyche and the reason. Though all are inescapably immortalized, they differ in the degree to which they are able to have their unifications and diversities preserved without alteration.

Sensibility encompasses a plurality of feelings. Sensibility's unity integrates the diverse feelings, altering what it must in order to have those feelings harmonize with one another. Unity adopts that unity as its own, so far as this is compatible with the adoption of other unities. The result is that the feelings are preserved by Unity in a form more or less altered from that which they had initially.

Finally, the spirit unites a plurality of assessors by means of a single, prescriptive assessment. The assessment requires some alteration on the part of the assessors before these can function as its unified content; the result of the union of the assessment with that content itself is content for Unity. Whatever is preserved in the assessment of the spirit is preserved via that assessment by Unity. The partial independence of this preservation from the others makes it possible for values to be preserved with one degree of modification while feelings, for example, are preserved in another degree.

The self is no mere aggregate of roles. It has a reality of its own. But if we wish to avoid confusing it with itself in its roles, we should speak of it by itself in terms distinct from those we employ when we refer to those roles. Instead, then, of saying that the self is an individual, it would be better to say that it is unique; instead of saying that it has rights, it would be better to say that it has importance; instead of saying that it is trued, it is better to say that it is authentic; instead of saying that it is self-identical, it would be better to say that it has integrity; and instead of saying that it is a unity, it would be better to say that it is singular. Or, alternatively, one should use 'individual,' 'rights,' 'truth,' 'identity,' and 'unity,' with special subscripts to distinguish the fact that these have an import in relation to the self different from what they have for the roles of the self. In either way, the fact that the self has a reality and function of its own, and that it encompasses the different contents possessed in its various roles, is allowed. The self is immortalized as encompassing them, but is altered so as to be compatible with what else is immortal.

Immortalization is a process taking place here and now. What occurs here and now has a place in what is forever. The self is a reality which exists in contrast with Unity and is able to be accommodated by it as an attenuated limit of itself. Unity accepts the self with more and more intimacy in the course of altering it so as to make it part of a single content. The result is preserved by Unity so far as this can be done compatibly with the preservation of others.

Immortality is not peculiar to man, or even to living beings, for even a physical entity has a unity which is congenial to Unity. The conclusion appears strange because man has overpersonalized the question of immortality, just as he has overpersonalized God. Yet, just as God is a finality whose reality ontologically grounds and is not dependent on religion or His religious viability, so immortality is an ontological result whose warrant does not depend on its ability to satisfy man's hopes or desires. If it be supposed that a man is immortalized through the action of a God, reasons should be provided showing that there is such a God, and that He engages in these actions.

Common expectations and desires with respect to immortality cannot be justified without the benefit of special knowledge beyond the reach of philosophic speculation, argument, or analysis. Those expectations and desires may require what is not compatible with what is the case. Nor need one adopt the common way of speaking of immortality as though it were a process by which a part of a man acquires an independent existence in a place outside this world, where it holds on to what it had been, unchanged or purged of irrelevancies and defects. If what is immortalized is placed somewhere remote from this world, there will be the problem of getting to that remote region, and of understanding how the separated entity can function there.

Actualities below the level of man, like man, are substances which instantiate and maintain themselves against Substance. Like man, they too are unique realities, insistent, resistant, self-enclosed, contributing to the constitution of appearances and able to sustain symbols of Substance. Since they have little or no power to unify content, they can be preserved only as comparatively empty units or as together. Rights, trued natures, identities, nevertheless can be ascribed to them. But since none of them is able to maintain itself against all the finalities, they are substances which lack the richness characteristic of a substantial man. Their rights, natures, and identities pertain to them as together with others, not as they are in themselves.

A man substantializes himself as a unity by internalizing a qualification imposed by Unity. Most of the other actualities are unable to internalize the qualification which Unity imposes on them, and are, therefore, unable to substantialize themselves as unities in themselves. They are immortal both as individual substances (which may have been partly enriched through an internalization of some of the qualifications they acquired from the various finalities), and as together with one another (and therefore as qualified by a common permanent Unity). Men, in contrast, are immortal as individual substances which have internalized the qualifications imposed by all the finalities. They alone are immortal as individuals who instance all the finalities. This, to be sure, is not the immortality that interests most men. They hope for an immortality in which there is a consciousness, and even a use of the mind, continuous with present uses. But consciousness depends on the presence and use of a living body, and it is this which is lost on death. Consciousness can not be immortalized except as possessed by Unity. But even then it would be no more than a residuum, unable to be quickened because detached from a functioning, living body.

A man is preserved in those roles which are non-bodily in nature, and so far as they are nonbodily in function. He is immortal as a psyche, reason, mind, sensibility, and spirit, encompassing and unifying appropriate content, all encompassed in a single unity. A richer or better or more desirable immortality can conceivably be vouchsafed by some special knowledge, acquired either from an encounter with those who have died, or with Unity itself, or with its messengers. But to get these one must pass outside the bounds of philosophic capacities.

Everything in this world is perishable; everything in this world, nevertheless, has a minimal immortality. The two differ as the separate differs from itself as continuous with a finality. As perishable, each is self-enclosed; as immortal, it is encompassed by Unity. Each is able to be immortalized without change the more harmonious it is.

When virtue is identified with what completes and solidifies, and vice with what destroys, separates, and conflicts, that man is most adequately preserved who lives a life of virtue. But he, too, will finally be overcome and reassessed within Unity as it exists in itself, for Unity reorganizes all that occurs, to make it all sum to a single maximum value. But we have no way of knowing exactly what Unity alters and how, whether or not Unity is conscious, and whether it knows or preserves the consciousness that men possess.

A man has immortality now while he lives. He then also has an individuality, rights, a trued self, and an identity. To accept him in these forms is the beginning of a humane wisdom. That matures the more he comes to know the nature of the various finalities, the way in which he and other actualities interplay with them, and how he and they internalize them to make themselves instances of and, thereby, acceptable to those finalities.

16

~~~~~~

MIND, BODY, MEN, AND MACHINES

~~~~~~

Controlling Summary: Actualities differ from machines in having single privacies. Men differ from other types of living actualities in having their privacies embody the different finalities, with the consequence that each has a psyche, reason, mind, sensibility, and spirit. When these are maintained in opposition to all else they are the subjects of individuality, rights, truth, identity, and immortality.

Understanding and awareness are distinct operations of mind. Both have objects and careers of their own; both are expressed in and through the body. It is therefore just as true to say that the human body is a self capable of public action as it is to say that the self is the human body at its most private.

Beyond the capacity of any machine to duplicate are men's capacities to be aware, to withdraw from the world, to wonder, and to creatively use what they encounter. They have a distinctive freedom which they can use to envisage ideals and to act to realize these. Their irreducible centrality and flexibility permits them to make new uses of old programs, and to produce new programs for old material. Allied with one another in opposition to all else, they alone can produce new appearances which make possible insights into the depths of actualities and finalities. And all are chargeable with doing less than they ought because all are measured by an ought-to-be that is beyond their power to realize.

~~~~~~

Individuality, rights, truth, identity, and immortality are not observable. Criteria are needed to enable one to decide whether or not they are to be credited to a man. If the criteria are not to be arbitrary, and, therefore, if they are not to authorize judgments which have nothing that answers to them, there must be criteria for the choosing of the criteria. But then, it would seem, we are led back and back over an infinite regress. The regress is avoided with the recognition that the criteria for the selecting of criteria are provided by the psyche, reason, mind, sensibility, and spirit; these provide distinctive groundings for man's individuality, rights, truth, identity, and immortality. Now, though, we seem to be caught in a vicious circle, since we are apparently using the objects of speculative judgments to tell us when we can accept something as the test that such objects are present.

Available occurrences are used to provide criteria, telling us whether or not those occurrences are themselves possessed by and do not merely accompany an individual; express a native right rather than a permission; sustain what is genuinely true rather than what is merely agreed upon; are part of the identical rather than of the merely continuous; and are caught up in immortality rather than in an ongoing. The occurrences, to yield the criteria, must be generalized, for criteria have multiple applications. The result will then have to be made specific and determinate in the course of particular uses, for otherwise it will not be pertinent to one particular item rather than another.

We grow up in a society where there are established criteria for what is not observable. What those criteria are we learn in the course of maturation. But we would be just mimics or actors or zombies or frauds if we did not possess a generic form of what satisfied the criteria. The generic is where the specific is; the indeterminate is part of what is determinate. But the generic indeterminate has a nature and status and role of its own. Normally no attention is paid to the generic form, but this does not preclude its operation in the acceptance of criteria which are to serve as tests for the presence of what is specific and private.

Criteria are observable occurrences used to report the presence of what is not observable. They can be acted on, controlled, and sometimes utilized by others. A special case is a sensation, a feeling, or an emotion. Pain may serve as an example. A generic pain—a pain which is not identified as a pain in the toe or the leg, as being due to gas or the heart—is used by the psyche to pick out specific occurrences such as swelling, discolorations, responses to further pressure; any or all of these are then used as criteria for the presence of particular pains. The unspecified pain itself does not allow one to discriminate one of these items from another. But were it not for its use, there would be no warrant for accepting what is evidently not a pain, but a mere change in the body, as a criterion for the presence of a particular pain.

The individualized psyche adopts a conspicuous confronted occurrence as a criterion for the presence of an expression of that psyche. To make the occurrence into a criterion, it not only has to attend to it as an observable, but to generalize it so that it can have multiple applications, and then must specify the result in use to make it signalize the presence of an expression. It thus provides an objective referent for the presence of what is private. Did the psyche not make such use of something confronted, whatever occurred could conceivably be irrelevant to the psyche and its expressions. There would then be no observable occurrence by means of which one could report to another that something private, of such and such a type, was taking place.

Implicitly we take all men to use the same considerations in picking out criteria for ascertaining what concretely each of us privately is. We are allied with one another socially so far as we all make use of similar criteria. Our private solidarity as men is supplemented by a social solidarity; in the one, there is an instancing of the same generic realities, while in the other there is an acceptance of similar, particular occurrences as the beginnings for justified references to what each is.

It is not because we have primary access to ourselves and suppose that other men are similar to ourselves that they are confidently taken to be individuals with their own rights, trued selves, identities, and immortality. There is no warrant for supposing that what we discover in ourselves is similar to anything in those we publicly confront. And when we come to know our public bodies we know them in ways we do not know the others; we feel with, in, and through them, but not with, in, and through the others.

We confront other men; we attend to their appearances. Apart from the symbolization by means of which we reach them as they are in themselves, we make use of some of their appearances as publicly available criteria to judge what they are in themselves, not as men standing apart from us, but as allied with us. As allied we all instance a common nature. Each of us distinguishes himself from the others by specific acts expressive of his irreducible determinate distinctness. Each of us uses the specific acts of others as criteria for determining just which specifications of the common nature are to be attributed to them. Ideally, the attribution will take the form of a symbolization; one then makes contact with them.

[2]

The self has a number of roles; the most important of these are the psyche, reason, mind, sensibility, and spirit. The psyche is the most interior of all; its successors on the list are more and more exterior to it. In turn each is interior to those that succeed it. And each has a bodily counterpart: the possessed, the bounded, the living, the sensitive, and the behaving public body. Some of these are themselves subdivided, and the result has further subdivisions. The divisions do not mark out compartments or faculties, but emphases which have had practical and historical importance. The main divisions are:

I SELF

1. psyche, 2. reason, 3. mind, 4. sensibility, 5. spirit

    3. A. intuition
       B. understanding
       C. awareness
       D. sensitivity
       E. attention

B. Understanding
  a. intention
  b. articulation
  c. reasoning
  d. judgment
  e. claiming

C. Awareness
  a. insight
  b. apprehension
  c. consciousness
  d. feeling
  e. intimation

II PUBLIC BODY

1. possessed,   2. bounded,   3. living,   4. sensitive,   5. behaving

3. A. readied
  B. lived
  C. organic
  D. feeling-tone
  E. interactive

B. Lived Body
  a. self-maintaining
  b. assertive
  c. purposive
  d. performing
  e. assessive

C. Organic Body
  a. immersed
  b. pivotal
  c. directed
  d. impulsive
  e. adoptive

Any of these, bodily or not, can be split into two, one unrelated, the other related to something beyond. The self (I) divides into a secret and an expressed self; judgment (I, 3, B, d) divides into the terminus and the residuum of an activity. The organic body (II, 3, C) divides into a used body and an observable one; the purposive lived body (II, 3, B, c) divides into an intentional and an oriented lived body.

The interior limit of a man is the psyche (I, 1); his exterior limit is his adoptive organic body (II, 3, C, e). What is between the two can be credited to the one or the other. The self can be taken to stretch from the psyche to the adoptive organic body, and to have exterior to itself only the organic body as approached from outside it. The organic body, equally, can be taken to stretch from the world in which it is involved to the expressed self, and have beyond it only the secret self.

The outermost reach of a man is inwardly held; the innermost core is outwardly involved. The organic body belongs to the self; the self belongs to the organic body. At every point we can distinguish an inner and an outer. Since the result can also be divided into an inner and outer, it is possible to distinguish inners and outers without end. That outcome is inevitable so long as inner and outer, unrelated and related, are put on a footing. It is avoided with the recognition that the outer is that at which the inner expressively arrives (through the help of the outer), and that the inner is the outer intensified and at which one symbolically arrives from the outer (through the help of the inner). Wherever we start we go through a series of inners and outers; that with which we end is an outer/inner, undivided and defiant.

The problem of inner and outer has, since Descartes, been treated mainly as one having to do solely with the relation of mind to body (or brain). But both of these are partly independent outers for a single more basic inner. They are both the self in different limited situations where it is occupied with what is independent of it.

If we ignore the self, the problem of body and mind assumes the guise in which it interests most thinkers today. Thereupon it is often unduly narrowed by the assumption that it then has to do only with the relation of particular meanings to observable or conditioning bodily occurrences. Not only are other dimensions of man then ignored, but no reference is made to the various finalities. Yet, without such a reference, it is not possible, I think, to do justice to the problem even in its current form.

Men differ from both machines and animals, primarily because their human inwardness is maintained against all the finalities preliminary to a relating of that inwardness to their more outward aspects, to other actualities, and to the finalities. This fundamental difference is exhibited in a number of distinctive ways.

1] Each man has a single inwardness; his psyche, reason, and the others do not divide it, but merely refer to it as engaged in special functions. A machine does not exhibit similar specializations, nor does it have a single inwardness. At best it has a plurality of inwardnesses, each belonging to a distinct physical part, or to their constituents. Animals, though, like men, have an inwardness. But theirs falls short of men's in richness, reach, and use.

2] Men can take a stand at their selves. Each has an inwardness with a being of its own, giving him a distinctive dignity. Machines, in contrast, have the status of aggregates, while animals are beings in a world with others. The most advanced of animals may, like men, be at once substances, meaningful, existent, and unitary, but, unlike men, they do not internalize the qualification to which Being subjects them.

3] Men impose conditions, provided by what is relatively interior, on what is relatively exterior. Machines may carry out conditions, but they do not impose them. Animals carry out conditions, but are unable to take themselves to be centers for all else.

4] Men are frequently thrown back into themselves by untoward events. Sometimes they deliberately withdraw into themselves. In either way they are open to a direct confrontation with finalities. They are then able to appreciatively wonder, and to occupy themselves with making the finalities known and used. The finalities are responded to emotionally, and are submitted to as so many controls. Neither machines nor animals can wonder, the one because it has no privacy into which it can withdraw, the other because it cannot withdraw far enough.

5] Men interrelate in many ways what is relatively interior with what is relatively exterior. Either the interior or the exterior may be dominant, and then in different degrees. Since machines have no privacy, and animals have none which is able to function independently of the observable, organic body, neither can distinguish self and body, or interior and exterior, and relate them as condition and conditioned.

[3]

Man creatively reaches out to and internalizes what is outer in a way that no other reality can. As a consequence, his body is distinguished in a number of ways in nature and use from the bodies of physical things, machines, and animals.

1] Because bodies are palpable, and some of their activities predictable, and because bodies are topics for the more exact and successful sciences, one is tempted, with the materialists, to try to free oneself from reference to anything but bodies, and then only as known by the sciences. The attempt must fail, since at the very least it presupposes what it seeks to deny. It necessarily acknowledges non-bodily items in order to have something to reduce. Did it not, there would be nothing for it to reduce. It must also attend to nonbodily items in order to express what it has achieved.

How awkward it is for materialism that its theory is not itself material, but a claim to truth based on evidences not identifiable with anything material, and referring to what itself is not material. For a materialism, too, there can be no prescriptive conditions dictating where divisions in bodies are to be made, or where different bodies can function as units in relation to one another. For it, therefore, there can be no laws, no organizations, no cosmos. But then there can be no world of material units all in the same space and time, caught in the same web of causality, to be understood in the same ways. Materialism also tacitly makes reference to what is not material in the form of experienced data on which it depends for content; it tacitly distinguishes meanings from existents, prescriptions from descriptions. It also tacitly presupposes the reality of actualities and finalities, for the objects in which it is interested are cosmic unities which the actualities and the finalities together constitute. Since it makes claims and communicates, it inevitably offers assertions, judgments, and arguments, which have the nonmaterialistic properties of truth or falsehood, validity or nonvalidity, and necessity or contingency.

What is confronted in experience or in daily commerce is the mottled surface of the bodies that are known to science. These bodies are the objective appearances of actualities, to be grasped by a non-material mind. Even if all actualities were without any interiority, or were not realities in their own right, they could not be known to exist except by one who had such a mind.

A substance not only opposes other substances, but Substance itself; it has an inwardness not reducible to its surface or its acts. A machine, no matter how well put together, is put together from the outside. It always remains a plurality of distinct entities. Each of these has the minimal inwardness of a physical thing, without the enrichment which is to be obtained by standing in opposition to finalities other than Substance. But that it is a substance, materialism cannot know, unless it allows for the use of nonmaterial powers by which to grasp realities transcending the experience of extended things.

Man's inwardness is unitary. It is one, not because his body is one, but conversely. His body is one because it is enlivened from within by a single inwardness. As standing apart from all finalities that inwardness is a self. This is open to and makes use of the very finalities in opposition to which it maintains itself as an independently functioning reality. The conscious mind is the self in one role; alternatively, the conscious mind is the organic body focused on meanings that are governed and interrelated prescriptively.

The human body is the self involved in public activities, interconnected in law-abiding and other prescriptive ways. Instead of the body one could, therefore, speak of the extended self; instead of the self one could speak of an individuated body. Nothing is altered in principle when one refers to the human brain instead of to the organic body, or to an attentive focusing apparatus instead of an awareness, for the brain, too, is exterior to the self. Nor is anything significantly altered when one abandons the term *self*, so long as a distinction is made between the body or brain as it is involved with what is external to itself, and between the body or brain as interior to this. But once that distinction is made, the existence of an awareness will compel a further distinction between the body or brain as it is possessed and as it is used. That distinction will entrain a further distinction between the body or brain as possessed or used and what possesses or uses it.

2] When machines are made to duplicate the publicly evident activities of animals and men, they do not then acquire bodily beings. They are still aggregations and combinations of physical units, without distinctive beings of their own. Animals have distinctive beings as together, but have no ability to make themselves function as central superior realities in terms of which all else is approached. Occupied with satisfying their bodily needs, they cannot take a stand away from their bodies. A man, in contrast, can hold himself away from his body. He can take a stand at his being, and look out at all else as beings, all coordinate in relation to him. His being, with its rights, is inward to his body, and can be expressed in and through it.

Because each man has a being in terms of which other actualities are credited with being (in relation to him), each has a dignity denied to other types of reality. The conjoint presence of all beings other than men contrasts with men as constituting a single human-kind. There each man faces the remaining actualities.

From the standpoint of Being itself, animals and things have beings equal to man's. But because man's ultimate inwardness has a being of its own, it can stand apart from and make use of what is relatively exterior, to make him distinctive, not reducible to an animal, thing, or machine. Their beings are entirely contextualized and cannot be maintained in independence of Being or of other beings.

A reason is an internally instancing being. Because neither a machine nor an animal can individually maintain itself against Being, neither can have a reason. Only man has a reason, because only he is able to internally instance Being itself. Only he, therefore, is able to be a bearer of rights—the native right to privacy, to be, to know, to experience, and to worship. Animals have the right to be living actualities in a world of actualities, but they do not internally possess rights, since they do not internally maintain themselves in contrast with Being. And, since they have no distinctive inwardness of their own, machines have no rights at all.

3] Men are not wholly self-enclosed. They are involved with other realities. That involvement can be brought under their control to some degree. As a consequence, it is possible for men to subject what lies outside themselves to themselves as apart from it. One result of this is consciousness. This is a special case of awareness. It is mind as exterior to both intuition and understanding, each of which can possess and qualify it.

A mind is an inward instantiation of Possibility. Strictly speaking, it is attributable only to men and animals. A machine can be credited with a "mind," though, when this is identified with a plan, or program, or arrangment. Such a "mind" is indistinguishable from an arrangement of the parts of a machine, from an outlining of the steps involved in the functioning of the machine, or from a way of determining the selections and rejections of externally presented items. A machine cannot use these prescriptively, or combine them with a consciousness. And though an animal can have a conscious mind, it cannot use this to understand Being or any other finality, since it is unable to withdraw fully from its involvement with actualities and finalities.

Possibility itself can be made the object of a conscious mind. It can be approached from the position of a particular meaning which takes Possibility to be but one of a number of subordinate meanings. This is what is done when men deal with Possibility in relation to other meanings. Possibility then is understood to be just the most comprehensive of meanings.

Possibility can also be dealt with as subordinating itself, in the guise of a particular meaning, to itself as all-comprehensive. It is then related to other meanings. This is done when one deals with the intelligible relations which Possibility has to other finalities and to actualities as, for example, when it is said that "Possibility is only one of many realities."

Possibility can also be treated as the final objective of inquiry, subordinating every identifiable form of itself as a particular meaning. In this and in the other cases, mind is in a primary position, with an incidental stress on Possibility in contrast with other finalities. Only man is able to engage in these different activities with relation to Possibility because only he has a self which can be disentangled from the world of actualities. Such disentanglement is necessary if he is to occupy himself appreciatively with any of the finalities.

The various roles of the self, through the help of Possibility, offer grounds for distinctive types of truth. Intellectuals are primarily interested in the truths grounded in the mind, but there are other types as well. There is a truth expressive of a sound psyche, another having to do with a sound reason, a third deals with the way in which one fits into the world, and a fourth relates to the degree of rectification that is necessary in order for a man to be a unity in harmony with others. It is possible to do justice to one of them at the same time that one fails to do justice to the others. All have their importance.

There is no truth that is pertinent to machines. By an extension of terms, though, one can speak of them as being trued to their tasks. Animals, because they have an inwardness, are more appropriately said to be true. But, unlike man, they do not and cannot assert truths because, unlike man, they are unable to withdraw from all finalities and actualities preliminary to getting a better grip on both. They are not even able to engage in inquiry, for this requires an attention to final, luring prospects, rooted in the various finalities.

4] Each self, in a different way, is engaged in the activity of reducing a multiplicity of diverse items to the selfsame result. Some men maintain an identity in mind by maintaining themselves in opposition to the demands of Possibility, while neglecting the identity they could obtain in opposition to the demands of the other finalities. Different men, consequently, become self-identical in different ways and with different results. But there is no self-identity possible either to machines or animals.

Machines persist through time. Animals are affected by their pasts, and turn toward the future burdened by those pasts. Men alone have an identity despite time, their spatial extensions, and the effects they suffer, because they use Existence to hold together what is spread out over regions of space, time, and causality. Machines may make use of memory banks, but they cannot use Existence to give their past a new import in the present. They cannot give themselves an identity, because they are unable to use a persistent Existence as an agent for unifying separated portions of Existence. They are therefore unable to have emotions, to undergo terror or joy. Animals, though, have emotions; they may undergo something akin to terror or joy, but they cannot isolate the appropriate objects of more basic emotions, because they cannot attend appreciatively to finalities as they stand apart from all else. Only men can wonder.

5] Machines are sustained by a technology which outlasts any of them; the unity of each, too, as the unity of an aggregate, is preserved within Unity. Animals are subservient to groups; the unity of each is

also preserved, but as insufficiently filled out. Men alone have individualized beings, natures, extensions, and unities. Each is immortalized as instantiating and standing opposed to all the other
finalities.

Things, animals, and men are able to have an immortal status
because Unity is not wholly sunk within itself, but holds on to
subordinate unities. Only men, though, are distinct substances which
stand away from all the finalities. Only they, therefore, are capable of
being preserved by Unity in that guise.

[4]

The relation of mind to body offers a special case of the problem
that arises when a finality, or a specification of it, is brought to play
on limited versions of itself. Were there no finalities, there would be
just singular actualities. But were there only these, there would be no
thing to which they were compelled to submit. Finalities make it
possible for the inner to control the outer in terms not available to
the outer. When the finality is Possibility, the result is a mind.

Mind and awareness are distinct. A mind without awareness is a
structure, an order, a rationale—a locus and not an act. An awareness
without a mind is a mere confronting of meanings. The best machine
has only a mind; it has no meanings to interlock with principles.
Were there sense-impressions they would be units for a mere awareness. But since no meaning can be isolated without the help of Possibility, or a specialization of it, there is no genuine awareness without
a mind.

A conscious mind is a locus and an act. As a locus it encompasses a number of interrelated meanings. As an act it makes use of a
principle to govern and relate meanings. In either way, it enables the
principles to become indirectly involved with the natures of things,
for those natures are just meanings ingredient in those things.

A principle is a prescription, applicable to whatever meanings
are distinguished; meanings are data to be prescribed to and related.
Since the connecting of a principle with meanings does not compromise the independence of the principle or the meanings, both
continue to exist outside the connection.

The private juncture of the objects of understanding and awareness is an idea. When the two factors are in equilibrium, the idea is a part of a subjectivity. But the equilibrium is only a momentary stop in a process by which the meanings lucidatively lead to Possibility. Though the meanings have been freed from their role in actualities, they are not entirely severed from them; it is therefore possible for the ideas, of which those meanings are constituents, to continue adumbratively into those actualities.

The acknowledgment of a meaning has an effect on man, and that effect can be given a role in a program. If its acknowledgment makes a man follow x by y, a machine can conceivably be made which, though it makes no such acknowledgment, nevertheless also follows x by y. So far, there is no distinguishing in kind between machines and other bodies. There is also, so far, no distinguishing in kind between bodies and minds. A distinguishing is required, though, when we refer to principles. These are meanings which control and relate meanings. If we credit a body with an openness to principles and with the power to use these to govern and connect other meanings, there will so far be no difference between saying that it has an awareness and an understanding and saying that it is just a body which functions in terms of meanings.

Machines can be made to deal with objects discriminately. But they are unable to extend the scope of their activities to include items not previously considered, although they can act on the new items as though they were similar to those previously accepted or rejected. A man kept to such narrow confines would still be able to deal with new items creatively, forging new unities of them and accepted meanings. The unities will sometimes involve the alteration of the items, the meanings, or both. There is no evident way to determine in advance which will occur, or to what extent.

The higher animals, like man, but unlike machines, are responsive. Machines merely interact. Animals group together because of what they intuit of one another; men make themselves centers for whatever they face. If machines are to be duplicates of the higher animals, they must act as though they had a desire to mate, to occupy themselves with the care of the young, and were attuned to the demands and desires of some of the other animals. If machines are to be duplicates of men as well, they must go further and subordinate the natures of actualities to the specification of Possibility that is their mind. They must not merely carry out programs, but control, organize, and interplay with meanings of which they are aware.

A number of machines can conceivably be built whose distinctive operations are interlocked with one another. A missile's arrival at a target can be the occasion for another machine to increase the amount of light that is displayed there. The two will then function as though they were one machine, terminating at a lighted target. If the machines are not linked, their different termini can be related through the action of a human mind. That mind will make it possible for a meaning to connect different termini and thereby produce a new meaning. To make a machine duplicate a man, it is necessary not only to duplicate the effects which some meaning has on him, but to give this the power to determine the relation that the machine's terminus will have to others which are determined independently of it. Always escaping machine control is the governance of the relation of specific independent meanings by an overriding principle.

Machines are made by men using their minds. The minds provide the arrangements of the parts of the machines, as well as the programs which the machines are to carry out. The minds then function somewhat as coaches and teachers sometimes do; a principle is imposed on what then proceeds to act in terms of it, but not necessarily because of it.

The human mind is to be distinguished from a body, not because it is a distinct substance, but because it makes Possibility bear on particular meanings and the embodiment of these. Possibility controls and connects the natures of bodies. But it takes a human mind or something which empowers it to abstract the meaning of those natures, and to use a specification of Possibility to relate those meanings to one another. The mind that is both aware and understands makes possible the production of a single, complex meaning. In the absence of such a mind and that on which it depends, there would be no distinguishable, organized meanings, but just a sequence of occurrences.

When thinking is equated with the production of rationally justified connections between what is otherwise independent, no machine can be credited with thought. Current machines can be said to think, only if thinking is taken to be identical with the re-presentation of what was already there to be externally joined together.

The question whether it is possible to construct a machine which has a mind able to use a principle to relate new meanings, is one with the question as to whether or not a manlike being can be created through artificial means. There is no reason why this can not be done. But when it is done, it will not mean that man has been shown to be nothing but a machine, a combination of chemicals, or a mere biological unity, but only that these are able to have human-like minds. If they can, they will so far be on a footing with men, because they will somehow have succeeded in being more than bodies, physical or living.

There is no action on the part of an animal that could not conceivably be reproduced by a machine. If the activities of the two were similar in all respects, we would have to allow that the machine also had some awareness and some form of understanding, or deny these of animals. The decision will be arbitrary. Since both have only limited repertoires, there is no way in which one can tell whether or not they could bring an understanding of their own to play on the items with which they deal, or are just programmed to go through a limited series of steps. But it will still be possible to distinguish men from both machines and animals. Confronted with unrelated novel items, the men can and the others cannot subject them to previously used principles to produce new unities.

A man or an animal can become habituated to the activities of another. The mother comes to expect what the infant will do, even though from its position what it does may have no known connection with what it had done. A machine can have a memory bank in which known combinations are stored; it may, when prompted to take one step, be ready to take another which anticipates what in fact is being independently produced. It could be so made that it will defeat any chess amateur; it has been so made that it will never be defeated in tic-tac-toe. One could conceivably have it make sounds and to gesture, or make sounds, advance, and retreat while playing these games. It will then appear to be functioning in the way a man does—but only if we unduly limit man.

The repertoire of men is endlessly extendable. Were all possible items envisageable in advance, it would be conceivable that a machine could relate them in the way a man does. On the hypothesis, there would be no items which would test the presence of a controlling meaning. A similar situation would result from the making of a machine which was able to reject every item but a selected few; there would then be no novel items which would serve to test the presence of a controlling meaning. But if there is no way to test the presence of a controlling meaning, there is no way to know if a humanlike mind is operative.

It is conceivable that a machine might be made that could learn in the sense that it not only corrected its errors but never repeated any. It might be made flexible enough to alter its course on the introduction of new items and demands. So far it would act in the way men can. But it would still not yet be wholly like a man, for a man uses his understanding to determine the import of that of which he is aware. He changes his course, not merely because he meets new items or new conditions, but because he has assessed them in a relation to what he already had in mind.

Man's use of understanding enables him to link distinguished items by necessity. That necessity is imitated but not duplicated in the form of a constant conjunction; it cannot be known except by attending to the difference which a prescriptive meaning or principle makes to whatever items are confronted. From the outside the necessity cannot be discerned since it is encountered only in the course of the alteration which the objects of awareness undergo in being understood. Evidences of its presence, though, can be conveyed in speech and action. These observations relate to understanding and consciousness. When other forms of mind and awareness are distinguished, the gap between animals and machines, and between both of these and men, widens considerably.

The gap between animals and machines can be narrowed beyond any preassigned degree, because the animals are not able to make free use of their understanding. But the gap between men and other actualities will always be unbridgeable, for men alone can subject any object of awareness to understanding, and thereby produce a new meaning without giving up the use of accepted principles.

The programs machines follow have a unity to them because of the unitary purpose of the men who make and use them. The organic body of an animal and its life also have a unity to them, enabling the animal to partly isolate unities in the objects with which it has to deal. But a man is able to function, under the governance of Unity, as a unity attentive to other unities. Machines have no power to isolate unities; animals have no power to make full use of Unity. Neither, consequently, is able to attend to unities as wholly separated from the realities where those unities are embodied.

A man has the ability to attend to new unities. Even in a world where a machine or animal functioned as though it were occupied only with connecting unities in the way men connect them, men would still differ from machines and animals because of their ability to make acknowledged unities be united with Unity.

Neither machines nor animals can function creatively in new situations; neither is able to provide more than factual connections between the items with which they are involved, because neither is able to make use of finalities. It is only man who can connect items with necessity, without effect on their identity, and as contributing, with him, to a final Unity.

There is nothing here which is inconsistent with the main contentions of an evolutionary theory of the origin of men. Material bodies, living beings, and men are all subject to finalities. Those finalities operate cosmically with respect to the physical bodies, and are specialized in the form of controlling principles governing the groups which animals form, both biologically and socially. The higher animals so far as they are receptive to those principles are enabled to have a consciousness which can confront partially separated aspects of what is encountered. Men, in addition, make active use of finalities, and therefore are not only able to have a degree of awareness not possible to the animals, but are able to institute binding relations in new situations. Their increase in awareness, with its associated increase in an appreciation of finalities, has survival value in enabling them in principle to bring together everything in an ordered whole. But there seems to be no survival value in man's ability to speculate. Apparently, it is just one of the benefits which accrue from his being able, with the advent of a developed social organization and its support of leisure, to stand away from the biological struggle for survival, then to become aware of the finalities, severally and together, and, by means of instances of these, to connect and govern that of which he is aware.

[5]

Faced with a prospective target and an independent source of light, a machine would not deal with that source unless it had already been programmed to do so. A man, instead, would be able to decide that the target would be more visible if that target were illuminated. We could say that he is programmed to deal with every possible item, even those which no one envisages; we will then speak of him as though he were a machine, but will credit him with powers machines do not have. If the linkage between a target and some unspecified possible source of light could be incorporated in a machine, that machine would embody the mind of the man who links the target with such a source. There would still be need to connect the illuminated target with other objects not yet linked to that target by any machine.

Related considerations help clarify the problem of our knowledge of other minds. We can attend to another's speech, actions, and above all to his productions, his anticipations, and his demands for still other independently produced items. When he attends to the very units we do, manifesting, through his speech and action toward those and other units, that he relates them as we do, we credit him with understanding us. When, in addition, he relates them in ways we do not, yet successfully anticipates what we do not, we credit him with having a better knowledge of ourselves than we have.

Those who are defective, radically incompetent, immobilized, are accepted as humans because they are recognized to have living bodies which could sustain an awareness capable of interplaying with an understanding. It may not be possible to tell from their words or actions that they are able to interconnect independent items in ways that are similar to those we employ, but if we penetrate to them from the position of their grimaces, gestures, and expressions of recognition, anger, pleasure, and pain, we can know that even if they are not aware of anything, they are in a position to become aware, and therefore are able to make use of some finality so as to connect particular items derived from independent events.

Some animals seem to exhibit behavior similar to that of men; they grimace, cry out, snarl, advance, and retreat. We therefore rightly take them to have an awareness and an understanding, even though they may not be able to do more than attend to aspects of a very limited number of occurrences, and are able to use only established relations to new items.

Because he internalizes not only qualifications imposed by Possibility, but those that are imposed by other finalities as well, a man is able to assume all the roles possible to a self. This he must do if he is to have an adequate apprehension of all the finalities. His body at the same time enables him to make an acquaintance with actualities. Initially he confronts the finalities and actualities as only dimly together, behind the particularities with which he is daily occupied. He then has only an emotionally toned grasp of them all inchoately together. But there are various enterprises in which he can participate, enabling him to discern something of the depths of finalities at the same time that he gains insight into actualities beyond that vouchsafed in the ordinary course of living. Making that union evident is the work usually of myth or speculation, the one unreflectingly produced by a people, the other by individual philosophers. To know it in the latter guise is to know the ought-to-be that is; the former, instead, offers a dramatic presentation of a realization of it that is relevant to a present stage of civilization. In between these two, and sharing in features characteristic of each, are the objectives of scientific inquiry and of social and political programs. These are occupied with only a part of an ultimate ideal condition, and envisage its realization in specific forms pertinent to the traditions, practices, and interests of limited groups.

The final ideal condition has one guise when approached from the position of actualities, a second from that of Substance, another from that of Being, a fourth from that of Existence, a fifth from that of Possibility, and the sixth from that of Unity. It is equally six ideal conditions, and one ideal condition viewed from six positions.

17

PERFECTION: THE FINAL CONDITION

Controlling Summary: The final condition is the minimal possible juncture of actualities and finalities in the role of a demand that it be enriched by the full harmonious presence of the actualities and finalities. The demand is a constant, measuring what is and what is to be done.

Some enterprises, such as religion, make one aware of depths to finalities not previously noted; others, such as biography, make one aware of unnoted depths to actualities; still others, such as celebrations, produce new appearances which open up unsuspected depths in both. The most adequate grasp of the final condition is mediated by these; they make evident the realities that can most completely satisfy the condition's demand. Philosophy encompasses those realities in a systematic conceptual account. It is therefore able to state the nature of the condition that those realities constitute when they are minimally together and which they can satisfy only by being maximally harmonized.

Actualities together make up a single world of actualities. What they individually exhibit is not altogether alien to what they are in relation to one another. The manner in which their exhibitions are publicly related to one another is determined by the context which finalities provide. The resulting appearances, consequently, are re-

lated in a common world in ways which reflect how the actualities
and finalities exhibit themselves and are connected. No one can read
off from appearances just what kind of relations their actualities have
to one another, or just what the source of a context is like.

Appearances are components in contexts where each supplements the other. It is not difficult to conceive of a better organization
of all appearances than that which now prevails. Defects in the world
of appearances, however, do not define that world to be unreal. If
they did, the defects would by that very fact also disappear into
unreality. To be real, it is not necessary to be perfect. Indeed, to be
anything at all, it is necessary to be less than perfect, for it is to be
other than the perfection which measures how excellent something
is, or it is to be the measuring perfection itself and therefore other
than what this measures. The conclusion holds equally of an eternal
God and of the most trivial, transient puff of air in a remote part of
the globe. A God, if he is the measure of all else, faces that which is
to be measured, and is so far other than that which is being measured.
He will, therefore, not be all reality; what he measures will be distinct from Him. If, instead, He is not the measure of all else but is
to be characterized—even as 'the perfect'—He stands in contrast with
the measure 'perfection', and by that very fact cannot be absolutely
perfect, but only the best of all real unities.

The common world is defective. So is the daily world. There is
much that is dark and confused, ugly, frustrating, disappointing,
hurtful in it. It constantly changes and is overrun with conflicting
activities. Items in it intrude and interfere with one another, apparently at haphazard; nothing supports or enhances all others consistently or fully. What happens at one place is largely irrelevant to
what is happening elsewhere.

Some men consider these defects to be so serious that they want
to dismiss the daily world as an illusion, a veil which the wise man
pushes away so as to leave him confronting something nobler and
more truly real. For others the defects offer a challenge, demanding
an effort at improvement. Those who dismiss it and those who are
challenged by it lead quite dissimilar lives, but both are in accord on
a fundamental point. Both make use of a standard of excellence,

a measure of worth, distinct from anything that can be found in the world. The standard, usually explicit for those who deliberately reject, and usually implicit for those who accept the daily world as real, permits them to measure that world as defective. This judgment requires that there be an excellence which the world fails to exemplify. The one, though, takes that excellence to be already achieved elsewhere; he sees how defective our world is by contrasting it with one which is more glorious and complete. The other takes the excellence to be a goal possible of attainment; he guides his actions and defines his hopes in terms of it, in the belief that the world can become or be made better than it is. In the end, both of these views are partly justified. There are better states of affairs than the daily world contains; the daily world can and ought to be improved.

If we reject all prospective better states of affairs, we are left with the world as it now is. Why not accept it in just that very form? Why take it to be defective? Why not just describe it, or at most systematically explore and deliberately organize it? The obvious answer is that it now contains much that is unwanted. It frustrates us; there are conflicts in it. What frustrates us is undesirable, except where it blocks what is itself undesirable—which is not always or everywhere. Conflicts jeopardize what is precious. The world is defective, we know, since its items are not now unfrustrated; they are not jointly and maximally harmonized.

The answers provoke questions of their own. Why object to frustrations and conflicts? Are they not desirable prods? Do they not prompt determination and effort? Do they not make for a desirable diversity? Do they not justify the pursuit of independent studies?

These questions themselves invoke standards of excellence. They assume that it is good that there be prods, effort, diversity, and the pursuit of independent lines of inquiry. Any other questions that one might substitute for these would be caught in similar difficulties. All tacitly or explicitly invoke measures of excellence in terms of which some position is taken to be better than others.

To refuse to submit to any standard or to use any measure is to be forced to say that nothing is better or worse than anything else, at the same time that one is prevented from claiming that this admission is desirable. It is possible to imagine oneself living in accordance with such a view, and, despite appetites and pains, tragedies and comedies, supposing all things to be without value. But the position could never be defended or even maintained without pushing aside other alternatives as less true, or less desirable, or less interesting, or less suitable for the purpose. To allow the rejected alternatives to be as good as one's own is in principle to give up one's own claim, and to end by judging nothing, including the desirability of doing this.

Might not, though, all standards be man's own creation, or hold only of what he cherishes? Might they not simply be reports of what men think more desirable, used to guide them in judgment and action? If they were, there would be no assessing of men's decisions. If any decision is judged to be good or bad, right or wrong, some measure of evaluation will have been employed. When men disagree with one another, one position can rightly be termed better than another only if there is a standard common to both in terms of which they are measured.

Were there someone bold enough to say that no one's decision is better than another's, he will inevitably judge his own position to be superior to one which says that there are some decisions that are better than others. Sooner or later he will have to allow or disallow all judgments as being on a footing. Whether or not this is done arbitrarily or on reflection, he will submit to a standard, justifying the excluding of the others even if that exclusion be based on no other grounds than that one does not care for it. Caring will then provide a standard for what is preferable.

It might be contended that all standards are like caring: they are either created by men or are merely functions of their interests. In either case, the men will stand outside their particular decisions and elections, measuring them as better or worse. A distinction will then have to be made between a judging and a judged self, the one possessing and perhaps presenting the standard in terms of which the other was measured. Even if the standard they used were the outcome of some empirical generalization, a substitute for some parental or societal practice or rule, or a restatement of their desires, the judging self and its standard would remain outside all that was being judged. Somehow, out of the transient, a position would have been won which outlasts and encompasses all the others. Eventually, one will be forced to say that it is good, or bad, or indifferent that use is made of it and not of some others.

Every use of content follows some procedure, implicitly or explicitly. The method may be rather straightforward, one of a number of long-established patterns of classification, dissection, or analysis. Or it may be the product of a number of these, intertwined or used in sequence. In both ways, the data will be collected, related, and ordered. Concerned with the use of the data by means of some such method, one then has no occasion to study or to justify the principles and operations performed. To carry out the method one must not stop to make it the primary object of study at that time. This does not mean that one must proceed uncritically, without self-control or self-reflection, but only that limited disciplines begin within limits.

Disciplined thinking demands self-criticism; a strong method makes provision for its own correction. The self-criticism and correction concern details, applications, particular uses of the method, and do not reach to its nature or its warrant. Rules are usually changed not because they have been made the object of study, but because they have led to difficulties that one seeks thereafter to avoid. And if one criticizes the method, or studies the rules, use will be made of what is then unexamined, until one comes to a final abstract measure. One can examine this in the terms it provides. That final abstract measure will, however, be itself measured as being defective, by the very items it governs, since it will lack their concreteness. The limit of all criticism is set by an abstract final measure; this is itself measured by what is concrete, and thus by that which the formal measure has shown to be formally imperfect.

[2]

All experiencing has a direction, but it may veer first in this way and then in that, making its course difficult to predict or to characterize. At each point, and sometimes throughout, there is a specific prospect which one is then acting to realize. That prospect is usually taken for granted; it operates but is not known. Rarely does one ever come to know it in detail or with surety. But it continues to operate, controlling the way data are divided, corrected, combined, classified, and evaluated.

Some men are lured by what in root are projections of their desires. They are then guided and sometimes controlled by what they themselves produce. The laws of nature, the dispositions of things, the nature of possibility, and the prescriptiveness of the unrealized ideals of truth, goodness, and beauty make implausible the view that all prospects are such projections of desires. But even if they were, it would still be true that they guide and even control men and their experiences. Relative to a particular situation and need they function as objectives, even if, apart from that situation, they are but intermediate goals for some more remote end.

It is possible to favor standards supporting deceit and incoherence. But one will then be maintaining with some honesty and clarity that it is good to spoil or to prevent civilized living or inquiry. It is true, of course, that civilized living and inquiry are not acceptable to all men. Living and inquiry have sometimes in fact been deliberately replaced by those which sanction self-expression, spontaneity, and just living. But if either side is chosen arbitrarily, it will not eliminate the other. A justified choice requires recourse to nonarbitrary ways of adjudicating claims. In either way, a standard will be invoked in terms of which it can rightly be said that things are not as they ought to be.

It makes sense, perhaps, to say that this or that personal experience is good or bad. But does it make sense to assert that the world itself has any value, that it is defective or excellent, bad or good? Perhaps it has no value at all? It seems silly to say that birds ought not to fly, or that frogs ought not to croak; perhaps it is equally silly to say that the Nazis ought not to have had gas chambers, or that incest is wrong? We might not like one or the other occurrence, but this will not affect the fact—if fact it be—that there is nothing right or wrong here.

Not all human satisfactions are desirable; some, like addictive drugs, begin a chain of distress. Not everything that serves the interests of the majority, the stronger, or an ongoing society, a scientific community, or even the entire present civilized world is to be accepted. Sometimes mankind goes in a wrong direction for quite a period. It is only recently that most of mankind has become convinced that slavery and child labor are wrong. Whether we accept this judgment or reject it, we recognize that the good is what measures up to some standard of excellence, and the bad is that which does not. We may not know how to assess the flight of birds or the croaking of frogs, apart from their convenience to us or their use to themselves, but this convenience and this use also have some value, pointing us toward a standard which enables one to measure that value.

Perhaps we should not look further than convenience and use? Perhaps a world other than that which now exists is not even possible? We are not Gods and do not make the world. Why then should we evaluate it, or speak of what it ought to be? But would it not be arbitrary to deny that evolution might have gone along now abandoned lines? Is it not odd to deny that it could have taken a better course? The very uses and preferences of beings might have been different, and perhaps might have been better than they are now. Men, at least, might have been kinder than they are, and from childhood on; they could have had stronger hearts, more intelligence, and be less prone to war. We can surely think of these alternative outcomes. If we wish to deny that they express a desirable state of affairs, we will still have to make use of a standard lying outside them.

If we can think of this or that item being changed for the better, we will have invoked a standard of value. And we can always think of any item being improved. It is not even necessary to examine it; no matter how good it is and how much it is improved, it will always be deficient in some regard. Every item is defective intrinsically, since it lacks the reality that makes it to be just that limited thing it now is. What limits an item has a reality and nature of its own. If either it or what it limits were annihilated, there would be a loss of value, or the annihilated items would be negative particles whose destruction ennobled what was left.

If anything is defective, must it always remain so? What in it is beyond all possible correction? If any part can be improved, why cannot every part? Why, therefore, cannot the whole be perfect? If perfection cannot be attained, a standard of perfection would be unrealizable; but what bearing could a standard have which could never be realized?

Even if every appearance and reality were made as excellent as it is possible for it to be, the result would not be an absolutely perfect world. Finalities and actualities are forever distinct from one another. Each requires the other to be without the reality it itself possesses, and therefore to be so far defective. The actualities and finalities could conceivably be together in better ways than they now are, either in the cosmos or in the daily and common worlds of appearances. But not only can men not unite them so that the result is beyond all possible improvement, but their distinctness from one another, and their distinctness from what was realized through their harmonious union, means that severally and jointly the realities necessarily lack some reality.

In a full realization of perfection, actualities and finalities in their concreteness would together fill out the union characteristic of that perfection. But while they filled it out, these realities would also stand away from it, or would destroy the meaning of a standard, final, conditioning perfection on attaining it. Because the realization of perfection requires that perfection, and what satisfies this, be distinct from the realized result, the fullest realization of perfection necessarily falls short of what is demanded by perfection. The realization of perfection must fall short of absolute perfection.

Perfection is a final condition, constituted by a minimal, constant union of actualities and finalities. Those realities are there inseparable, merged parts of a single whole. They are not there in their concreteness; only aspects of them are now united and are, therefore, constituents of the Ideal condition. In their concreteness, the realities maintain themselves in opposition to one another and to the condition, but aspects of them are intimately and firmly together, thereby constituting a single conditioning perfection. Alternatively, in their full concreteness, the realities constitute the final condition by being logically conjoined, at the same time that, in their full concreteness, they stand away from it, as realities together disjunctively, not fully harmonized.

The minimal constant unity of realities is a final condition for the disjunct realities in their full concreteness; it demands of them, as disjunct and concrete, that they be logically united and still remain concrete, thereby repossessing aspects of themselves. That demand is integral to the minimal union, for it is nothing less than a reference to what would make that final condition be satisfied—which is to say, also, it is a reference to what would substantialize the united aspects. The realities in their full concreteness also make a demand. They demand of the final condition that this become integral to them, and thereby make them complete—which is to say, also, that they demand that their aspects, as now harmonized, be returned to them.

The realities, as demanding the presence in them of the final condition that is now distinct from them, are alone able to act; the realization of the condition could be achieved only by them. The completion of those realities, and the satisfaction of the condition would have to be attained at the very same time and in the very same act, by having the realities in their full concreteness harmoniously together. Because the realization of the condition is identical with the self-realization of the real, the necessary failure of the one is identical with the necessary failure of the other.

The final condition demands a realization of itself, but itself is not that realization; actualities and finalities together can together fully satisfy the condition, but only by destroying it and themselves. What is now, what ought to be, and the realization of what ought to be are all defective, the one because it is not fully harmonized and, where harmonized, does not involve realities in their full concreteness; the second because it is constituted by the minimal juncture of the realities as demanding the presence of those realities without reserve; and the third because the condition and the realities continue to be outside anything that they might constitute together.

[3]

The qualia of actualities, and the contexts in which they are together, constitute a world of appearances. Made up of the contributions of actualities and finalities, that world lacks some of the reality of both. The final condition, constituted of the actualities and finalities as minimally together, is in fact not fully realized in the world of appearances. But even if it were fully realized there, it would still be defective, for it would still continue to be a minimal juncture of the actualities and finalities, demanding that they be together in their full concreteness.

The world of appearances is not as good as it could be. The appearances are not yet related to one another in the best possible way. If each appearance were to be as excellent as possible, it could still be in conflict with others; and all of them could be together in the best possible way, without themselves being at their best, since that best possible way could require that they be muted and greyed. Both alternatives must be precluded before the appearances of actualities can be as excellent as possible. And then that world will be far from being what perfection requires.

Actualities and finalities in their depths, while apart, are logically together. Despite their concreteness and richness, their juncture has only the most minimal concreteness and richness, that of a logical union. As having such a minimum, it provides a measure of itself, of its members, and of what is to realize it. Without losing any of their concreteness or content, the finalities and the actualities are required by their aggregated totality to fill up its emptiness. Perfection is a standard constituted by the actualities and finalities. That excellence measures the attempt to conceive it, as well as everything else, as comparatively good or bad. It does this whether or not men think of it, and no matter how men think of it. If they fail to think of it or if they misconstrue it, it measures them as thinkers who are not as good as they could have been.

In itself perfection is not absolutely perfect, since there are realities external to it. So far as those others are defective, it must be defective in still another sense, since it still needs realization through them. But if it is imperfect, by what could it be measured? If it is defective it must be measured by something other than itself; yet if it is the measure of everything, what is there to measure it? The answer to this vexatious problem has already been anticipated. The perfect is always defective because there always are realities distinct from it. It measures itself, both as realized and as unrealized, as that which stands in contradistinction from all else. Though it is nothing more than the minimal juncture of the actualities and finalities, it does not stand alongside them, but overarches them.

If one were to suppose, instead, that perfection was already realized in such a way that nothing was lacking to it, one would, with Bradley, have to say that it was beyond all comprehension as well—and that would be a defect. If, instead, with other Hegelians one thought that the imperfect was now the case, but that it had no reality of its own, one would be driven to suppose that it was a product of self-deception on the part of what was real. This is not a great improvement on Plotinus, who held that defective forms of the perfect were inevitably precipitated out of it, inexplicably.

[4]

Perfection is specified in the form of a number of distinct standards of excellence and measures of what is good and bad.

1] The standard of an *improvable common world* measures the degree to which appearances are to be altered under prevailing conditions. That standard is constituted by the conjunction of the appearances in their severalty with the contexts that now govern them together. Whatever muting is now required in order for the appearances to be harmoniously subject to the same common conditions is now voided; the standard will be met when the appearances are reordered, restructured, given new locations in space and time. That result men should try to bring about. They can and do approximate it when they change the present relations appearances have to one another for others which allow those appearances to be better harmonized.

2] The standard of an *improvable cosmos* measures the degree to which actualities are to be altered under the prevailing cosmic laws. That standard is constituted by the conjunction of the several actualities with the finalities as now manifest. Actions designed to enhance certain actualities without thereby injuring others help meet that standard. Though the number of actualities on which men could act is not very large, it is larger than the number of actualities on which men in fact do act. And though the amount of change men could produce is not very great, it is greater than the amount they in fact bring about. The standard cosmos measures men as deficient to the degree that they fail to alter all actualities so as to make our cosmos maximally good.

3] The contexts that now govern appearances do not control them as fully as they could. The standard of a *better conditioned world of the appearances of actualities,* constituted by the conjunction of present qualia and the prevailing contexts, should guide men in their social planning. If it did, the men should then back it with power of their own. But they rarely do this, and when they do, they do not back it maximally. Mankind is criticizable for having developed only a limited technology, and for giving this insufficient or inadequate use.

4] The finalities, which are behind the contexts that govern the appearances of actualities together, can be more effectively expressed than they are. The standard of a *better controlled world of appearances* is constituted of the appearances as subject to forces emanating from finalities. Those forces can be and are, to some degree, utilized by men when they symbolize those finalities and return to the world of appearances enriched by that experience. They do not attend to those forces as much as they might, and when they do attend to them the men do not make use of them as much as they could. If they did, they would be more alert to the resonances, the reality, the rationale, the consequences, and the coherence of appearances than they are.

5] In the ordinary course of life, finalities are reached by starting with their appearances. But in taoism, mysticism, theoretical science, art, and religion sometimes sudden insights are achieved into finalities as they stand apart from all else. One becomes aware that there are depths to them which have not been exhibited but which cannot be brought to bear on actualities or appearances. They provide the main constituent of a standard *transcendentalized world* which demands that actualities and appearances be governed in a way that no action by men could realize.

6] The reciprocal of 5 (above) is a standard of *unused resources of actualities*. This is known when, through sympathy, love, and cooperative activities, one probes beneath the appearances into depths of actualities not probed before, and envisages the result in union with the prevailing laws. One is then aware that actualities should be involved in the cosmos to a degree greater than they now are. Men are criticizable for not doing all that needs to be done to make an excellent cosmos, even if they have no way of bringing this about. "Ought" implies "can," but "you ought" does not imply "you can." If it did, stupidity, ineptitude, ignorance, self-indulgence, would cut down one's obligations. "You cannot" does not mean you have so far freed yourself from an obligation.

7] A combination of the last two standards is equivalent with perfection. This demands that finalities and actualities be maximized together in their full concreteness. We can envisage this juncture of all the finalities with actualities, at their most concrete, only to the degree that we have insight into the finalities and actualities. Since we have never probed either to their depths, we cannot yet envisage the satisfaction of perfection fully. We must continue to engage in those enterprises which reveal what more there is in both actualities and finalities which they could conceivably contribute to the realization of a perfection that measures every reality and appearance, every achievement and every failure.

8] The condition which is most usable by men is that of a *civilized world*, where men in alliance with one another act to satisfy the first four standards, while remaining conscious of the requirements of the final condition. Every stage of civilization is fringed by a consciousness on the part of some of its members of that condition. It is one of the tasks of civilization to make possible the facing of a more demanding form of it than had been envisaged before. Philosophy expresses what actualities and finalities are at their most concrete, and thereby makes possible the formulation of the nature of their perfect union. But men normally require the final condition to have a dramatic demanding form; they therefore present it in the form of folklore and myth. The hope of civilization lies in the happy absorption of the philosophic formulations of the final condition, perfection, into the dominating dramatic guides of a civilized mankind.

Perfection, the final condition, is constituted by all the finalities and actualities, not only by those that interest men. Though men cannot realize it, they can take account of those realities and the nature of their minimal, their present, and their desirable union. Each man has already within him something of the finalities. Each can act as a representative of other men and eventually of all other actualities. The posture that he assumes in order to experience appearances is supported by his internal instantiation of the finalities. His judgments and actions are supported by his assumption of a representative status for all actualities. That is one reason why he can do more than other beings to realize perfection. But no matter how good men are, and how much they accomplish, there is always still more to be done.

INDEX OF NAMES

INDEX OF SUBJECTS

INDEX OF NAMES

INDEX OF SUBJECTS

244; definition, 233; Kant on, 234; absolute, 234–35; men and, 248, 312, 349, 363; unity and, 253; contexts and, 257; symbols and, 261, 266–67; dialectic and, 272; Being, 276, 332; global terms and, 290–91; internalization and, 292–93, 311; self and, 314; subhuman beings, 342; materialism and, 351; Possibility and, 354; animals and, 355; mind and body, 356–58. *See also* Penetration
Firsts, 106
Focused, the, 24, 26, 39, 58, 60, 84, 124, 175, 185, 236–43 passim, 250, 251, 253
Force, 249–51
Form, 35–36
Formal, the, 45
Formalism, 327
Formulae, 326
Freedom, 216
Frustration, 367

Generic, 345
Generosity, 57, 98
Genetics, 309–10
Global terms, 290–91
God, 36, 37, 39, 44, 79, 80, 95, 119–20, 155, 169, 252, 271, 280–82, 296–97, 317, 336–37, 341, 366
Good and evil, 46, 370, 375
Grain, 89, 109
Grammar, 236, 253
Grit, 109

Habit, 359
Harmony, 168
Here, 7, 258

History, 21, 322
Humility, 17

Ideal, the, 199, 216, 329
Ideal excellence, 206–7, 209–10, 215
Idealism, 33, 43, 106, 159, 237, 300
Ideality, 271
Ideas, 326–29, 357
Identity, 32–33, 327, 333–36, 355
Ideology, 196–97
Illusion, 46
Immortality: finalities and, 338; diversified unity, 339; mind and, 339–40; men and, 342; mentioned, 337, 341
Indeterminate, the, 151–52
Indifference, 43, 86
Individuality: knowable substances and, 53; actualities and, 77, 311–12, 318; space and, 165; traces of, 169; biology and, 309–10; Unity and, 314; of men, 315–17, 356; sensibility, 317; state and, 322; identity and, 335
Infinity, 281–82
Inquiry, 6–7, 14–15, 33, 49–51, 225, 294, 355
Integrity, 65, 91, 152, 159
'Intentionality,' 61
Intentions, 213
Interesting, the, 17, 49, 56
Intermediaries, 281–82
Internalization, 99, 310–11, 319, 350
Intuition, 330
Involvement, 334
Inwardness, 233, 242, 251, 271–72, 296–97
Irreducibles, 65
Isolated thing, 60